Linux Routers

ISBN 0-13-086113-8

90000

Prentice Hall Series in
Computer Networking and Distributed Systems
Radia Perlman, editor

Linux Routers

A Primer for Network Administrators

Tony Mancill

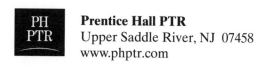

Prentice Hall PTR
Upper Saddle River, NJ 07458
www.phptr.com

Library of Congress Cataloging-in-Publication Data

Mancill, Tony.
  Linux routers : a primer for network administrators / Tony Mancill.
      00p.   cm. -- (Prentice Hall series in computer networking and
distributed systems)
Includes bibliographical references and index.
  ISBN 0-13-086113-8
  1. Linux. 2. Routers (Computer networks)   I. Title.   II. Series.
  QA76.76.O63   M348   2000
  005.4'4769--dc21

                                                    00-058450

Editorial/production supervision: *Faye Gemmellaro*
Acquisitions editor: *Mary Franz*
Editorial assistant: *Noreen Regina*
Development Editor: *Jim Markham*
Marketing manager: *Julie Tiso*
Manufacturing manager: *Maura Goldstaub*
Cover design director: *Jerry Votta*
Cover designer: *Anthony Gemmellaro*
Cover illustration: *Tom Post*
Composition: *PreTEX, Inc.*

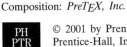

© 2001 by Prentice Hall PTR
Prentice-Hall, Inc.
Upper Saddle River, NJ 07458

Prentice Hall books are widely used by corporations and government agencies
for training, marketing, and resale.

The publisher offers discounts on this book when ordered in bulk quantities.

For more information, contact:
Corporate Sales Department
Phone: 800-382-3419   Fax: 201-236-7141
Email: corpsales@prenhall.com

Or write:
Prentice Hall PTR
Corporate Sales Department
One Lake Street
Upper Saddle River, NJ 07458

All product names mentioned herein are the trademarks of their respective owners.

Printed in the United States of America

10 9 8 7 6 5 4 3 2 1

ISBN 0-13-086113-8

Prentice-Hall International (UK) Limited, *London*
Prentice-Hall of Australia Pty. Limited, *Sydney*
Prentice-Hall Canada Inc., *Toronto*
Prentice-Hall Hispanoamericana, S.A., *Mexico*
Prentice-Hall of India Private Limited, *New Delhi*
Prentice-Hall of Japan, Inc., *Tokyo*
Pearson Education Asia Pte. Ltd.
Editora Prentice-Hall do Brasil, Ltda., *Rio de Janeiro*

Contents

Preface

This book is the culmination of over two years of dodging the obvious: I needed to write a HOWTO to document the things that I was using Linux for in my work, particularly concerning the use of Linux as a router in a variety of scenarios. But the book is not only about routers, it's about running Linux in production and all of the non-technical details which go along with it. This book is not intended to be the authoritative "be-all end-all" of what can be accomplished with Linux routers, but a HOWTO describing what has worked for me and my employers over the past few years. I have tried to record all of the stupid mistakes I have made along with the arbitrary parts of configuring and running a Linux router so that you won't have to learn them on your own. I fully expect you to far exceed the contents of this book as you further the state of the art.

ACKNOWLEDGMENTS

I had the opportunity to hear Richard Stallman speak in 1998 about the Free Software Foundation and the work he has done to develop, support, and promote the GPL. I found his talk very inspiring, and although this book is not released under the GPL, it is nevertheless inspired by, and possible because of, the work of Richard Stallman, Linux Torvalds, and the GNU/Linux community at large.

Specifically, I would like to thank the technical reviewers Todd O'Boyle, Tom Daniels, Mark Thomas, Radia Perlman, and David Mandelstam for working through the manuscript repeatedly and for setting me straight on technical inaccuracies. Radia Perlman gets double thanks, along with Jim Markham, for the thankless job of helping me improve my writing. Mary Franz and David Mandelstam (again) are to thank for being constant sources of encouragement and putting the idea of a book in my head in the first place. Last, and certainly not least, thanks to Melissa, Java, and Grommit for support and dealing with my weird writing schedule and moodiness due to sleep deprivation.

FEEDBACK

As an active professional in the IT industry and an advocate of Linux, I am interested in your commentary about the contents of this book. Please feel free to contact me by email to provide feedback, contribute ideas, or discuss your criticisms of either the material or my method of presenting it. The following address should find me: <tony@mancill.com>.

Happy Hacking!

Introduction

Router configuration has long been an arcane art possessed by the few (and the lucky—at least in the eyes of the interested yet unchosen). One reason for this is that routers were expensive, and required specialized training. They were also the sort of equipment that was found only in small numbers in larger companies. Unix, while not quite as inaccessible in terms of cost, has also frequently been considered a black art for the few. Linux, of course, has turned all of this on its ear and delivered a GNU[1] operating system to the masses. There used to be a couple bookstores in a big city with a decent selection of Unix books. Now every mall bookstore has a Unix/Linux section.

Routers, although not quite ubiquitous, are also much more prevalent in recent times too. The explosive growth of the Internet has every business, large and small, scrambling to get connected. Even completely non-technical organizations POP their email from their ISP over a dial-up link several times a day. And people use more networked computers in general nowadays. People now even have routers in their homes, pehaps to provide Internet connectivity via a cable modem to multiple computers in the home.

Interestingly (but not surprisingly), Linux delivers a router platform accessible by the many, almost as easily as it has resurrected the word "Unix." Although "traditional" routers are special-purpose hardware running embedded real-time operating systems, there has always been a group using Unix-based operating systems running on general-purpose hardware. Linux has helped expand this group immensely by providing a full-featured and robust TCP/IP stack and hundreds of device drivers— all of which run on commonly available computing hardware. Another important factor is the GNU/Linux community's basic tenet of sharing ideas and knowledge instead of hoarding them. The truly amazing part is that all of this is available without expensive licensing costs or non-disclosure agreements. With these good tools and some know-how, anyone can build an inexpensive, stable router platform capable of performing a variety of functions within any organization.

---

[1] "GNU's Not Unix," although it's more Unix than anything else that claims to be. The complete text of the GNU General Public License appears in Appendix E.

If you're asking yourself, *What's a router?*, do not despair! This book will try to cover most topics in enough depth and with enough references that you will not be left stumped. If it fails to do this, please let me know. Traditionally, a router is defined as a layer 3 switch. That is, it looks at the layer 3 packet headers and decides where to forward them. (Layer 3 refers to the OSI "network" layer.) For TCP/IP networks, the router examines the IP headers to determine the destination IP address of the packet, the TTL (Time To Live), among other things. In this strict definition, the type of packet—TCP, UDP, ICMP, etc.—is immaterial. However, routers have evolved beyond this function and can now take into account the layer 4 (transport layer) headers when deciding what to do with a packet. Some other things that routers do:

- Transfer traffic between two different types of physical networks. An example of this is forwarding packets from Ethernet to Frame Relay and vice-versa, as is done by a WAN router.

- Restrict the flow of traffic to/from certain addresses or networks. This is commonly known as **packet-filtering**. Often, the router will examine more than just the IP headers to make filtering decisions. TCP and UDP headers and other layer 4+ packet fields, are fair game.

- Rewrite source addresses so that traffic appears to originate for an address other than the original sender. Under Linux, this is known as **masquerading**, and the router acts as a **NAT** (Network Address Translator). The task includes unmasquerading replies flowing in the other direction.

- Act as a BOOTP or DHCP server issuing IP addresses and other configuration parameters for workstations on your network. Throughout this book, we will use Linux routers to do much more than this.

The focus of this book is admittedly not on definitions, but on how to accomplish (or at least get started on) a certain task. You may find that knowing the correct technical definition for something is not the same as successfully configuring and administering it in a production environment. If you're just getting started as a network administrator, be confident that a lot of technical know-how can be only learned through experience (a.k.a. "the hard way"). Do not be intimidated by the lack of a formal body of knowledge; just admit when you don't know the answer and strive to figure it out.

0.1 FROM WHENCE LINUX?

The progress on operating systems implementation has been much more dramatic during the 1990's, thanks to Linux. If you are interested in the "early" history of Linux and can stomach discussions of OS design, you should check out the following:

- *http://www.educ.umu.se/˜bjorn/mhonarc-files/obsolete/* This is a flame-war between Linus Torvalds and Andy Tannenbaum, a well-established researcher, professor, father of *MINIX*, and author of several (good) OS-design books.

- *http://www.educ.umu.se/˜bjorn/linux/misc/linux-history.html* This is a collection of Linux-relevant postings made to `comp.os.minix` about building an OS.

The way I understand the early history of Linux, it boils down to this: Linus Torvalds had an Intel 80386-based PC and some free time. He set out to write an operating system that would capitalize on the new features of this processor, ignoring backwards compatibility with the 8088 and the 80286. (Other PC operating systems of that era were struggling with some design trade-offs that were imposed by the limitations of the predecessors of the 386. In all fairness, they did this to maintain backwards compatibility with software written to run on those systems.)

Another incentive for writing his own OS from scratch was to take advantage of the large body of excellent "free" software being developed by the Free Software Foundation. This is the (first) connection between Linux and Richard Stallman, who founded the GNU project in 1984 and has lent both philosphy and code to the effort. The system software which Linus used for his new kernel is commonly known as the GNU toolset. These tools include most of what is commonly thought of as standard "Unix" system tools.[2] This collection of software had the tremendous advantage of being available in source code form and being delivered with a license that allowed early Linux developers to modify the source and redistribute it.

In the early 1990's, the Internet crossed over from being an academic/scientific tool to being the most powerful communications medium ever available to the general public. The ability to communicate, collaborate, share, discuss, and debate has never before been available to such a large percentage the world's population. Why the sentimentality about the Internet? If Linus Torvalds conceived Linux, and it spent a while in the "womb" of academia, then the Internet is its home—where it will play, grow, and mature. But it has become more than a user of the Internet; it has become part of it, and is now being used to propagate itself.

0.2 WHY A LINUX ROUTER?

At this point, you may be thinking that this is all well and good and apropos in some sort of cosmic sense—the child has grown up to take care of the parent, etc., and so on—but what makes a Linux router any better or different than other routers? As with most interesting questions, the answer is: "it depends." Primarily, it depends upon what your definition of "better" is.

- Linux routers are inexpensive. For about $500 plus a meagerly equipped PC, you have a WAN-router capable of running several different protocols at T1 (1.5Mbps) speeds and higher. For a bit more, you can route multiple T3s. License costs are nil. Ongoing hardware maintenance costs are typically nil. Linux runs on the most widely-supported and lowest-cost hardware available.

- Linux routers are flexible. Try running a copy of *Apache* (the world's most popular HTTP daemon) on a "traditional" router, or integrating a "traditional" router into your in-house developed security infrastructure. At best, you will pay your router vendors handsomely for the privilege of letting them port your code to their systems. Otherwise, you're probably out of luck.

---

[2] Remember, "*GNU's Not Unix.*"

- Linux routers are stable. Whereas the TCP/IP implementation of others has been reviewed by, at most, a few hundred capable programmers, Linux's TCP/IP stack has been reviewed by literally thousands. More importantly, because Linux is a "labor of love" for most of its contributors, its quality is based on pride and technical excellence, not hampered by deadlines and office politics.

- Linux routers are easy to administer. If you can navigate a shell (you can pick the shell of your choice), you have already completed level one of your router training. With other solutions, you need to learn a new command-environment and set of tools. Linux is the same whether it's acting as a web server, workstation, or router.

- Linux routers are based on proven, widely-available technology. Because the system hardware and adapters are being produced for such an enormous market, costs are low and time-to-market cycles are as short as possible.

- Linux routers provide investment protection beyond that of their "traditional" counterparts. If you've worked in computer support for any length of time, you've probably experienced a vendor discontinuing a product line, phasing out support for a particular version, not adding features that you desperately need, or simply not responding to bug reports. With Linux, there is no vendor who can strong-arm you into accepting any of these. You always have the option of modifying the source yourself or choosing not to upgrade and remaining at the version which suits you best.

- Linux routers are expandable. Because you can use almost anything that you can attach to a PC, you never have to worry about whether or not your router chassis can support a third BRI ISDN adapter. Just add a serial expansion card and attach the third adapter.

- Linux routers are adaptable. One thing the computer industry has shown us by now (or taught us the hard way) is to expect change. Where is IBM's MCA? Whatever happened to 100VG-LAN? The next big thing to hit the market will be ?? Whatever it may be, you can be pretty certain that it will run on a Linux platform and be supported by Linux.

0.3 GOALS OF THIS BOOK

This book aims to promote Linux as a router by telling you how to set up and manage your own Linux router based on my experiences using them in production environments. Different "types" of routers are illustrated through a series of examples, each of which introduces the functionality and configuration of that router. For instance, Chapter 3 describes a router used to route traffic between two LAN subnets, while Chapter 5 details the configuration of a Frame Relay (WAN) router. Because the fine details of "how" change continually, every attempt is made to maintain a level of detail that will be useful for more than just the next point-release of the kernel. (However, the specific examples in the book are for the 2.2.x kernel series. See Section 0.6.1.)

Alongside the configurations are general discussions about running Linux in production, as well as coverage of some applications that help support the network infrastructure (like traffic analysis and system monitoring). For me, Linux is about enabling people to do things that they would not have been able to do (or afford to do) otherwise. Because of this, the book also contains some background information suited for "newbie" administrators who have never done network administration. While this information will be familiar to experienced network administrators, I feel that it's important because technical elegance is pointless without sound administration practices.

In what I believe is the "true spirit" of Linux—sharing information, ideas, and accomplishments instead of hiding them—references to publicly available resources will be made whenever such sources exist (and I am aware of them). Many of these are collected as a list of links in Appendix A. Another element of this spirit is the attitude that "whatever it is I need to accomplish, Linux is a sufficient toolset to succeed." Having faith in your toolset and in your ability to use it effectively to solve business problems are crucial to you performing your work well and enjoying it, too. This book aims to help you establish some faith in the toolset by offering knowledge about how to use it. I hope this book will help you find ways in which you can:

- Reduce the total cost of ownership (TCO) of your current environment.
- Deploy Linux routers in organizations which might not be able to afford the "traditional" hardware or the associated license and maintenance costs.
- Solve problems not addressed by "traditional" routers.
- Keep your Linux production environment healthy, saving yourself time and unexpected trips into the office.

THE LINUX DOCUMENTATION PROJECT

The *Linux Documenation Project*, or *LDP* as it's commonly known, is an invaluable resource for Linux documentation. The project aims to make high-quality documentation freely available to all. This means not covering a wide range of topics at various depths and skill levels, but making sure that the documentation is current and correct.

This documentation covers a wide variety of topics, from general hardware compatibility to specialized software configurations. The documentation takes several forms, from the informal FAQs and mini-HOWTOs to the regular HOWTOs and the longer guides. If you're not already familiar with this site, bookmark it—I will refer to documentation found there throughout this book.

http://www.linuxdoc.org

0.4 NON-GOALS OF THIS BOOK

This book does not aspire to incite the masses to riot and replace all "traditional" routers with Linux systems. (Throughout this book the term "traditional" should be taken to mean special-purpose router hardware based on a closed, proprietary system interface or "operating system." This would include the fine family of Cisco products, Nortel, Ascend Communications, et al.) These products have their place, and they have played the crucial role in paving the way for existence of Linux and the Linux router. In many instances, depending upon either the specific application or your corporate culture, traditional routers are the right choice for your production environment. On the other hand, a sound business philosophy is to pick the best tool for the job within the budget constraints given—the tool that will result in the lowest total cost of ownership. Realistically, cost is the overriding factor for most business ventures, and Linux-based solutions will often have the advantage.

This book does not attempt to thoroughly teach TCP/IP or fully explain routing protocols used in TCP/IP networks. Nor does the book thoroughly address firewall configuration or security. They are simply beyond the scope of this book, and other people have done fantastic jobs of covering these topics (much better than I could). I do heartily recommend a thorough understanding of TCP/IP and networking in general for anyone considering administering a TCP/IP network, regardless of the equipment used. For an authorative treatment of networking and routing, see *Interconnections* by Radia Perlman. Finally, the book you now hold covers only routing with TCP/IP (although Linux is capable of handling other protocols). If you need to support something other than IP, know that you are not alone, and that much of the software and hardware specifically supports protocols besides IP.

0.5 LAYOUT OF THIS BOOK

Chapters 1 and 2 discuss topics which are generic and applicable to all Linux routers, while Chapters 3–8 each cover a type of Linux router as I have used it in production and highlight what I learned in the process.[3] Of these six chapters, the first three are basic LAN, extranet, and WAN routers, while the remaining chapters address more advanced topics such as connecting to the Internet and making routers do more than just route.

Within each router chapter, the router first is introduced by its function, and then technical details of configuration are discussed. Throughout the book, several threads of related topics are presented and developed alongside the routers themselves. These topics include choice of hardware, choice of software, strategies for high-availability, TCP/IP niceties of Linux available in the kernel, and monitoring configurations and software. Different chapters have different components and requirements, but generally have the following layout:

- hardware
- software required and configuration
- kernel configuration
- support/high-availability
- monitoring

---

[3] There should probably be a chapter called "Franken-router" for the router configurations that did not work. A HOWNOTTO of sorts. Adventurous readers will be able to write this chapter themselves... :)

The appendices address topics either too general or too specific for the main text, from how to compile the Linux kernel (Appendix B) to using *VMware* to augment your testing strategies (Appendix C) to ethical considerations of a network admin. Finally, there may not be a single "flavor" of router presented in this book that fits your application. If that is the case, do not shy away from combining configurations presented here into something new. (Just remember to share them with others!)

0.6 TYPOGRAPHICAL CONVENTIONS

Every technical book has this section and I almost never read it, as it seems that all of the publishers must have sat down together a few years back and worked this out once and for all. On the other hand, I find that I am free to use conventions of my choice. Hopefully, you will find these to be straightforward. If you're still reading, here goes:

Table 0.1 Typographical Conventions

bold text	is used to introduce new terms and keystrokes which are not command names. (e.g. **CTRL-D** or **ESC**).
italics	indicate file, directory, and command names when they appear in the body of a paragraph. They also are used to highlight options to commands appearing in the body of the text. Beside that, they carry the normal meanings of *emphasizing* a word or phrase and marking URLs and email addresses, etc.
`fixed font`	is used for the contents of files, the output from commands, and general things that appear on the shell prompt.
`fixed bold`	is used for things that should be literally typed by you if you are following along with an example.
`fixed italic`	signify keywords, options, or other text which are variable and should be replaced by the user to fit the situation at hand.

0.6.1 A Note to 2.0.x Kernel Users

Initially, this text encompassed the 2.0.x and the 2.2.x versions of the kernel. As the book went through various stages of editing (and time passed), it became clear that the main text should appeal to the broadest userbase without forcing the reader to switch back and forth between the details of two different kernel versions. This is particularly true for the sections on masquerading and firewalling (Chapters 4, 6, and 8). For this reason, and because all of the major Linux distributions at the time of writing run on 2.2 kernels, the decision was made to remove the 2.0 specific portions of the text and make them freely available.

If you support a 2.0 Linux shop, you will still find value in the book, but you may want to access the specific configuration examples and text for the 2.0.x kernel at *http://www.prenhall.com/mancill/linuxrouters/*.

0.7 NAMING OF CHAPTERS

You might have already noticed something odd about the names of the chapters in this book. Maybe they make you want to check the cover to make sure that this isn't a science textbook. Selecting a naming motif for Unix systems is a tradition that seems to have been around for quite a while. Perhaps one of the hacker subculture deities knows its origin. (See *The New Hackers Dictionary* by Eric Raymond if this sort of computer trivia interests you.) If you haven't already guessed, I've named my routers after elements in the periodic table.

The periodic table has a few characteristics that make it suitable for naming. First of all, there is a large pool of names, many of which sound cool. (Unless you are dealing with a large environment, you shouldn't run out of names for a while.) Every name has a short yet unique "symbol name" associated with it, e.g., *gold* is **Au**, *carbon* is **C**. These can be used as a sort of shorthand, along with aliases (CNAMEs) in DNS to save keystrokes.

Routing Building Blocks

Whatcame before the router? What comprises the router? Or, for those of you with philosophical aspirations, which came first, the router or the packets? For the purposes of this chapter, we will conceptualize the router as consisting of three different components:

- The **hardware**, upon which the router runs.
- The **environment** and environmental considerations. This portion does not actually do any routing, but is important all the same. Without it, the router hardware and software may not be able to perform their specific tasks.
- The **software**, which directs the packets and may perform other useful functions.

This chapter will cover aspects of Linux routers common to almost all variations on the theme. Having the right mixture of these three basic building blocks is important for building stable elements described in later chapters. A large part of administering high availability systems is strategy and planning. Effort put into this up front can save a lot of (down)time and rework down the road. As we talk about the hardware, environment, and software, I will introduce some principles I have picked up while administering production systems. As with most opinions, YMMV (Your Mileage May Vary), so take the applicable parts and expand on them. Leave the rest.

1.1 ROUTER HARDWARE

It is likely that what first comes into your mind when you think about "hardware selection" are things like processor generation and speed, RAM, and Ethernet adapters. All of these are important to a router, but there are some even more fundamental aspects of hardware selection you should take into consideration. A router has different uptime requirements than a workstation. If a workstation is down for an hour, you've affected only a single user, or at most a single group of users. The same outage with a router will affect all users and will not go unnoticed. Maintenance windows are also smaller, since any nightly batch job or system backup that relies on the network depends upon the router. Should a component in a router fail, chances are likely that you will be under considerable stress to return it to service as quickly as possible. Therefore, consider the following when selecting your hardware:

1.1.1 Case

The case should be easy to open and have a consistent type and size of screw-head. The main components—hard drive, add-on cards, power-supply, and RAM—should be easy to reach without having to remove other components such as daughterboards, etc. Typically, big-name manufacturers do a better job of this than the low-cost offerings, but not always. Also, different product offerings from the same manufacturer can vary greatly. Probably the only way to know if the case is suitable for you is to take a system apart yourself. In environments where you will have multiple production systems, use the same case/vendor for all systems, if possible. The more alike the cases are in size and in configuration, the easier it will be to find a way to neatly stack or shelve them. Rack-mounted systems can make for extremely tidy installations, but can be expensive and difficult to service while still mounted in the rack.

1.1.2 Power-Supply and Fans

The power-supply should be adequately sized (in watts) for all of the components in your system. If it is difficult to replace, realize that you might be stuck migrating the hard drive and add-on cards to another system if it fails. The fans should provide adequate airflow in case of harsh environmental conditions (typically, extreme heat) outside of the system. Remember that a good fan is worthless if you place the entire unit such that air cannot enter and exit the case.

1.1.3 Motherboard

The choice of main system board for your router is probably less important than other components. For one, compatibility is typically not an issue with Linux, although I would steer clear of some of the more exotic motherboards and bus architectures.[1] Secondly, a router is less likely to use some of the fancier motherboard features, such as AGP bandwidth and USB support, which may be differentiating factors for non-router systems. If you are worried about a motherboard's compatibility with Linux, a good starting point is *http://www.linux.org/help/beginner/platforms.html*.

1.1.4 BIOS

Linux does not do much with BIOS after the machine bootstraps itself and starts loading the operating system. The BIOS must be able to recognize your hard drives and assign base addresses and IRQs to your PCI devices. Beyond that, a BIOS that

---

[1] There is support for the MCA (Micro Channel Adapter) systems from IBM, but I have not used them.

supports a password to get into the BIOS configuration menu might be useful if physical security is a concern, although hopefully you can solve these issues in other ways. Power-on passwords may also be necessary if physical security is a concern. Every BIOS is different, so here are some basic guidelines on configuration:

- Turn off any "Windows *XX*" features.
- Turn off any "15–16MB memory hole" feature.
- Turn off all of the APM (Advanced Power Management) features; routers never sleep. The BIOS should not be continually stopping and restarting your hard drive, as this will definitely shorten the lifespan of the drive. Also, a router should be able to process an interrupt from a communications adapter quickly, and waiting for APM to wake up system components may take too long to avoid packet loss. If you are environmentally conscious, try to purchase components with low power requirements, or use fewer components.
- Disable unused on-board adapters such as integrated USB ports or parallel ports. These use interrupts, which you may need for communications adapters. (On the other hand, do not disable things that you may need, since re-enabling them will require you to reboot the system while at the console.)
- Use the PCI bus controller configuration (if available) to explicitly set the interrupt to be given to a PCI slot. This will prevent quirky things from happening, like adding an Ethernet adapter and then finding out on your next reboot that the IRQs assigned to your adapters have changed (and no longer match the values you are using when loading device driver modules).
- *Consider* using power-on passwords and BIOS configuration passwords. I would tend to shy away from power-on passwords unless you have a facility that is staffed 24×7. These are a good idea for physical security, but can be troublesome when you desperately need to reboot a router from a remote site.

    A BIOS configuration password is a good idea as long as you can find the password when you need it. One way to keep these passwords safe without having to keep track of many (potentially dozens of) different passwords is to send a PGP-encrypted email containing the password to yourself (and your back-up administrator or manager).
- The BIOS on some older Compaq systems (Deskpro XLs) relocates the PCI address space to a location in memory that Linux will never find. There is a documented work-around for this which you can find via the *LDP*.

1.1.5 Hard Drive

Because a router should never be disk I/O bound,[2] your choice of hard drive is fairly arbitrary. Many people swear by SCSI drives for both reliability and performance. I prefer to use IDE drives for routers due to their low cost and easy configuration, and

---

[2] A state when other system activities must frequently wait for the completion of reads and/or writes to the disk subsystem. This waiting is also known as **blocking**.

because I have had good luck in terms of reliability. SCSI drives work well too—just make sure that your SCSI controller is supported by the kernel.

DRIVE RELIABILITY IN THE REAL WORLD

> Donald Becker, the father of a large number of the Ethernet drivers in the Linux kernel and leader of the *Beowulf* project, had some interesting things to say about IDE hard drives during a talk about Beowulf clusters at the 1998 Atlanta Linux Showcase. In his experience, which includes large numbers of IDE drives running continuously for long periods of time, drive failures are unrelated to the MTBF statistics listed by the manufacturer.
>
> According to him, drives come in either good batches or bad batches—i.e., different production runs, regardless of manufacturer, are a more important factor in drive reliability than the manufacturer. He went on to say that power consumption also seems to play a very important role in drive reliability, and that the lower the average power consumption, the more reliable the drive. (Power consumption is related to the spindle speed (RPM) and the mass of the platters themselves.)
>
> In case you are wondering, a Beowulf cluster is a group of Linux machines networked together to build a system capable of performing like a supercomputer. What started as an experiment in the cost-efficiency of such a solution has been very successful, and there are now many dozens of such clusters in use. See *http://www.beowulf.org/* for more information.

Partitioning Hard Drive Space   Overall drive capacity is not a primary concern for most router applications, and depends primarily on the amount of logging required. Most of my production routers use a single 1GB or 2GB drive. If there is a second drive, it is a backup for the primary drive. Still, the question of how to partition drive space is a common one among those new to Linux and Unix. Although there are lots of opinions on this, each founded by its owner's experience, my answer for routers with a single disk is simple. Assign 400–600MB for the root partition, between 64–128MB of swap space, and everything else to */var*. This results in a partition table that looks like:

```
Device Bootflag   Mount point   Size (MB)       File System
/dev/hda1    *        /            400            ext2 (Linux native)
/dev/hda2            n/a           64             Linux swap
/dev/hda3            /var          all remaining  ext2 (Linux native)
```

There are several reasons to allocate so much space to */var*, and why the root partition and */usr* do not need to be very large:

- All logging is done to */var*. Even if you use *syslog* to log remotely, you should have enough space to log locally for cases when you need to do some serious debugging or packet capture.
- Most package managers do all of their work in */var*, including using it for a cache of recently loaded packages. You'll need some space here if you want to upgrade between releases.

- Packages you may add to your routers, such as *sendmail*, *Apache*, and *Bind*, all use space under */var* to hold their files.

- Without users, */tmp* space is not a concern. Well-behaved Linux packages do not use */tmp* for anything of consequential size.

- Compared to */var*, */usr* remains fairly static, although it does grow when you add more packages (and therefore system executables).

- Because items in */var* are dynamic, it has a chance of filling up and needs to be a separate filesystem.

For those of you who want to allocate a separate filesystem for */usr*, there is no harm in this as long as */var* is also its own filesystem and is of ample size. When sizing */usr*, include space to hold a copy of the kernel source,[3] unless you know that you'll build your kernels elsewhere. Until Linux has support for filesystems, which can be grown dynamically "on-line," you'll need to take any special features of your system into consideration before you carve up your disks into partitions. (This sort of support is imminent, and it should be available by the time this book goes to press.)

NOTE: VERY LARGE HARD DRIVES

The full range of cylinders in very large drives may not be recognized by the BIOS in older systems. If your boot partition is located in an area not accessible to the BIOS, your system may not be able to boot by itself. You can circumvent this problem by making and using a boot floppy. (Once Linux is running, it does not use BIOS, nor does it have this problem with larger hard drives.) Since a router should rarely be rebooted, a few extra seconds during the boot-up sequence should not be too high a price to pay. If you find a boot-floppy inconvenient or otherwise inelegant, refer to the *LDP*'s *Large Disk HOWTO* for other strategies (like creating a small */boot* partition at the beginning of the disk).

1.1.6 SCSI Adapter

Normally, I do not use SCSI devices in my routers. (I do recommend SCSI tape drives for backups, but these are normally done over the network to another machine.) If you do require a SCSI adapter in your system, check the *LDP*'s *Linux Hardware Compatibility HOWTO* and consider an adapter that supports bus-mastering DMA transfers. Bus-mastering greatly reduces the load on the processor and the bus while accessing the device(s) by allowing the adapter to read and write data from memory directly. Without bus-mastering support, the CPU has to manage these transfers, which necessitates transferring the data from the device to the CPU and then from the CPU to memory to complete a read.

---

[3] The kernel keeps growing—sizes at the time of writing can be found in Appendix B.

1.1.7 Video Adapter

This is an area where almost nothing is more than enough. You merely need an adapter capable of supporting an 80×25 text-mode console. Starting with version 2.2 of the kernel, the use of a serial port as a console is supported—thus eliminating the need for any video adapter whatsoever (almost). The caveat is that you won't be able to modify the system BIOS without a video adapter (on x86 architectures), and a few systems may refuse to boot without a keyboard attached. Configuring your system to use a serial port as the console requires three steps:

1. You need to enable serial console support in the kernel. (Although you can compile the serial support as a module, I recommend against it since you will want to see the boot messages before any modules are loaded.)

```
Character devices --->
    <*> Standard/generic (dumb) serial support
    [*]     Support for console on serial port
```

2. Configure your boot loader to tell the kernel which serial port to use as the console by supplying `console=device,baudrate` as an argument to the kernel during the boot sequence. You should use the device name shown by *dmesg* (not the path to the device in */dev/*). Use 9600 for the baudrate. If you are using LILO, add the following line to your configuration and then rerun *lilo* to update the boot sector:

```
append = "console=ttyS0,9600"
```

3. Configure a getty process to run on this port by adding the appropriate line to */etc/inittab*.

```
T0:2345:respawn:/sbin/getty -L ttyS0 9600 vt100
```

After you reboot so that these settings are active, you can access your serial console by attaching the specified port to any dumb terminal or to the serial port on another system and running a terminal emulator such as *minicom*.

1.1.8 CPU

Processor speed can be quite important for certain types of routers, while others seem to barely touch the CPU at all. Routers that need more processing power are ones with lots of firewalling or masquerading rules and those that must also perform heavy statistics collection or monitoring. CPU requirements depend not only upon load, but also upon the number and type of adapters in the system. Adapters capable of DMA (and that have Linux drivers which support bus-mastering) can significantly reduce the CPU requirements by being able to move data to and from main memory without involving the CPU. In the case of WAN adapters, some of these are capable of running the link protocol on the card itself, which means that there is less code in the device driver and correspondingly lower CPU requirements.

In this matter, my recommendations are based purely on experience. At the time of writing, I have never needed to use anything faster than a P6/180 (which was for a packet-filtering firewall). For WAN routers, a 486/66 has proved itself adequate, exposing its relative sloth only during kernel compiles. Because it really does depend upon your application, you should keep a close watch on marginally-sized systems using tools like *top* and *vmstat*. Remember that routing and network transfers that occur in the kernel are recorded as system CPU time.

LINUX ROUTER SHOOTOUT!

Several people have suggested conducting a benchmark to determine the relative speed of Linux routers compared to traditional offerings. This is a good idea because I believe it would allay the fears of those reluctant to consider Linux as a router. On the other hand, speed is only part of the equation, since Linux offers low cost and flexibility. Furthermore, speed is relative; a couple of milliseconds may be bad news latency for a gigabit switch, but it's peanuts for a 128kb ISDN link.

1.1.9 Bus Architecture

There is a lot of theory that goes into a discussion about the relative strengths of the different bus architectures. In the final analysis, I think it boils down to the following points:

- PCI >> ISA 16-bit > ISA 8-bit (where > means "is faster than"), so use PCI adapters when possible. Hopefully, there are not many 8-bit ISA Ethernet cards out there, but if there are, find some other use for them besides in your router.

- Interrupts *are* important—you should particularly avoid having an Ethernet adapter at a lower interrupt priority than a slow device, such as a parallel port or a serial port. Typically, interrupts 3, 4, 5, 7, 9, 10, 11, and 12 are available to you. The relative priorities, from highest to lowest, are 9, 10, 11, 12, 3, 4, 5, and 7.[4]

1.1.10 RAM

You should have enough RAM to ensure that your router will not be swapping at any point during normal day-to-day operations. This means at least 8 MB for a plain router and definitely more if you intend to run other services or do any monitoring. Of course, faster memory is better (e.g., using 8ns DIMMs instead of 70ns SIMMs).

---

[4] For more information about interrupts, see *http://www.linuxdoc.org/LDP/LG/issue38/ blanchard.html*.

1.1.11 Network Interface Card (NIC)

Your choice of network adapter is a topic that warrants some discussion, although much less nowadays than it used to.[5] The Linux kernel natively supports a wide variety of adapter types, including ATM, FDDI, ISDN, token ring, Wireless LAN, ARCnet, Appletalk, infrared, amateur radio, WAN, and a slew of Ethernet cards. The amount to which different devices are supported seems to be proportional to the probability of encountering those devices; i.e., the more popular the device, the more fully developed and tested the driver. Ethernet, of course, reigns supreme, but there is an impressive amount of support for the other types of devices too.

If you're interested in trying something new or perhaps a bit out of the ordinary, check for driver availability in the most recent stable kernel release. (I do not recommend using development kernels for routers.) If the driver is not in the kernel source, you should check with the hardware manufacturer to determine if they have Linux support. Sometimes they have drivers that either have not yet made it into the source, or have license restrictions which prevent them from being incorporated into the main source.[6] You can also refer to the *Linux Hardware Compatibility* or to the *NET-HOWTO* on the *LDP*.

1.1.12 Ethernet Adapters

Because Ethernet is so ubiquitous, let us spend a moment talking about it, although some of the comments apply to all adapters. For most applications, a well-known PCI 10/100 card is the right choice. Here are things to keep in mind:

- Look for PCI cards that support bus-mastering DMA. You can also look for cards with more on-board RAM. This is used for buffers and can normally be found on the "server" cards. The extra buffer space is a Good Thing when your router gets busy.

- When one side of the router hosts a relatively slow communications link, a 16-bit ISA adapter should suffice. (On average, you cannot send or receive data at rates any higher than the rate of the slower interface.)

- Always compile your device drivers as modules. This will allow you to upgrade the device driver without having to generate a new kernel or reboot your machine. It also makes it possible to unload and reload the device driver should you need to reinitialize the driver for some reason. For a more in-depth discussion of kernel modules, see Section B.5 in Appendix B.

- To get the most out of your device driver (modular or not), you should read the comments at the beginning of the driver source code in the kernel. This is traditionally where the most current (and complete) driver documentation is kept. The drivers are stored in *./drivers/net/*`driver_name.c` relative to the

---

[5] Many thanks to all of the people who have contributed to the impressive amount of support and stability of the network device drivers for Linux.

[6] If they provide no Linux support whatsoever, take the time to send them a note. It may be that someone in-house has developed the driver, but it has not yet been made public. Also, companies don't know about demand unless you make that demand known.

root of the Linux source tree. Of particular interest for router admins will be documentation on initializing more than one card of the same type per system. (Another benefit of using modular drivers: If you specify the parameters incorrectly for a built-in driver, you'll have to reboot to test another syntax or combination—not so with modules.)

- Plug-and-Play (PnP) ISA cards are not going to save you any time whatsoever. They only confuse the issue of base-address and IRQ selection, and there are some behaviors that are very difficult to trouble-shoot if the card is left in PnP mode. If you have a PnP card, immediately disable the PnP functionality and set the base address and IRQ manually. Typically, this can be done with the DOS-based setup utility which comes with the card. Some cards have their configuration utilities ported to Linux. Such tools for several very common cards can be found at *http://cesdis.gsfc.nasa.gov/linux/setup/*. If you're wondering how to find out what IRQs and base-addresses are already in use on your system, `cat /proc/interrupts` and `cat /proc/ioports`, respectively.

That completes the general hardware selection notes for your Linux router. Just as with network adapters, it is advisable to stick with devices that are supported in the stable kernel releases unless you like to roll up your sleeves and hack driver (and kernel) source code. In any event, do not belabor your decision about hardware for too long. Most of the work and decision-making takes place during the software configuration, so save your time and energy for that.

1.2 THE ENVIRONMENT AROUND YOUR ROUTER

Now we will step back and look not at the router itself, but at some of the elements that surround the router. This encompasses not only the physical surroundings, but also procedures and policies.

1.2.1 Power Source

You should have a good, stable source of grounded power. A UPS is an important investment towards keeping your system up and protected from power outages, brown-outs, lightning strikes, and other dangers to electronics. Several major UPS vendors provide Linux versions of their software, so you should do some research before you purchase one.

1.2.2 Physical Installation

Like any other production system, your router(s) should be in an area which can be physically secured (i.e., locked), is temperature-regulated, and is low-traffic. (By "low-traffic" I mean a place where people are seldom to be found.) You should use either a rack or a cabinet to house the system, if possible, but make sure that there is adequate airflow around the case. It may sound pedantic, but a neat installation is less likely to be accidentally taken offline by a clumsy mistake. (People are also less likely to be inclined to touch or disturb a neat installation.)

1.2.3 Testing

No matter how careful, everybody makes mistakes. I heard it said that *human error* is the cause of over 80% of production computer outages. It is important to admit this fact from the very beginning and work with this in mind if you want your production environment to have a minimum of downtime. For this reason, any changes should be thoroughly tested before you roll them out to your production environment. The problem is that networks are not always easy to test adequately. It is often difficult and expensive to duplicate aspects of your environment, such as network load and circuit types, particularly when you are running protocols that involve networks controlled by others (e.g., Frame Relay with your provider or connecting to the Internet).

You can limit your vulnerabilities by being confident about any changes you make. Part of this is testing, while another component is following sound **change management** procedures. As opposed to providing a lengthy discussion on change management, I've relegated some ideas about that and more information about testing strategies to Appendix C.

1.2.4 Backups

It's a boring job, but *you* have to do it. There are lots of ways of generating backups; some are simply more useful than others. I recommend reading the section on UNIX backups in *Practical UNIX & Internet Security* by Garfinkel and Spafford[7] before deciding on a strategy.

If you decide that you need full backups performed on your router, I've had good success using 4mm DAT drives on SCSI interfaces together with *BRU 2000* from EST, Inc. But backups to removable media are not your only option. Other strategies particular to routers and other (almost) data-less systems are presented in Section 7.4.2 of Chapter 7.

1.2.5 Logs

You should maintain a log file of all major changes you make to your production systems, including software loads and configuration changes, password changes, hardware changes, in addition to any outages, odd behavior, security breaches, etc. Even if the event is not directly related to your system(s), you might want to note it. (This is really all part of change management.)

Keep at least one log per system, and, depending upon the size of your environment, one or more overall logs related to each service you provide your users. These logs will help you see how changes in one part of the network affect the other parts. You may store these as files, but you should keep them in a safe place, possibly encrypted and definitely backed-up at regular intervals. Some stress hardcopy as a necessary component, but you cannot *grep* hardcopy, nor can you quickly transfer it to other members of your team, and it is quickly outdated. Whatever the final for-

---

[7] See the Bibliography for the complete reference.

mat is, do not forget to include things like essential system files, a copy of a working routing table, and any known bugs or odd behaviors. As with backups, this topic is well-covered in *Practical UNIX & Internet Security*.

1.2.6 Scripting

Regardless of your choice of scripting language, thoroughly document your scripts; well-documented code saves time down the road. Your code should contain comments within the code and a modification history at the top which tracks changes made to the script over time. You can save yourself some typing by developing or borrowing a script template to use as a starting point for all of your scripts. I include the header I use for *ksh* scripts here:

```
#!/usr/bin/ksh
#
# <name of program>
#     <description of program>
#
# <license/copyright information>
#
# modification history:
#
# 19990514/tm  initial release
# 19990608/tm  reworked error message code
######################################################################
```

The main point is that changes in the script are noted so that others (or even you) will not have to guess at what changes have occurred when the script suddenly stops doing what you expect it to do. Use a common date format so that changes can be quickly spotted by a human or match a regular expression.

1.2.7 Planning

Examples are planning upgrades, outages, migrations, and the like. Take the time to list out the steps required to complete some task—say, for example, adding a NIC to a router migrating a remote office to a larger Frame Relay link, or upgrading the hubs in your equipment room without affecting the users. You may never use the list, but the act of taking the time to write out the steps required will often lead you to consider how those actions will interact with your environment, and remind you of things you might have overlooked had you started the task without explicitly listing the steps required. Roadblocks take many forms—a piece of equipment that needed to be ordered, or a hostname which should have been registered with the InterNIC, or simply a lack of ports on a hub. Speaking from personal experience, you can save yourself a lot of frustration by just jotting down the sequential actions you need to take to complete a job and then review these before you start the task.

1.2.8 Security

While password and network security receive a lot of attention, physical security is often neglected. Different types of organizations have differing needs, but as a minimum you should have a room with a lock on the door and a list of those who have the key.

And thus concludes our brief discussion of system environmentals. Much of being a good system administrator is being conscientious about things like documentation and backups, being aware of how changes to one system might affect the systems around it, and having a contingency plan should things go wrong. (And things will go wrong.) Therefore, it is prudent to control the things you can since there will be many that you cannot. This leads us to our next topic: software.

1.3 ROUTER SOFTWARE

The term *router software* might be a bit misleading since it is the Linux kernel itself that performs the actual routing of network packets. In other words, there is no program, per se, that has to be running for routing to occur. The routing takes place in **kernel-space** (as opposed to daemons and most services which run in **user-space**). Still, there are a host of programs which help make this happen, and make it easier for humans to manage. This section contains a discussion of the different Linux distributions and what you might want to consider when you go about selecting one.

The selection of a Linux distribution can be the source of great anguish and gnashing of teeth, and you will find that it is as much a religious debate as a technical one. If you're asking yourself, "What's a distribution?", it is a set of pre-compiled binaries and **package tools** (tools that are used to load and upgrade software on the system) which work together and have been tested as a whole to give us a complete operating system. In Linux-lingo, they are called **distros**. Realize that the Linux kernel itself is only a small part of the distribution (or what we commonly think of a "Linux"). The remainder is comprised of compilers, shells, applications, servers, and systems software so that we can actually do something useful with the kernel. I've divided the discussion of distribution into two parts: *full-sized distributions*—distributions intended to be run from a hard drive and are general-purpose in nature—and *mini distributions*, which normally fit on a single floppy diskette and are sometimes special-purpose.

1.3.1 Full-Sized Linux Distributions

There are at least a half-dozen very stable, successful full-sized distributions available. You are not likely to go wrong with any of these, and your choice is largely a matter of personal preference. Since routing is performed in the kernel, I am not aware of a distribution that couldn't act as a router. However, keep in mind that production systems have different requirements than a personal workstation or home system, so some distros are better suited than others. The following is a list of properties which I believe are important for a production Linux distribution:

- **dependencies** — Be sure to choose a distribution that supports package dependencies (i.e., uses a scheme to notify you when you are loading software that depends upon some other software or library, or perhaps a certain version of a library.) Most of the "modern" distributions do this automatically via their **package manager**. It is vital for this piece of software to prevent you from upgrading pieces of software which may have adverse effects on other software on the system.

- **upgradability** — Closely related to dependencies, make sure that you choose a distribution which is committed to providing upgrade paths between versions. There is a certain sinking feeling you might be familiar with—that feeling you get when you realize that there is no (or at least no sane) upgrade path between the OS version that you currently have and the next supported version. Don't be bitten.

- **support** — Unless you have a lot of free time on your hands or very special requirements, choose a distribution which is being actively maintained and developed. There should also be a forum for submitting bugs, asking questions, and making suggestions for improvements. For an active distribution, users beget questions, which beget FAQs, which beget gurus. If you (or your management) require it, do some research to determine if there is commercial support available.

- **stability** — The better tested the distribution, the less "testing" you'll do on your own. This also points towards the more popular distributions, although another component to consider is the value of simplicity over complexity. The more complicated a piece of software, the less likely that any organization or number of people will be able to test it thoroughly. Of course, you can quickly make a stable distribution unstable by taking matters into your own hands and deciding to upgrade software outside of the confines of the package management scheme.

- **security** — Security goes hand-in-hand with testing and support. A distribution should have provisions for you to file security bugs against it, and provide documentation for running a (more) secure version of the base distribution.

- **licensing** — Because Linux is inexpensive in the grand scheme of things, an extra copy here or there should not break the bank. However, you should be cognizant of the licensing policy of the distribution you use.[8] Software piracy continues to exist, even in the world of OpenSource.

- **extensibility** — Although you might not initially be thinking of writing your own software packages, when you do, it would be nice to be able to distribute your custom software via the same mechanism as the rest of the OS. Therefore, your distribution should make the same tools used to build packages for the released version available to you so that you can also build packages. This saves you the time and effort of producing documentation about how to compile, install, and configure software which is not available in the distribution.

- **target audience** — Linux is growing in popularity, and as such, distributions are emerging with specific target audiences in mind. Not all of these will be the right choice for your production router.

---

[8] Furthermore, I think that you should fundamentally agree with it.

Loading Linux   As I stated earlier, any of the modern distributions should suffice for a router. Choose what suits you and learn how to use that distribution's tools and features. Being able to find what you're looking for when you're trying to fix things is more important than whether or not the file is in the "right place." When you load your system, remember to select tools and avoid unnecessary toys. With the variety of distributions and their various schemes for loading software, it is difficult to list exactly what you should select from your system. The following guidelines should help:

1. You will very likely need C development environment (at least *gcc*, *make*, and the *bin86* tools [assembler, etc.]). In other words, enough to compile a kernel. Some distributions will automatically load the required tools if you select a kernel source package. If you find that loading an entire development environment just to compile a kernel is overkill, you can forego this and compile your kernels on another system. In my experience, having the ability to compile a kernel on the router is useful.

2. You should not need an X-server or a window manager, although X libraries are not a bad idea if you will be throwing xterms and running other X clients from your system.

3. Load all of the networking tools you can find, at least until you learn which ones you like and don't like. Examples of what to load are mentioned throughout the book.

4. Do not load "network server" parts of the distribution unless you know that you need these things—typically, packages like *Samba*, *Apache*, and other things for network *servers*. Once you're up and routing, you can go back and add these things if needed. Until then, they are a security risk and an extra load on your router.

Once you have loaded your system, take some time to familiarize yourself with what you have loaded. Sometimes, the distribution will come with tools that you are not even aware existed. All of the distributions that support dependencies will place information specific to the packages loaded somewhere on your system. For example, if you're running Debian, you can use `dpkg -l` to see what packages are loaded. For every package loaded, there is a directory */usr/share/doc/*package which contains documentation for that package (or a pointer to it), in addition to the license and a changelog.

1.3.2 Mini Linux Distributions

The mini distributions offer several advantages over their full-sized counterparts. Many are small enough to fit on a single floppy disk and can be tried without disrupting the system configuration on the hard drive. They can be easier to master because there is less to learn, and they are small enough that you can take them all apart and look at how they work. Their size also makes them more likely to be both secure and fully tested (less to crack and less to break). Because they can be placed on removable media, they are not subject to hard drive failures. For this reason, they are an excellent choice for physically demanding environments which might be too rough for a hard drive.

Of course, these advantages come at certain cost. Namely, these distributions lack some of the flexibility and conveniences of their larger cousins. (Do not expect to find half a dozen different shells plus a Perl interpreter.) Also, many of the commands have to be scaled down and recompiled against leaner versions of *libc* to save space. This means that some commands might behave a little differently than they do on the full distributions. Still, for a router, they can be a good fit. They are also excellent instructional aids; several of them cater to this purpose. Another way to use them is to use full-sized distributions for day-to-day production systems, and have a mini distribution ready to take over in case the hard drive dies.

Here is a partial list of the mini distro offering:

- **LRP**— The Linux Router Project. This distribution is directly targeted at the network administrator of production routers. It is well-done and capable of supporting more than just basic routing. Examples include packages for *Bind*, *GateD*, and an *SNMP* daemon, among others. Furthermore, it is loosely based on the Debian distribution. You can find out more about it at *http://www.linuxrouter.org/* as well as in Chapter 3 in Section 3.4.

- **tomsrtbt**— *http://www.toms.net/rb/* This single floppy distribution provides a nice set of commands which can be used to perform rescue activities as well as configure a router. I have used this distribution in the past to put together single-purpose diskettes—for tasks at remote sites without sysadmin staff for which some special action is needed, which cannot be performed over the network.

- **Trinux**— *http://www.trinux.org/* This is based on multiple floppies (two or three) and focuses on providing a network security and monitoring tools. It supports an impressive amount of network tools and is ideal for quickly producing a working sniffer on almost any machine without damaging the host OS.

- **muLinux**— *http://sunsite.auc.dk/mulinux/* This fits on a single floppy with optional "add-on" floppies. Like Trinux, it is also targeted for workstation use, but contains enough tools to be useful as a basis for a router.

- **floppyfw**— *http://www.zelow.no/floppyfw/* Here is another networking-centric single floppy distribution which is designed to act as a packet-filtering router. It caught my eye since it supports the latest kernel (2.2.x, while many of the other minis are still running 2.0.x) with the newer **ipchains** interface to masquerading and firewalling. It also happens to be based on Debian.

This list is by no means complete. A more comprehensive list can be found on the **tomsrtbt** homepage. To my knowledge none of the mini distributions is a commercial effort or has any sort of financial backing. Keep this in mind if you find that they are lacking some of the gloss and polish that the full commercial distributions have. Since the authors volunteer their time, they might not be able to incorporate features or answer questions as quickly as you would like. Do not let this dissuade you from their use. Like so many other things involved with Linux, they have merit *because* they are non-commercial. They are usually a labor of love, and their high quality reflects this. If you really want to see something in the distribution, submit a patch. Clear as mud? The choice of distribution can seem unwieldy if you do not already have an opinion.

1.3.3 My Choice of Distribution

The examples in this book should run on any of the distributions, although there is some value-added information about Debian, since that is what I have always used. In my experience, Debian GNU/Linux meets the criteria listed at the beginning of this section as desirable to have in a Linux distribution.[9] Its package manager enforces dependencies in a consistent and straightforward manner. Debian is committed to being upgradable. (And this is something I have had occasion to verify often.) Its stability is ensured by the Debian QA group and a large body of developers who beat up on it daily and hash out design decisions in open mailing lists.

   Debian is security-minded, and is bold enough to make its bug-list completely open, including security holes. This is a strong statement of the belief that by making things completely open the group can flush as many bugs and holes out of the system as possible. Besides being completely open, Debian is completely free—not only in terms of cost, but in terms of the licensing and source code availability. Having the source code for both the binaries and the packaging greatly aids its extensibility. Should you require a slight modification, all you need do is retrieve a copy of the source package, make the desired changes, and use the Debian developer's tools to repackage the software. I've done this for several packages, allowing other administrators who were loading their systems to receive the latest versions pre-configured for our environment. Debian's target audience seems to be those who agree with the philosophy of a 100%-free Linux distribution and who value the technical precision that is fostered by openness and constructive criticism. (They claim no particular target.) See *http://www.debian.org* for more information.

1.4 SUMMARY

This concludes the section on router software, and with it the chapter. We covered a large range of topics, trying to provide an overview for newcomers, so let's quickly review. You should be armed with enough knowledge to get started:

- gathering hardware (page 1) and selecting a network adapter card (page 8).
- preparing your management for the sticker shock of the UPS and other environmentals you will need that cost more than the router (page 9).
- selecting a Linux distribution (page 12), be it a full-sized distribution or a mini distribution.

   This knowledge classifies you as "dangerous." The next chapter continues taking about routers in general. It covers basic IP subnetting and routing principles and terminology surrounding digital telephony. If you would like to be "really dangerous," please turn the page now.

---

[9] To be completely honest, in some ways, it has defined them.

IP, Ethernet, and Telephony Basics

$\mathbf{T}$his chapter covers some background concepts before we dive into configuring a router. First, we'll review IP subnet terminology and the related base–2 math. This is a prerequisite for the discussion on principles of IP subnetting used by workstations and routers. After that, we'll switch gears for a short discussion of Ethernet, including how machines find each other and the difference between Ethernet hubs and switches. The chapter concludes with an introduction to WAN links, based on digital telephone circuits.

2.1 ROUTING 101

For the purposes of this book, a router is anything that transfers TCP/IP packets between different IP subnets, regardless of their physical media-type or the media-protocol. In short, a router is something used to connect two distinct IP subnets.

What's an IP subnet? What's a physical media-type? What's a media-protocol? These are all questions first of terminology, but also of *layers*. Networking can be discussed in terms of layers and how each layer acts as an interface, performing communication between the layer above and below it. This is done for numerous reasons, but I believe the most important are reuse and flexibility. It is useful to be able to differentiate between the layers and to agree on a common terminology to be able to talk clearly about building networks and routers. The most common taxonomy for networks is defined by the OSI networking model. If you are not familiar with the OSI networking model, see the first chapter of *Interconnections* by Radia Perlman. The complete reference can be found in the bibliography. To get started with routing, you don't need to memorize all seven layers of the model. Just understand the concepts in the following definitions:

physical medium — in most cases a wire, or perhaps an RF link. It is generally associated with a specific physical interface. As an example, think of a normal serial cable used to connect a DB9 serial port to a DB25 external modem.

physical protocol — the protocol (normally electrical or optical) which runs on the **physical medium**. RS–232 is an example for a serial cable, or IEEE 802.3 for Ethernet.

link-layer protocol — the protocol used to negotiate a connection (or a **link**) between two machines sharing the same physical medium. Examples are PPP, HDLC, Frame Relay, and Ethernet. The link-layer does not dictate which networking protocol you run on top of it, but it does need to know about it. This is why you might find different PPP implementations for IP and IPX.

networking protocol — the protocol which dictates addressing of nodes and packets, and the way that packets are routed between endpoints. Examples are IP and IPX.

transport protocol — the protocol which interfaces the networking protocol to the operating system and processes within it (also known as an **end-to-end protocol**). In the case of TCP/IP, there are multiple protocols which comprise the **protocol suite**—namely, TCP and UDP.

application protocol — the level of protocol created by applications programmers, often where users get involved. They invoke commands such as *telnet*, which define a sequence of TCP transactions, which in turn are realized through a series of IP events (which define transmissions between Ethernet hosts, which in turn result in electromagnetic waveforms propagating through a piece of twisted-pair). Other application protocols are NFS, HTTP, NTP, NNTP, SNMP, SMTP, FTP, and many others.

Figure 2.1 illustrates each layer encapsulating the layer above it. When everything is configured properly, the different layers work together as a cohesive whole, and the user doesn't even think about these things. In contrast, you need to understand what's happening at the different layers to be able to effectively design and trouble-shoot your network. As an example, not being able to make a connection

Figure 2.1 Layered Network Model

to a remote machine does not necessarily mean the network's "down," at least not if the problem is with the user's DNS configuration. By correctly assessing the level at which the problem exists, you eliminate the need to test other layers, whose problems are merely symptomatic of the root problem. The end result of a good understanding is less time spent on wild goose chases.

2.1.1 IP Subnetting

An IP subnet is a collection of network addresses which can communicate directly with each other without having to refer to a router to accomplish the communication. In other words, the media-protocol drivers support direct communication between all systems in the same subnet. Transmitting data between two separate subnets requires a router, often called a **gateway** in this context. To determine whether or not two systems are in the same subnet, do the following:

> Perform a binary AND of the IP address of machine A and the subnet mask of machine A. Now do the same for machine B. If the resulting network addresses are identical for both machines, then these machines can speak over TCP/IP to each other without using a gateway.

If this is Greek to you, you should review the remainder of this section. It introduces enough base–2 math to get you started with IP addresses, the subnet mask, what is meant by a network and broadcast address, and how to calculate them.

The IP Address & Base–2 Mathematics   An IP address is a collection of 32 bits, divided into four groups of 8 bits for convenient presentation in the form of 4 unsigned integers (really, *decimals*, since the presentation is in base–10). Each grouping of 8 bits can be expressed as a value between 0 and 255. Almost everyone is familiar with the dotted-decimal notation used for 32-bit IP addresses: $w.x.y.z$, where $0 \leq$ w,x,y,z ≤ 255. This is done primarily for humans; the computers couldn't care less about the decimal values. Here is an example IP address:

As you see it (base–10):

$$215.38.181.126$$

As the computer sees it (base–2 or binary):

$$11010111001001101011010101111110$$

Split into 4 groups of 8 bits:

11010111	00100110	10110101	01111110

Each bit represents a successively greater power of two as you move from right to left. Note that the powers of two, which are listed below, start at 2^0.

2^7	2^6	2^5	2^4	2^3	2^2	2^1	2^0
128	64	32	16	8	4	2	1

A "1" in a given bit position indicates that the corresponding power of two counts towards the final value. A "0" in a given bit position means to ignore that position. If we label the bit positions b_7–b_0 (moving from left to right), we can write out a formula for our binary-to-decimal conversion.

$$128*b_7 + 64*b_6 + 32*b_5 + 16*b_4 + 8*b_3 + 4*b_2 + 2*b_1 + 1*b_0$$

Thus, the binary-to-decimal conversion of 11010111 works as follows:

128*1	+	64*1	+	32*0	+	16*1	+	8*0	+	4*1	+	2*1	+	1*1
128	+	64	+	0	+	16	+	0	+	4	+	2	+	1

which equals 215.

As you can see, the bit positions where there was a "1" contributed to the final value; the positions containing "0" did not. Converting the other three values in our initial example (oftentimes referred to as **octets**, as they are groupings of 8, but most commonly known simply as **bytes**) yields:

$$00100110 = 38$$
$$10110101 = 181$$
$$01111110 = 126$$

TIP: HELP WITH BASE–2 CONVERSIONS

> If you are not accustomed to making these conversions (or counting in 2's), I encourage you to perform these conversions on your own so that you can be certain about how they work. Most scientific calculators can help, as will some calculator programs—notably *calctool* (written by Rich Burridge).

The reason the computer does not use the decimal representation is because it is easier only for humans. The hardware in the computer (and on the NIC) is designed to operate on bits. In fact, it can work *only* with bits. One good thing about bits is that digital hardware can do things with them incredibly quickly. Routers like speed and efficiency, so router admins get to work with bits.

To review, an IP address is 32 bits that are often represented as four groupings of 8 bits each. At least, that's the simple answer. The next section covers how these 32 bits can be split into network and address fields.

The Subnet Mask   The subnet mask is a topic which seems to cause considerable confusion when it comes to configuring a TCP/IP stack. The **subnet mask** is used to divide the 32 bits into two parts. The left portion is the **network address**. The remaining part is the **host address**. The subnet mask simply tells the computer how many bits (from left to right) are in the network address. The remaining bits comprise the host address. This can be seen in Figure 2.2.

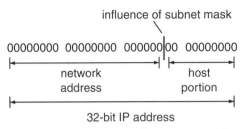

Figure 2.2   Network and Host Portions of the
IP Address

In the olden days there were three types of networks: class A, class B, and class C, each with its own fixed subnet mask. Period. This meant that there were three ways to divide the 32 bits in an IP address into a network and a host address. Because this resulted in extremely restrictive groupings of IP addresses, **CIDR** (Classless Inter-Domain Routing) was born. With CIDR, you can divide the IP address almost anywhere within its 32 bits. You can think of it as drawing a line in the sand and proclaiming: *"All bits to the left of this line comprise the network address, and all bits to the right of this line comprise the host address."*

The delineation between the two fields of the IP address is presented with the subnet mask. The idea is similar to cutting a hole in a piece of paper and then placing it over a page of this book. The larger the hole, the more of the book you can see through it. In the case of a subnet mask, the part you see through the hole is controlled by the number of "1"s, and corresponds to the network address of the subnet. The remainder is the host address. To "look through the mask," the computer performs a binary-AND operation of the IP address and the subnet mask. Here is a quick example:

	11010111	.	00100110	.	10110101	.	01111110	*IP address*
bitwise-AND	11111111	.	11111111	.	11111100	.	00000000	*subnet mask*
	11010111	.	00100110	.	10110100	.	00000000	*network address*

As you can see, where there is a "1" in the subnet mask, the bit in the IP address is copied into the network address. "0"s in the subnet mask remain "0"s. That's **masking**, and it is something that can be performed very quickly by computer hardware. Although the subnet mask is always a string of bits inside the computer, people get tired of writing out all of those ones and zeros, so there are three different representations for human use.

- The first is just like a dotted IP address. For example, **/255.255.252.0**. This is easy for humans, and it is the most common format used when specifying the subnet mask in commands and configuration files.

- The second is the format used in the example—i.e., all bits written out as four groups of eight bits (**/11111111.11111111.11111100.00000000**). It is rarely written out except when you need to calculate network addresses by hand.

- The third representation counts the number of "1"s before the "0"s start, which we can call **maskbits** notation. The subnet mask in our example has 22 "1"s, and would be simply written as **/22**.

Table 2.1 Subnet Mask
Lookup Table

dec	binary	# of bits
255	11111111	8
254	11111110	7
252	11111100	6
248	11111000	5
240	11110000	4
224	11100000	3
192	11000000	2
128	10000000	1
0	00000000	0

Note that there cannot be a "0" followed by a "1" in a subnet mask. Recall that the subnet mask is telling us how many bits (from left to right) are in the network address. Because the **network** and **host** fields are contiguous, and all bits must be used, there are no gaps. For all three representation it makes no sense to specify a network address without a subnet mask, or vice versa, so a slash (/) is used to separate the two.

Converting Between Subnet Mask Representations   Table 2.1 contains a list of subnet mask numbers that can help you perform conversions between the different subnet mask formats. Use this for each octet in your mask separately. If you encounter 255.255.224.0 as a subnet mask, you can use the table above to quickly calculate that it is equivalent to $8 + 8 + 3 = 19$, or /19, or if you need the binary, 11111111.11111111.11100000.00000000.

Parameters Related to the Subnet Mask   Given an IP address and its associated subnet mask, we can determine anything we need about the properties of the IP subnet. In addition to the network address, which we calculated in the prior example, the following parameters can be calculated:

host address — This is the portion of the IP address that does not correspond to the network address. If you were to invert the subnet mask (exchange "0"s with "1"s and "1"s with "0"s—this is known as the **1's complement**), and calculate the bitwise-AND of this with the IP address, the result would be the host portion. There is no point in calculating this parameter, because people never use it.

broadcast address — The broadcast address is a reserved address in each IP subnet which can be used to speak to all of the IP hosts via a single packet (called a **broadcast**). For a given subnet, it is the network address together with the bits in the host portion of the address all set to "1". Put another way, it is the highest (or last) host address in the subnet. It is easiest calculated by performing a bitwise-OR of the IP address and the 1's complement of the subnet mask.

number of host addresses in this IP subnet — This quantity is used for planning deployment of address space. (We will use it later, on page 25, for this purpose.)

The value is calculated by raising two to the power of the number of "0"s in the subnet mask. But because the first address in the subnet is always reserved for the network address, and the last address for the broadcast address, you should subtract two from this value to find the maximum number of hosts. You can use these formulae:

$$\# \ of \ host \ addrs \ = \ 2^{(32 - maskbits)} \tag{2.1}$$

$$\text{max \# of hosts} \ = \ 2^{(32 - maskbits)} - 2 \tag{2.2}$$

Calculating Network Parameters with CIDR   The rub when working with network addresses is that humans do not like counting in two's as much as computers do. The way the subnet mask splits the string of 32 bits is pesky for the human operator's decimal-to-binary and binary-to-decimal conversion circuits. It may clear things up to work through a few examples:

Example #1

IP address:	192.168.40.31
subnet mask:	255.255.255.0 (or /24)

Calculation of the network address

```
              11000000 . 10101000 . 00101000 . 00011111   IP address
bitwise-AND   11111111 . 11111111 . 11111111 . 00000000   subnet mask
              11000000 . 10101000 . 00101000 . 00000000   network address
```

or **192.168.40.0/24** (converted to dotted-decimal notation)

Calculation of the broadcast address

```
             11000000 . 10101000 . 00101000 . 00011111   IP address
bitwise-OR   00000000 . 00000000 . 00000000 . 11111111   ! subnet mask
             11000000 . 10101000 . 00101000 . 11111111   broadcast address
```

or **192.168.40.255** (converted to dotted-decimal notation)

This example is easy because the subnet mask ends on a dot-boundary, so you can just read off the answers by knowing how the subnet mask works. Note that "!" is a way of indicating the inverse or 1's complement of a value. For single bits, it means to flip the bit. For multiple bits, flip each of them individually, as was done with the subnet mask. For the next example, let's use the same IP address but with a different subnet mask.

Example #2

IP address:	192.168.40.31
subnet mask:	255.255.240.0 (or /20)

Calculation of the network address

	11000000 . 10101000 . 00101000 . 00011111	*IP address*
bitwise-AND	11111111 . 11111111 . 11110000 . 00000000	*subnet mask*
	11000000 . 10101000 . 00100000 . 00000000	*network address*

or **192.168.32.0/20**

	11000000 . 10101000 . 00101000 . 00011111	*IP address*
bitwise-OR	00000000 . 00000000 . 00001111 . 11111111	*! subnet mask*
	11000000 . 10101000 . 00101111 . 11111111	*broadcast address*

or **192.168.63.255**

Now, just for the sake of completeness, how about the host portion of the address? You can calculate it by ANDing the complement of the subnet mask with the IP address.

Calculation of the host address
Calculation of the broadcast address

	11000000 . 10101000 . 00101000 . 00011111	*IP address*
bitwise-AND	00000000 . 00000000 . 00001111 . 11111111	*! subnet mask*
	00000000 . 00000000 . 00001000 . 00011111	*host address*

or **0.0.8.31**

So the host address is 0.0.8.31?!? I can assure you that no one writes out host addresses this way. In fact, no one really bothers with host addresses at all when working with CIDR.

Class A, B, and C Networks   Now that you've learned the right way to think about subnets, it is safe to introduce the traditional "classed" subnet definitions. In the early days, these conventions dictated the values of the first four bits in the address (known as the **prefix**), which, in turn, implied how the 32-bit address space was separated into network and host portions. This way, routers could share network route information with each other without including the subnet mask. (An initial savings that would end up costing a lot later in terms of confusion and rework to implement CIDR.)

The different designations split the address on octet boundaries, which lessened the need for base–2 math skills on the part of the network administrator. The designations are listed in Table 2.2.

Table 2.2 Subnet Class Designations

	prefix	bits in subnet mask
class A	0	8
class B	10	16
class C	110	24
class D	1110	n/a
class E	1111	n/a

Thus, a class A address must have the first bit set to zero, and it uses the first 8 bits for the network address and the remaining 24 bits for the host address. Classes B and C each set another bit in the prefix and shift the subnet mask over by 8 bits. Class D is used for multicast addresses (11100000 in binary equals 224 in decimal, if that rings a bell). Class E is reserved for future use.

Because the prefix places certain limitations on the network address, you can easily identify which class an address is in by looking at the first octet. So if you see 151.30.22.12 and you know that your network is following the class conventions, you instantly know that this is class B network and that the subnet mask is /16. The ranges are listed in Table 2.3.

Table 2.3 Class Address Ranges

class	network address range	host address range
A	0–126	0.0.1–255.255.254
B	128.0–191.255	0.1–255.254
C	192.0.0–223.255.255	1–254

Although I'm not much of a fan of the class designations, it is important to be familiar with them in order to communicate with others who use the terminology.[1] Probably the most frequently used term is "class C." People often use this to refer to any network with a 24-bit subnet mask and 8-bit host address, although properly, it includes only those network addresses that begin with 110.

Carving Up IP Address Space with CIDR   Sometimes you will need to take address space allocated to you and divvy it up into several IP subnets. You have to choose either the number of separate subnets you want to create, or how many hosts should be in each subnet. To divide the original subnet, you add bits to the network address (thereby removing bits from the host portion of the address) until you have the desired number of subdivisions in the original address space. It should come as no surprise that everything happens in powers of 2, and that more base–2 math is lurking around the corner.

If you choose to create N subnets, you need an additional $m = \log_2 N$ 1's in the subnet mask. An easier way to think about the math is to realize that adding m bits to the subnet mask will result in 2^m additional subnets.

Example A   Let's take the address space 192.168.18.0/24 and carve it up into 8 subnets. $N = 8$, so $m = \log_2 8 = 3$, which is the number of bits to add to the subnet mask. The result is 8 subnets with network addresses of *192.168.18.x/27*.

Now we need the 8 values for x: x_1, x_2, x_3, x_4, x_5, x_6, x_7, x_8, so that we can write out the network address for each subnet. The first one always starts where the original address space started, in this case 0. The subsequent values for x_n are found by adding the number of hosts in each subnet to the preceding value of x. To calculate the number of hosts, refer back to the equation on page 23. In this case, the

---

[1] I have to admit that I also use them sometimes due to laziness on my part.

number of host addresses is $2^{(32-27)} = 2^5 = 32$, and we can write out our network addresses accordingly:

x_1	192.168.18.0/27
x_2	192.168.18.32/27
x_3	192.168.18.64/27
x_4	192.168.18.96/27
x_5	192.168.18.128/27
x_6	192.168.18.160/27
x_7	192.168.18.192/27
x_8	192.168.18.224/27

The number of usable host addresses in each subnet is 30. You could calculate the broadcast address for each of these, although they can be written down by inspection. Since the broadcast address is the last address in the subnet, it must be one lower than the next network address. For x_1, it would be 192.168.18.31; for x_6, 192.168.18.191, and for the special case, x_8, 192.168.18.255 (because the next network address would be 192.168.19.0/255).

You won't be able to use the maskbits representation of the subnet mask for most networking commands, so you should go ahead and convert it back to decimal (using the chart on page 22, if needed). Remember that the 27 bits must be contiguous, from left to right, so they must be 11111111.11111111.11111111.11100000, which is 255.255.255.224. You don't really have to write out the full 32 bits each time, just start subtracting 8 from the maskbits. Each time you can subtract 8, copy down 255. When you are left with a number less than 8, look it up in the table and copy down the decimal representation. If you have not yet written down 4 decimal values, then write down "0"s for the rest.

Before we move on to the next example, let's look at one more property of the subnet mask and the network address that you can use to double-check your work.

11000000 .	10101000 .	00010010 .	01100000	*network address* (192.168.18.96)
11111111 .	11111111 .	11111111 .	11100000	*subnet mask* (255.255.255.224)

Notice, when you line up the network address and the subnet mask, that the network address is all "0"s to the right of the subnet mask's last "1". This will **always** be the case. If it's not, then you have made a mistake. Simply put, you are in a completely different subnet. Recall that the purpose of the subnet mask is to divide the IP address into network and host fields. The bits in the host field are reserved for hosts, so let not network bits appear there, lest the stack complain bitterly and functioneth not.

Example B   When we started this section, I said that you could also pick the number of hosts you would like in the subnet and use this to calculate the subnet mask and network address. Let's assume that you need a subnet with at least 1400 addresses. Since we have to pick a power of two, and 1024 is not large enough, we have to take 2048. A subnet that has 2048 host addresses in it needs to have $\log_2 2048 = 11$ bits to hold the host address. There are 32 bits total, so this leaves 21 bits for the network address.

Now that you know the subnet mask, chances are good that you'll need to carve it out of some private address space. If you want to take this space from the RFC 1918[2] allocation for private class A (10.x.x.x) or class B (172.16–31.x.x) networks, you have no worries. The class A network space has 24 bits of host address—more than plenty. The same is true for any of the 16 different private class B networks. They each have 16 bits of host address. (Remember that we need only 11.) Just choose an unused one, slap on the /21, and start CIDRing.

However, if you want to use an aggregate of private class Cs (the 192.168.x.x address space), things can get a little sticky. The last example included a prologue which showed that the network bits cannot run over into the host portion of the IP address. That wasn't so tough when we had a network and wanted to carve out addresses. But now we have addresses and want to fit them into a network. The first thing to do is to write out the subnet mask in binary.

$$11111111.11111111.11111000.00000000$$

Now, we want to find a network address that does not have a "1" in any of the last 3 bits of the third octet. (If a "1" appears here, the network address is spilling into the host position.) This is not as difficult as it sounds once you write out the subnet mask in binary. Using 0 (binary 00000000) for the third octet will meet the criterion. If this address space is not available, then the next choice is to copy down the octet with the right-most "1" in the subnet mask intact, and everything else "0"—so in this case 00001000 (8). Any multiple of this value will also meet the requirements, up to copying down the octet from the subnet mask itself (11111000). So we are free to choose from:

```
192.168.0.0/21     11000000 . 10101000 . 00000000 . 00000000
192.168.8.0/21     11000000 . 10101000 . 00001000 . 00000000
192.168.16.0/21    11000000 . 10101000 . 00010000 . 00000000
192.168.24.0/21    11000000 . 10101000 . 00011000 . 00000000
          ⋮
192.168.248.0/21   11000000 . 10101000 . 11111000 . 00000000
```

Each of these has room for 2046 hosts and will have its own broadcast address. If you are still unclear on calculating the broadcast address, try calculating it for 192.168.64.0/21. You should come up with 192.168.71.255.

If you try to start anywhere in the address space, e.g., at 192.168.2.0/21, you'll have problems. Let's write this network address out in binary and align it with the subnet mask:

```
network address    11000000 . 10101000 . 00000010 . 00000000
subnet mask        11111111 . 11111111 . 11111000 . 00000000
```

As you can see, the network address spills over into the host portion of the address (to the right of the last "1" in the netmask). By doing this, you specified a

---

[2] More information about RFC 1918 can be found in Section 2.1.5 on page 33.

host within the subnet, and not a network address. If you ever try something like this with Linux, it will let you know:

```
$ route add -net 192.168.2.0 netmask 255.255.248.0 eth0
route: netmask doesn't match route address
```

More Subnet-Related Definitions   The material covered in Section 2.1.1 may have seemed a bit obtuse, but it truly is useful when designing networks. Here are a few more notes on terminology before we get to routing.

- The term **supernet** can be used to refer to subnets containing more addresses than a normal class C. Sometimes this helps to remind people that 255.255.255.0 is not always the subnet mask.

- I have attempted to be consistent in my use of terms. The term **subnet mask**, however, is equivalent to **netmask** (as it appears in most command names), **network mask**, and sometimes even just **mask**. In the routing table, it appears as **Genmask**.

- An **IP subnet** and a **network** are the same thing, unless there is some special distinction made about the type of network.

- A **workstation** is a generic term for any node on a network that is not part of the routing infrastructure. It sounds better than saying **PC**, and **node** is being saved for Frame Relay routers. Sometimes I call workstations **machines**.

- The next session talks about **gateways** and **routers**, which are equivalent. Typically, users configure their workstations with a **gateway**, whereas a router talks to another router.

- **Forwarding** and **routing**, are, in most cases, the same thing.

2.1.2 Workstations—To Gateway or Not to Gateway

Every machine on your network with a TCP/IP stack has a configuration setting for *gateway*. This is so that it can reach IP networks other than its own. When it detects that the destination is part of a remote network, it sends the packet to the gateway for forwarding. For destinations in the same subnet, it will send the packet directly to the other machine. How does a workstation determine if a destination is part of the same or a different IP network?

First it ANDs the destination address of the packet with its own subnet mask. If the resulting address matches its own network mask, then the destination is in the same subnet, and the TCP/IP stack tells the card to send the packet directly to the destination machine. (Actually, more than this occurs in order to send the packet directly, but it's no longer part of TCP/IP, but Ethernet. This is covered in Section 2.2.) If, however, the calculation shows that the destination is part of another network, then the sender makes use of its gateway to transmit the packet. In effect, the sender is saying, *"I do not know how to deliver this packet; can you please deliver it for me?"* The gateway accepts the packet and then goes through a similar procedure. (That procedure is known as **routing**, and there will be plenty more about it later.) Here

Table 2.4 Address Information for Workstation Routing Examples

workstation	IP address	network/netmask	gateway
A	192.168.16.4	192.168.16.0/22	192.168.16.1
B	192.168.17.20	192.168.16.0/22	192.168.16.1
C	192.168.30.4	192.168.30.0/24	192.168.30.1

are a few examples of the workstation's decision-making process (the workstation IP and network information is in Table 2.4):

workstation A sends to workstation B   Workstation A knows its own network address/subnet mask is 192.168.16.0/22. Workstation A calculates the *local-subnettedness* of the destination packet as follows:

Are A and B in the same subnet?

	11111111 . 11111111 . 11111100 . 00000000	*subnet mask of A*
bitwise-AND	11000000 . 10101000 . 00010001 . 00010100	*IP addr of dest (B)*
	11000000 . 10101000 . 00010000 . 00000000	*network of dest*
compare	11000000 . 10101000 . 00010000 . 00000000	*network of A*

they are equal—both **192.168.16.0**

Because the network address of the sender matches the result of this calculation, the packet is sent directly to machine B.

workstation C sends to workstation B   Workstation C knows its network address/subnet mask is 192.168.30.0/24. Machine C checks to see if the destination packet falls within its subnet:

Are C and B in the same subnet?

	11111111 . 11111111 . 11111111 . 00000000	*subnet mask of C*
bitwise-AND	11000000 . 10101000 . 00010001 . 00010100	*IP addr of dest (B)*
	11000000 . 10101000 . 00010001 . 00000000	*network of dest*
compare	11000000 . 10101000 . 00011110 . 00000000	*network of C*

they are not equal—**192.168.17.0** $\neq$ **192.168.30.0**

In this case, the comparison fails. The sender, C, has no choice but to send the packet to its gateway. (If you take the time to do the calculation, you discover the gateway is in machine C's subnet. In fact the gateway must always be in the sender's subnet; otherwise, the sender could not send to it either!)

2.1.3 A Workstation's Routing Table

Even workstations with a single interface have a routing table and must scan it before deciding what to do with a packet. The tests above are performed multiple times—once for each entry in the workstation's routing table. Note that having a routing table does not necessarily mean that the workstation can route; it is simply the means for determining how to send packets. Here is an example routing table from a workstation. The `Destination` field contains the network address, and the `Genmask` field contains the subnet mask. By reading this table from top to bottom, you make decisions about what to do with a packet just like the kernel does.

```
$ route -n
Kernel IP routing table
Destination     Gateway         Genmask         Flags Metric Ref    Use Iface
192.168.18.0    0.0.0.0         255.255.254.0   U     0      0      869 eth0
127.0.0.0       0.0.0.0         255.0.0.0       U     0      0        2 lo
0.0.0.0         192.168.18.1    0.0.0.0         UG    1      0      182 eth0
```

1. All packets for the network 192.168.18.0/23 (remember that /23 is just another representation of /255.255.254.0) are sent out via interface *eth0* without using a gateway. This is denoted by `0.0.0.0` in the `Gateway` field and the lack of a G flag in the `Flags` field.

2. All packets for the network 127.0.0.0/8 are sent out via interface *lo*. This is known as the **loopback interface**, and it is reserved for sending packets to the local machine.

3. Any other packet will be forwarded to the gateway address (192.168.18.1), which is accessible via interface *eth0*. If you look at the `Destination` field, you will notice that the network is 0.0.0.0 with a `Genmask` of 0.0.0.0. This matches every packet, and is known as a **default route**.

   When the kernel encounters this entry, it notices that the G flag is set, which means that the packet is to be sent to the IP address listed in the `Gateway` field for forwarding.

Note that the table is sorted in reverse order by the number of bits in the `Genmask` (subnet mask) field. This is so the kernel walks the table in most-to-least restrictive order (the last entry will always be the default route). As soon as a suitable `Destination` and `Genmask` (really, subnet and subnet mask) pair is found, the packet is sent via that interface. The routing table on a router functions exactly the same way, which is the topic of the next section.

2.1.4 A Gateway's Routing Table

To forward packets, a router consults its routing table much like a workstation and sends the packet on its way over the appropriate interface. Where a router differs from workstation is in what sort of traffic it will accept. When routing is enabled in the Linux kernel, the router will accept packets destined for its Ethernet address, but with IP destination headers pointing somewhere else. A machine without routing might accept these packets from the wire (because of the correct Ethernet address), but would then discard them when it discovered that they were not destined for its IP address. The router knows that its job is to forward, so it accepts the packet and examines its headers to find out where it's headed. A routing table on a router looks like this and is taken from the router depicted in Figure 2.3.

Figure 2.3 Sample Router

```
$ route -n
Kernel IP routing table
Destination      Gateway          Genmask          Flags Metric Ref    Use Iface
192.168.5.20     192.168.10.7     255.255.255.255  UGH   1      0      180 eth1
192.168.1.81     192.168.10.5     255.255.255.255  UGH   1      0      187 eth1
192.168.10.0     0.0.0.0          255.255.255.0    U     0      0    63311 eth1
192.168.18.0     0.0.0.0          255.255.254.0    U     0      0   753430 eth0
192.168.64.0     192.168.10.5     255.255.192.0    UG    1      0    47543 eth1
192.168.128.0    192.168.10.7     255.255.192.0    UG    1      0    89011 eth1
127.0.0.0        0.0.0.0          255.0.0.0        U     0      0      564 lo
0.0.0.0          192.168.10.20    0.0.0.0          UG    1      0   183436 eth1
```

We can tell a lot about this router by looking at the routing table (even without the aid of the illustration).

- The first two entries are known as *host routes*; they can be used to access only a single destination IP. This is denoted by the H in the Flags field, and the fact that the Genmask is 255.255.255.255 (or /32). Both of these routes have a metric of 1 and a gateway on the 192.168.10.0/24 network, which is why the Iface is set to eth1. When the kernel encounters a packet destined for one of these exact IP addresses, it will be forwarded to the specified gateway over the *eth1* interface.

- The next entry is just like the entry that a workstation has for its network interface. It is a network route for the locally connected network, 192.168.10.0/24. You can tell this because the gateway is set to 0.0.0.0 (which implies a local interface), and there is no G in the Flags field. We can safely assume that the *eth1* interface has an IP address in the 192.168.10.0/24 subnet. The figure confirms this; the interface is 192.168.10.1.

  For those of you familiar with other Unices, this is one point where Linux differs. It does not need to use the IP address of the interface as the gateway for locally connected networks (although this type of configuration will also

work). It automatically uses the interface listed in the `Iface` field. By looking
at the figure, we might surmise that the 192.168.10.0/24 network is a network
for routers.

- The fourth entry is just like the third, except that it is for interface *eth0*, which
we can see is connected to the 192.168.18.0/23 network. This is the network
where the workstations are—the LAN.

- The next two (fifth and sixth) entries are network routes which point out over
gateways on the router network. All traffic which falls into IP address ranges
denoted by the network address (`Destination`) and subnet mask (`Genmask`)
will be forwarded to the appropriate WAN router. A safe bet would be that
these correspond to IP address space in use in other locations. If you notice their
`Genmask`, you will understand why they first appear now in the routing table.
The table is sorted from most-restrictive to least-restrictive, and 255.255.192.0
is the *widest* subnet mask yet.

- The next to last entry in the table is for the loopback device, *lo*, just like on a
workstation.

- The last entry is the **default route**. Just like workstations, routers have these
in case they do not know where else to forward a packet. In our example, the
default route points to the 192.168.10.20 machine, and is heavily used (note the
`Use` field). 192.168.10.20 could be the Internet router or a firewall.

Preference for Two Equivalent Routes   Note that the table is sorted in reverse
order by the number of bits in the `Genmask` field (just as it is on a workstation). The
kernel checks each entry in the table against the destination IP address of the packet
it received, and it forwards the packet on the first match it finds. This means that
multiple (static) routes to the same destination are not used if you have simple static
routing. In the case of a tie—two entries with identical `Destination` and `Genmask`—
the one with the lower metric value is chosen. Should the metrics be equal, the more
recent entry is chosen. The kernel doesn't remember when the entries were made
for static routes, but it knows that when someone enters a route equivalent to an
existing route, the intention is most likely to use the new route. This is convenient
if you need to temporarily route around a particular gateway or have some other
testing in mind. You can enter the temporary route, and it will be used. When you
delete it, the previous route is used.

Unroutable Packets   Each of the other routers must also have routing table entries for the network(s) and host(s) it is expected to forward. If they don't, then
they will either use their default route, or, if no default route exists, they will reply with an `ICMP: host unreachable` message. The pathological case is when the
route points back to the sending router, which forms a loop. (Router$_A$ sends to
router$_B$, which sends to router$_A$, and so on. . .). Fortunately, IP packets all contain a
TTL (Time To Live) field which is decremented every time the packet is forwarded.
Eventually (actually, very quickly), the packet will be discarded. Nonetheless, such
misconfigurations mean that the packet will not find its destination, which results in
performance degradation for correctly routed packets on the network. Just say *No*
to routing loops!

Misconfigured Routes—ICMP Redirects   Another situation arises when router$_A$ forwards a packet to router$_B$ when it could (and should) have forwarded it directly to router$_C$. That is, all three routers are on the same subnet, but router$_A$ is ignorant of (one or more of) router$_C$'s routes. When router$_A$ forwards a packet to router$_B$, and router$_B$ notices that the packet should have been sent directly to router$_C$, it forwards the packet, but alerts router$_A$ to the fact with an `ICMP: redirect` message telling router$_A$ how to forward packets of that type in the future. Router$_A$ notes this by adding a new (host route) entry in its routing table. You can quickly spot these entries because they have the `UDGH` flags all set. Of note is the D, which indicates that the route was added either dynamically or due to a redirect.

Static vs. Dynamic Routing   There are two methods of configuring a routing table. If the table is populated by you (or by a script on your behalf) using the *route* command, then it is known as **static routing**. If it is populated automatically by a daemon such as *routed*, you are using **dynamic routing**.

I am a fan of static routing, because the reassurance of knowing exactly what the router will do with a packet at all times is worth the extra effort on my part. However, static routing cannot be used in every situation, and is by no means the only way to do things with Linux. (More information about dynamic routing daemons for Linux can be found in Section 8.4.)

If this material is new to you, hopefully you're feeling more acquainted with TCP/IP routing than you were before. If you're not, there are many good tutorials on TCP/IP subnetting available on the Internet, as well as numerous books on the subject. One such tutorial is at *http://www.sangoma.com/fguide.htm*; another is the *IP-Subnetworking mini-HOWTO*, part of the *LDP*.

Being able to calculate network addresses, subnet masks, and being able to convert subnet masks from binary to the # of maskbits representation are all important day-to-day things for network admins. The next section is about private address space—address space which you can use to build your own IP network, as long as you keep it isolated from the Internet.[3]

2.1.5 RFC 1918 Private Address Space

Under the current IP addressing scheme (often known as IPv4, eventually to be replaced by IPv6), the address space is divided into two types: public address space and private address space. Understanding the difference is important and useful for a network administrator, especially if your organization is connected to the Internet.

All of the **public address space** (IP addresses) routable via the Internet are managed by one of the three *Regional Internet Registries* (RIRs). Each of these is responsible for a geographic region. (Don't confuse these with the InterNIC

---

[3] Several sections of this book deal with *how* to keep your private networks isolated from the Internet. They are the sections on IP masquerading (Sections 4.2–4.4) and proxy servers (Section 8.1).

[*http://www.internic.net*] and its designated registrars, such as *Network Solutions, Inc.* They handle **domain name** registration, not address registration.)

- North and South America, the Caribbean, and sub-Saharan Africa are managed by the *American Registry for Internet Numbers*, or simply: *ARIN. http://www.arin.net*
- Europe, the Middle East, and other parts of Africa are managed by *RIPE* (*Réseaux IP Européens*). *http://www.ripe.net*
- *APNIC*, the *Asia Pacific Network Information Centre*, handles the Asia Pacific region. *http://www.apnic.net*.

You must request address space, and they will either grant or deny your request. Alternately, you can request the address space from your ISP (who then, in turn, allocates you from its ARIN-allotted address space, or makes the request on your behalf).

This is done to preserve address space and provide a central authority to prevent address-space collisions. When you are using a public address, you can send to and receive from all (non-broken) parts of the Internet. This means that all routers in the Internet have an idea about how to route your IP address towards you. Because of this, not all address space is **portable**. If you own your address space, you can authorize an ISP to route it for you, but there is a chance when you change providers or locations that it will no longer be possible to route your IPs to that new location. (So you might want to check before you travel with your address space.)

In any event, the public address space has been divvied up and allocated to countries, companies, universities, ISPs, other organizations, and individuals. A small part of the overall address space has been classified as **private address space**. It is also known as **RFC 1597** or **RFC 1918** address space, after the RFCs that describe its proper use. Private address space is intended for use by anyone, but on private networks. The subnets themselves will be familiar to many of you, even if you were previously unaware that they corresponded to private address space. According to RFC 1918 (which obsoletes the well-known RFC 1597), the private subnets are:

IP address range	network/mask	number of address
10.0.0.0–10.255.255.255	10.0.0.0/8	16,777,216 (2^{24})
172.16.0.0–172.31.255.255	172.16.0.0/12	1,048,576 (2^{20})
192.168.0.0–192.168.255.255	192.168.0.0/16	65,536 (2^{16})

The 10.0.0.0/8 network is a single class A network. 172.168.0.0/12 is a set of sixteen class B networks. 192.168.0.0/16 represents 255 contiguous class C networks. For organizations with private networks which are connected to the Internet, this means:

1. They can run TCP/IP without any danger of address conflicts with the outside.
2. They can allocate address space from the private address space in a manner which makes sense for them (perhaps geographically, maybe organizationally).

3. Their internal networks are (somewhat) shielded from Internet-based attacks. An attacker has more difficulties launching an attack against IP addresses which cannot be routed.

4. Their machines with private addresses cannot directly communicate with the Internet. This necessitates the use of a proxy or masquerading mechanism, which can help perform logging and prevent unauthorized access.

5. They do not have to go through the hassle of changing IP addresses should they change ISPs, nor do they have to apply for address space when they need more.

Every network admin should have a copy of the latest RFC describing the private address space (for IPv4). An official source for this document is *http://www.ietf.org/rfc*. Debian has provided a copy if you've loaded either the **bind-doc** or the **doc-rfc** package.

Allocating Private Address Space Internally   Keep private address space in mind when planning your network. If you work with other network admins at your organization, draw up an allocation scheme for your environment and have all involved agree to abide by it. The time-savings down the road could be substantial. Another benefit is that you can prevent clutter in your routing tables. If you use CIDR to divide the address space into large aggregates of subnets which are based on geographic boundaries, you can reduce the number of routing entries at each router.

For example, imagine a Frame Relay router located in Europe with PVCs to North America and the Pacific Rim. The site in Europe acts as the hub—i.e., the two leaf sites send data to each other via the site in Europe. Each site has four class C subnets, and all sites communicate with all other sites. If all three sites grew up at about the same time, and you allocated the subnets sequentially, you would have:

Europe	North America	Pacific Rim
192.168.10.0/24	192.168.14.0/24	192.168.18.0/24
192.168.20.0/24	192.168.24.0/24	192.168.28.0/24
192.168.30.0/24	192.168.34.0/24	192.168.38.0/24
192.168.40.0/24	192.168.44.0/24	192.168.48.0/24

The router in Europe would then have four class C subnets to route per PVC. But the router in North America would have eight, as would the router on the Pacific Rim. At this scale, the issue is still a manageable one, but consider what happens when each site has 10–15 class C networks. If you plan ahead and assign each location a larger block of class C networks, you could have the following:

region	range of addresses	subnet	# of subnets
Europe	192.168.0.0–192.168.63.255	192.168.0.0/18	64
Pacific Rim	192.168.64.0–192.168.71.255	192.168.64.0/21	8
North America	192.168.128.0–192.168.159.255	192.168.128.0/19	32

Now Europe has only two routing table entries: 192.168.64.0/18 (all 64 class C's towards the Pacific Rim), and 192.168.128.0/17 (the remaining 128 class C's towards

North America). North America has only a single routing entry, 192.168.0.0/17, which points towards Europe. And the Pacific Rim also has two routing table entries: 192.168.0.0/18 and 192.168.128.0/19. A little time spent up front can alleviate the need for large static routing tables or dynamic routing daemons for your internal network.

When you're allocating network space, leave yourself room for growth. It is difficult to know in advance how much address space a site will need, so spread things out at first. (If you need to reclaim the unused address space later, it will still be there.) As a rule of thumb, allocate a class C for every existing 100 devices, and if the site expects growth, double the existing address space by taking another bit from the subnet mask.

2.2 ETHERNET 101—SWITCHES AND HUBS

This section drills down and looks at how packets flow across an Ethernet LAN, and specifically how machines on the same Ethernet segment communicate with each other. This case is analogous to the concept of IP subnets, except that Ethernet segments are groupings based on physical topology, while IP subnets are groupings based on configuration. This communication is the same mechanism used by the workstation to contact the router (or gateway) for that segment—which is why the gateway must be on the same physical Ethernet segment.

A common mechanism for connecting machines together nowadays is over twisted-pair (either 10-BaseT or 100-BaseT), where each machine is connected via its own dedicated wire to a port on some sort of "network port concentrating device." This "device" comes in two basic flavors. A **hub** emulates a broadcast bus—what is sent to one port is available for all ports to see. (Technically, this is a **repeater**.) A **switch** emulates a crossbar switch—the sending port and receiving port are directly connected to each other for the length of the packet transmission. (This acts like a very short-lived **bridge**.) There is more on the differences between a hub and a switch covered in Section 2.2.3.

2.2.1 The MAC Address

Of primary interest is how communication takes place between two systems on the same Ethernet segment, since it's a quantum of much of the network communications we're concerned about in this book. The answer is that machines send Ethernet packets directly to one another by specifying the 6-byte Ethernet address of the destination system. This address is often called the **hardware address** or the **MAC address** of the Ethernet card. "MAC" is an abbreviation for "Media Access Control." On any given LAN, every MAC address must be unique. This should not be a problem, because the MAC address is programmed in by the NIC vendor, and there is a system by which NIC vendors ensure that the addresses they program into their cards are unique.

All vendors have their own address block(s), which is designated by the first 3 bytes of the address field.[4] Each vendor code encompasses $2^{24} - 2$ (16,777,214)

---

[4] */usr/share/karpski/datfiles/vendor_codes.dat* has a complete list of these assignments. The file is part of the **karpski** Debian package, which is a GUI packet-sniffer covered in Section 4.5.3.

addresses after you take out the reserved *ff:ff:ff* broadcast address, and many vendors have multiple codes. (To be completely accurate, not all cards have their own MAC address—on some systems, such as Sun Microsystems, the MAC address is stored in NVRAM and assigned to whatever network face is plugged into the system. This way, the MAC address for a system doesn't change, even if the physical card does.)

To determine the **hardware address** of the NIC corresponding to *eth0* on your system, use the command `ifconfig eth0` and look at the *HWaddr* field. It should look something like:

```
$ ifconfig eth0
eth0      Link encap:Ethernet  HWaddr 00:60:97:8F:EE:01
          inet addr:192.168.101.4  Bcast:192.168.101.255  Mask:255.255.255.0
          UP BROADCAST RUNNING MULTICAST  MTU:1500  Metric:1
          RX packets:0 errors:0 dropped:0 overruns:0 frame:0
          TX packets:0 errors:0 dropped:0 overruns:0 carrier:0
          Collisions:0
          Interrupt:11 Base address:0x300
```

The hardware address is normally expressed with each byte represented in hexadecimal format and separated by colons, like *ff:ff:ff:ff:ff:ff*. The chances of having two Ethernet cards with the same MAC address are slim, but it seems to happen occasionally. The result is chaos on the affected segment.

2.2.2 Address Resolution Protocol (ARP)

ARP, the Address Resolution Protocol, is the means by which an Ethernet sender finds the desired recipient. The ARP protocol uses a simple broadcast mechanism to learn the address of the recipient. This Ethernet broadcast packet is called an **ARP request**, and it is seen by all systems connected to that Ethernet segment. To generate an Ethernet broadcast, the system sets all of the bits in the destination address to one (which yields *ff:ff:ff:ff:ff:ff*, similar to an IP broadcast) and the IP address of the recipient it desires. The host that has that IP address replies—all others remain silent (even if they know the answer)—with an **ARP reply**. Unlike the request, the reply is sent directly to the machine that issued the ARP request.

Now the sender knows the MAC address of the recipient, so it stores it in a cache called an **ARP table**. (You can save your system the step of using broadcasts to find MAC addresses by storing the mappings in */etc/ethers*, but this is rare nowadays). Periodically, entries in the host's ARP table expire (for instance, when a machine changes its IP address). For Linux 2.2, the default timeout is 5 minutes. You can view the contents of your system's ARP table using the command *arp*, as in the following example (the -n switch suppresses name resolution of the IP addresses):

```
$ arp -n
Address         HWtype  HWaddress           Flags Mask   Iface
192.168.1.2     ether   00:E0:29:32:5A:95   C            eth0
24.8.66.1       ether   00:10:F6:DA:6C:10   C            eth1
192.168.16.6    ether   00:50:56:CB:9C:2B   C            eth2
```

Packet Sniffing ARP Requests   Packet sniffers are programs that "watch" everything that flows across the network segment, and are covered later (Section 4.5).

If you're monitoring your network and watching for ARP traffic, your sniffer will report them with messages like:

```
arp who-has 192.168.16.1 tell 192.168.16.2
arp reply 192.168.16.1 is-at 0:50:56:8a:0:0
```

The first packet is the ARP request, issued by 192.168.16.2 in an attempt to contact 192.168.16.1. 192.168.16.1 replies that it has hardware address 00:50:56:8A:00:00. Because ARP is a link-layer protocol, there are different specifications for each type of link. For example, FDDI uses a different ARP specification than the one for Ethernet. If you would like to read the ARP specification for Ethernet, it is *RFC 826*.

RARP **RARP**, or Reverse ARP, can be used by a machine that does not know its own IP address to learn it from a machine that does. It generates a broadcast which appeals to a machine running *rarpd* (the Reverse ARP Daemon) to answer back with its IP address. The answering machine has a list of MAC addresses along with the corresponding IP addresses to assign to them. It is typically used in environments with disk-less workstations and Xterminals. If you need this functionality, you should look into the **BOOTP** and **DHCP** protocols too. If nothing else, you should be aware of its existence and function.

2.2.3 Ethernet Switches and Hubs

Although, from the users' perspective, there is little difference between switches and hubs (perhaps additional performance when using a switch), there are significant differences for network administrators.

A switch differs from a hub in that the former maintains a mapping of ports to the MAC address(es) attached to them. It uses this table to "switch" packets between ports by connecting the sending and receiving port using its crossbar circuitry. In contrast, a hub is simply an electronic conduit, which forwards anything received on one port to all other ports. In general, switches can do everything that a hub can do, plus the following:

- They provide protection against people running packet sniffers on other ports on the same device. See Figures 2.4 and 2.5.

Figure 2.4 Eavesdropping with a Hub

Figure 2.5   Preventing Eavesdropping with a Switch

- Some offer the ability to partition sets of ports into multiple isolated segments. This can be useful in the server room when you might need several different segments with only a few machines on each.
- Switches should always offer the same performance as hubs, and they typically offer much better performance. Why not always better? Imagine a configuration where all systems on the switch want access to the same port. An example is when all of the ports on the switch are allocated to clients, except for one, which is the server. If all clients speak only to the server, and not to each other, then the performance gain by using a switch will be marginal. Some clients may even be worse off than with the hub, depending upon the algorithm that the switch uses to choose the next user.
- Switches often allow you to mix 10Mbps and 100Mbps ports on the same unit. This is relatively easy for them to do, since they have to be able to perform buffering. (There are some hubs which provide this capability, too—you could call them hybrids.)
- Because there are more circuitry and higher costs involved, many switches come with features such as network-based management modules for configuration and statistics gathering. (Many hubs offer this too.)
- **However**, by virtue of having a direct connection between the sending and receiving ports, a given port cannot watch (or "sniff") traffic not destined for it. What you gain in security may be lost in trouble-shooting and other network monitoring functions. Some switches have features to compensate for this, such as the ability to define a monitoring port.

Certainly you should be using switches for your servers and your router(s) if they are available to you. Just remember that you will be unable to monitor network connections between systems on the same device unless it supports a monitoring port, and unless you are willing to configure a system to use it. Also, you might not need to go to the expense of switches unless they are truly warranted. As an example, a **perimeter net** (the network outside the firewall where external web servers and mail gateway, etc., are located) might only have three or four machines on it. If the hub can be physically secured (i.e., no one can walk up and plug into one of its ports), then a simple hub may have advantages over a switch, such as:

1. Beyond the initial cost savings, hubs are inexpensive enough to keep spares in stock.

2. Any of the machines on the perimeter net can act as a sniffer. This relieves the router from having to do all of the monitoring work, and even it would not see all of the traffic. For example, there may be DNS traffic between two machines on that network which would not be visible to the router.

3. At its simplest, a hub is truly *dumb* in that it doesn't look at the packets, it just passes them. Many switches being sold today offer features such as network-based configuration and statistics. While this might be neat and handy, it also poses a security risk. If hackers attack the switch itself, they can reconfigure it, monitor data undetected, cause outages, etc.

4. Along those same lines, switches have firmware, i.e., software packaged in silicon. This software occasionally has bugs—bugs that potentially cause network outages.

In summary, you should understand the difference between hubs and switches, and keep them in mind when deploying them in your network. My advice is to get the right equipment for the task at hand, and do not fall into the trap of believing that more features are better, or that expensive hardware is somehow always worth it. If you're not going to use any of its extra capabilities, then you're doing nothing more than wasting money and increasing the probability of failure of your network.

2.3 WAN Basics 101

Many organizations need to span greater physical distances than those possible using normal LAN technologies, so they deploy a **WAN** (Wide Area Network). Linux routers feel right at home acting as LAN or WAN routers, or as an interface between the two. Because Linux routers can provide functions in addition to routing, WAN links are an application where they shine in comparison to the alternatives. More about this in Chapter 7. But before you start deploying them as WAN routers, you will need to be familiar with some of the terminology and technologies used in a WAN environment.

There are an impressive number of communications technologies available today, and I cannot profess to having mastered even a reasonable subset of these. Therefore, I present only the mainstay for use in corporate WANs today—namely, the digital T-carrier and its common variants. After introducing it, we will talk about how you tie yourself into public and semi-public networks, including interface equipment and billing. This section concludes with a few potential issues to keep in mind when planning your WAN links.

2.3.1 Telephony 101

When you use an ordinary telephone in the United States, you are using what is generally referred to as an **analog line** or **POTS** (Plain Old Telephone Service). The analog telephone network was designed for carrying voice conversations of frequencies up to 4000 Hz.[5] In fact, it attenuates frequencies outside of the 300 to 3400Hz range so effectively as to filter them out almost completely. Digital data will not pass unless it is encoded to "fit" in this frequency range, known as the **passband**.

Because of its bias towards human voice frequencies, a POTS line is often referred to as a **voicegrade** circuit. This is where a modem comes into play; it converts digital pulses into a format compatible with voicegrade circuits. But for the moment, forget about modems, bandwidth, and signal waveforms. There is something else particular about the ordinary telephone network.

Switched Access   A POTS circuit is an example of **switched access**, which means it is a connection to a public network that can make a connection to any of multiple other sites. In the case of the public telephone network, you can literally connect to hundreds of millions of destinations (one at a time) using your single connection. This is the **switched** part, meaning that the network can switch your destination for you based on your input. **Access** in this context is a noun, and refers to the facility you are using to connect your telecommunicating device (in this case, the device is a telephone) to the public network. One property of switched access is that you need to tell the network where you would like to go, i.e., you must *dial* it before you make a connection to it. The most commonly used switched networks are the analog telephone network, ISDN (which is integrated into the analog network), and the X.25 packet-switching network. Charges for switched services are normally a base rate plus usage-based—you pay for it when you use it. Also, switched networks are not necessarily designed so that every node can be used simultaneously (as in the infamous *I can't get a line out on Mother's Day* problem). To save costs, there is limited capacity in the backbone (or the "switch") of the network.

Dedicated Access   Compare switched access to its counterpart, **dedicated access**. Here, you have a circuit which runs from point A to point B. (Note that the point B is not necessarily the remote location you are trying to connect to—more on this later). This circuit does not need to be dialed because its endpoints are fixed. Dedicated access is often known as a **leased-line**, because you are paying for all of the bandwidth of the circuit, all of the time. Leased-lines are typically digital **telco** circuits, but you can also lease a copper pair or a fiber optic cable running between two points from any suitable provider.[6]

There are two overall categories of telco leased-lines available in the United States: analog and digital. While analog circuits were widely used in the past, and may still be very cost-effective for certain applications, advances in analog modem technology (for use on voicegrade circuits) and the proliferation of digital circuits (due to the decreasing cost of broadband telco infrastructure) have made them less

---

[5] Ever wondered why music sounds so different (and bad!) over a telephone? It's because the higher (and lower) frequencies have been filtered out. Try turning the treble and bass controls of your stereo all the way down. This acts like a bandpass filter similar to that used on a analog voice circuit.

[6] But often the only providers are PTTs, an acronym for Post, Telegraph, and Telephone, frequently used generically to refer to the service provider in an area.

common. You may still want to use them for point-to-point links which span large physical distances, but the number of data network service providers in the U.S. which will allow you to connect to their networks using such a circuit is decreasing.

Still, a dedicated analog circuit has several advantages over a switched one (i.e., a POTS circuit). First, it is not subject to the same bandpass filters that voicegrade circuits are. Because more frequencies are allowed to pass, the result is higher bandwidth and throughput. Another advantage is that these circuits are four-wire circuits, which means that they can operate at full-duplex (they can send and receive simultaneously at the full bandwidth of the circuit—voicegrade analog modems present the illusion of this as best they can over two wires). If you know you're going to need to use analog leased-lines, you should do some research about the capabilities and equipment.

Dedicated Digital Access   The second category of dedicated access is digital access, and it represents a much broader class of circuits. Examples of service offerings are DDS (DS0), T1s, T3s, and so on, up to things like an OC–48 (a 2.5Gb SONET standard). The proliferation of digital circuits is largely due to advances in fiber-optic technologies used in the backbone of the world's telecommunications networks (and some changes in industry regulation). The benefits to you are lower bandwidth costs and improved reliability. The results are that more and more digital telco circuits are being used to build wide area networks. Although costs have decreased, they may still constitute a sizable fraction of your connectivity bill, and because most services are priced based on the length of the access circuit, what might be reasonable for one location may be cost-prohibitive for another.

Despite the advances in fiber optics, the legacy of the voice network is still present—in fact, the two are still largely integrated. The T-carrier was originally designed to allow a single digital circuit to simultaneously carry 24 voice conversations. This reduces the number of circuits required between a residential area and a **CO** (central office), and also between COs. It is achieved by digitizing the voice waveform via **PCM** (Pulse Code Modulation) and using **TDM** (Time Division Multiplexing). The T1 communicates by sending frames—a frame can be sent in a fixed amount of time and contains a fixed number of bits. Each of the 24 conversations is periodically sampled and the results are loaded into the frame, which is sent to the receiver. The receiver demultiplexes the signal by separating the frame into 24 pieces, each of which is decoded to reconstruct the voice signal corresponding to each of the 24 conversations being sent. Each of these "conversation channels" is commonly referred to as a **channel** (and sometimes as a **trunk**). Under normal conditions, a channel carries a single voice conversation.

If you bypass the PCM conversion, you can send digital data directly over the circuit, as long as the other end knows when to expect the digital portion and when to expect the voice portion. Each of the 24 timeslots in a frame can be virtualized as a channel, labelled 1–24, each of which can be used independently. This is what makes the T-carrier so versatile. You can mix voice and data on a single circuit simply by allocating a subset of channels (really just timeslots) to different applications. As long as both ends agree about how to multiplex and demultiplex the applications, no one will ever know the difference.

T-Carrier Bandwidth   The bandwidth of each channel is 64kbps. Although it may seem to be a nice round number, designed with data applications in mind, the origin is the PCM conversion which samples each voice conversation 8000 times per second (at 8000 Hz) and encodes the result in an 8-bit value.[7] Furthermore, data applications are not limited to using one channel at a time. The circuitry which interfaces with the digital circuit can aggregate channels to achieve higher data throughput. It is safe to say that the T-carrier scheme has been wildly successful and ubiquitous. Here are some common flavors of digital circuits:

- A **DDS** (or **DS0**), which is a digital circuit running at 56/64kbps (or one channel). (Note that this is not the same as a POTS circuit.)

- The **T1** (or **DS1**), which is $N \times 56/64kbps$, where $1 \leq N \leq 24$, up to 1536Mbps in increments of either 56kbps or 64kbps. The quantum is 56 or 64, depending upon the signalling protocol used on the T1.

  A T1 can be viewed as (24) DS0s, each of which is called a **channel**. A **full T1** is all 24 channels. A **fractional T1** is a subset of these channels.

- A **T3** (or DS3) is a digital circuit designed to carry 672 simultaneous voice conversations (channels). When used for digital transmission, it has a bandwidth of almost 45Mbps.

- An **E1** is a European standard similar to the T1, but instead of 24 trunks it has 32, corresponding to a data rate of 2.048Mbps.

- **FT1 access**, or **fractional T1 access**, is a service offering that does not correspond to a physical circuit. Still, the jump from 64kbps to 1.536Mbps is too wide a gap for some applications, so it is in the PPT's interest to provide such a product. If you order fractional T1 service, then the telco will run a full T1 and give you part of it. If possible, it will use the remaining bandwidth for another customer at the same facility. This sort of offering is common in Europe.

  Note, do not confuse fractional T1 *access* with fractional T1 *ports*, which are data services which use less than all 24 channels.

Digital circuits are your friends, your lifeline connecting you to the world. It helps to know the terminology because you will find that the people maintaining the access circuit are not the same ones selling you the circuits or the same ones responsible for the data services which ride them. (Services often "ride" T1s, in the jargon.) The next section takes this piece of the puzzle and places it in the context of a data link like one you would use to connect to a network service provider (like an ISP).

---

[7] The Nyquist sampling theorem states that you need to sample a waveform at a frequency at least $2\times$ the highest frequency in the waveform to be able to faithfully reconstruct it without data loss. If you recall, the original voicegrade circuit may have frequencies up to 4000Hz, so 8000Hz is the "magic number."

2.3.2 Data Links and Digital Access

Consider the situation where we have a group of machines in locations A and B—separated by 800km—that would like to speak TCP/IP to each other. We're going to need some way to tie our routers together so that they can speak to each other and trade packets. Unless you have the capability to build the network infrastructure yourself, meaning everything from erecting microwave towers to burying cable, configuring repeaters, bribing the local officials, and who knows what else, you're going to have to get your bandwidth from some sort of provider. What you purchase, and why, depends on myriad factors, so let's try to take this apart, step by step.

There are many different physical methods of moving bits from point A to point B. The partial list includes fiber-optic cable, copper cable, satellites up-links, microwave, coaxial cable, and other forms of RF, either through the air, a wire, or some other waveguide. What you use is often dictated by economics and physics, so unless you really can build your own network, you do not always have control over what will be used. For most circuits, your data will end up traveling over a combination of these anyway. This should not be an issue unless you have an application which is sensitive to latency, which is discussed in Section 2.3.5.

To establish a link between our sites, we could order a dedicated digital circuit which connects them directly to each other. This is known as a point-to-point configuration. It is depicted in Figure 2.6.

In this scenario, we would be leasing 100% of the circuit between the sites and could run whatever protocol we like over the link (as long as it is compatible with being used over a digital telco circuit—e.g., CHDLC, Frame Relay, or PPP). This sort of configuration is also known as a **back-to-back** configuration, because you control both ends, and all of the active network elements between them. You also have the full bandwidth of the circuit at your disposal, and you can perform whatever type of compression suits you. This arrangement is great because we are confident that the only other people who have access to the circuit are telco technicians whom we trust not to monitor our packets. If we think even they might be snooping, we can always use some sort of encoding or encryption. However, with most access circuits, you pay the telco based on the distance between the sites and the bandwidth of the circuit. If locations A and B are distant from each other, this can become prohibitively expensive.

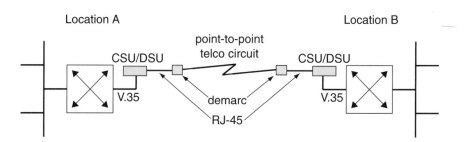

Figure 2.6 Point-to-Point Connection of Remote Sites

An alternative is to turn to a service provider which has **POPs** near both locations and purchase two access circuits—one between location A and its nearest POP,
and the other between location B and its corresponding nearest POP. POP stands
for "Point Of Presence," which is the title given to your provider's nearest geographical presence. We then pay the provider to route traffic on their internal network
between the POPs (and thus between our sites).

Now our dedicated access circuit costs are lower, because we only have to pay
for the distance between each location at its nearest POP. The difference now is that
we don't own the entire path between your sites. This has its own benefits and drawbacks. Apart from cost-savings, the benefits are that the provider will have many
POPs, and it becomes quite easy to add locations C, D, and E to our network. We
also do not have to worry about maintaining anything more than the node (endpoint)
routers.

However, because there are other routers (which belong to our provider) between our sites, we have to comply with their protocols and configuration guidelines.
This means that we cannot use all types of data compression (we can still encrypt
and/or compress IP payloads, but not link-layer protocol packets). More notewor-
thy, however, is that because we are using the provider's network, we have to pay for
that bandwidth. And the more we want to use, the more it will cost. But, because
our provider has orders of magnitude more bandwidth than we want, she can offer
us equivalent bandwidth for far less than what it would cost us to lease the same
dedicated bandwidth using a point-to-point. In this scenario, our WAN link looks
like Figure 2.7. In the case of Internet access, the cloud is the Internet, and many
providers are connected.

Figure 2.7 Connection of Remote Sites via Provider POPs

The Path Between You and the POP   The path your packets take between your router and the provider's POP for a typical T1 access circuit includes the following pieces of hardware and steps:

1. Your router will have a synchronous WAN interface card in it. This is typically an add-on adapter which has a high-speed serial port and a processor on-board to handle the protocol for synchronous communications.

2. A CSU/DSU which interfaces the synchronous WAN interface to the digital telco circuit. Details about CSU/DSUs are in Section 2.3.3.

3. A RJ–45 connection between the CSU/DSU and the telco access point, often known as either **demarc** or a **smart-jack**. The term demarc has its basis in the fact that everything on your side of that interface belongs to you, and is referred to by the telco as **CPE** (Customer Premise Equipment). The demarc is either a self-contained unit (normally a metal box mounted on the wall) or a card in a chassis which holds several demarcs. A smart-jack is the same as a demarc, except that the interface card (the circuitry which terminates the access circuit) is in a closet somewhere, and only the RJ–45 jack has been extended out to your site. When the circuit is installed, it should be labelled with the circuit ID of the access circuit.

4. The CSU/DSU handles the **channelization** of your data—i.e., it takes the stream of bits from the WAN interface and builds frames (with data only in the timeslots which correspond to the channels in use on the circuit). The CSU/DSU also converts the electrical signals for transmission over the T1.

5. This bit stream is transmitted through the telephone network through some combination of central offices and switches until it reaches its destination, which is the demarc at the POP. Because the data are digital, they can be reconstructed any time it is required to rebuild the signal strength or switch media within the telco network (for example, if a portion of the circuit is on fiber instead of copper).

6. The process is reversed on the other side. The bit stream flows through the demarc into their CSU/DSU where it is converted into signal levels that their router's WAN interface understands and expects.

7. From there, the packets flow on the provider's internal network until they find the appropriate exit point (also known as **egress**). The egress point from the provider's network depends upon the type of service you have. If this is your ISP, then your packet should end up on the Internet. If this is a Frame Relay link, then it will appear on your provider's router at the POP on the remote end of the link, so that it can be transmitted to your location B.

Looking back at the block diagram (Figure 2.7), it is functionally very similar to that of analog modems. The cables are new, the protocols are different, and what is really happening on the line is *entirely* different, but it feels the same (if you squint at the picture).

2.3.3 CSU/DSUs

As you noticed in the previous section, a T1 circuit requires an interface before it can be attached to your router. This device is known as a **CSU/DSU**, or a Channel Service Unit/Data Service Unit. CSU/DSUs range from being a simple black box that interfaces the two media types to complicated devices containing multiplexors, inverse multiplexors, SNMP daemons, "phone home" functionality, and circuitry to failover to backup access circuits. CSU/DSUs range in cost from a few hundred dollars to several thousand.

Some routers come equipped with an integrated CSU/DSU, and many service providers will provide a CSU/DSU as part of your service or will lease one to you. You should be aware that some T1 CSU/DSUs can interface only a full T1—i.e., they are permanently configured for all 24 channels. There are also T1 CSU/DSUs that are called "drop-and-add" units, which can be used to multiplex a single T1 for multiple applications. For example, you can order a T1 that has 8 channels of long-distance voice circuits and 16 trunks (1024kbps) of Frame Relay. The "drop-and-add" CSU/DSU makes sure that the signalling is not confusing to either your router or your PBX. Like a T1, a DDS circuit also requires an interface, but it contains only a DSU (since there is only one channel, and is therefore not compatible with the T1 variety).

The CSU/DSU almost always interfaces to the telco circuit via a straight-through twisted-pair cable with RJ–45 connectors on each end. In other words, any CAT5 Ethernet cable that isn't a crossover cable will do. On the "router-side" of the CSU/DSU there is typically a V.35, RS–232, or X.21 connector. Make sure that you get the right cable to interface your router.

Configuring the CSU/DSU   If your service provider does not do it for you, you'll have to configure the CSU/DSU yourself. This is done either through a (second) RS–232 interface or the front panel. Things you will need to know from your provider about your T1 access circuit are:

- framing (ESF or D4) [**ESF**]
- encoding (B8ZS or AMI) [**B8ZS**]
- line build-out (expressed in either distance in feet or dB signal-loss) [**0–133ft** or **0dB**]
- which channels carry the data circuit, in the case of fractional T1
- clocking (internal or external) [**external**] (For anything not in a test lab, the clocking must be driven externally, i.e., from the telco circuit.)

Once you have these values, you'll configure the CSU/DSU to multiplex/demultiplex frames on the T1 as required for the circuit. If you haven't a clue what the values should be, try the bolded values in the list. For the channels, if there is no other application on the circuit, they are typically configured consecutively from channel 1 to N, where $N = bandwidth/64kb$. If this material is new to you, don't worry too much about it. The configuration will be intuitive once you understand the background.

2.3.4 Billing of Digital Services

As the network administrator, you will probably have to validate the charges on the invoices, since you are best prepared to interpret them. Although it sounds like a mundane task, it is important to understand where your money is going. You will need this to be able to compare offers from other service providers.

Access can be expensive, and it is often a source of confusion. Some providers will try to hide access charges by charging a single price for the service, regardless of its distance from the POP (within reason, say 10 miles). This could be a good deal for those relatively distant, and a bad deal for others. Other vendors will separate the access out—perhaps even invoicing it separately. If your organization has contracts for voice service, the access circuits may fall under that contract. Because the FCC tariffs access and data services differently, access may be discounted separately, too.

Other potential complications arise when access is provided by a third party. Often the data service provider will not own the "last mile" and will lease the access circuit on your behalf. In this case, you may see things like "COC" or "Central Office Coordination" charges on your bill. These charges represent the fees your provider has to pay the access provider for co-locating in their facility. They are often not subject to discount terms in your contract. Finally, there is often an opportunity to save costs by multiplexing a single access circuit for both voice and data.

Once you get beyond access costs, there are fees for the data services themselves. In general, the cost of using a vendor-provided service with a leased-line includes:

- monthly access costs (possibly including COC fees)
- one-time access install charge (sometimes waived)
- monthly port costs (for the service itself)
- one-time port install/setup charge (sometimes waived)
- per-byte charges if your port/service is usage-based

It adds up quickly. A vendor should be able to explain all of the costs related to the service. It is in your best interest to collect and organize as much documentation about the link, and the various vendors' services which comprise it, as possible. When there are troubles and questions, you may be ultimately responsible within your organization.

2.3.5 Potential Datacomm Issues

Between having to unravel the secrets of what to order, solve CSU/DSU configuration problems, cope with physically down circuits, and audit incorrect billing, you'd think that a WAN administrator had enough to worry about. (After all, you're just supposed to configure the router.) The following sections address other topics which you may need to consider.

Latency   When you are working with extreme physical distances, the different media paths your packets take through a provider's network become important. Latency is a measure of the time it takes for a packet to travel from location A to location B, and is independent of bandwidth. For example, you can place a small packet into a very large pipe (say, a 45Mbps link) between two points, but it could still take a "long" time (maybe 600–800ms) for a packet sent to emerge from the other end. Latency is partially due to the delays introduced by switching elements, which require some time to look at the packet and pass it on. But a significant cause of latency is a physical limitation—namely, the speed of light.

A satellite geosynchronous orbit has an altitude of almost 38000km. If you could beam light directly at it in a vacuum, it would take about an eighth of a second to get there. Multiply this by two to go up and come back down. And because you won't be directly under the satellite for both trips (otherwise, you'd be sending it to yourself), you should factor in another $\sqrt{2}$, plus the switching delays. Now you're well past 350ms, and all of this just to get to the destination. If you're working interactively, you'll need to wait for a reply, too.

Compare this to the latency for fiber-optic half-way across the face of the earth, and you'll see why it makes good sense to stay on the ground. Of course, with fiber-optic, you'll be taking more hops (more switching time) and not travelling directly from location to location. Fiber-optic links can also be more expensive to deploy (and therefore more expensive to use) than RF or satellite links. In most circumstances you have little control over the path your packets take once they leave your facility, but be aware that more bandwidth does not always equate to "fast" for your users.

Link Security   Where there is networking, it seems that a security discussion is not far behind. The basic goal is always to exchange data between two or more machines, but the security measures required vary, based on the nature of the connection (and the data).

When you dial up an ISP and use the Internet to connect to your office, you are making a point-to-point connection via a public network that is, for the most part, unregulated. You must guard not only the data you transfer, but also the machines themselves.

Compare this to some of the private IP networks, which are known as dial-IP solutions. Access to a private network is controlled, either physically or by some authentication mechanism. For these networks, the users of the network all know each other; at least that is the illusion. Much more likely is that they are all customers of the same service provider. Furthermore, the service provider should go to some effort to ensure that customer X cannot take a peek at the traffic customer Y is sending. Therefore, a better classification would be a **semi-private** network. If you are dealing with very sensitive information, you cannot completely guarantee that an acutely interested competitor might not find a way to infiltrate your provider's network (admittedly paranoid, but conceivable).

Frame Relay is also a semi-private network, although most treat them as private networks. Once your packets are on your provider's network, they travel alongside packets from anyone else. It is conceivable that, through some social engineering, someone on the inside could be listening. My guess is that most providers would wag their heads very convincingly that these sorts of things never happen, but then again, you never know. This very topic came up during the deployment of a world-wide personnel system which was to be used only on the internal network. The objection was that the use of the WAN violated the German data security law (*Datenschutzrecht*) because it allowed information about employees to pass between sites over unencrypted links. An interesting proposition, even though the links between our sites belonged to an uninterested third party.

Are these sorts of links truly insecure? That will be for you to decide, depending upon your application. My personal belief is that there are far easier (and less expensive) methods of spying, but that may be my naiveté. If these sorts of things make you perk up, consider using a strong method of encryption of your IP packet payloads. There are several **VPN** (Virtual Private Network) solutions for Linux; here are a few links to get you started:

- **CIPE** (Crypto IP Encapsulation) is a lightweight protocol that allows you to connect two subnets via an insecure middle network. It is based on encapsulating all of the traffic within UDP packets and does this through a Linux kernel module. See its homepage at *http://sites.inka.de/˜W1011/devel/cipe.html* for more information.

- **Linux FreeS/WAN** is an implementation of the IETF's IPSEC (Internet Protocol SECurity) for Linux. It is also implemented in the kernel (like CIPE) and comes with a set of tools and utilities for its use. Its homepage has some very good documentation about configuring and using the software (*http://www.xs4all.nl/˜freeswan/*).

- The **VPN HOWTO**, part of the *LDP*, covers using Secure Shell (*ssh*) and a pty redirector to easily build a private network using the standard PPP daemon. It is a good example of an "IP-encapsulated-within-IP protocol," similar to **PPTP** (Point-to-Point Tunnelling Protocol).

2.4 SUMMARY

This chapter covered some of the background material which, hopefully, will help you increase your comprehension of what you are doing as a network administrator. The chapter began by defining the difference between a physical (media) protocol, a link protocol, and a networking protocol. While the definition presented is somewhat informal, the concept should stick in your mind. "Frame Relay" is a link protocol which ties routers together. "IP" is a networking protocol which supports the TCP and UDP transport protocols. V.90 is a physical protocol (used by two modems talking to each over an analog telephone line).

The next topic was IP subnetting. You should revisit that section or appeal to other sources if the concepts and math of CIDR are not clear. You cannot balance a checkbook without being able to add and subtract; you cannot design a network without being able to calculate subnet masks.

From there, the next topic was, "How does a workstation decide if it needs to use a router, and how does a router make its decisions?" We then talked about the hardware used to glue routers and workstations together when using Ethernet—hubs and switches—and some security considerations when using them.

Zooming out from the LAN, we looked at the WAN, including general types of access, information about digital telco circuits, the interfaces required to use them, and the general layout of a WAN link. The section also noted a few gotchas about billing, round-trip packet delay, and security. From here on out, we'll build routers!

## CHAPTER 3

Silicon—LAN Router

"Silicon" is the name of one of the busiest and most heavily used systems I have ever administered. As the main LAN router and the primary internal DNS server, this system is involved with almost every action that a user can perform with a networked computer. If you wonder how someone comes across the idea to use a PC running Linux as a LAN router in a production environment, the initial answer was one of economics. Silicon's total cost was less than that of upgrading the existing router, and the DNS server was a free bonus. The fact that it was successful started something exciting and added reasons such as stability, ease of maintenance, and flexibility to that answer. You can use the information here as a starting point for deploying this and more interesting topologies.

The first example in this chapter covers how to configure a Linux router to route between two physical subnets. For this example, we will work up the configuration in detail, hopefully with enough information for those just getting started with routers. Later examples will go much more quickly. After we have our LAN router configured, we extend the idea of routing between physically separate subnets, and introduce **IP aliasing** and the idea of **multi-netting**. This is used to route between multiple logical IP subnets on a single physical segment, and the technique can ease migrations from one set of IP addresses to another. Next, we cover the IP accounting facility in the kernel—the basis for some of the traffic analysis tools available for Linux. Having mastered these topics, you will be ready to route. The chapter concludes with an introduction to the **LRP** Linux distribution. LRP is *networking-centric* and fits on a single floppy-diskette, making it an alternative to using a full Linux distribution for your router.

3.1 CONFIGURING A **LAN ROUTER**

Silicon is a good place to start talking about production Linux routers because its hardware configuration is very simple and it requires no software other than the Linux kernel and network utilities which are included in the base installation of all common distributions.

In Section 2.1.2, we studied the degenerate case of how a single workstation sends a packet directly to another workstation on the same subnet. We noted that if the destination's IP subnet does not match that of the sender, then the sender needs to use a gateway. Here we configure that gateway, routing between two physically separate Ethernet segments, each with its own IP subnet. (Connecting two physically separate physical segments which are part of the *same* logical IP subnet is known as **bridging**. The Linux kernel provides bridging support, but it is not covered in this book.)

NOTE: PRIVILEGES FOR ROUTING COMMANDS

For the procedures in this chapter (and most things in this book), you have to become the super-user on your system to be able to execute the commands. Save yourself some hassle and make sure that your **PATH** contains both */sbin* and */usr/sbin*, since most of the network configuration commands are in these directories. If you'd like to keep a record of the commands executed, try the *script* command.

3.1.1 Defining Our LAN Router

The first thing you should do whenever starting any project is to figure out what it is you need to accomplish, noting any specific conditions which must be met or limitations to consider. This helps in mapping out your solution, and will keep you from losing sight of your goal as you become engrossed with the myriad details and smaller obstacles which present themselves. (I cannot tell you many times I have started a project only to realize upon its completion that I spent 80% of the time working on 20% of the functionality, and forgot to implement another 20% of the functionality altogether.) Our goal in configuring silicon is:

> Connect two separate IP subnets via a router. Each IP subnet is on its own physical 10-BaseT Ethernet segment. Subnet$_A$ is 192.168.16.0/24; subnet$_B$ is 192.168.18.0/24. Both subnets are to have full access to each other. The IP addresses 192.168.16.1 and 192.168.18.1 have been reserved as the gateway addresses for subnet$_A$ and subnet$_B$, respectively.

It can be quite helpful to draw a picture. Even if you understand the topology and what is happening, others will want to grok it. Try to be consistent when depicting your network graphically—a single and easy-to-draw set of conventions is easy for others to follow. A picture *can be* "worth a thousand words" (of documentation), but spending eight hours to produce a very fancy drawing is usually a waste of time. The conventions I use are in Figure 3.1. Using these conventions, silicon's topology is depicted in Figure 3.2.

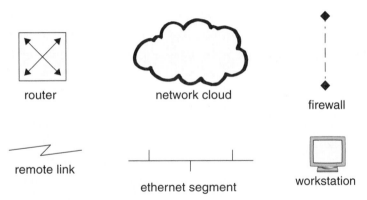

Figure 3.1 Conventions Used When Drawing Networks

3.1.2 Configuring the Base Platform

Now that we know what we want to do and have a picture, we can list the hardware required. We need a system with two Ethernet adapters, one for each segment, and cables to attach the router to the segments. The system itself doesn't need to be much; a P5/166 with 16MB of RAM should be sufficient for this configuration. (Refer back to Section 1.1 if you have questions about the hardware.) For this example, we use (2) 3com 3c905 10/100 PCI Ethernet adapters. You need to load your router with your favorite distribution of Linux. This example will be presented using Debian GNU/Linux. There is no need to load a slew of packages on your router; the base load will suffice.

Enabling IP Forwarding for Kernel Version 2.2.x   You need *IP forwarding* enabled in your kernel for your system to act as a gateway and to be able to route between multiple interfaces. The following kernel options should be selected, in addition to whatever other device support you may need:

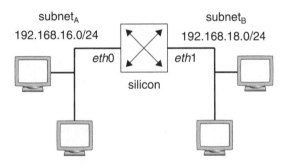

Figure 3.2 LAN Router with Two Subnets

```
General setup --->
    [*] Sysctl support

Networking options --->
    [*] TCP/IP networking
    [*] IP: optimize as router not host

Network Device Support --->
    [*] Network device support
    [*] Ethernet (10 or 100Mbit)
    [*] 3COM cards
    <M> 3c590/3c900 series "Vortex/Boomerang" support

Filesystems --->
    [*] /proc/filesystem support
```

These options should seem straight-forward. You are configuring a kernel to support TCP/IP and a specific Ethernet card. The IP: optimize as router not host setting is not needed, but recommended for performance. (This option tells the kernel that the packet is more likely to be forwarded than passed up the stack to a socket on this machine. This information is passed on to the network driver, which potentially changes the way in which it allocates memory to store the packet.) Support for the /proc filesystem and Sysctl support are required if you intend to do any routing. (Sysctl enables the /proc/sys hierarchy.) They provide a window into what is happening within the kernel and offer the ability to set certain kernel parameters through the filesystem. /proc will also be used later for IP accounting and other kernel features.

What's missing from this picture so far is a setting that tells the kernel that it is allowed to route packets—i.e. accept packets sent to it but not destined for its IP address, and forward these packets according to its routing table. (In version 2.0.x of the kernel, this could be done by enabling IP: forwarding/gatewaying. For 2.2.x, this is controlled via the value of /proc/sys/net/ipv4/ip_forward.

HINT: INSTANT ROUTING SUPPORT

The /proc filesystem offers a quick way enable or disable routing on any Linux system where you have superuser access. (In fact, it is the *only* way to do so shy of editing the kernel sources starting with kernel version 2.2.) Enable it with echo "1" > /proc/sys/net/ipv4/ip_forward. It can be disabled again by writing a zero to this file. Pretty neat, eh?

If you haven't already done so (and need to), build the kernel. Once this is done, reboot the system with **shutdown -r now** so that you are running on the new kernel. You will know you are using the new kernel by executing the command **uname -a**, which shows you the date and time that the currently running kernel was built.

HINT: THE STOCK DEBIAN KERNEL

> The stock Debian kernel comes with many options (such as firewalling support) and all of the modular device drivers. This eliminates the need for compiling a new kernel from the source for this example. However, the stock kernel is compiled for the 386 architecture and probably contains (disk subsystem) driver support that you do not need. To decrease the size of the kernel's memory footprint and to fine-tune other options to suite your environment, you should get into the habit of compiling your own. (Refer to Section B.4 in Appendix B for detailed instructions.)

If you are not running your new kernel, make sure that you wrote the new kernel to your hard drive with the `make {b}zlilo` step. You can call *lilo* explicitly from the command line with **lilo -v** to see what is happening. You might also want to check if perhaps you left either a rescue floppy or a boot floppy in your system which came with your Linux distribution.

3.1.3 Loading Modular Device Drivers

Once we have routing support, we need to load the device drivers for our Ethernet adapters so that we can use them. It is highly recommended that you use modular device drivers—for a list of reasons why, see the discussion in Appendix B on page 303.

The modules are placed in */lib/modules/$*`(uname -r)`*/net/3c59x.o* during the `make modules_install` phase of the kernel build. *insmod* should be smart enough to figure this out, and you should have to type only **insmod** `modulename`. If you happen to have 3c905 cards like those in the example, loading the driver is as simple as **insmod 3c59x**. If you have a different type of NIC (or NICs), you should load the appropriate modules.

Dependent Modules   Be aware that some modules use services (really, code) from other modules and must be loaded in what is called a **stack of dependent modules**. A very common example is the NE2000 card and its many clones. The modules *ne.o* cannot be loaded until a module it depends upon, *8390.o* has been loaded. Fortunately, you do not have to memorize this. Every time the system boots, *depmod* is called and writes the current list of module dependencies to */lib/modules/$*`(uname -r)`*/modules.dep*. You may look in this file to see what dependencies exist between modules. Each line in the file lists a module in the first field followed by a ":" and then a list of space-delimited module names. If nothing follows the ":", then the module has no dependencies. Otherwise, the dependent modules are required.

modprobe uses the contents of the *modules.dep* file to load any dependent modules that might be required before loading the module name you specify. You simply give it the name of the module to load as its argument, followed by any options you would normally specify to that module when using *insmod*. For example, `modprobe ne` will load *ne.o* and *8390.o*. Using the `-r` switch reverses the sense and removes a module along with any of its dependent modules (not in use by other modules or processes).

Module Parameters   Many modules accept configuration parameters, which can be specified on the command line when they are loaded. The parameters often tell the driver where to search for the card (at what IRQ and base address), as well as set options such as whether or not the card should use full-duplex mode, which transceiver to activate, and so on. Not all modules use the same keywords, although most support `io=baseaddr` and `irq=irq` for setting these values. Unfortunately, the manner in which options must be specified when you have multiple interfaces is completely up to the driver author. In these cases, it is best to refer to the documentation accompanying the driver or in the driver source code itself. These may be found in the kernel source tree (usually */usr/src/linux*) in *./Documentation/networking/* and *./drivers/net/*driver.c, respectively. Since not all driver names are the same as the card they support, it is helpful to *grep -i* through this directory for the name of your card to locate the right file(s). It also may not hurt to read through */usr/src/linux/Documentation/modules.txt*.

Problems Loading Modules?   What to do if you have the correct driver support and the cards still are not recognized? Chances are it has to do with incorrect parameters or a resource conflict (IRQ or base address). First, recognize that PCI and ISA cards are different. PCI cards receive their IRQ assignments from the BIOS on the motherboard, and most (worthwhile) BIOSes produce a list of IRQ assignments to PCI devices just before booting the operating system. If you still suspect an IRQ conflict with a PCI device (probably with an ISA device), check the contents of */proc/interrupts* to see if the interrupt you are using to initialize the card is already in use. (This is not foolproof, because the ISA card causing the conflict may not be initialized by the OS either.) The base address should rarely pose a problem. The range of addresses assigned to PCI devices is different than that used for ISA cards.

ISA cards are another matter altogether. For one thing, be certain than **PnP** (Plug and Play),[1] is turned **off** for any card in the system. Many network cards come with a configuration utility (which typically runs under MS-DOS) that will do this for you and let you set the IRQ and base address. Some of these tools are available for Linux; I would start my search at *http://cesdis.gsfc.nasa.gov/linux/*. Older cards have jumpers, which you can use to set to the base address, IRQ, or sometimes both. In the worst case, just use two interfaces with different driver types. You should keep in mind that most cards of the same brand and model default to the same **base address** and IRQ settings, so you will have to take some action to avoid the conflict.

If none of these things helps, break down and RTFM to find out if the card is supported by Linux at all. Odds are that someone else has had the same problem, and perhaps documented their experience at the *LDP* site (either in the *Ethernet*

---

[1] "Plug and Pray" for those who have suffered its arbitrary nature.

HOWTO or the *Hardware Compatibility HOWTO*). You can also pose the question to the support structure(s) of your Linux distribution. (See Appendix A.)

3.1.4 Detecting Ethernet Interfaces

As soon as you have loaded your device drivers, you will want to make sure that the kernel recognized and initialized the Ethernet adapters (or **NIC**s). The kernel always names the first NIC it finds *eth0*. Subsequent adapters are numbered consecutively as *eth1*, *eth2*, etc. There are several different ways to determine whether the kernel has already detected your NICs.

1. The contents of */proc/net/dev* will show all network devices which are currently configured on the system.

```
silicon:/root> cat /proc/net/dev
Inter-|   Receive                    |  Transmit
 face |packets errs drop fifo frame|packets errs drop fifo colls carrier
   lo:    4378    0    0    0     0    4378    0    0    0     0      0
 eth0:   27520    0    0    0     0   26367    0    0    0     1      0
 eth1:      31    0    0    0     0      17    0    0    0     0      0
```

This shows that the devices *eth0* and *eth1* do exist (along with the *lo*, the **loop-back** device which, by convention, has the IP address 127.0.0.1). If a device appears in this table, then we can configure it with an IP address and use it. Unfortunately, */proc/net/dev* does not tell us much about settings of the device driver or the NIC.

2. The *dmesg* command, which displays messages generated by the kernel during the boot sequence and thereafter, often gives more information. A sample output of *dmesg* follows:

```
silicon:/root> /bin/dmesg
8<------(lots of removed for clarity)------8<
3c59x.c:v0.99E 5/12/98 Donald Becker
 (http://cesdis.gsfc.nasa.gov/linux/drivers/vortex.html)
eth0: 3Com 3c905 Boomerang 100baseTx at 0xfcc0, 00:60:97:da:8d:91, IRQ 11
 8K word-wide RAM 3:5 Rx:Tx split, autoselect/NWay Autonegotiation interface.
 MII transceiver found at address 24, status 786b.
 Enabling bus-master transmits and whole-frame receives.
eth1: 3Com 3c905 Boomerang 100baseTx at 0xfc80, 00:60:97:26:6b:c7, IRQ 10
 8K word-wide RAM 3:5 Rx:Tx split, autoselect/NWay Autonegotiation interface.
 MII transceiver found at address 24, status 782b.
 Enabling bus-master transmits and whole-frame receives.
```

Notice that *dmesg* displays a good amount of information about the driver. The first line shows the version of the driver and its source. Then each device is listed as it is detected by the driver. In our case, two NICs are detected. For each device, *dmesg* shows us its base address, MAC address, the IRQ being used, the amount of RAM on the card, how that RAM is divided into buffers (Receive:Transmit), the type of negotiation enabled on the interface, the type of transceiver being used, and whether or not bus-mastering is being used. (The amount of useful information contained in the message depends upon the author of the device driver. In this case, Mr. Becker does a very good job.)

Be aware when using *dmesg*, however, that it reads from a circular buffer. If there have been a lot of kernel messages generated since bootup, the messages may have "wrapped-around" and started overwriting the messages from the boot sequence. Also, do not be misled into thinking that *dmesg* contains the startup messages for all subsystems (e.g., daemons and services) on your router. It shows only kernel messages.

3. The results of *ifconfig* are useful if the devices are, in fact, being initialized by the kernel. If the command returns an error like:

```
silicon:/root> ifconfig eth0
eth0: unknown interface.
```

then you know that either the driver module is not loaded, or it is being loaded but is not detecting the NIC. On the other hand, if the kernel does detect the devices and they are configured, then *ifconfig* will return something like:

```
silicon:/root> /sbin/ifconfig eth0
eth0      Link encap:Ethernet  HWaddr 00:60:97:DA:8D:91
          UP BROADCAST RUNNING MULTICAST  MTU:1500  Metric:1
          RX packets:0 errors:0 dropped:0 overruns:0 frame:0
          TX packets:0 errors:0 dropped:0 overruns:0 carrier:0
          Collisions:0
          Interrupt:11 Base address:0xfcc0
```

ifconfig tells us a lot about the interface—basically, everything except for the driver type. (Normally it also shows the IP configuration, but at this point, the IP address has not been configured.)

4. *netstat -ia* will show you an abridged version of *ifconfig*'s output. Note that with just -i, you will see all of the interfaces which are **up**, along with some statistics. Using the -a switch shows all of the network interfaces registered with the kernel, regardless of their status of **up** or **down**.

```
silicon:/root> netstat -ia
Kernel Interface table
Iface  MTU Met RX-OK RX-ERR RX-DRP RX-OVR TX-OK TX-ERR TX-DRP TX-OVR Flags
lo    3584   0    21      0      0      0    21      0      0      0 BLRU
eth0  1500   0     0      0      0      0     0      0      0      0 BRU
eth1  1500   0     0      0      0      0     0      0      0      0 B
```

5. In a roundabout way, *lsmod* will show us what is going on, too. Since we are using modules for our NIC device drivers, our NICs will not be detected until the module is loaded. For each *ethX* device detected by that module and configured **up** by *ifconfig*, the `Used by` field is incremented by one. Thus, in the following output, we would surmise that two 3c59x devices are **up**.

```
silicon:/root> lsmod
Module          Pages    Used by
serial             7         0
3c59x              4         2
```

The converse, however, does not hold true. Just because the module name does not appear in the output of *lsmod*, or the value of `Used by` is 0, does not mean that the NICs are not able to be detected. The most probable explanations are that the module has not been loaded (or could not load for some reason), that the devices have been deconfigured with `ifconfig ethX` down, or that it has not yet been configured up. Last but not least, the driver support could simply already be compiled into the kernel.

3.1.5 Configuring Ethernet Interfaces

Before you can go any further, you need to have a system where *dmesg* shows that both *eth0* and *eth1* are recognized. In other words, you should be able to execute **ifconfig eth0** and **ifconfig eth1** and see meaningful output. If you do not, make sure that you have support in your kernel for the NICs you are using, and that you've loaded the appropriate modules.

Now that we have gone through all of this trouble-shooting material, you might be wondering, "What was the question again?" Refer back to Figure 3.2 on page 55 to see the picture of our problem statement. We need to configure our router to route between the 192.168.16.0/24 and the 192.168.18.0/24 subnets, and we have reserved the .1 address in both subnets for the router. The next step is to assign IP addresses to *eth0* and *eth1*. Different distributions provide different ways to do this, although the underlying mechanism for configuring a card with a fixed IP address is the same and is based on *ifconfig*. *ifconfig* is easy to use. If its manpage seems intimidating at first, it is because there is so much that you can do with it. For configuring our adapters, it is quite simple. The usage is:

```
ifconfig device ipaddr broadcast bcastaddr netmask netmask up
```

Let's configure *eth0* first:

```
silicon:/root> ifconfig eth0 192.168.16.1 broadcast 192.168.16.255 \
                        netmask 255.255.255.0 up
```

Verify that the device is correctly configured by entering **ifconfig eth0**. The results should look like:

```
silicon:/root> ifconfig eth0
eth0      Link encap:Ethernet  HWaddr 00:60:97:DA:8D:91
          inet addr:192.168.16.1  Bcast:192.168.16.255  Mask:255.255.255.0
          UP BROADCAST RUNNING MULTICAST  MTU:1500  Metric:1
          RX packets:216 errors:0 dropped:0 overruns:0 frame:0
          TX packets:2 errors:0 dropped:0 overruns:0 carrier:0
          collisions:0 txqueuelen:100
          Interrupt:11 Base address:0xfcc0
```

If the interface settings do not look correct, you can run *ifconfig* repeatedly until things are right. Let's look at the output listed above line-by-line to learn about the command and what parameters it controls.

Line 1 shows the interface name, the type of interface, and the **MAC address** of the interface. There is nothing on this line which is controlled by *ifconfig* (for an Ethernet card).

Line 2 shows the IP address, broadcast address, and subnet mask of the interface—all of which are controlled by *ifconfig*. You may notice that the broadcast address is calculated from the IP of the interface and the subnet mask directly. Note, however, if you specify a broadcast address using the keyword **broadcast**, and miscalculate, you will receive no warning of your error. Furthermore, once the broadcast address is set (either by you or by *ifconfig*), it will not change until you explicitly do so with the keyword **broadcast**.

HINT: AUTOMATIC ASSIGNMENT OF THE SUBNET MASK

If you are not using CIDR networks, there is no need to specify the broadcast address or the subnet mask. As with most Unices, *ifconfig* will assume you want a class A, B, or C network, depending upon the IP address assigned, and assigns the subnet mask and broadcast values accordingly.

Line 3 shows which flags are set for the interface name, along with the **MTU** and **metric**. MTU stands for Maximum Transfer Unit, or max size in bytes for a packet which will be generated by this interface. The metric is a way of specifying which of two (or more) similarly configured interfaces is preferable and should be used by the kernel first. The flags for an Ethernet device are:

UP indicates that the interface is available to be used for sending and receiving packets.

BROADCAST indicates that this interface can receive all broadcasts. You can disable this by issuing **ifconfig eth0 -broadcast**.

RUNNING indicates that the driver for the interface is running.

MULTICAST indicates that the interface is capable of multicast. You can set[clear] (for some devices) this with `ifconfig eth0 [-]multicast`.

PROMISC indicates that the interface is listening to *all* traffic on the network visible to it. This effectively turns the interface into a network sniffer. *tcpdump*, *ethereal*, and other programs use this mode to have a look at all of the packets flowing past the interface. (See Section 4.5.) You can set[clear] this by issuing the `ifconfig eth0 [-]promisc` command.

ALLMULTI indicates that the **all-multicast** mode has been set, and that all multicast packets on the network will be received by the interface. This is similar to **promiscuous** mode, but for multicast.

Lines 4, 5, and 6 are mostly statistics for the interface. Zero values in these fields (except **RX packets** and **TX packets**) are Good Things. The last field, **txqueue-len**, is the number of packets allowed to buffer in the send queue before the sending process blocks. This value can be tuned down for low-speed links to help interactive performance.

Line 7 contains information from the driver about the IRQ and base address of the hardware. (Some drivers support changing these values with *ifconfig*, but I recommend using driver module parameters.)

3.1.6 Adding Routes—the *route* Command

The next step is to add what is known as a **network route** for the interface. Think of this as telling the Linux kernel about the IP subnet connected directly to the interface. But because this is done so commonly, and because all of the necessary information is available when you *ifconfig* the interface, Linux kernel[2] takes care of this itself. You can verify this by checking the contents of the **routing table** before and after configuring your interfaces. Do this with either `route -n` or `netstat -rn`—the command results are almost identical.

```
### before any interfaces are configured
silicon:/root> route -n
Kernel IP routing table
Destination     Gateway         Genmask         Flags Metric Ref    Use Iface
127.0.0.0       0.0.0.0         255.0.0.0       U     0      0       20 lo

### after eth0 has been configured
silicon:/root> route -n
Kernel IP routing table
Destination     Gateway         Genmask         Flags Metric Ref    Use Iface
192.168.16.0    0.0.0.0         255.255.255.0   U     0      0        0 eth0
127.0.0.0       0.0.0.0         255.0.0.0       U     0      0       24 lo
```

---

[2] Starting with version 2.2 of the kernel.

Note that you do not need a **host route** for the interface as you do for other Unix variants. If you are not running a 2.2 kernel, or inadvertently flush your routing table, you can re-add the network route for *eth0* with:

```
route add -net 192.168.16.0 netmask 255.255.255.0 eth0
```

Note that the *route* command for Linux has some slight differences when compared to other versions of Unix. Mainly, you can add network routes directly to interfaces, bypassing the step of establishing a host route for the interface before adding the network route via the gateway of the IP address of the adapter. This "trick" also works for point-to-point links. (More about this in Section 5.3.5.) Also, the syntax is a little different. Let's cover some of the options.

```
route [add|del] [-net|-host] target netmask nm [gw gw] intf
```

Basically, you can either **add** or **del**ete routes, of type either **-net** or **-host**.[3] For network routes, you will want to use the **netmask** keyword unless you are using only class A, B, or C networks, in which case the command will look at the **target** and determine a default value for the netmask (like *ifconfig* will do when configuring the interface). Because many applications are a mix of CIDR and standard class C networks, you should always specify the netmask explicitly. The **netmask** must be specified in dot-notation.[4]

If you need to specify a gateway, use **gw** followed by either the IP address or the hostname of the gateway. Once again, you should be explicit and type out the IP address. If you get into the habit of using hostnames, make sure that they are in the local */etc/hosts*, not DNS or NIS names. Although these names will work fine as long as the name resolution succeeds, you may have to wait through some long timeouts if you specify a DNS name for the gateway for a route, and your DNS server is somewhere beyond that gateway.

The last argument is the *interface* to use for this routing table entry. You may use the **dev** keyword before it and list it anywhere in the command-line,[5] but placing it at the end of the line and omitting the **dev** seems to be a popular convention. If you do not specify a gateway, you will have to specify an interface, but in most other cases, the kernel can figure out which interface it should use from the IP address of the gateway.

3.1.7 Defining Multiple Interfaces

So, we have one interface up and configured, and a route to the local subnet over that interface. Before moving on, we need to do a little housekeeping. We have *eth0* configured, but which card in the PC is *eth0*? Take a moment and label the physical interface card corresponding to *eth0* so that there is no confusion about which physical card corresponds to which interface. This is a good time to do this,

---

[3] Used for a single IP address, in which case you do not have to specify a netmask.

[4] Anyone want to write a patch to let you use *lmaskbits*?

[5] In fact, most of the options may be shifted around to suit your taste.

because the second card is not initialized with an IP address, so even if you have both cards attached to hubs, only the first card could be the one being used. You should attach the card you believe to be *eth0*, and `ping` an IP address on that network. (Note that the Linux version of *ping* must be terminated with **CTRL-C** [unless you use the **-c** *count* option].) If you did not specify IRQs or base addresses when loading the device driver modules, use *dmesg* (or *ifconfig*) to note the IRQ of *eth0* so that you can specify it explicitly in the future. This way, you can be certain that the kernel's *eth0* is the same card you expect it to be. Once you know which interface is which, label them both, and connect them to their respective hubs.

Moving onto the second interface. . . . We simply repeat the process for the *eth0*, but for *eth1* and changing IP addresses and network addresses as appropriate. First, *ifconfig* the interface with **ifconfig eth1 192.168.18.1 netmask 255.255.255.0 up**, and check to see that all is well.

```
silicon:/root> ifconfig eth1
eth1      Link encap:Ethernet  HWaddr 00:60:97:26:6B:C7
          inet addr:192.168.18.1  Bcast:192.168.18.255  Mask:255.255.255.0
          UP BROADCAST RUNNING MULTICAST  MTU:1500  Metric:1
          RX packets:0 errors:0 dropped:0 overruns:0 frame:0
          TX packets:0 errors:0 dropped:0 overruns:0 carrier:0
          collisions:0 txqueuelen:100
          Interrupt:10 Base address:0xfc80
```

Remember that the kernel will automagically add the network route for the interface, so your routing table should now look like:

```
silicon:/root> route -n
Kernel IP routing table
Destination   Gateway   Genmask         Flags Metric Ref    Use Iface
192.168.16.0  0.0.0.0   255.255.255.0   U     0      0        0 eth0
192.168.18.0  0.0.0.0   255.255.255.0   U     0      0        0 eth1
127.0.0.0     0.0.0.0   255.0.0.0       U     0      0       24 lo
```

That's it! You now have a router. You should configure workstations in each subnet to use their router—either 192.168.16.1 or 192.168.18.1. If you have Linux workstations, you can add a route to a workstation in subnet $_A$ to find subnet $_B$ with **route add -net 192.168.18.0 netmask 255.255.255.0 gw 192.168.16.1 metric 1**. Alternately, you could add a default route to that workstation in subnet $_A$ with **route add -net default gw 192.168.16.1 metric 1**. Use a similar command for a workstation in subnet $_B$ so that it can find subnet $_A$ before you test. Once this is done, the workstations should be able to speak TCP/IP to each other via the router.

What?!? They can't talk to each other? Are you certain that IP forwarding is enabled? In otherwords, is */proc/sys/net/ipv4/ip_forward* set? If it's not (i.e., if `cat /proc/sys/net/ipv4/ip_forward` yields 0), then set this bit with `echo "1" >/proc/sys/net/ipv4/ip\_forward`.

3.1.8 Making Configuration Changes Permanent

But before you announce your victory, you need to make sure that what you have done will be there the next time that the machine is restarted. One common question I have heard is, "Where is the routing table stored?" In the case of static routes, it is stored in memory, and unless you record the same commands you issued during the example in a startup script somewhere, you will be starting over again from the beginning whenever you reboot the router. Let's review what we have done, thereby noting the configuration changes which need to be made permanent:

1. We built a kernel with modular support for our NICs, Sysctl, and proc filesystem support. No action is required to retain this support.
2. We loaded our device driver modules. Modules can be loaded in several different ways. With Debian, you can:
   (a) Let the kernel load them automatically.
   (b) Add them to */etc/modules*, which is parsed by */etc/init.d/modutils* during system startup.
   (c) Add statements to */etc/init.d/network* (up through Debian 2.1).
       There are other creative things you might do, but the ones listed above make the most sense. Of these options, I choose the third, because it places almost all of the information about the network configuration in a single file. I tend to shy away from allowing production boxes to autoload device driver modules, so the first choice is out (for me anyway).
3. We *ifconfig*'d the interfaces with their configuration. This is normally done in */etc/init.d/network* on Debian systems (up through Debian verison 2.1—edit */etc/network/interfaces* starting with Debian version 2.2)
4. We added network routes to the router. This is also done in */etc/init.d/network* on Debian systems before version 2.2, albeit in a relatively workstation-centric manner. We shall repair that presently.
5. We set `/proc/sys/net/ipv4/ip_forward` to "1."

   I believe that all of the network configuration information to be kept in a single file, when feasible. This means that you can reconfigure a system's network parameters by editing a single file. For this reason, I use a modified */etc/init.d/network*. A version for the configuration of silicon so far follows.

```
#!/usr/bin/ksh
#
# /etc/init.d/network
#
# modification history:
#
# 19990213/tm    complete rework for new silicon box
############################################################################
Intf_up()
{
   [ -z ${INF} ] && echo "failure - INF not set" && return 1
   [ -z ${IPADDR} ] && echo "failure - $INF IPADDR not set" && return 1
   [ -z ${NETMASK} ] && echo "warning - $INF NETMASK not set"
   [ -z ${BROADCAST} ] && echo "warning - $INF BROADCAST not set"

   echo "    configuring ${INF}=${IPADDR}"
   ifconfig ${INF} ${IPADDR} netmask ${NETMASK} broadcast ${BROADCAST}
   route add -net ${NETWORK} ${INF}
   return
} # end Intf_up()
```

```
case "$1" in
    start)
        echo "Starting ethernet networking support:"
        echo "    configuring lo"
        ifconfig lo 127.0.0.1
        route add -net 127.0.0.0
        echo "    loading device drivers"
        insmod 3c59x        # eth0 and eth1
        # eth0
        ######
        INF=eth0
        IPADDR=192.168.16.1
        NETMASK=255.255.255.0
        NETWORK=192.168.16.1
        BROADCAST=192.168.16.255
        Intf_up
        # eth1
        ######
        INF=eth1
        IPADDR=192.168.18.1
        NETMASK=255.255.255.0
        NETWORK=192.168.18.0
        BROADCAST=192.168.18.255
        Intf_up
        echo "    enabling IP forwarding"
        echo "1" >/proc/sys/net/ipv4/ip_forward
        echo "end of network start"
        ;;
    stop)
        echo -n "Stopping ethernet networking support:"
        ifconfig eth1 down
        ifconfig eth0 down
        rmmod 3c59x
        echo "."
        ;;
    restart|force-reload)
        echo -n "Restarting networking driver support:"
        $0 stop ; $0 start
        echo "."
        ;;
    *)
        echo "Usage: /etc/init.d/network {start|stop|restart}"
        exit 1
        ;;
esac
exit 0
```

3.2 IP ALIASING FOR MULTI-NETTING

The Linux kernel supports a functionality called **IP aliasing**, which is a means of mapping a single MAC address to multiple IP addresses. It is useful for situations when you want to create the illusion of having more interfaces than physically exist.

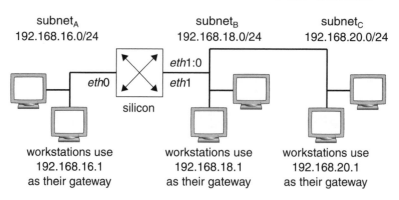

Figure 3.3 Multinetting LAN Router

One such use is **multi-netting**. The term refers to running multiple logical IP subnets on a single segment. Useful examples of this capability include preparing for and executing piecewise migrations to other IP address space (as opposed to having to work all weekend for a flash-cut), and planning for future growth by using more IP address space than you currently need to support your clients.

First take the IP address space migration.... If you need to migrate to a different address-space, you can create additional "virtual" interfaces (really aliases) on top of your existing interface(s) and convert your users to their new IP addresses and gateways over time. Another scenario: If you are planning network growth at some point in the future, you might want to assign separate IP ranges to different departments or physical areas in your building. If there are currently only 10–15 people in each department, it would be overkill to have a separate router interface for each department. However, if you expect growth to 80–100+ devices in this area, you would be wise to go ahead and assign a class C subnet address space to this department (254 IP addresses) so that you will not have to go back and reassign addresses later when you do decide to give that department its own segment and interface. Finally, if you have no free slots for additional interfaces in your router, but need to add an IP subnet, you can use IP aliasing as a stopgap measure.

In this section, we will use the second case as our example, and add an IP subnet to the 192.168.18.0 segment of silicon. Once again, let us begin with a short description of the work to be completed and a sketch of how the network will look after the configuration change (Figure 3.3).

> Create a new IP subnet, 192.168.20.0/24 which will share physical Ethernet segment B with 192.168.18.0/24. The 192.168.20.0/24 subnet, subnet$_C$, should have full access to the other subnets.

Now we know what we want; to accomplish it, we must first enable IP aliasing in the kernel. Note that the kernel configuration options listed build upon the configuration we used for silicon's first kernel. (In other words, you need all of the options from the previous configuration '+' the option below.)

IP Aliasing for Kernel Version 2.2.x

```
Networking options --->
+    [*] IP: IP aliasing support
```

If you are familiar with the 2.0.x kernel, note that for version 2.2.x, you no longer have to select `Network aliasing` in order to be able to select `IP aliasing support`. Nor do you have the option of compiling it as a module. If you select it, it is compiled directly into the kernel. You will have to rebuild your kernel and reboot your system before you can use the new functionality.

3.2.1 Using IP Aliasing

IP aliasing works by assigning additional virtual interface names to existing interfaces. IP aliases for a given interface are indicated by appending **:N** to the interface name. Thus, the syntax *ethX:N* is used to specify the aliased interface name, indicating that the virtual interface is part of physical interface *ethX*, where ($0 \leq N \leq 9$). You use *ifconfig* to create additional virtual interfaces. For example, to add a virtual interface to the real interface *eth1*, as in our example, use:

```
silicon:/root> ifconfig eth1:0 192.168.20.1 netmask 255.255.255.0 \
                        broadcast 192.168.20.255 up
```

Check the interface with *ifconfig* just as you would any real physical interface. Note that all of the address settings and flags are present, but that the interface statistics are not. (If you need to keep track of these, you can do so with **IP Accounting**, introduced in Section 3.3.)

```
silicon:/root> ifconfig eth1:0
eth1:0  Link encap:Ethernet  HWaddr 00:60:97:26:6B:C7
        inet addr:192.168.20.1  Bcast:192.168.20.255  Mask:255.255.255.0
        UP BROADCAST RUNNING MULTICAST MTU:1500  Metric:1
        Interrupt:10 Base address:0xfc80
```

Just as with a real interface, the kernel will automatically register a network route for the aliased interface when you configure it up.[6] However, if you look in the routing table, you'll notice that it uses the real name of the interface, not the IP aliased name.[7] If we take another look at the routing table, we'll see that our new subnet is routed out over *eth1*:

```
silicon:/root> route -n
Kernel IP routing table
Destination     Gateway         Genmask         Flags Metric Ref    Use Iface
192.168.16.0    0.0.0.0         255.255.255.0   U     0      0        0 eth0
192.168.18.0    0.0.0.0         255.255.255.0   U     0      0        0 eth1
192.168.20.0    0.0.0.0         255.255.255.0   U     0      0        0 eth1
127.0.0.0       0.0.0.0         255.0.0.0       U     0      0       24 lo
```

---

[6] For the 2.0 kernel, you need to do this by hand.

[7] This changed between kernel versions 2.0 and 2.2, and I'm not sure why; I thought it was clearer to be able to see the virtual interfaces in the routing table.

You can delete IP aliased interfaces the same way that you would for a real interface. In this case, *ifconfig eth1:0 down*. Appropriately, this also removes only the network route corresponding to the virtual interface. As with any actions you take which modify the running kernel, you need to incorporate them into your startup script(s) in order for them to be consistently executed upon startup. Because IP aliasing is an extension of the physical interface configuration, you can place the commands in */etc/init.d/network* alongside the rest of your network configuration.

IP aliasing is quite a useful tool to have at your disposal. Should a group of contractors show up onsite and require immediate access to the network, you can add a virtual interface, with its own firewalling and accounting rules, in a matter of minutes. The next section covers accounting, another neat feature of the Linux TCP/IP stack used to collect statistics about the traffic the router is forwarding.

3.3 IP ACCOUNTING

IP accounting is a facility available in the Linux kernel which will accumulate the number and sizes of network packets that match a given set of criteria. By specifying particular combinations of pattern-matching criteria, also known as **rules**, you can collect all kinds of statistics about the packets flowing through your router. Examples include what percentage of the network traffic crossing the router consists of people using HTTP browsers, or what percentage is inbound FTP, or NFS traffic between servers. The only trick is learning how to configure the rules, which are called that because they are set up in the same manner as packet-filtering rules. In fact, IP accounting is just a piece of the **IP firewalling**, **IP forwarding**, and **IP masquerading** facilities in the kernel. The same kernel code is used to determine if a packet matches the specified criteria—in the case of accounting, a counter is incremented; for firewalling, forwarding, and masquerading, more sophisticated actions are taken.

The underlying kernel code which supports IP accounting changed between versions 2.0.x and 2.2.x of the kernel. The 2.0.x facility is known as **ipfw**, and uses *ipfwadm* to configure the rules. The 2.2.x facility is **ipfw_chains** or simply **ipchains**, and uses the command *ipchains* to configure the rules.[8] For a good understanding of the interaction between rules and packets, you should review the copies of the manpages for these facilities and commands.

HINT: NICE PRINTOUTS OF MANPAGES

> An easy way to generate nice-looking printouts of manpages is to use `man -t` *manpage* `>/tmp/manpage.ps`. This will produce a PostScript file which will be nicely formatted when printed. If you do not have a PostScript capable printer, use the **magicfilter** package to configure your printer to automatically invoke *ghostscript* before spooling the file for printing.

---

[8] There is an implementation of *ipchains* for the 2.0.x kernel. It is distributed as a set of patches. Visit the IPCHAINS homepage if you need this functionality.

3.3.1 Packet-Matching Criteria

You can specify the criteria to match just about any part of the headers on an IP packet, the TCP or UDP headers, and combinations thereof. They include:

- source or destination IP address (or a range of IP addresses, specified in network/subnet mask notation)
- source or destination port (or a list, or a range of ports)
- protocol of TCP, UDP, ICMP or *all (all is the default when no protocol is listed)
- physical interface used to send or receive the packet
- the status of the **SYN** and **ACK** bits. The significance of **SYN=1 & ACK=0** is that this type of packet is the first packet used to establish a TCP/IP connection. If ACK is set (equal to 1), then this packet is part of an established connection.

3.3.2 Summary of IP Accounting Concepts

Before we get into configuring IP accounting on silicon, let's quickly summarize the concepts.

- IP accounting is built into the Linux kernel. Because of this, there is no process which must be running to collect the statistics.
- Counters may be incremented any time a packet traverses the networking stack. A counter is incremented depending upon whether or not the packet meets a certain set of criteria.
- These criteria are called **rules**. Rules are specified by using a command-line interface which enters the rules into the running kernel. (There are other interfaces available for entering rules, but they are all based upon the command-line interface.)
- Packets can be matched based on the contents of the TCP/IP protocol headers, such as source IP address and destination port.
- The kernel code which supports IP accounting changed between versions 2.0 and 2.2 of the kernel. The old code used *ipfwadm* as its configuration tool; the new code uses *ipchains*.

Compiling Support for IP Accounting into the 2.2.x Kernel   The only additional option required to use IP accounting with the 2.2.x version of the kernel is to enable IP firewalling.

```
Networking options --->
+   [*] IP: IP firewalling
```

3.3.3 Configuring IP Accounting Rules with *ipchains*

If you are comfortable with *ipfwadm*, then the flexibility of *ipchains* can take a bit of getting used to. It might help to think of *ipfwadm* as a subset of *ipchains* where there are only four chains (accounting, input, output, and forwarding), and these chains are always configured. Unlike with the 2.0 kernel, *ipchains* does not come preconfigured with a chain for accounting; it is up to you to create one (or more). The chains it does have are **forward**, **input**, **output**, plus any that you create.

Another difference between 2.0 and 2.2 with respect to IP accounting is that the *ipfwadm* accounting "chain" allowed you to differentiate specifically between **in**, **out**, and **both** directions for packets. In this regard, it was sort of special. With *ipchains*, you need to create the chains yourself, and you will need to create one each for inbound, outbound, and bidirectional traffic. We will feed our chains by adding rules to the built-in chains **input** and **output** that target our chains. This means that any packet which traverses the input and output chains (by definition, *all* packets must traverse these) will also be forwarded down (or visible to) our user-defined chains.

Here is a list of ways in which you can manipulate chains:

- `ipchains -N` *mychain* creates a chain named *mychain*.

- `ipchains -X` *mychain* deletes a chain named *mychain*. *mychain* must not be referenced by (be the target of) another rule.

- `ipchains -F` *mychain* deletes all rules on the chain named *mychain*.

- `ipchains -L` *mychain* lists all rules on the chain named *mychain*. There are several display options related to `-L`.

    `-v` generates verbose output.

    `-n` generates numeric output. In other words, supresses any name or services lookups.

    `-x` expands numbers in the packet and byte counter fields. No more pesky K, M, and Gs to try to hack around in your Perl script!

- `ipchains -A` *mychain myrule* **A**ppends *myrule* to *mychain*. Rule specification is similar to rule specification with *ipfwadm*, but has been expanded with some nice features.

    `-p [!]` *protocol* specifies a protocol, which must be **tcp**, **udp**, **icmp**, or **all**. '!' does what you think it would; it is the logical opposite of the condition. For someone used to *ipfwadm*, this jumps out immediately as a useful improvement.

    `-s [!]` *address[/mask] [!]* *[port...]* specifies a source address as with *ipfwadm*. The port can be an ICMP type (`ipfwadm -h icmp` will list them for you). Nice enhancements are that the ICMP type can be listed by name, and inclusive port ranges—specified with ":"—default to either 0 or 65535 if the lower or upper bound is omitted.

    `-d [!]` *address[/mask] [!]* *[port...]* specifies the destination address in the same way as `-s`.

    `-i [!]` *interfacename* indicates that the packet must (not) traverse *interfacename*. A wildcard can be specified by ending an interface name substring with "+". For example, *eth0+* will match eth0 and any IP alias of eth0.

-b makes the rule apply bidirectionally. What really happens is that two rules are entered—one the way you specified it on the command line and the other with -s and -d reversed.

[!] **-y** matches packets where SYN=1 & ACK=0 & FIN=0, in other words, packets initiating a TCP connection (or ! not).

[!] **-f** matches packet fragments 2–N of a fragmented packet. This is necessary because fragments do not contain ports (neither source nor destination) or ICMP types, so it is not possible to match them with other rules.

[-j] *target* sends the packet to chain called *target* if it matches it. This is how we send packets through our user-defined accounting chains. Beside a user-defined chain, *target* can be one of the built-in targets. These are **ACCEPT**, **DENY**, **REJECT**, **MASQ**, **REDIR**, and **RETURN**. Of these, **RETURN** is of interest for IP accounting. This is a way to not count packets which match the criteria specified in the rule, because it RETURNS the packet to the calling rule on the calling chain.

- ipchains -D mychain {myrule|rulenum} **D**eletes *myrule* from *mychain* or *rulenum* from *mychain*. Rules are numbered consecutively starting with "1".

- ipchains -R mychain rulenum myrule **R**eplaces *rulenum* with *myrule* in *mychain*.

- ipchains -I [rulenum] mychain **I**nserts *myrule rulenum* into *mychain*. If *rulenum* is omitted, then the beginning of the list is assumed.

Phew! *ipchains* packs a lot of functionality, and we have scratched only the surface. We need to do something with it before we lose track of all those options.

3.3.4 Choosing Packet Criteria for IP Accounting

Let's continue to introduce the concept of IP accounting by deciding on some packet criteria and then configure the system to count all matches. Fundamental to making sense of IP accounting is to understand TCP/IP's use of different source and destination ports to differentiate between protocols. In other words, IP accounting is not going to configure itself; you have to know what it is you are looking for, and what that means at a protocol level. For example:

- establishing a TCP socket connection to port 23 is the first step in starting a *telnet* session.
- sending a UDP packet to port 53 is used to get things going with DNS.
- connecting to TCP port 110 implies that you want to talk to a POP3 daemon.
- talking to TCP port 80 will more than likely get you a connection to a HTTP daemon.

There are several books which cover this topic in considerable detail and clarity; *Building Internet Firewalls* by Chapman and Zwicky is one that does an excellent job of putting the pieces together. It is important to have a good understanding of the protocol to configure accounting rules which detect the *network events* you are interested in capturing.

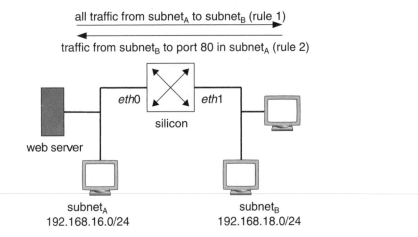

Figure 3.4   IP Accounting Example

For our example, we are going to configure our router to keep track of the number of packets (and bytes) traveling between subnet$_A$ and subnet$_B$. Futhermore, because all of our intranet web server is located on subnet$_A$, we would like to know the volume of traffic generated by users in subnet$_B$ accessing web services in subnet$_A$.

3.3.5 IP Accounting in Action—An Example

To implement the example, follow the script below. The first few steps are just to set up the user-defined chains. After that are the accounting rules which keep track of the traffic between our two subnets. The configuration is depicted in Figure 3.4.

```
# create accounting chains "in", "out", and "both"
# and hook them into the built-in chains (input and output)
# by making them targets of these (the built-in) chains
###############################################################
# create a (N)ew chain "in"
ipchains -N in

# (I)nsert a rule for the input chain
# which (j)umps to target chain "in"
ipchains -I input -j in

# create a (N)ew chain "out"
ipchains -N out
ipchains -I output -j out

# create a (N)ew chain "both"
ipchains -N both

# (I)nsert a rules into the input and output chains
# that (j)ump to target chain "both"
ipchains -I input -j both
ipchains -I output -j both

# acct rule 1
#############
#
```

```
# monitor traffic from subnetA destined for subnetB
#
# (A)ppend a rule to the "in" chain which counts all inbound packets
# from (s)ource 192.168.16.0/24 to (d)estination 192.168.18.0/24
#
# note that this could have been an "out" rule too
ipchains -A in -s 192.168.16.0/24 -d 192.168.18.0/24

# acct rule 2
#############
#
# monitor HTTP traffic between clients in subnetB and
# servers in subnetA
#
# (A)ppend a rule to the "out" chain count all packets
# from (s)ource 192.168.18.0/24 (generic client port)
# to (d)estination 192.168.16.0/24 (HTTP server port)
# of (p)rotocol tcp, and (-b) vice versa (server to client)
# and entering/exiting the router via (i)nterface eth0
#
# note that the (s)ource port range upperbound defaults to 65535
ipchains -A out -s 192.168.18.0/24 1024:        \
                -d 192.168.16.0/24 80        \
                -p tcp -b -i eth0

# acct rule 3
#############
# count the number of telnet sessions initiated in subnetA
# to hosts located in subnetB
#
#
# (A)ppend a rule to "in" to count all packets
# from (s)ource 192.168.16.0/24 (generic client port)
# to (d)estination 192.168.18.0/24 (telnet daemon port)
# and entering/exiting the router via (-W) interface eth0
#
# as in rule 2, an interface (or direction) is
# specified to avoid counting the traffic twice
ipchains -A in -s 192.168.16.0/24 1024:        \
                -d 192.168.18.0/24 23        \
                -p tcp -i eth0
```

3.3.6 Viewing IP Accounting Rules with *ipchains*

IP accounting rules created with *ipchains* are viewed using the -L switch and its various options as listed above. For our example rules, sample output looks like:

```
### first list the rules for each user-defined chain
silicon:/root> ipchains -L in
Chain in (refcnt = 1):
target  prot opt     source            destination      ports
-       all  ------  192.168.16.0/24  192.168.18.0/24  n/a
-       tcp  ------  192.168.16.0/24  192.168.18.0/24  1024:65535 -> telnet
silicon:/root> ipchains -L out
Chain out (refcnt = 1):
```

```
target  prot opt    source             destination        ports
-         tcp ------ 192.168.18.0/24  192.168.16.0/24  1024:65535 -> www
-         tcp ------ 192.168.16.0/24  192.168.18.0/24  www -> 1024:65535
### we did not add any rules to the "both" chain
silicon:/root> ipchains -L both
Chain both (refcnt = 2):
### (L)ist the rules in chain "in" (v)erbosely with (n)o name lookups
silicon:/root> ipchains -L in -vn
Chain in (refcnt = 2):
 pkts bytes target  prot opt    tosa tosx  ifname  mark  outsize  \
  624 24960 -       all  ------ 0xFF 0x00  *                      \
  606 24240 -       tcp  ------ 0xFF 0x00  eth0                   \
        source             destination        ports
        192.168.16.0/24    192.168.18.0/24    n/a
        192.168.16.0/24    192.168.18.0/24    1024:65535 -> 23
### hmm... telnet traffic accounts for most of the packets
### list the "out" chain with statistics
silicon:/root> ipchains -L out -v
Chain out (refcnt = 2):
 pkts bytes target  prot opt    tosa tosx  ifname  mark  outsize  \
    6   264 -       tcp  ------ 0xFF 0x00  eth0                   \
    0     0 -       tcp  ------ 0xFF 0x00  eth0                   \
        source             destination        ports
        192.168.18.0/24    192.168.16.0/24    1024:65535 -> www
        192.168.16.0/24    192.168.18.0/24    www -> 1024:65535
### wow, our webserver must be down.  There were 6 packets sent to the
### www port, but no replies.
```

The counters can be reviewed in two ways. You can use the commands as illustrated in the examples. Alternately, you can access the counters directly by reading the contents of the appropriate file in the */proc* filesystem. For kernel version 2.2.x, that file is:

$$/proc/net/ip\_fwchains$$

Of course, keeping detailed statistics with either *ipchains* or by periodically reading from the */proc* filesystem will require some additional development on your part. Before you start on that project, you might want to conduct some research and perhaps try some of the packages listed below.

Debian Packages/Commands Related to IP Accounting

ipac is a set of commands which script the things that you would most likely end up scripting on your own if you wanted to use IP accounting to generate reports on a regular basis. To use it, load the **ipac** package and read the manpages for *ipacset*, *ipacfetch*, and *ipacsum*.

netbase contains a command called *ipfwadm-wrapper*. This package will be installed on your system as part of the base OS, but it is nice to be aware of the ipfwadm-wrapper when converting to *ipchains*.

net-acct provides a user-level daemon, *nacctd*, that logs all traffic passing the machine it runs on. It does not require IP accounting support in the kernel; instead, it functions more like a sniffer (by placing the interface in promiscuous mode).

wmnet is a network monitor for WindowMaker using kernel IP accounting. It polls */proc/net/ip_acct* and displays the results as an X client. One nice feature is that it works with both *ipfwadm* and *ipchains*, so it works for both 2.0 and 2.2 systems.

dotfile-ipfwadm (requires **dotfile**). This package uses a Tcl/Tk interface to allow you to graphically "build" your own accounting, forwarding, input, output, and masquerading rules. It can be very helpful for quickly developing a set of rules, which it outputs to a file. You can then tweak the rules if needed. Note: It allows you to select only options which are applicable to your running kernel. Because of this, you need to have options which you will be using already enabled. (This is currently useful only for 2.0 kernel users.)

That concludes the introduction to *ipchains* for use with IP accounting. For an alternate discussion of *ipchains*, and information about migrating from *ipfw* to *ipchains*, please see the *IPCHAINS-HOWTO* at either the *LDP* site or the *ipchains* homepage at: *http://www.rustcorp.com/linux/ipchains/HOWTO.html*.

3.4 LRP—The Linux Router Project

Silicon has an emergency floppy diskette which waits patiently for the day when it will be used to resurrect the system after a catastrophic hard drive failure. The rescue floppy was created using the Linux Router Project (LRP)[9] distribution, which fits on a single 1.44MB floppy disk. But LRP is more than just for rescue floppies—this versatile and capable mini-distribution can be used as the basis for all of your routers. In this section, we are going to configure silicon again, but this time using LRP.

Unlike a router based on a full-sized Linux distribution, you will need to build your LRP boot disks on another machine. This machine does not have to be a Linux machine, since the LRP boot disks are FAT (MS-DOS) formatted floppies.

I recommend getting a copy of the latest distribution *sans* the source tree (unless you really want to know what's going on!) with a program like *lftp*.[10] *lftp* can mirror an entire directory tree with a single command, and it supports some nice extensions, such as extended regular expressions in the filespecs and restarting an interrupted mirror job. The commands to retrieve LRP version 2.9.4 look like:

```
$ lftp ftp.linuxrouter.org
lftp ftp.linuxrouter.org:~> cd linux-router/dists/2.9.4
lftp ftp.linuxrouter.org:/linux-router/dists/2.9.4> mirror -x source/*
```

Once you have the files that make up the package, you will need the floppy tools mentioned below to make your LRP boot floppy. The idea is: Build the floppy, boot

---

[9] *http://www.linuxrouter.org*

[10] Available in the **lftp** package for Debian.

Table 3.1 Debian Packages Useful for Working with LRP Images

syslinux	supplies *syslinux*, used to make the LRP boot disk bootable.
mtools	contains the *mformat* command, which provides the same functionality as the *mkdosfs* command listed in the LRP documentation.
fdutils	contains the *superformat* command for low-level formatting of floppy disks.
lftp	FTP client able to retrieve entire directory trees in a single command (optional)

from it, configure the system the way you see fit, and then use the LRP provided utilities to back up your configuration changes to the boot floppy. The next time you boot from this floppy, your saved configuration is used to configure the system.

This section presents two different ways to configure your LRP boot disk. The first is the easy way, using the "idiot image" available the *linuxrouter.org* site. The standard trade-off applies—the second way is more complex than the idiot image, but also more flexible. The second method will also give you more insight into how LRP works. Before diving into the two examples, there are a few tools you will need to have on your system to be able to work the LRP disks, listed in Table 3.1.

As previously mentioned, the LRP disks are standard MS-DOS formatted disks, and they use *syslinux* as the boot loader. Because of these, it is helpful (but not necessary) for your workstation to have FAT filesystem support in the kernel. If you do have MS-DOS compiled into your kernel, you will be able to mount your LRP disk and copy files to it as needed. Both examples presented here assume that you do have FAT filesystem support.

3.4.1 Quick-n-Dirty LRP Configuration

The quick-n-dirty configuration is a shortcut to getting a LRP system running (at the expense of understanding why or how it works like it does). To build this config-uration, you need to retrieve the disk image from the LRP FTP site, and also the corresponding kernel tarball, found in the *kernel/* directory. The tarball I retrieved was named *kernel/2.0.36pre15–1.tar.gz*.

Start with two 1.44Mb floppy disks; Label one *LRP root* and the other *LRP modules*. Perform a low-level format of both of these with **superformat /dev/fd0**. Note, you will have to be the superuser (or have access permisssions to write to */dev/fd0*) for this procedure. Also, the device file given is for the first floppy drive on your system. Adjust */dev/fdX* accordingly.

Creating an Idiot Image Diskette   You need to transfer the idiot image to a floppy disk. Notice the word *transfer* and not *copy*. The image is a complete image of the floppy disk used to boot LRP. You do this with *dd*. Insert the *LRP root* disk, and from the directory where you have the LRP files,

```
$ dd if=./idiot-image_1440KB_2.9.4 of=/dev/fd0 bs=8192 conv=sync ; sync
```

You can use this command to duplicate any 1.44Mb disk, regardless of the filesystem on it, simply by reversing if (**I**nput **F**ile) and of (**O**utput **F**ile) as required. The last *sync* ensures that all of the data blocks to be written to the floppy drive are flushed before the command prompt returns. This will prevent you from ejecting the floppy disk from the drive prematurely.

dd—THE MULTIPURPOSE DISKETTE DUPLICATOR

> You can use *dd* to create an exact duplicate (or **image**) of any floppy disk (or other type of disk or file), regardless of the operating system on it. (Note that "dd" does not stand for "Diskette Duplicator.")
>
> To read in the image, specify the device file of the device with the data to be read as the argument for `if=`. The block size (`bs=blocksize`) is quantum of data to be read—if you don't know better, use either 512 or 8192 for floppy disks. The output file (`of=/path/to/image`) will contain the image being read.
>
> To write the image to another diskette, make sure that the disk has been low-level formatted and then call *dd* again, swapping the arguments for `if` and `of`.

The LRP root image is a bootable Linux system. It already has the kernel and all commands needed for the mini-distribution. What it lacks are the device driver modules needed for the various Ethernet cards, filesystems, and other devices. If these were all included in the idiot image, the image would be too large to fit on a single floppy.

Creating a Modules Diskette   The reason you need an *LRP modules* disk is to transfer any needed device drivers over to your LRP system. Create it as follows:

Go to the start of the directory tree where you downloaded the different LRP files, and **export LRP=$(pwd)**. This way, you can refer to this directory as $LRP throughout the session. The command paths assume that you downloaded LRP with the directory tree intact. Take the *LRP modules* disk (which is already low-level formatted), insert it in your floppy drive, and create a MS-DOS FAT filesystem on it with mformat a:.[11] Once this is done, mount the filesystem with **mount -t msdos /dev/fd0 /floppy**. Now, with our modules floppy ready to go, we are going to load it with pre-compiled modules from the LRP distribution.

```
$ cd $LRP/kernel
$ tar xzvf 2.0.36pre15-1.tar.gz
$ cd 2.0.36pre15-1/modules

### Customize the following filespec to suit your particular needs.
### Not all of the modules will fit on a single floppy, so you
### might want to create multiple module floppies for your
### day-to-day general use.  This filespec copies all Ethernet
### device drivers and the IPv4 modules.

$ find ipv4/* net/* | cpio -pdm /floppy ; sync
$ umount /floppy
```

---

[11] Note that this depends upon */etc/mtools.conf* being properly configured for your floppy drives. The default configuration on my system required me to add the string *1.44m* along with the *exclusive* flag so that the line looked like `drive a:file=''/dev/fd0''` `exclusive 1.44m` before it worked without supplying all of the various command-line switches to describe the geometry of a 1.44Mb FAT format.

Configuring LRP to Be Silicon   To configure the LRP-silicon; just follow these steps:

1. Boot your router system with the *LRP boot* floppy. You will notice the banner message which can be customized by replacing *syslinux.dpy* (on this diskette) with your own ASCII art.

2. Login to the router as *root*. Intially, there is no root password, but we will set it soon.

3. You will be presented with the LRP configuration menu. This menu allows you to edit configuration (by navigating the filesystem for those who are not familiar with their locations). You can (**q**)uit the configuration menu and work directly on the command line and return to the configuration menu at any time with **lrcfg**.

4. Hit **q** to exit to the command line.

5. Use the *passwd* command to change the root passsword.

6. Eject the *LRP root* floppy and insert the *modules* floppy. Mount it with **mkdir /tmp/mnt ; mount -t msdos /dev/fd0 /tmp/mnt**.

7. Copy the required modules from */tmp/mnt* into place in */lib/modules*. Do **not** create *net/*, *ipv4/*, etc., subdirectories underneath */lib/modules*. All modules must be in */lib/modules*, as this is where the LRP version of */etc/init.d/modutils* expects them to be. For silicon:

   ```
   myrouter# cd /tmp/mnt
   myrouter# cp net/3c59x.o /lib/modules
   myrouter# cp ipv4/ip_alias.o /lib/modules
   myrouter# cd
   myrouter# umount /tmp/mnt
   ```

8. Go ahead and eject the *LRP modules* so that you do not inadvertently try to write to it later on when you back up your configuration for your *LRP root* disk.

9. Edit */etc/modules* to load both of these modules by adding/uncommenting the lines `3c59x` and `ip_alias`. The editor that comes with LRP is *ae*.[12] It is has *vi*-esque and *emacs*-esque modes; the one you get depends upon how you invoke it. **vi** will act like *vi*, while *ae* is the *modeless* mode. If you need help, hit **F1**.

10. Next you need to configure networking on your system. You can either edit */etc/network.conf* from the command line, or restart *lrcfg* and select **1)** `Network settings,` **1)** `Network Configuration (auto).` In either case, you to make the following changes:

    (a) set `IPFWDING_KERNEL` to `YES`

    (b) `CONFIG_HOSTNAME=YES`

    (c) uncomment `IF0_IFNAME=eth0`

    (d) set `IF0_IPADDR` to `192.168.16.1`

    (e) set `IF0_NETMASK` to `255.255.255.0`

---

[12] The same editor found on Debian and other rescue floppies.

(f) set IF0_BROADCAST to 192.168.16.255

(g) modify IF1 as you did IF0, except use the correct values for silicon's *eth1*.

(h) set HOSTNAME to a name of your liking

11. Your work is almost done. All you need to do is to save your configuration to your *LRP root* disk and test. To write your configuration, go back to the main menu (or restart *lrcfg*) and hit **(B)**ack-up ramdisk. Then select **2)** etc and **5)** modules. When queried as to whether or not there will be enough space on the *LRP root* disk, answer **y**.

12. Reboot the system, either with **CTRL-ALT-DEL** or by logging into a shell prompt and executing **shutdown -r now**. Test your system after the reboot to make sure that it functions as you would like it to.

13. If you find that you need other commands to be executed during the router configuration, the easiest place to add these is to */etc/network_direct.conf*. Do not forget to back up your etc configuration after you make the changes.

3.4.2 Manual LRP Configuration

Manual configuration of LRP is really not so bad, and you gain the personal satisfaction of having not used the idiot image. Instead of starting with the idiot image, you are going to build your own disk, and then copy over the LRP packages you would like. The procedure after that is similar. But to help illustrate how the LRP packages (the .lrp files) work, we will assemble our *modules.lrp* on our workstation and then transfer it to the *LRP root* disk. By knowing how to take apart the LRP packages, you can do much of your configuration on your own workstation. The basic steps are:

1. Use *superformat* and *mformat* to prepare your *LRP root* floppy. Mount it on your workstation with **mount -t msdos /dev/fd0 /floppy**.

2. Using the LRP tree you retrieved earlier, cd $LRP ; cp base/* /floppy ; cp boot/* /floppy. The *base/* directory includes the files you need for a minimal LRP system. The *boot/* directory contains the files needed for *syslinux*.

3. Copy the LRP kernel to your *LRP root* disk. Depending upon the version of LRP you are using, there may be several different kernels.[13] The kernel images are in the *$LRP/kernel/2.0.36pre15–1.tar.gz* tarball. Extract this archive, and copy the image to the floppy disk, making sure to name it *linux* on that filesystem. For example:

```
$ cd $LRP/kernel
$ tar xzvf 2.0.36pre15-1.tar.gz
$ cd 2.0.36pre15-1
$ cp 2.0.36pre15-1-LRP-zImage /floppy/linux
```

Note that the zImage file is just like any other normal kernel image, except that it was built from LRP-patched sources. For those of you who want to build

---

[13] If you have an older 486-class machine without a built-in FPU, you need use the kernel with FPU (Floating Point Unit) emulation support.

your own kernel images, make sure that you used the LRP patch or else your system will not know where to find *init*. There is a -config file in kernel tarball which will help you get started.

4. Extract a copy of the *modules.lrp* in a safe place where you can work on them. I chose *$LRP/work*. Note that the .lrp files are gzipped tarballs in disguise.

```
$ mkdir $LRP/work
$ cd $LRP/work
$ tar xzvf $LRP/etc/modules.lrp
```

5. Now add the files you would like to be in the modules LRP package. You can do this by copying the file to its destination. Do not add completely new directory trees unless you know what you are doing and want to hack the files in *var/lib/lrpkg/*. For the silicon configuration, all we need is the module with our NIC driver and the IP aliasing module. Continuing from the example above:

```
$ cd $LRP/work/lib/modules
$ cp $LRP/kernel/2.0.36pre15-1/modules/net/3c59x.o .
$ cp $LRP/kernel/2.0.36pre15-1/modules/ipv4/ip_alias.o .
$ cd ../..
```

6. After you make sure that you have changed the current directory back to *$LRP/work/*, you can build your new *modules.lrp* tarball, and write it directly to the floppy: **tar czvf /floppy/modules.lrp ***

   You can perform this same step for any of the LRP packages; just make sure that you do not move or delete important parts of the system. One application of this would be to localize the *etc.lrp* module (or edit the *local.lrp* module).

7. To make your *LRP root* floppy bootable, run *syslinux*. The only argument it requires is the device name of your floppy drive (probably */dev/fd0*). It automatically knows to look for the *syslinux.cfg* in the root of the filesystem on that device.

8. Unmount the floppy disk from your workstation, configure, and then test your LRP system.

The ultra-manual LRP configuration would be having to start from scratch. Thanks to Dave Cinerge and other volunteers at the LRP for creating such an attractive alternative to this option. There is a selection of *packages* available for LRP from their website. If you would like a quick introduction on how to use packages which are not part of the base LRP distribution, see Section 5.6.1 in Chapter 5. For more infomation about LRP, visit the LRP webpage and subscribe to the LRP mailing list.

3.4.3 LRP and High Availability

High availability is not always easy to obtain. Many (sales)people think that it can be accomplished with a showcase of hardware redundancy. In reality, the hardware, software, and adminstrative practices all need to be mature and working in concert to realize the goal.

LRP addresses each of these aspects (although I have to admit that my initial attraction was merely to mitigate the risk of hard drive failure). Because of its widespread use, it is well-tested, and because it is smaller than a full-sized Linux distribution, it is easier to test more completely. A side-effect of its size is that it is easier to document, easier to customize and harden (with respect to security). Because it is open, it is feasible for you to review *all* of the code used to build the distribution to check it for security holes, etc.

You can base your entire Linux router infrastructure on LRP. There are LRP mailing lists, and the author is actively involved in support. If you decide to do this, do not forget to contribute when and where you can. Answering common questions on the mailing list might not seem like a lot, but it reduces the workload on others who might be contributing to development.

3.5 SUMMARY

As the first router chapter concludes, we have covered how to do some fairly general things with our Linux router. Silicon can route physical and virtual IP subnets, and it can keep track of how much traffic is being passed between them. It can be implemented on a low-end system without a hard drive. But do not let the simplicity of this example implementation discourage you. A Linux LAN router can be used to connect two or more Ethernet subnets together, connect 10Base-T to coax Ethernet, connect Ethernet to token-ring, Ethernet to FDDI, FDDI to ATM, or almost any conceivable combination. Use your imagination, and let the solution fit the problem at hand. And don't forget to keep track of how much money and time you've saved. . . .

Erbium—An Extranet Router

Erbium is an example of an **extranet** router, which is used to connect your network to other networks of other organizations (not including the Internet). It was configured in response to the need for a dial-out point for a product support group at my employer's so that they could access client networks to validate and research problems. Although the support staff had access to a modem server from their desktops, which provided them PPP and terminal dial-out capabilities, this arrangement had certain limitations:

1. Access into a client site was limited to a single person/machine, making collaborative efforts difficult.
2. Direct access from the Unix development servers was not possible without undertaking extensive configuration efforts and opening questionable security holes.
3. All users who required access to the remote system had to set up the access themselves, an inefficient use of time which further resulted in more time spent assisting with configuration (and repairing broken configurations).
4. Controlling use of the dial-out connections via a modem-server solution in use was difficult. Users could dial anywhere, potentially creating security holes or accumulating excessive toll charges.

In summary, the environment was not conducive to productive trouble-shooting for the support staff. They spent more time making their tools work than using them to help clients. We needed a method of dialing into the client sites and reconfiguring the network so that access from all of the support group's workstations and the Unix servers over that single dial-up link was possible.

This chapter presents a solution that addresses these capabilities both as they apply to erbium and in general. Key to that solution is the ability to "masquerade" the IP addresses of the workstations connecting via the extranet router since the target network is not expecting them. This feature is often known as **NAT**, or Network Address Translation, and is frequently used to allow Internet access from private address space. And because not everything always goes as planned, the final section goes into detail about the **packet sniffers** available for Linux. These programs are used to "see what's on the wire" (the network), from the protocol headers to the packet payloads. Specifically, the chapter is divided into the following major sections:

- Erbium's hardware, software, and scripting configuration
- IP masquerading concepts
- Configuring IP masquerading on Linux
- Using IP masquerading every day
- Packet sniffers available for Linux, and how they are useful for trouble-shooting

NOTE: LINUX AS A MODEM OR DIAL-IN SERVER

Note that this chapter is not a discussion of using Linux as a true modem server—although support for this is available. Likewise, using Linux as a dial-in server, either for an ISP or as a remote access server, is not covered. Many people are using Linux very successfully in this role, and you should be able to find ample documentation concerning this configuration. You can start with the *LDP* if you are looking for resources.

Why Linux for an Extranet Router?   An extranet router is faced with a daunting list of tasks. Its job after establishing a connection is to make *n* different workstations appear as a single dial-up client. It needs to be flexible in terms of both security and networking standards. After all, you cannot tell your clients that they must implement protocol XYZ with product ABC so that you can access their network for support. They have several other vendors who need access, their own security policies to enforce, and their own dial-in solution investment. An extranet router should be customizable, so that you can cater to the needs of your users and their needs, and it should be able to grow along with the rest of the technology world. Finally, it should offer some security, even though its primary role is to connect your network to external ones.

Linux has a lot to offer in this role since many have long prized how effectively you could connect it to other machines. Open standards for dial-up connectivity are already implemented, and in dire cases, you have the source to roll your own. The benefits of using a popular hardware architecture means that your selection of interface devices is plentiful and economical. You can customize your dial-out server with your own shell scripts, Tcl/Tk, or a full-blown GTK-based GUI front-end. And if you need to, you can lock it all down with packet-filtering and integration to the security mechanism of your choice.

4.1 ERBIUM'S DESIGN

The basic idea is to have a router configured to dial-up analog and ISDN links so that we can connect to customer networks as if from a single workstation. This allows support links to be set up very quickly, since most of the target networks already have provisions for point-to-point remote access. In this case, erbium dials the connection and appears to the target network as a single workstation. In reality, it populates the routing table on our local LAN router with information about systems in the customer's network available for support access.

When a user accesses destinations in the remote network, the LAN router forwards this traffic to erbium and then out over the dial-up link toward the destination in the customer's network. However, this accomplishes only half of the goal; **IP masquerading** does the second half. The issue is that the customer's machine doesn't know how to respond to an IP address in our internal network. After all, the remote access wasn't designed for this type of use. IP masquerading takes care of this by modifying all packets destined towards the remote network so that they appear to have originated from erbium's dial-out interface. Because the customer network knows this IP (it issued it), it can respond. When erbium receives the response, it knows what traffic is for it and what is for our internal workstations and forwards the workstation traffic appropriately.

4.1.1 Choose Your Weapons—Dial-Out Hardware

Erbium's hardware won't come as any surprise. It's off-the-shelf equipment, similar to what you might use for a home PC.

- A Pentium 90 with 32MB of RAM—which is more than adequate. The system has very little overhead or CPU demands.

- A 1GB IDE hard drive—we need a little bit of space for logfiles and as a staging area for file transfer between the networks.

- Two external analog modems, both of them are *U.S. Robotics V.Everything* modems for analog dial-out. Whatever you do, do not go out and buy the cheapest modems you can find. (And remember that Winmodems will not work because their manufacturers provide no drivers for Linux.)

  A less expensive modem might seem like a good deal, but when you are trying to establish a connection over a very noisy, high-latency satellite link, you will find out where the difference in price went. External modems are also a good idea because they can be moved between machines without having to shut anything down.

- A SpellCaster Datacommute/BRI ISDN board in the machine for ISDN dial-out. This is an ISA card, so it doesn't require a third serial port (the two we have are taken by the modems). The vendor is committed to providing Linux driver support, which is a pleasant surprise when shopping for ISDN adapters in North America.

4.1.2 Dial-Out Software

Once the hardware is set up, you need something to glue it all together. Before anything else, you need a way to dial out. (Note, the boldfaced items are Debian package names.)

- **ppp**, which contains the PPP daemon, *pppd*.
- **minicom** for dialing into terminal servers, gettys, and BBS-style systems.
- *Babylon*, which is a product from SpellCaster. It contains drivers for the *Datacommute/BRI* and programs to configure and dial ISDN PPP and MPPP links.
- A utility for configuring PPP links. (Actually, not a necessity, but potentially a big time-saver. Some of these are introduced in Section 4.1.3.)

In order to give your users the ability to perform certain super-user actions associated with bringing the link up and configuring the routing and masquerading, you need a controlled mechanism for allowing normal users to execute commands with root privileges. (On erbium, the only commands users may execute as root are the custom shell scripts which dial the link and set up the routes.) The following packages are related to this purpose:

- Access is regulated with **sudo**. (There are several other choices, such as **super** and **secure-su**.)
- **ssh** is needed as a secure alternative to *rexec* for running commands on nearby routers.

Last but not least, we turn to another cool feature of the Linux kernel, IP masquerading (covered in Sections 4.2–4.4), and employ some custom scripts to make it easier for the user to set up and tear down connections.

4.1.3 *pppd*—The PPP Daemon

At the heart of our analog dial-out capability is the ability to connect to other dial-in solutions. Many such solutions assume that remote users will connect to their networks using a machine running a Microsoft operating system,[1] so we have to accommodate this. Enter *pppd*, the Point-to-Point Protocol Daemon, which does a pretty good job of pretending to be most any type of PPP dial-up client. It supports the **PAP**, **CHAP** (or **CHAP–5**), and **MS-CHAP** (also known as **CHAP–80**) forms of PPP-based authentication, in addition to being flexible about chat-based (`ogin:` `assword:`) mechanisms. It is, of course, compatible with other (non-Microsoft) dial-in solutions as well.

Instead of going into a droll description of *pppd* and how to configure it for dial-out, I offer you some references to some nice configuration utilities. (Just let me tell you that it used to be much more difficult—barefoot in the snow, 20 miles, uphill in both directions, all that good stuff.) To get *pppd* running on your system, you will need the *pppd* software and probably one of its configuration utilities. *pppd* itself is in the **ppp** package, which is part of the Debian base installation. The configuration

---

[1] A silly assumption, if you ask me.

packages available will vary, based on the distribution you are using; the list below uses the names of the Debian packages.

PPP Configuration Packages

pppconfig is the tool I use most frequently. It has an *ncurses* interface and supports any number of different connection configurations. Once the package is loaded, you invoke it by running *pppconfig* as the super-user. The rest is self-explanatory.

xisp is a nice GUI-based dial-out tool, suitable for standard PPP links and links which require a combination of terminal interaction (e.g., to use a hard token) and PPP. It's not designed to be used to build configurations for use by other dialers, but is very useful for one-off situations.

ppxp was not available when I was configuring erbium, but had it been, I think that I would have taken a very close look at it. According to the package description:

> PPxP is a user-space PPP program. It provides easy setup, on-demand dial-up, IP masquerading, IP filtering, DNS relaying, and more. It can work as a PPP server, using either the *userlink* or *ethertap* kernel modules.

> There are X11 and Tck/Tk console (management) packages available (**ppxp-x11** and **ppxp-tcltk**), as well as a development package, **ppxp-dev**, for building your own management console interface. If it delivers all that it claims to, then it could save an impressive amount of work.

wvdial was the first of these configuration tools I encountered to support automatic modem detection. It is (currently) geared towards a single dial-up connection, so it's not that well suited for an extranet server.

dunc is aimed at the newbie and for people connecting to Microsoft RAS sites.

HINT: FINDING SOFTWARE FOR NON-DEBIAN USERS

If you are not a Debian user and have trouble locating the source of a package, you can visit Debian's website, search for the package, and view the package copyright information, which will point you to the original source. To do this, point your browser to *http://www.debian.org/* and select the "Debian Packages" link. Scroll to the bottom of this page, and use either "Search Package Directories" or "Search the Contents of the Latest Release." The former will search through the list of package names, and present you with a clickable link to any packages which match. The latter searches through all files in the current distribution and will show you the filename, section, and package name which contains the package. Once you have located the package, you can download the source or view the copyright file. If you still do not find what you need, try searching for the software on *http://www.freshmeat.net/*.

4.1.4 Kernel Support for PPP

To be able to use any of these, you will need PPP support in your kernel. The default kernel supplied with most Linux installations should already have this compiled into it. But when you reconfigure the kernel, do not forget to include PPP support, which is the single option `PPP (point-to-point) support` under the `Network Device Support` heading. If you compile PPP support into the kernel as a module, realize that it is part of a dependent module stack, so load it with *modprobe*. Because I used to always forget to load the *bsd_comp* module (which provides software compression if it is supported on the other side), I just use `modprobe bsd_comp`, which loads everything. On a 2.2.x system, the modules loaded are:

```
ppp_deflate         38516   0
bsd_comp             3468   0
ppp                 19324   2   [ppp_deflate bsd_comp]
slhc                 4128   1   [ppp]
```

4.1.5 Using Debian's PPP

O.K., now that you have compiled support in the kernel and have loaded the PPP modules, you need to configure a dial-up link for each client. We're going to use these configurations in the dial-out script we write for our users. Debian's **ppp** package comes with two handy commands: *pon* and *poff*. Despite their funny names, they are useful abbreviations for the most common tasks involved with PPP links—bringing them up (*pon*) and shutting them back down (*poff*). A third command, *plog*, will *tail* the last bits of */var/log/ppp.log* so that you can see what is going on. Their usage is simple.

- *pon* takes one argument, the name of the link to dial. This is the same name of the file which appears in */etc/ppp/peers/*, and is the name you gave the connection while configuring it with *pppconfig*. If you do not specify an argument, the PPP peer of "provider" is assumed.

- *poff* can take several options followed by the name of the link to disconnect. See the *poff* manpage for details. Be aware that without any options, it kills all active *pppd* connections.

- *plog* displays the last 10 lines of */var/log/ppp.log* so that you can see what is happening. *pppconfig* by default configures all of your PPP option files (the files in */etc/ppp/peers/*) with the keyword **debug**, so there should be something in the file. *plog* optionally takes any argument that *tail* takes. Of these, `-f` to follow the file is probably the most useful.

Configuration of PPP links can be frustrating. When things don't work, sometimes it is not abundantly clear how to fix them. Be sure to use the documentation resources at your disposal before you get too irritated. As unlikely as it may seem, someone else really has already run into the problem you are experiencing; hopefully they were thoughtful enough to share their experience in a HOWTO somewhere. The documentation in */usr/share/doc/ppp* can be very helpful. There are several HOWTOs as part of the *LDP* which cover PPP, modems, serial ports, etc., in detail.

Also, do not forget to enable debugging if you turned it off in the configuration file. You can do this quickly, without having to stop the link and edit the file with `poff -d linkname`. This way, you'll know what to look for in the documentation.

Before we start configuring the actual links for erbium, we should take a moment and consider the network surrounding erbium and how the different components should interact with each other.

4.1.6 A Sample Network Topology for an Extranet Router

One key to erbium's functionality is the fact that it requires no changes to the user workstations whatsoever. Once the link is up, a user can *telnet* to the client's machine as if it were part of the local network. But for this to function, you need to make sure that the client can find the remote machines, and this takes a little bit of design work. Because a typical workstation network configuration consists of a routing entry for the local subnet and another for the default gateway, your choices are to update either the workstation or the gateway (or other gateways upstream of that gateway). Because modifying the client's configuration is tricky at best, and potentially downright foolhardy, I opted for the latter. The topology is displayed in Figure 4.1.

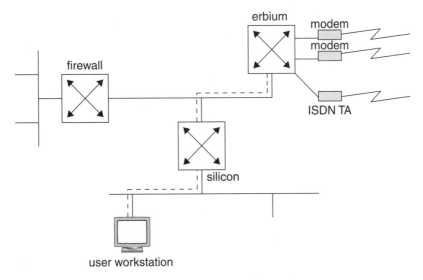

Figure 4.1 Erbium Network Topology

In this topology the extranet router is located at least one **layer** removed from your local LAN. When extranet links are active, erbium updates silicon's routing table to include routes to the customer's network. When the link goes back down, erbium removes the routes. In both cases, the changes are performed using shell scripts which invoke *ssh* to make the changes on silicon.

4.1.7 A Dial-Out Script for Extranet Connections

Now that we know where erbium fits into our network, we can start the configuration. So that we can focus on the integration piece, let's assume that we already have PPP configurations so that you can connect to our client(s). Furthermore, we'll take for granted that we have worked out any required routing and masquerading statements. Now we need a way to let our users start and stop these links.

Scripting dial-out access presented a few challenges. First, a lot of the documentation about *pppd* was geared towards dial-in solutions, and I couldn't find any documentation about dynamically choosing from a pool of available modems for dial-out. After choosing a modem and dialing the link, masquerading had to be configured on erbium and routes had to be added to both erbium and silicon. Finally, I wanted the script to be easy to use. For analog PPP dial-out, the result was a single script with the following properties:

1. A single script without requiring the user to remember options necessitated a "script of many names." The script infers the action to be taken based on the name by which it was invoked.

    The usage is simple—either `dial_client` or `hangup_client`. The code to accomplish this is:

    ```ksh
    #!/usr/bin/ksh
    prog=$(basename $0)      # program name without a path component
    ACTION=${prog%*_*}       # get the string up to the '_'
    TARGET=${prog#*_*}       # get the string past the '_'

    case $ACTION in
       dial)
          pon $TARGET
          ;;
      hangup)
          poff $TARGET
          ;;
       *)
          # a user should not be able to call this script such that
          # their intention is not known - we control the arguments!
          echo "something is wrong!"
          ;;
    esac
    ```

    To add links, simply create symbolic links or hard links back to the main script. Having one script is useful because when you want to make changes or add functions—for example, to perform extra logging—everything is updated for all connections simultaneously.

2. Using more than one modem for dial-out is one of the few options you cannot set in a *pppd options* file. The device name listed in the file is the one which will be used. To remedy this, the script went under the knife again to take advantage of UUCP device-locking semantics. *pppd* and other well-mannered applications which use the modem will write lockfiles to */var/lock/* as long as you don't configure them not to.

All we need to do is to find out which devices are not locked, and then fix up the options file to use one of these. The result is a function which uses *sed* to fix the options file before the link is dialed. The function is added to the beginning of the prior code snippet; the code below it is called as part of the *dial* case.

```
MODEMS="ttyS0 ttyS1"        # list of available devices

# function to walk the list of MODEMS to see which
# have lock files
Find_Free_TTY()
{
    FREE_TTY="none"
    for TTY in $1
    do
        if [[ ! -f /var/lock/LCK..${TTY} ]] ; then
            FREE_TTY=${TTY}
        fi
    done
    echo ${FREE_TTY}
    return
}
# a cheap hack to find a free modem
MODEM=$(Find_Free_TTY ${MODEMS})
if [[ $MODEM == "none" ]] ; then
    Error "Sorry... all modems are currently in use"
else
    # fixup the options file with the right tty
    cp -p ${OPTFILE} ${OPTFILE}.presed
    echo "s/^\/dev\/ttyS./\/dev\/$MODEM/" >${SEDFILE}
    cat ${OPTFILE}.presed | sed -f ${SEDFILE} >${OPTFILE}
fi
```

3. Now add routes and configure masquerading. This is done by calling an additional function. First, routes are added to the local system, then masquarading is configured and then routes are added to silicon. Tearing down a connection is the same set of steps in reverse.

```
Setup_Connection()
{
    # assert:  TARGET is a global, and is set
    case $TARGET in
        client1)
        route add -net 10.34.2.0 netmask 255.255.255.0 $DEV
        route add -host 209.54.2.2 $DEV
        ipchains -A forward -j MASQ -i $DEV
        ssh silicon route add -net 10.34.2.0   \
                netmask 255.255.255.0 gw erbium
    ;;
client2)
    :
    ;;
    esac
}
```

4. Hold on a minute! How did the value of $DEV get set to the right value? You know that it's the name of the PPP device created by *pppd*, but the catch is that the name is not always *ppp0*, since you may have multiple concurrent sessions. The work-around is to take advantage of the */etc/ppp/ip-up.d/* directory, which executes all scripts located in it after the link is dialed and configured up. We will add a script, */etc/ppp/ip-up.d/list_device*, which looks something like:

```
# the PID was just patched by sed - watch out for race conditions
CALLER_PID=123
# write the device into this file
echo $PPP_IFACE >/tmp/pppdevice.${CALLER_PID}
```

Our main script can modify the script above with *sed* to set the PID to its executing PID, and then read the device as */tmp/pppdevice.$$*. Once it's read, delete the temporary file.

Mocked up into its final form, the script looks like:

```
# header with modification history
# function definitions
# code to get $ACTION and $TARGET
case $ACTION in
   dial)
       # code to find a free modem
       # code to sed the "list_device" script with our PID

       pon $TARGET             # dial the link
       sleep 30                 # wait for it connect
       Setup_Connection        # setup masquerading
       ;;

   hangup)
       poff $TARGET            # hangup the modem
       Teardown_Connection  # unconfigure masquerading
       ;;
esac
```

Once everything is coded and tested, we cannot forget that giving users dial-out privileges is not sufficient if they also have to add routes, run masquerading commands, etc. To do this, we need to configure *sudo* to allow our users to **sudo dial_client**. A little bit of user education and we're ready to turn them loose. . .

4.1.8 ISDN Dial-Out with Spellcaster's Babylon

Erbium also needed to be able to dial ISDN links. Because both of the serial ports on erbium are used for analog modems, I had to find an ISDN solution other than the standard terminal adapter (TA) with a serial interface. One such device is the *Datacommute/BRI* from Spellcaster, Inc., an ISA add-on card with Linux driver support.

Although it is a complete departure from the status quo Linux support for ISDN, the board works well. The folks at Spellcaster have put a lot of effort into designing an entire system around their cards. You use their utility to configure the card once with the SPID information for the ISDN circuit, and then edit a configuration file which sets the parameters for your various dial-out (or dial-in) sessions. After that, you dial the link with one of their software commands—similar to using *pon* and *poff* with *pppd*. The software, which is called *Babylon*, has support for multiple devices, which can be grouped into pools, and MPPP (bridging the two BRI B-channels to form a 128kb link).

The Babylon software is very easy to use. Note that Spellcaster produces a range of ISDN equipment, including PRI boards which could be used for larger-scale dial-in or dial-out solutions. For more information, visit its website at *http:// www.spellcast.com*.

Erbium in Restrospect   How well did all of it work? The IP masquerading works like a charm, at least for all of the applications we were using (normally FTP, telnet, IRC, and SQLnet connections). The biggest single problem I had was the users forgetting to hang up the connection after using it. This ran up toll charges and left the routing tables and masquerading entries cluttered. It is easy enough to script around this—probably the easiest thing to do is to issue an *at* job to bring the link down automatically after a period of time.

If I'm allowed a complaint, it would be that *pppd* doesn't have exit codes which tell you the results of the command. What I was looking for was the ability to check the return code to see if the link dialed, or if no modem was available, etc. This would have made things easier on the user, who sometimes had to use the *plog* command to see what was going on. But I shouldn't complain, since I have the source and can compile my own version to suit my needs. The privilege of having the source code comes with the responsibility of making things better instead of just griping about them. . . . And with that, we conclude the discussion of erbium and shift the focus to more general topics useful for extranet routers. The first of these is IP masquerading, a topic crucial not only for this type of router, but also for many Internet routers.

4.2 IP MASQUERADING CONCEPTS

IP masquerading is a facility in the Linux kernel which can manipulate packets so that they appear to originate from addresses other than the original source. Before you think that this is some hacker tool, the masquerading is performed only during the *forwarding* of a packet. (It would make no sense if the router itself originates the packet or if the router were the destination of the packet.) The kernel performs some acrobatics to make the process transparent to both the sender and the receiver. It does a good job in all but a few rare cases.

Before we talk about configuring IP masquerading, let's start with an example of why one might need it, and what happens to a packet when it is masqueraded. The primary function of masquerading is to obscure the IP address of a client from a server located on a separate network. The reasons for doing this vary. The most common one is that the client has an address such that the server either would not or could not respond to a connection request originating from that client. This situation is depicted in Figure 4.2, where the client can contact the server, but the server response will never reach the client.

Figure 4.2   A Scenario for IP Masquerading

Remember that the private address space may be used by any private net, and as such, may be routed internally at B's network to some other machine with the address 192.168.24.17. To remedy the situation, the router alters the packet so that it appears to have originated from its external interface R_B, which is an Internet valid address. When the server sends a response, it is routed to R, which then forwards the packet on to the client A. The topology, of course, is usually much more complex than that depicted; there may be many hops between the router and the server. The result, however, is the same. The packet appears to have an Internet-valid source address and will find its way back to the router to be unmasqueraded.

4.2.1 IP Masquerading Under the Hood

Now that we are motivated to use masquerading, we can talk about what is really happening to the packet when it is masqueraded. As an example, let's say that client A would like to connect to server B using either TCP or UDP.[2] The client is going to send from port x to port y on the server. In order to reach B, A first sends the packet to its gateway, which has address R_A. The gateway interface on the B side is R_B.

If you take a close look at such a transaction, there are three different types of addresses involved. First, each machine has an Ethernet address, useful only for transmission of frames to other machines on its local subnet. The next layer includes the IP address of the source and the destination. Finally, for the TCP and UDP protocols, there is a specific port on both the client and the server. Normally, the client port is not significant and is a value between 1024 and 65534, arbitrarily chosen by the operating system.[3] However, the server response must arrive on the port where the client expects it—otherwise, the client doesn't know that the packet is a response to its send.

---

[2] The client/server designations refer to the system's role in the transaction. The client originates the connection request with the server, and the server responds to it.

[3] If the send port is not specified in the code, Linux starts at 1024 and simply increments the value each time a client binds to a new port for sending.

Forwarding without Masquerading   Let's list the sequence of a send/respond transaction when no masquerading occurs, and then follow the values of the three addresses in Table 4.1:

1. Client A wants to send to the service running on port y on server B, so it builds a packet with B's IP address as the destination. Because B is part of a different subnet, client A knows to forward the packet to its gateway, R. It does this by setting the destination in the Ethernet frame to R.

2. R receives the packet and notes that its destination is a remote IP address. Because R is configured to forward, it accepts the packet and determines which interface to use to forward the packet. It then places B's Ethernet address as the destination address in the Ethernet frame and sends the packet. (In the general case where B is still several hops away, it determines which gateway is the next hop and sends to it, where the same procedure takes place.)

3. Server B receives the Ethernet frame and notes that the destination address for the packet is its own. Therefore, it accepts the packet and sends it to the process which has a socket bound and listening to the destination port y in the TCP packet header.

4. The same procedure is executed in reverse for the response. This time, the TCP header destination port is x, and the source port is y. The IP packet header has B as the source and A as the destination. The Ethernet frame headers take on the appropriate values as the packet makes its way back to client A.

Forwarding with Masquerading   Now take the same situation and configure the router to masquerade traffic from subnet$_A$ or traffic to subnet$_B$. The following steps will occur during a transaction between client A and server B:

1. **client send/router receive**—A sends a packet to B via its gateway R.

2. **router masquerade**—The packet pattern-matching on the router R notices that this connection should be masqueraded. It builds a new set of IP headers for the packet payload in which the source IP address of the packet is replaced by the IP address of the forwarding interface on R. R opens a free port, z, and fixes up the packet so that it now originates from $R{:}z$.

Table 4.1 Protocol Headers During Normal Forwarding

Ethernet addr		IP addr		TCP port	
src	**dst**	**src**	**dst**	**src**	**dst**
A	R_A	A	B	x	y
router forwards					
R_B	B	R_B	B	x	y
B	R_B	B	R_B	y	x
router forwards					
R_A	A	B	A	y	x

3. router forward/server receive—The newly massaged packet is forwarded to B.

4. server reply/router receive—B's server process receives the packet and builds a packet to reply to it. The reply is to R at port z, because these are the source values B sees in the packet headers. B puts this packet on the wire to R.

5. router unmasquerade—The kernel on R recognizes the packet as a response to a previously masqueraded send by the destination IP and port tuple (R, z). When it opened the socket corresponding to port z, it left special instructions there to forward responses to that port to A at port x. Therefore, it **unmasquerades** the packet by fixing up the headers and then forwarding it to client A. The fix-up includes replacing the source IP address to be that of B, and the sending port to be y.

6. router forward/client receive—R puts the packet on the wire. A receives the server response, which automagically appears to have come directly from the server at B. Neither A nor B is the wiser.

In summary, forwarding involves fixing up the link-layer headers, while masquerading is the act of fixing up network-layer headers (IP address) and transport protocol-layer headers (port). Table 4.2 and Figure 4.3 illustrate the step-by-step exchange explained above. The items in the table which are changed by the masquerading router are marked*.

Table 4.2 Protocol Headers while Masquerading

	Ethernet		IP		TCP	
	src	**dst**	**src**	**dst**	**src**	**dst**
1)	A	R_A	A	B	x	y
2)			router masqs			
3)	R_B	B	R_B*	B	z*	y
4)	B	R_B	B	R_B	y	z
5)			router unmasqs			
6)	R_A	A	B	A	y	x*

The values reported in the tables are the same values you would see in the output of a packet sniffer (covered in Section 4.5) if you traced such a transaction. In this case, there are four different points where you could monitor the packet flow (at A, R_A, R_B, and B). If you were to watch all four, you would see that both interfaces on subnet$_A$ see the same traffic, as do both interfaces on subnet$_B$. I point this out to show that the kernel modifies the packets *in-between* the interfaces—i.e., while it internally forwards the packet from one interface to another. The upswing is that you can perform your monitoring directly on any interface on the masquerading router.

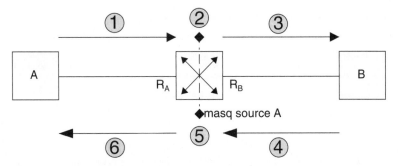

Figure 4.3 IP Forwarding and Masquerading over Ethernet

4.2.2 Protocol-Specific Masquerading

You can fool some of the packets some of the time, but you can't fool all of the packets all of the time. The example presented above represents one class of TCP/IP connection: a TCP stream. What about masquerading UDP and ICMP? As long as they are *well-mannered*, the IP masquerading code in *./net/ipv4/ip_masq.c* handles all three without any additional configuration. What do we mean by *well-mannered*? IP masquerading works "out of the box" for all TCP and UDP-based applications based on a single fixed server port and arbitrarily chosen client port, where the machine being masqueraded (the client) is the initiator of the connection.

How far does this get you? It handles telnet, ssh, rlogin, HTTP, pings (ICMP) and traceroutes (a combination of ICMP and UDP), DNS (often UDP, but can be TCP), NNTP, and many others. But, as you already know, it's what *doesn't* work that people notice. The first notable exception is FTP. FTP likes to open connections from the server back to the client, contrary to the direction you are trying masquerade (and/or firewall).

To handle a case like this, the masquerading code needs to understand something about the application protocol so that it can watch for the beginning of a transfer and know to connect the inbound socket connection to the client, not to the router. Remember, the process running on the client is expecting that inbound connection, not the router. To make things even more complicated, the FTP protocol also has a **passive mode** in which this inbound connection does not occur. The client and server negotiate a new pair of ports and use these to build a stream connection for the data transmission.

The Linux kernel developers weren't satisfied with IP masquerading without FTP, so they added `Protocol-specific masquerading` support. Code, in the form of modules, can be loaded into the running kernel to provide masquerading for the less well-behaved protocols. These modules are automatically built when you select `IP: masquerading` during kernel configuration—all you have to do is load them. Pretty spiffy, eh? The list of modules and protocols supported includes, but is not limited to:

- **CUSeeMe** with the module `ip_masq_cuseeme.o`
- **FTP** with the module `ip_masq_ftp.o`
- **IRC** with the module `ip_masq_irc.o`
- **Quake** with the module `ip_masq_quake.o`[4]
- **RealAudio** and **RealVideo** with the module `ip_masq_raudio.o`
- **VDO Live** with the module `ip_masq_vdolive.o`

To use one of the protocol modules, simply load it with `insmod modulename`. Because they need to be loaded to be useful, I add them to my */etc/init.d/network* file so that they are loaded during the startup sequence. Although you may rarely need to use it, several of the modules support the ability to listen to more than just the well-known port for their respective protocol. This is useful if you would like to provide FTP services on more ports than just port 21 by adding the argument to `ports=x1,x2,x3...` to the command line with using *insmod* to load the module. If you want to specify more than `MAX_MASQ_APP_PORTS` different ports, you will have to modify the value in */usr/src/linux/include/net/ip_masq.h* and recompile the kernel and the modules. Several other masquerading modules related to **IP port forwarding** are covered in Section 8.2.3 and **transparent proxying** in Section 8.2.2.

4.3 CONFIGURING IP MASQUERADING

Now that you know what masquerading can do, and have an idea about how it does it, you need to know how to go about enabling support for it and configuring masquerading rules. As with other kernel facilities, you must select it during the kernel configuration process, compile a new kernel, and then reboot to be able to use IP masquerading.[5]

The generic IP masquerading code is in */usr/src/linux/net/ipv4/ip_masq.c*, and handles the straightforward TCP, UDP, and ICMP protocols. When you compile a kernel only with `IP: Masquerading`, you will have support for TCP and UDP. You should set `IP: ICMP masquerading` if you also want ICMP packets to be masqueraded. (This enables some conditional parts of the code in *ip_masq.c*.)

In either case, be sure to set `IP: always defragment` whenever using masquerading. This has the effect of coalescing any packet fragments into the original (larger, unfragmented) packet before handing them to kernel's forwarding code. This is necessary because the masquerading code in the kernel will not be able to recognize fragments from masqueraded connections without knowing the source and destination IP and ports. Additional protocol support is automatically built as modules when you build a kernel with masquerading support. (Just don't forget to load into the running kernel before using them.) The full set of options follows:

---

[4] It is absolutely essential for popularity with developers and fellow administrators that this is working!

[5] The stock Debian kernel comes with masquerading enabled, as may others.

Compiling Support for IP Masquerading into the 2.2.x Kernel

```
Networking options --->
    <*> Packet socket
+   [*] Network firewalls
    <*> Unix domain sockets
    [*] TCP/IP networking
    [*] IP: advanced router
+   [*] IP: firewalling
+   [*] IP: always defragment (required for masquerading)
+   [*] IP: masquerading
    --- Protocol-specific masquerading support will be built as modules.
+   [*] IP: ICMP masquerading
Filesystems --->
    [*] /proc filesystem support
```

4.3.1 Configuring IP Masquerading with *ipchains*

As with IP accounting and firewalling, once you have a kernel with masquerading support, you use *ipchains* (for 2.2.x kernels) to configure **rules**. In this case, the rules are part of the packet-forwarding mechanism (as compared to the input, output, or accounting mechanisms). The syntax for *ipchains* is identical to that covered in Section 3.3.3, but we use some different arguments for masquerading.

Managing rules consists of entering them, viewing them, editing them, and removing them. Entering them involves specifying pattern-matching criteria along with the option(s) to tell the kernel to perform masquerading when a match occurs. Recall that *ipchains* uses the concept of **targets**, so masquerading occurs when a packet matches a rule with a target of MASQ. Furthermore, only packets that are being forwarded can be masqueraded.

Adding IP Masquerading Rules with *ipchains* All packets being forwarded automatically traverse the built-in forward chain. To masquerade them, add a rule to the forward chain with a target of MASQ. Alternately, you can add a rule to the forward chain which has a user-defined chain as its target, and somewhere along this chain is a rule with the built-in target MASQ. Perhaps a few examples will clear this up:

```
# masquerade EVERYTHING
### insert a rule that masquerades everything that the
### kernel forwards, using the built-in "forward" chain
###
### (note that not specifying any matching criteria means
### that all packets will be matched)
erbium:/root> ipchains -I forward 1 -j MASQ

# masquerade packets forward out over ppp0
### create a user-defined chain named "ipmasq" and append it to
### the built-in "forward" chain, and then add a rule to masquerade
###  packets which will be forwarded over the ppp0 interface
erbium:/root> ipchains -N ipmasq
erbium:/root> ipchains -A forward -j ipmasq
erbium:/root> ipchains -A ipmasq -i ppp0 -j MASQ
```

You may want to masquerade traffic only from certain subnets or traffic destined for a particular subnet. To do this, use the -s and -*d* switches (among others) to specify some packet matching criteria. For example, for erbium, we might find it conceptually simplest to masquerade only traffic bound for the client's network instead of trying to figure out what interface is forwarding the traffic. So we would use rules such as:

```
# masquerade packets destined for host 10.10.34.216
### use the /maskbits notation for the subnet mask
erbium:/root> ipchains -A forward -d 10.10.34.216/32 -j MASQ

### is equivalent to:
erbium:/root> ipchains -A forward -d 10.10.34.216/255.255.255.255 -j MASQ

### is equivalent to:
erbium:/root> ipchains -A forward -d 10.10.34.216 -j MASQ
```

Sometimes it is easier to specify what it is that you do not want to masquerade. For example, you may have a topology where the firewall is performing masquerading, but there are several machines located outside the firewall that have routes for your internal networks. You do not want connections to these machines from internal machines to be masqueraded because any meaningful information about the source IP address is lost. If the internal network you need to masquerade is 192.168.0.0/255.255.0.0, and the external network is 210.56.12.64/255.255.255.192, you can set the rules as follows:

```
# masquerade everything from the internal network
# to everywhere except the perimeter net

### masquerade for almost all destinations
erbium:/root> ipchains -I forward -s 192.168.0.0/16      \
              -d ! 210.56.12.64/25 -j MASQ

# OR, an alternative solution

### masquerade for all destinations
erbium:/root> ipchains -A forward -s 192.168.0.0/16 -j MASQ
### forward _without_ masquerading to the perimeter net
erbium:/root> ipchains -I forward -d 210.56.12.64/25
```

By using user-defined chains and the special targets MASQ and RETURN, you can create very intricate rulesets which masquerade only certain types of connections and provide accounting for different aspects of the process. Refer to the manpage for more information about managing rules using *ipchains*.

Modifying IP Masquerading Rules with *ipchains*   A little time spent with the *ipchains* manpage, and you will be familiar with methods of manipulating existing rules. Being able to make modifications to chains, such as inserting rules into chains at arbitrary locations, is quite handy, since, unlike IP accounting, masquerading rules are sensitive to order. Here's a synopsis of useful command forms:

`ipchains -R` *chain n rule*	replaces the nth rule for chain *chain* with the new rule specified by *rule*. (Rules are numbered starting at 1.)
`ipchains -D` *chain n*	deletes the nth rule from chain *chain*. If you'd rather specify the rule explicitly, just use it in place of the number.
`ipchains -I` *chain n rule*	inserts the rule given into the nth position for chain *chain*, moving each of the existing rules down. (Rules are numbered starting at 1.) Omitting the position argument defaults to the first position in the list.

Viewing IP Masquerading Rules with *ipchains* You can view the counters associated with rules by listing (`-L`) the rules on a chain along with some switches to increase the amount of detail (normally `-v`, `-n`, and `-x`).

```
### list masquerading rules
### (headers/output split into two lines)
erbium:/root> ipchains -L forward -n -v
Chain forward (policy ACCEPT: 33 packets, 1686 bytes):
 pkts bytes target  prot  opt    tosa tosx  ifname     mark    outsize
   33  1686 MASQ    all   ------ 0xFF 0x00  eth1

                 source      destination ports
                 0.0.0.0/0   0.0.0.0/0   n/a
```

Some additional notes about viewing the rules:

- `-n` prevents name resolution from occurring.
- `-v` makes the output more verbose, adding the packet (`pkts`) and byte (`bytes`) counter fields, the interface field (`ifname`), the TOS masks (`tosa` and `tosx`), and the `mark` and `outsize` fields.
- `-x` is useful only in combination with `-n`. It prevents conversion of the byte and packet counters into larger units of K, M, or G.
- If you do not specify a *chainname*, all chains will be listed. If you want only to see rules which result in masquerading, *grep* the output for `MASQ`.
- If you do not specify the verbose switch, you will not see the interface field (an oversight, in my opinion), which is important unless you do all of your masquerading based solely on source or destination address.

Viewing Active Masqueraded Connections You may view the current list of masqueraded connections with *ipchains*. The syntax is:

> `ipchains -M -L [-n] [-v]`:

- The `-n` (once again) switch prevents hostname and port name lookups. Its use is optional.
- use `-v` (verbose) if you would like to see the `initseq delta prevd` fields in the output.
  - `initseq` — is the initial sequence number
  - `delta` — the difference between the client's opinion of the current sequence number (read from its most recent packet) and the server's opinion of the current sequence number.
  - `prevd` — the previous delta value

```
# ipchains -M -L
IP masquerading entries
 prot expire   source             destination         ports
TCP  03:57.94 192.168.107.223    195.20.227.241      3160 (62041) -> 80
TCP  01:22.40 192.168.104.221    193.71.196.106      1185 (62057) -> 80
TCP  01:22.46 192.168.104.221    193.71.196.106      1182 (62054) -> 80
TCP  14:27.44 192.168.104.221    193.71.196.101      1184 (62056) -> 80
TCP  11:58.10 192.168.108.220    204.71.200.55       1099 (63099) -> 5050
UDP  01:57.29 192.168.101.14     24.112.240.60       1076 (62219) -> 53
```

Each line of the output represents a masqueraded connection. As you can see, there are five actively masqueraded connections at this time. Looking at the 192.168.104.221 client, you will notice that a **masqueraded connection** refers to every unique port pair between a client and server; there are two active connections from this client to the same server.

There are two fields which should be noted. The `expire` field is the wall clock time remaining before the masquerading is taken down for this connection. It is in *minutes:seconds.hundredths*. The `ports` field is in the format *client (router)* → *server*. The router port is the port to which the server will reply to a client request. After unmasquerading the packet, the router sends it back to the client at the client port.

What Is the Expire Field and Why Is It Necessary?   If someone initiates a TCP connection, but then some evil befalls him/her and he/she is not able to take down the connection gracefully, the masquerading router will sit there forever waiting for more packets because it never saw the stream taken down properly. Since UDP is stateless, the situation is even more dire; the router is never able to intercept any information about the final packet in a UDP sequence. However, during their normal operation both types of masquerading use up ports on the router. If the masquerading never timed out, some of these ports would linger forever... or until the next reboot, which would probably have to occur when all 65535 ports on the system were exhausted. The expire timer is reset each time the connection is used. They then start counting down. If they reach zero before another packet is sent or received via the connection, the masquerading for that session is torn down.

Modifying Masquerade Expiration Timeouts with *ipchains*   You can modify the expire timeout values to something other than the defaults set in *ip_masq.h*. Those defaults are 15, 2, and 5 minutes for TCP sessions, TCP in the FIN WAIT state (after receiving a FIN packet), and UDP packets, respectively. There is also a default for ICMP (about two minutes), which may be set only by modifying the header file and recompiling the kernel. The syntax to modify the TCP and UDP values is:

ipfwadm -M -S *tcp tcpfin udp*

Note that you must specify all three of the timeout parameters, which have the unit of seconds. If you want to leave a value set to its current value, you can specify a timeout of 0. You may find tuning this useful if you have the habit of logging into a remote site over a masqueraded connection and do not want to be logged out after 15 minutes of inactivity.

4.3.2 IP Masquerading Information in /proc

Another way to view rules, counters, and expire timeouts is to poke around in the /proc filesystem. The amount of information you can find here has been increased with the 2.2.x kernel. Some highlights are listed below; all pathnames are relative to /proc/net:

file	description
ip_fwnames	lists all chains, including the chain name, default policy, reference count, packet count watermarks (high and low), and byte count watermark (high and low).
ip_fwchains	contains all rules from all chains (the chainname is the first field). This is merely a quick way to list all active rules.
ip_masquerade	lists the current masqueraded connections in raw format, along with the number of free ports available for UDP, TCP, and ICMP masquerading. (See the sample output after this list for more information.)
ip_masq/app	contains the active reference counts for the kernel built-in masquerading protocol modules. It has four fields: <ul><li>**prot**—one of TCP, UDP, or ICMP</li><li>**port**—the port which needs to be monitored to properly masquerade the protocol</li><li>**n_attach**—the number of active masquerading connections using the module and port</li><li>**name**—the protocol name, i.e., the protocol modules name *sans ip_masq_*</li></ul>
ip_masq/icmp	available when CONFIG_IP_MASQUERADE_MOD is enabled in the kernel— provides support for special modules that can modify the rewriting rules used when masquerading. It gives the user-space program *ipmasqadm* access to the kernel data structures.
ip_masq/tcp	see *ip_masq/icmp*
ip_masq/udp	see *ip_masq/icmp*

Probably the most interesting of these for day-to-day use is */proc/net/ip_masquerade*. Besides displaying the actively masqueraded connections in raw format, it shows the number of ports available for masquerading each type of connections.

```
erbium:/root> cat /proc/net/ip_masquerade
Prc FromIP    FPrt ToIP      TPrt Masq Init-seq  Delta PDelta Expires
(free=40959,40956,40960)
TCP C0A80102:0464 D08C7063:006E F658 00000000      0      0      479
TCP C0A80102:0466 1801F046:006E F65A 00000000      0      0     1145
UDP C0A80102:0434 1801F021:0035 F30B 00000000      0      0    18839
TCP C0A80102:0448 D0EDB215:0050 F65B 00000000      0      0    88925
TCP C0A80102:0465 D11E0216:006E F659 00000000      0      0      847
```

From this output, we see that there are 40959 ports available for masquerading UDP connections, 40956 for TCP connections, and 40960 for ICMP connections. We also see the five connections currently masqueraded and the number of clicks remaining for their expire timers (expressed in $\frac{1}{100}^{th}$s of seconds).

If you suspect that you are low on ports for masquerading, you: **a)** might want to remember to check here to see what the kernel thinks, **b)** might have a busy site, and **c)** may want to compile a new kernel to adjust the number of ports available. The values you need to change are PORT_MASQ_BEGIN and PORT_MASQ_END in */usr/src/linux/include/net/ip_masq.h*. After modifying the source, you will have to recompile the kernel and reboot for the change to take effect. (For those of you who worked with the 2.0 kernel, you'll notice that the number of free ports assigned to masquerading by default is increased by a factor of 10 for the 2.2.x kernel versions.)

One last note about using *ipchains* to configure your rules. You will need to store the rules in a script once you get them the way you want them or else they will be lost during the next reboot. You may even want to save a hard copy of the forwarding/masquerading rules. If you don't like the idea of configuring these rules by hand, check the following section for information about configuration tools.

4.3.3 IP Masquerading Configuration Tools

IP masquerading is a very commonly performed task. As such, a lot of work has been put into making it easier to configure. Now that you know what lies underneath, here are some packages which might aid you in configuring it for your system.

ipmasq is a native Debian package based on the scripts in the LDP's *IP Masquerade mini-HOWTO*. If you would like to use the package without running Debian, you can retrieve the source from any Debian mirror site. The following is taken from the description which accompanies the package:

> By default, this package configures the system as a basic forwarding firewall, with IP spoofing and stuffed routing protection. The firewall will allow hosts behind the firewall to get to the Internet, but not allow connections from the Internet to reach the hosts behind the firewall. However, **ipmasq** now features a very flexible framework where you can override any of the predefined rules if you so choose. It also allows you to control if the rules are reinterpreted when *pppd* brings a link up or down. This package should be installed on the firewall host and not on the hosts behind the firewall.

dotfile-ipfwadm is a module for **dotfile**. This package uses a Tcl/Tk interface to allow you to graphically build your own accounting, forwarding, input, output, and masquerading rules. It can be very helpful for quickly developing a set of rules, which it outputs to a file. You can then tweak the rules as needed. It allows you to select only options which are applicable to your running kernel. For non-Debian systems, check to see if *dotfile* is available, otherwise visit *http://www.imada.ou.dk/~blackie/dotfile/*. (Note, this currently supports only *ipfwadm* commands for the 2.0 kernel.)

netbase contains a command called *ipfwadm-wrapper*. This package will be installed on your system in any event, but it is nice to be aware of *ipfwadm-wrapper* when converting to *ipchains*.

MasqDialer (Debian package **masqdialer**) is suited to replace the scripting work I had to do by hand for erbium. The description from the Debian package is shown below. I wish it had been available back when I started on that. `<sigh>...`

> The masqdialer system is designed to provide easily accessible control of multiple dial-out modem connections to the members of a LAN using IP Masquerade for their Internet connectivity. The system is a client/server design, so as long as a client can be written for a particular platform, that platform can take advantage of masqdialer's offerings. The masqdialer daemon runs on the Linux machine, and upon an authorized client request, carries out the user's request.

> *MasqDialer's* home website is *http://cpwright.villagenet.com/mserver/*. There is a GUI front-end for managing the server available in the Debian package **tkmasqdialer**. You will also need the **mclient** package, which is a command-line client used to communicate with the server.

4.4 USING IP MASQUERADING EVERY DAY

Masquerading is great when it works and can be miserable to trouble-shoot when it doesn't. Things can go wrong if you've specified rules that masquerade too much, not enough, or in the wrong direction. It may also be that the protocol doesn't lend itself to masquerading and is not supported via a protocol module. But in my experience, bad rules are often to blame.

First, think about what you want to accomplish. For a dial-up connection into another corporation, you will probably want to masquerade everything headed from your network into theirs so that it can be returned back to you. The easiest way to do that is to masquerade everything that is leaving that interface. Something like `ipchains output -I -j MASQ -i ppp0` seems like it would do the trick. The rule means that everything that leaves the system over interface *ppp0* is masqueraded, regardless of its source or destination. Unfortunately, that will not work because the `-j MASQ` target is valid only for rules on the `forward` chain. If you use the same format with a forwarding rule (without specifying a source or a destination), you will be masquerading in both directions, or will you? And should you be masquerading in both directions anyway? (This *might* be ok, but before you jump on it, you need to determine if you want traffic coming back into your network from the PPP link to appear to originate from your extranet router.)

Instead of waxing philosophic about how to provide rules, I believe that they are easiest to understand by looking at pictures of what works and what doesn't. Masquerading is a topic with a lot of subtleties, and for me it was sometimes easier to grow accustomed to how to use it than to understand all the details of how it worked. Throughout this section, the router is shown to have two Ethernet devices, *eth0* and *eth1*. That both of these are Ethernet devices is purely arbitrary. The concepts are

Figure 4.4 Masquerading Interface Is Chosen
Based upon Packet Destination

valid if either of the interfaces were to be replaced by an interface of another type.
The convention in the drawings is that *eth0* is on the *inside* and *eth1* is on the *outside*,
when such a distinction is applicable.

Secret #1 *The Linux kernel is smart about what to masquerade.* When you have
a rule that instructs the kernel to masquerade packets matching a particular source
network/mask, it chooses the IP address to place in the headers, depending upon
which interface is used to forward the packet. As an example, see Figure 4.4.

Instead of replacing the packet's source IP with any IP on the system, it always
uses the IP of the interface over which the packet will be sent.[6] This is the same
interface that appears in the routing table for either the gateway route or network
route which must be used to reach the destination IP. If you think about it, this is
exactly what you want to happen. Any other action would be nonsensical, because
the packet would not be routed back to you over the same interface, if at all.

Secret #2 *Masquerading is directional with respect to client-server transactions.* A
client-sever transaction refers to the paradigm where the client initiates the connection to the server, sends to the server, and the server responds. Shown in Figure 4.5,
we can represent such a connection as a pair of arrows, first from client to server and
then from server to client. The router in this picture is configured to masquerade
any packets with a source address in subnet$_A$. The masquerading bends the arrows
a bit (because of the port changes), but the connection precedes correctly.

It should come as little surprise that if the packet source address does not match,
then the packet is not masqueraded. What about the reply? It has a source address
from subnet$_B$, not from subnet$_A$. However, the reply is unmasqueraded correctly
because the kernel is expecting and because it arrives on a special port.

What's interesting is when a client on subnet$_B$ tries to *open* a connection to a
server on subnet$_A$, as depicted in Figure 4.6 (For this example, let's assume that the
host on subnet$_B$ has a valid route to subnet$_A$, which will not always be the case.)

The packet passes from client to server untouched by the router because the
source address did not match any of the packet criteria for masquerading. The server

---

[6] If you want to explicitly specify the interface to be used, then you can do so when you configure
the IP masquerading rules with *ipchains*. However, you will see that it is unnecessary unless you want
every connection going out over that interface to be masqueraded.

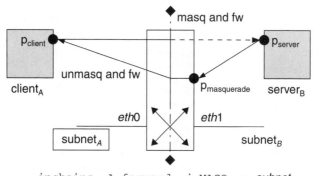

ipchains -A forward -j MASQ -s *subnet*_A

Figure 4.5 Masquerading Is Directional—Inside Out

on subnet_A formulates a response to the client and sends it. But, now the packet matches the masquerading code. The kernel knows that something is amiss, since this is not the *direction* implied by the arguments given when establishing the rule, and it throws the packet into the bit bucket. The same situation depicted differently is shown in Figure 4.7.

You can verify this independently using packet sniffers—the server on subnet_A will respond, but the response never gets forwarded by the router. One of the reasons to mention this case, is that not all masquerading routers are positioned between only two networks. If you used source-based rules without explicitly defining forwarding rules for the nets which should be able to communicate unmasqueraded, you may experience problems. This can be further compounded by the fact that ICMP, e.g., *ping* and UDP, e.g., *traceroute*, which use both, will traverse this configuration in both directions without a problem. This can be alleviated by using interface-based masquerading rules, but know that they also have an implied direction and nuances.

ipchains -I forward -j MASQ -s *subnet*_A

Figure 4.6 Masquerading Is Directional—Outside In

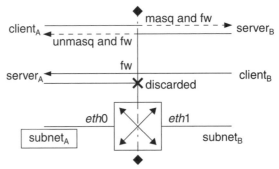

ipchains -I forward -j MASQ -s *subnet_A*

Figure 4.7 Masquerading Is Directional

Secret #3 *Masquerading for an interface occurs only when the interface specified is the* **forwarding interface**. Figure 4.8 depicts a configuration where masquerading is set up to be performed on the *eth1* interface, which we will call the *outside*. The interface on the inside is *eth0*.

As you can see from the arrows in Figure 4.8, connections from the inside out are masqueraded, but those from the outside in are not. To complete our terminology, the **forwarding interface** is the interface on the router that *sends* (forwards) the *outbound* (inside → out) connection. The packets which emerge from this interface will be masqueraded, provided that they met any other criteria in the masquerading rule (such as protocol, source, or destination addresses). For an *inbound* connection, *eth1* is the receiving interface, not the forwarding interface. Note, in addition to the definition of the forwarding interface, that the situation is identical to source-based masquerading example with respect to direction. Client to server connections which are forwarded by the masquerading interface will succeed. Client to server connections which use the masquerading interface as a receiving interface for packets in the client → server direction will be swallowed by the kernel.

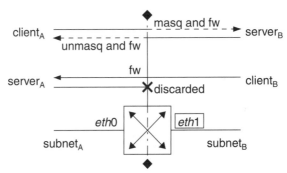

ipchains I forward -j MASQ i *eth1*

Figure 4.8 Interface Masquerading Must Occur on the
Forwarding Interface

So what do the secrets mean? That depends upon your masquerading application. Perhaps they might save you some time when configuring masquerading on your system. Packet sniffing, presented in Section 4.5, is an excellent way to troubleshoot masquerading problems, but you'll need to be monitoring on both sides of the masquerading router to get the complete picture of what is happening. Other things to keep in mind when trouble-shooting masqueraded connections so that you don't spend all day chasing ghosts are:

- The problem may not be with your rules configuration, but may be because you have failed to load the correct module to masquerade the protocol being used.

- The protocol you are using might not have masquerading support in the kernel at all. Watch out for protocols where the server tries to open a connection with the client.

- When dealing with extranet connections, sometimes the problem is either the NAT or some firewalling on the remote side (although masquerading a masqueraded connection does work when correctly configured).

- Firewalling rules and masquerading rules are executed sequentially, in the order defined by your configuration. Take care that you are not filtering out part of the masqueraded connection (perhaps by blocking part of the masquerading port range).

- Proxies are an excellent way of avoiding the issue for Internet masquerading. One drawback is that you may have to give up some of the standard services you run on that system (e.g., telnet), or train your users to telnet to a different port when connecting to a client. However, not everything can be proxied. See Section 8.1 for more information.

- There are tools available to aid you in configuring masquerading—sweet, nourishing tools! (See Section 4.3.3.)

4.4.1 Why Masquerade?

This chapter introduces IP masquerading in conjunction with the configuration of erbium. It was used to overcome a technical snag in connecting two corporate networks. Whether the IP addresses were private or not was not always the issue; it was often a question of coordination with the other network administrator. Neither of us wanted to exchange network information, worry about address space collisions, or expend efforts reconfiguring our networks for an infrequent (although important) application. In short, erbium uses IP masquerading because of its convenience.

The most common motivation for its use, however, is for Internet access from clients on private subnets. If your organization is using any of the private subnets listed in RFC 1918 (see Section 2.1.5), you will be required to either provide proxy servers or perform masquerading for these clients to access the Internet. Even if you can get Internet routable address space, you may choose to use private address space. After all, it is nice to have all of that address space at your disposal when planning your network. For both of these reasons, you will often see IP masquerading discussed side-by-side with packet-filtering firewalls and proxies as part of discussions for using it on an Internet gateway. But aside from allowing access from machines where access would not normally be possible, you may find yourself using IP masquerading for applications where the traffic could have been routed normally. In essence, you are obscuring the identity of the sender from the receiver, which has a couple of tangential benefits. First, it is a security measure. Second, it can be used to *condense* traffic.

IP Masquerading as a Security Measure   Say that a user on your network is using a web browser to access a less than reputable website. Web browsers have loose tongues and almost always reveal the operating system of the sender. Should someone on the receiving side have unscrupulous ideas with regards to users of this particular operating system, he/she may launch an attack against the sender. In the case of masquerading, he/she will not have access to the IP of the true sender. Instead, he/she will launch an attack against the wrong system. Although perhaps not the most quieting of examples, it is the Right Thing to limit attacks against users.

IP Masquerading to Condense Traffic   Although its applications are less frequent, there may be times when you do not want to know the IP address(es) of those who are contacting you, even if routing is not a problem. In this case, you are purposefully masquerading incoming traffic before it enters your network. One reason may be because your servers are having a hard time performing (reverse) name lookups on the IP address coming over the link, resulting in long DNS timeouts for client connects. Another reason may be for logging purposes, when you would like for all connections from a certain site or IP range to appear to originate from a single point. If you wanted to get an idea of the amount of web traffic the group on the second floor generated on the proxy server, you could configure IP masquerading from that router interface to the HTTP proxy server at port 80. This might not be your *modus operandi*, but you could configure it for a day just to generate statistics. A third reason would be to bypass a problem in your network. Refer to Figure 4.9 as part of the following scenario.

When everything works, each site routes over its link directly to the other site. Now imagine that the link $_{BC}$ goes down in the middle of B's night. C is in the office

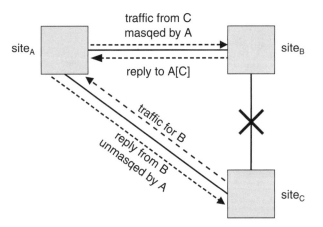

Figure 4.9   Re-routing Traffic with IP Masquerading

and unhappy about not being able to access B, and A is on the phone and unhappy about being the only WAN admin available for comment. Here's one solution:

- Login to C's router and reroute traffic towards A over link$_{AC}$.
- Configure the router$_A$ to masquerade all traffic originating from C and bound for B.
- B's servers will see traffic from router$_A$ and respond to it, avoiding link$_{BC}$. Make sure that you have the protocol modules loaded on router$_A$ so that things like FTP will work.
- Send an email to the users at C that not everything is going to work wonderfully in this scenario, but most services (anything that can be masqueraded) will.
- Go back to bed, but make sure that you get the password for router$_B$ for future reference.

By nature of its incredible usefulness, and therefore popularity, there are many resources available to assist you in configuring IP masquerading. A quick search on most any web search engine should produce hundreds of hits (in at least a dozen languages), so you should not have any problem locating resources. If you do, try the Linux Documentation Project.

4.5 IP Monitoring Tools

Having access to the data on the line is invaluable when you are trouble-shooting a variety of network problems. Sniffers can operate on all different network layers, or be configured to operate at only a certain layer. Imagine all that is happening on an Ethernet segment when machine A tries to telnet to machine B and nothing goes wrong. . . .

1. First, machine A might need to resolve the hostname of machine B, requiring it to perform a DNS hostname lookup. When it calls `gethostbyname()`, a UDP packet is formatted to be sent to the DNS server.
2. For our example, let's assume that the DNS server is on the same IP subnet, and is known as machine C. This means that the IP stack is not going to use a gateway to transmit the packet. It will send the packet directly to the DNS server. To contact the DNS server, machine A will have to issue an **ARP request** to locate the address of machine C. The ARP request is sent to media address *ff:ff:ff:ff:ff:ff*, which is the broadcast address for the Ethernet segment. The ARP request is `Who has IP address of machine C?`
3. Machine C will answer with an **ARP reply** which contains its Ethernet hardware address.
4. Machine A can now send its UDP packet to port 53 on machine C as an IP packet. Machine C's reply goes out immediately because C already knows machine A's Ethernet hardware address. The **ARP table** on machine C should have been updated with this information when it received the packet from machine A.

5. Now machine A has the IP address of machine B, which, to make things interesting, is located in another IP subnet. The telnet client on machine A formats its packet to send to port 23 of machine B.

6. The IP stack on machine A looks in its *routing table*. (Machine A has a routing table of sorts. Although it is not necessarily a gateway, it uses the same mechanism to determine where to send a packet as a router would.) Machine A notes that the destination address is not part of the IP subnet attached to its *eth0* and it has only one NIC, so it will have to use the default gateway.

7. Now the process to contact the default gateway (which is known by its IP address) begins, once again with an **ARP request**, assuming that machine A has not used the gateway before, or possibly it has, but the entry in the ARP table has already expired.

8. Once the gateway receives the packet, it checks the packet's destination and sees that the packet must be sent to machine B, which, for your (the reader's) sake, is on an Ethernet segment directly connected to another interface on the gateway.

9. The gateway must perform an ARP request (on the other interface) to learn machine B's Ethernet address so that the packet can be forwarded.

10. Machine B performs the same process in reverse to send to machine A, except that machine B already knows the IP address of machine A and the Ethernet address of the gateway.

Simple, eh? With a packet sniffer, you can watch all of this unfold before you in frighteningly verbose detail. Use packet sniffers to explore what is happening at the **link-layer** (Ethernet), the **network-layer** (IP, ARP, RIP, etc.), and the **transport-layer** (TCP, UDP, etc.). A few examples of uses are:

- You can detect Ethernet segment problems such as hosts configured with incorrect gateways, hosts which are continually generating broadcast messages, and perhaps even hosts which are generating malformed packets.

- You can quickly detect routing and firewalling problems by seeing if the packets you expect are on the line. If there is a lot of activity on the segment, use a filter to restrict what is monitored to only the IP address of host(s) in question. You can further restrict what is monitored by specifying a certain protocol and/or port. (If you are connected via the network to the machine where you are performing the sniffing, be sure to exclude traffic to and from your machine unless you want to see all of the results of the trace *in* the trace.)

- You can measure the volume and latency of the packet exchange required to complete a transaction. Because a sniffer prints very precise timestamps along with the packet headers, it is not difficult to write another script to calculate where in the sequence there are delays, and from that present a detailed analysis of where the latency was occurring.

- As the network administrator, sometimes you will be asked to perform odd functions. A user once came to me because he had forgotten the password for a POP3 account a mail client had been automatically checking from his workstation at the office. The user asked me if I could sniff the password when the mail client checked his mail the next time. `ipgrab -i eth0 port 110 and host` *userip* to the rescue...

I will introduce a few of the popular packet sniffers, of both command-line and GUI flavors. All of these are based on *libpcap*, a packet capture interface library brought from the Network Research Group at the Lawrence Berkeley National Laboratory. If you would like to look at the source, visit *ftp://ftp.ee.lbl.gov/libpcap.tar.Z*.

There are a few things to remember when using packet capture programs. First, they can show you only what they see on the wire. If you are plugged into a switching hub, you may see only IP broadcasts, some Ethernet broadcasts, and traffic to and from your workstation. (Refer to Section 2.2.3 for a more detailed description of why this is.) Second, sniffers work only when they are run as the super-user. Without this the interface cannot be put into **promiscuous** mode, nor can the interface be read by a normal user. Third, it is not ethical to go about sniffing other people's packets just because you can. See Section D.1 in Appendix D for more on this.

A good way to start is with one of the command-line sniffers. They can unlock the details of the network without generating a lot of overhead on the system they are running on. Later on, we'll look at the GUI-based tools.

4.5.1 tcpdump

tcpdump could be called the *original* packet sniffer. It was written by the same folks responsible for *libpcap*—Van Jacobson, Craig Leres, and Steven McCanne—and it runs a slew of different versions of Unix. In its most basic form, you can start it without any arguments and it will dump the packet headers being sent and received on the first Ethernet interface it finds (normally *eth0* for Linux) onto *stdout*. Of course, you can adjust where the sniffer gets its input, how the output looks, where the output goes, and what sort of filter the sniffer should use. Here are some of the common options used with *tcpdump*:

```
tcpdump [ -adeflnNOpqStvx ] [ -c count ] [ -F file ]
             [ -i interface ] [ -r file ] [ -s snaplen ]
             [ -T type ] [ -w file ] [ expression ]
```

Controlling Where *tcpdump* Gets Its Input

-i *interface*—a network interface with an encapsulation format supported by *libpcap*. This is most anything except for Frame Relay and ATM.
>   OR

-r *file*—read the *file* for input. *file* should have been created by `tcpdump -w` or a program that writes the same format. Specify "-" to read from *stdin*.

-c *count*—read only *count* packets from the input source before exiting.

-s *snaplen*—specify a different number of bytes to be read from each packet. Typically, *tcpdump* reads only enough bytes to make sure that the headers are saved, but you may want to increase this value, especially if you intend to use `-x` down the road.

[**expression**]—is an expression used to limit the scope of the patterns matched by *tcpdump*. By default, all packets are displayed. The format is known as the "Berkeley packet filter expression" format. Although it is different from the filtering expressions you use with *ipfwadm* and *ipchains*, and different again from the filtering expressions you have to learn if you want to use *diald* or *sniffit*; this one is very intuitive and is used by several popular sniffers. The expressions look like English phrases in many cases.

The expression syntax is one or more **primitives**, combined by **and**, **or**, or **not**, which are also known by **&&**, **||**, and **!**, respectively. Primitives may be grouped using parentheses, but when you do this, you will need to either quote to otherwise escape the (and) to prevent the shell from misinterpreting them. So you can do things like $p_1\&\&!(p_2||p_3)$. But what exactly is a **primitive**? It consists of an **identifier**, potentially preceded by a **qualifier**. And this is where it gets complicated. . . . The authoritative source on this subject is the manpage and whatever works for you on the command-line. A synopsis is provided below:

Berkeley Packet Filter *qualifiers*

type—specifies the type of the *identifier*. It can have the values of **host**, **net**, or **port**, with **host** being assumed.

direction—is one of **src** or **dst**, with the default (when no direction is specified) being **src or dst**, which is like **both** for *ipfwadm*. Therefore

```
tcpdump -n -i eth0 src or dst port 110
tcpdump -n -i eth0 port 110
```

are equivalent. Keep in mind that **src** and **dst** do not apply to just IP headers. They can also apply to other protocols, such as **ether** (and thereby indicate a source or destination Ethernet address).

protocol—is one of **ether**, **fddi**, **ip**, **arp**, **rarp**, **decnet**, **lat**, **sca**, **moprc**, **mopdl**, **tcp**, and **udp**. I typically stick to **tcp** and **udp**, and if I'm feeling a little froggy I might use **arp** or **ether**. Of course, your needs will guide you to the protocols you need to sniff. If you do not specify a **protocol**, then any protocol type which makes sense for the identifier will match. Therefore, if you specify only a **port**, then both *tcp* and **udp** protocols are implied.

Types of Berkeley Packet Filter *identifiers*

host *host*—indicates the IP address of *host*. Qualifiers that make sense with this are **src** and **dst**—remember that the default means that *host* can be either the source or the destination. *host* can also be a DNS name which resolves to multiple IP addresses, in which case all of them will match. Note that **host** is the keyword and *host* is the value of the identifier.

ether host *ehost*—indicates an Ethernet address. Once again, **ether host** is the keyword and *ehost* is either a 6-byte Ethernet (MAC) address in the format *xx:xx:xx:xx:xx:xx*, or a name from */etc/ethers*. The **dst** and **src** qualifiers apply as they do for a **host**.

gateway *host*—generates a match if the packet being examined was forwarded by *host* acting as a gateway, or is about to be (next hop *only*) forwarded by *host*. The *host* specified must appear in both */etc/hosts* and */etc/ethers*. BTW, */etc/ethers* is not so wonderfully documented. On my glibc2.0 system, the only whitespace allowed between the Ethernet address and the ehostname is a single space. This is not so important for specifying an *ehost* since you can use the 6-byte format. But **gateway** will not work without the same *host* appearing in both files.

net *net*[*/masklen* | **mask** *mask*]—this is merely one of several different ways to specify an IP subnet. The keyword **net** is required, while the */masklen* (the same "number of ones" format covered back in Chapter 2 and used by *ipfwadm* and *ipchains*) and the **mask** *mask* (the dot-format used by *ifconfig*) is optional. The **dst** and **src** qualifiers apply.

port *port*—indicates *port* is on one end (or both) of an IP packet. *port* can be an integer port number or a service name from */etc/services* or equivalent. The **dst** and **src** qualifiers apply as usual, optionally *preceded* by **tcp** and **udp**. Note that the order of the qualifiers before the keyword **port** is important, as in the following examples:

```
erbium:/root> tcpdump -n -i eth0 tcp src port 110    # correct
erbium:/root> tcpdump -n -i eth0 src tcp port 110    # WRONG
```

less *length*—matches packets with a length (in bytes) less than or equal to *length*. Note that the length is the payload + the transport headers, so you cannot use *less 1* to catch empty packets (ACKs and what not). Because different protocols have different header lengths, you might have to experiment a bit to find the magic number. My rule of thumb is to add 64 to whatever length you are looking for when you're sniffing an Ethernet device, and 40 for PPP devices.

greater *length*—matches packets with a length (in bytes) greater than or equal to *length*. The same comment about headers made for **less** applies.

ether broadcast—matches the packet if it is an Ethernet broadcast—any packet with an Ethernet destination address of *ff:ff:ff:ff:ff:ff* (e.g., an **ARP request**). The keyword **ether** is optional, but since I find it easy to confuse with the next option, I recommend using it.

ip broadcast—matches three different types of IP broadcasts.

    1. packets sent to 255.255.255.255 (all ones)

    2. packets sent to 0.0.0.0 (all zeros)

    3. packets sent to the local subnet broadcast address (as is applicable for the -i interface being listened upon).

ether multicast—matches Ethernet multicast packets (I've personally never come across one of these. . .).

ip multicast—matches ip multicast packets.

expr relbinop expr—is a way to get inside the packets to compare either 1, 2, or 4
bytes of the packet header with some known quantity. The first *expr* should be
a *protocol*[*offset:size*] where:

- *protocol* is one of the protocols listed among the protocols in *types of
  qualifiers*
- *offset* is the number of bytes from the beginning of the header implied by
  the *protocol.*
- *:size* is optional, as *size* will default to 1

  relbinop is a relative binary operator from the list of >, <, >=, <=, =, !=,
  and the second *expr* is an integer mathematical expression (no variables!) in
  C syntax.

  If that sparks your interest, then go for it. It might be useful as a training
  aid, or to watch for some rare condition (perhaps a suspected protocol violation). I consider it for full-blown gurus, so I'll leave it up to you to figure out
  how to use it.

Controlling How *tcpdump* Formats Its Output

-e—**e**xtend the output to include the link-layer headers for each line of output. (You
can also remember this by thinking of **e**thernet headers.)

-n—**n**o name resolution of IP addresses or service names (ports). This can save a lot
of time, especially when running *tcpdump* with output going to *stdout.*

-N—do not print FQDNs (Fully Qualified Domain Names), but instead only print
the hostname portion. Obviously, this makes no sense if you have specified -n.

-q—a less verbose mode of output. This skips the sequence numbers and a lot of the
protocol flags. The output (when used with -n) will fit nicely in an 80-column
terminal window.

-S—print absolute TCP sequence numbers, which might be useful for calculating
packet counts during a given session.

-t—do not generate a timestamp on each line.

-tt—display the 32-bit timestamp value instead of the wall-clock time. (Warning, not
valid after the year 2038!).

-v—display more verbose output, including IP TTL and TOS header information.

-vv—display even more verbose output, including protocol information when *tcpdump* knows about the protocol.

-x—print the packet payload in hexadecimal, up to the number of bytes set by -s
`snaplen`. This is one reason why *tcpdump* might be considered more polite
than other sniffers that display the data in ASCII. You will not just happen
across the contents of someone's email or his/her password with the data in hex

without making an effort to decode it. (If you can *read* hex-formatted ASCII, you need to get out of the office more.)

-w *file*—write the output to *file*. *file* will be in binary and can be parsed by specifying it as the input for `tcpdump -r`. This eliminates the overhead of writing to a terminal, so you might prefer using `tcpdump -w` and then `tcpdump -r` on busy machines. *tcpdump* is clever enough not to even try to perform host or service name lookups while in this mode to further increase performance. It will do them for you while reading the file back in if you do not turn them off. Specify "-" to write to *stdout*.

Examples of *tcpdump*   If you didn't absorb all of those options all at once, you might want to work through the examples below.

```
### capture all ARP packets on a given interface
###
### notice how a machine asks 3 times (once per second) before
### giving up - in this case 192.168.16.7 must be offline
erbium:/root> tcpdump -i eth0 arp
22:47:45.825740 arp who-has 192.168.16.7 tell 192.168.16.1
22:47:46.820064 arp who-has 192.168.16.7 tell 192.168.16.1
22:47:47.820068 arp who-has 192.168.16.7 tell 192.168.16.1

################################################################

### capture all traffic from the telnet daemon on the server yeti
###               do not show domain (N)ames, use (q)uiet output
###
### (e.g., we want to see how many different telnet sessions
###   connect to yeti in a given period)
erbium:/root> tcpdump -q -N -i eth0 host yeti and tcp src port 23
tcpdump: listening on eth0
22:34:11.429987 yeti.telnet > baer.4006: tcp 0 (DF)
22:34:11.597841 yeti.telnet > baer.4006: tcp 12 (DF)
22:38:43.030749 yeti.telnet > cygnus.1024: tcp 0 (DF)
22:38:43.205024 yeti.telnet > cygnus.1024: tcp 12 (DF)
22:38:43.277924 yeti.telnet > cygnus.1024: tcp 0 (DF)
22:38:43.283733 yeti.telnet > cygnus.1024: tcp 15 (DF)

### It's a dirty hack, but you could take the output above
### and pipe it into:
###
###                         awk { print $4 } | sort -u | wc -l
###
### to count the number of telnet connection attempts.

################################################################

### somebody thinks it's cute to start his workstation with the
### IP address of the default gateway before he goes home at night
### and then change it back in the morning, causing IP conflicts
### during this period
###
### we're going to find out the hardware address of this system
### by looking for packets from the gateway's IP but not from
### the gateway's MAC address
```

```
erbium:/root> tcpdump -n -e -i eth0 ip src 192.168.16.1          \
    and not ether host 00:50:56:94:00:00
tcpdump: listening on eth0
23:05:52.460772 0:50:56:95:65:2 ff:ff:ff:ff:ff:ff 0806 42:        \
    arp who-has 192.168.18.22 tell 192.168.18.1
23:05:57.742258 0:50:56:95:65:2 ff:ff:ff:ff:ff:ff 0806 42:        \
    arp who-has 192.168.18.22 tell 192.168.18.1

### Aha!  Now we know the MAC address of the culprit.  It was
### disclosed when the .22 box tried to use the gateway.
###
### now we set another trap for our user the next morning:
erbium:/root> tcpdump -i eth0 ether host 0:50:56:95:65:2
tcpdump: listening on eth0
08:13:18.251493 cygnus.mancill.com.1314 >                         \
  silicon.mancill.com.domain: 51522+ (33)
08:13:18.780158 silicon.mancill.com.domain >                      \
  cygnus.mancill.com.1314: 51522* 1/2/2 (153) (DF)

### we'll use this information (the IP address of the culprit)
### to track them down.  If we don't know it already, we can
### do something like firewall them at the router so that they
### will call in a trouble ticket
###
### spend the rest of the morning planning on how to stunt the
### political future of the cygnus' master
```

You can use -w *filename* to perform non-interactive monitoring. This generates less system overhead than redirecting the normal output to a file, and it also gives you more options when you review the file. To do that, you can use -r *filename* and specify options to vary how the output is filtered and displayed. For example, you can log all of the traffic and then use options such as -q, -n, and packet filter expressions during multiple *tcpdump* runs to produce different views of the data.

Learning how to use *tcpdump* is probably half the battle. The other part is learning efficient ways to parse and condense its output into reports and other things consumable by humans. Computers can generate meaningless data extremely quickly. *Perl* is a natural choice, but don't overlook its capable forerunners, *awk* and *sed*. It all depends upon how you look at the problem. There are some very nice example scripts in */usr/share/doc/tcpdump/examples* (which I wish that I had known about before trying to imitate their functionality).

4.5.2 ipgrab

ipgrab is another command line packet sniffer available for Linux based on *libpcap*. IMHO, it is a good example of a program which has not succumbed to creeping featurism.[7] It uses the same filtering mechanism as *tcpdump*. It dumps all of its output to *stdout*, which may be redirected to a file.

---

[7] Earlier distributed versions did not include filtering support.

Usage for *ipgrab*

```
usage: ipgrab [ -bplntm ] [-c cnt] [-i if] [expr]
  [ -c ] [ --count ] Exit after receiving 'count' packets
  [ -i ] [ --interface ] Listen on interface 'interface'
  [ -b ] Make stdout buffered
  [ -p ] Dump packet payloads
  [ -l ] Don't print link-layer headers
  [ -n ] Don't print network-layer headers
  [ -t ] Don't print transport-layer headers
  [ -m ] Minimal output
  [expr] Berkeley packet filter expression (see tcpdump manpage)
```

As you can see, it supports a limited number of options. So why use *ipgrab* instead of *tcpdump*? It is smaller than *tcpdump* and has a uncomplicated command line interface. Its output is also nicely formatted and easy to follow, making it a bit less imposing than *tcpdump*. It does this without sacrificing detail, since it goes to great lengths to *dump every relevant header field possible*, as the author states in the README file that accompanies the package. Mr. Borella goes on to say:

> I expect that this code can be used for detailed packet level debugging of existing or new protocols. Also, I imagine that it could be a useful teaching and instruction tool for TCP/IP or security courses. I've made an effort to make the code readable, sometimes even at the expense of efficiency, so that one can use it to learn about the *pcap* library calls and the header field data structures.

I looked over the source code for *ipgrab*, and it is indeed well-documented and easy to follow. This makes it good reading for those who want to know what is really happening, bit for bit, at every step along the way (i.e., at the link, session, and protocol/transport layers). Instead of being condensed, the output format is designed for human consumption. If you want to grab the latest copy of the sources for *ipgrab*, point your browser at *http://www.xnet.com/~cathmike/MSB/Software/*.

sniffit   *sniffit* is actually a hybrid—it supports a great deal of options on the command-line, making it similar to *tcpdump*, but it also has an *ncurses* interface which runs in a terminal window. According to the documentation, *sniffit* was written "to demonstrate the unsafeness of TCP." *sniffit* does make it easier to look at the packet payloads because by default it stores 300 bytes from the start of each session it sees. It even has a logging mode specifically configured to catch FTP and telnet session passwords. Also of note is that *sniffit* will summarize duplicate information about connections. It supports packet filtering via its configuration file format (man 5 sniffit) and it has support for (application layer) protocol plugins. The package ships with a DNS plugin.

Some people have taken exception to *sniffit*'s built-in support for collecting passwords. As a system administrator, I have to admit that it does not comfort me to think about developers with Linux workstations sniffing passwords off of the network. However, the author's point is well-taken—that many of the TCP/IP protocols, as implemented, offer a false sense of security when they are not implemented alongside physical security and encryption. As is the Linux tradition, the belief is that exposing security holes is healthier in the long run than ignoring them or trying to hide them. Some people have called *sniffit* dangerous and a hacker's tool. They do this because it takes even *less* skill to sniff passwords with *sniffit* than with other packet capture tools. There is little point in this, since any of the comparable tools are capable of the same thing, and the amount of skill required in either case is very little indeed.

One thing that is for certain about *sniffit* is that, although it performs a very similar function, it is completely different code than either *tcpdump* and *ipgrab*, and it takes some getting used to if you normally use *tcpdump*. *Sniffit* does have a filtering mechanism, but it is not the Berkeley packet filter syntax. It supports writing to *stdout* and logging to a file. The naming convention for the output files is *x.x.x.x.p-y.y.y.y.o*, where *x.x.x.x* is the sender's IP address and *p* is the sending port. *y.y.y.y.o* indicates the same for the receiver. So, instead of having one file with all of the traffic in it, the traffic is already separated into each connection.

You may not use *sniffit* as your primary network debugging tool (those @#$% options!), but some of its features would be time-consuming to implement on top of other sniffers, so keep it in mind. Also remember that `sniffit -i` will start the interactive *ncurses* mode which may be sufficient for a low-powered router when you do not want to incur the overhead of the full-blown GUI sniffers we discuss next.

4.5.3 karpski

karpski was the first of the two GUI packet sniffers I encountered, and I was completely blown away. As I previously mentioned, I always felt that *tcpdump* was a victory for Linux. *karpski* takes it to the next level. As soon as you enable monitoring with the **Start** button on the lower left corner of the screen, you will see that packets start to appear. If you see something that interests you, you can highlight it and then select **Watch** (or hit **w**—there are keyboard shortcuts for all of the buttons), which will follow that specific stream. You can limit the protocols being monitored in the **Config** → **Configure Protocols** menu to select which protocols should be monitored. The protocol list appears to be very complete. You can select a MAC address and then monitor all connections to and from it. You can also select a stream and follow it, as well as save results. The packets in the stream are displayed in great detail, similar to the output of *ipgrab*. *karpski* seems to be for interactive active monitoring. It throws lots of windows.

See *http://mojo.calyx.net/ btx/karpski.html* for more information about *karpski*, or load the Debian package **karpski**. It does have a capture-only mode which can be configured in the */usr/share/karpski/datfiles/capture_filters.dat* (which seemed a bit buggy at the time of writing).

4.5.4 ethereal

ethereal is a little different than *karpski*, but to me, even more impressive. That might have to do with my tastes—the two sniffers are different approaches to the same task. *ethereal* states to be an interactive sniffer, which I interpreted to mean a sniffer that displays data in real-time, the way *karpski* does. However, for *ethereal*, this must mean interactive packet analysis, which is the first big difference between the two.

To start monitoring with *ethereal*, you toggle the capture function via the menu section **Tools** → **Capture**. This will present you with a dialog box where you can select the interface and, if you would like, a filter. The filters use the same syntax as a *tcpdump* **expression**, and you can name a filter and save it, so that you can recall it during other sessions. You may also specify the number of packets you would like to collect. Once the sniffer is in capture mode, a window pops up and displays protocol statistics for the data being captured. This window has a **Stop** button that you can use to toggle off the capture. During the capture, the capture dialog box will not refresh until some data which matched my filter made their way through the sniffer. The same was true for the main windows. As soon as something has been captured, you can **Stop** the capture in the capture dialog. At this point (again), everything seems to hang. This turns out to be the time during which *ethereal* is resolving hostnames. Once the capture has stopped, the packets will be displayed in the upper section of the main window. When you highlight a packet in this section of the main window, you will notice that the middle section changes to reflect the type of packet, and the bottom section displays the data in the packet in raw hex and in ASCII. Here is where things get very neat.

The middle portion of the window presents detailed information about the packets and protocols via expanding hierarchical lists. As you travel down the middle section, which contains the list of header flags for each of the layers in the hierarchical format described earlier in this section, you can explore each of the layers by expanding and collapsing the headers. When you click on an item in the list, you view its value. For things like flags which are part of a bitmap, you will see the value of the flagword, and then when you click on that, you'll see the status of each of the bits in the flag. The top-level choices for a TCP packet are:

```
+ Frame (# of bytes on wire, # of bytes captures)

+ Ethernet II

+ Internet Protocol

+ Transmission Protocol
```

You will notice that when you highlight one of these, the corresponding portion of the packet (in the bottom section) is boldface so that you can see which bytes correspond to which layer. When you expand one of the protocols in the middle section, you will notice that selecting the individual header fields within that protocol highlights the exact bytes which represent that field in the packet. Very cool!

Another cool feature is the ability to select a packet in the upper portion of the window and then pull down the Tools menu and select `Follow TCP stream`. This will walk the TCP stream from start to finish, stripping away headers and protocol information, and present just the data payloads in a dialog box. Say goodbye to any unencrypted passwords you may use. *Anybody* could use this to sniff a password... (However, that's not what makes the feature cool.)

The only complaint I had about *ethereal* was the inability to switch off DNS lookups for the IP packets being captured. I was testing connections that did not have good (reverse) DNS lookups, and there was an annoying pause after the data capture and before it was displayed, as I mentioned earlier. I had started up *ethereal* and was looking under the **Edit** → **Options** menu to change the setting. As it turns out, there is a command-line switch (duh. . . -n, just like for every other networking command) that handles this. I should have RTFM first. If you cannot load the Debian package (called, appropriately enough, **ethereal**), then visit *http://ethereal.zing.org* to hunt for sources and binaries. You won't be sorry you did.

Before we conclude the section on packet sniffers, there is one point I would like to make about the nice GUI sniffers and your routers. Sniffers are a natural fit for laptops, because often you would like to go to the area where someone is reporting the trouble (e.g., like the duplicate IP address for the gateway example presented with *tcpdump*). This way, you can plug the sniffer into the same hub where the problem exists to get an idea of what is happening. However, for environments with switches instead of hubs, many times you will want (or need) to run the sniffer directly on the router itself to obtain the information you require. This can place extra load on the router, especially if you use one of the GUI sniffers. Just to give you an idea, I've listed the memory footprints of the sniffers covered in this chapter in Table 4.3. The values listed there do not include the data from the packet capture, which for the command-line sniffers is a small amount (because it passes right through), but can be significant for a GUI-based sniffer. This is not to say that you cannot run these sniffers on your routers, but do not leave them running all of the time, perhaps causing your router to swap. There are alternatives. *ethereal* allows writing to files (it's a command-line switch; read the manpage), and you can perform your monitoring on the router and then run the GUI on another workstation. Another option, if you have the resources, is to purchase a switch with a monitoring port and perform your monitoring from a central monitoring station. (Maybe it will be the same workstation you configure MRTG on in Section 5.5.)

Table 4.3 Packet Sniffer Memory Requirements

packet sniffer	size (in kB)
tcpdump	412
sniffit	620
ipgrab	628
sniffit -i	1088
karpski	1820
ethereal	2504

4.6 SUMMARY

So now we have a Linux router taking care of the LAN and dial-up connections to external networks. We can generate statistics about the amount of traffic sent using IP accounting, and view the contents of that traffic with packet capture tools like the sniffers mentioned in this chapter. We can also use private IP addresses to talk to public networks by means of IP masquerading. The next step is a general purpose WAN router, which is the topic of Chapter 5. This router can be used to connect our network to others (public or private) over high-bandwidth connections and traversing long distances.

Zinc—A Frame Relay Router

$\mathbf{Z}$inc has been up and routing IP over Frame Relay since late 1996, and has proven itself a "bread-and-butter" production Linux application. The heart of the router is a S508 router card manufactured and sold by Sangoma Technologies, Inc. This card, a 90MHz Pentium-based PC with 16MB of RAM,[1] plus a little Linux-kernel *glue* make an excellent low-cost Frame Relay router—one which is easy to administer, even for the first-time WAN administrator, yet offers the flexibility of a general-purpose platform. Zinc's configuration should give you a good basis for building your own Frame Relay router.

Before we dive into building our Frame Relay router, we first cover some Frame Relay concepts for those of you who have not worked with it before, followed by a short introduction to the S508 card and other WAN adapters available for Linux. The bulk of the chapter discusses configuring a Frame Relay router using *WANPIPE*, the software drivers and toolkit that accompany the Sangoma cards, and trouble-shooting using this software. Related topics covered at the end of the chapter include using *MRTG* monitor link performance and running *WANPIPE* in conjunction with *LRP*.

5.1 FRAME RELAY BASICS—DLCIs, PVCs, AND CIRs

Frame Relay for the WAN admin is pretty simple stuff, once you get the hang of it. The only confusing part is getting a handle on the terminology and understanding the different layers which make up a link. Essentially, you are dealing with an easy-to-configure version of PPP (although it's more complicated for network providers and other more complex topologies). First, let us define some terms (some of which are a review of Section 2.3.1); these terms are put to use in Figure 5.1.

---

[1] Actually, zinc ran fine on a 486/66 with 8MB for almost two years.

Figure 5.1 Frame Relay Terms

access—This refers to the digital telco circuit that runs between your location and your Frame Relay provider's nearest **POP**. Access is also known as the **local loop**.

POP—Point Of Presence means any sort of network service provider (not just Frame Relay) facility which is available for you to connect to its network. This connection is your **access**.

port—This card or port on your provider's switch that is connected to your router via your **access**. Ports have speeds associated with them, indicating the maximum speed at which your provider's switch will accept packets from you. Note that the port speed does not always coincide with access speed.

DLCI—Data Link Connection Identifier is the address used to specify the endpoint of a PVC (which corresponds to one of your **nodes**). This address is single integer and is used by your router to indicate which of potentially several different PVCs configured at your provider's switch is the correct recipient of the frame. (Note that you still need DLCIs, even if you have a single PVC in your network.) The DLCI should be a value between 16 and 1023. Many providers will allow you to request the DLCIs you would like to use for your network.

CPE—Customer Premises Equipment is a term for your router.

node—This is another term that refers to your router. A Frame Relay node typically has a single DLCI associated with it. Of these, **CPE** is probably better terminology, since your provider may use **node** to refer to network entities other than your router.[2]

PVC—Permanent Virtual Circuit is a path between two nodes on the network, set up by the provider so that they can talk to each other. (Actually, how the packets are routed through the provider's network is not known to you, but the PVC gives the illusion that the two nodes are directly connected to each

---

[2] Although I frequently use the term **node** for my routers, and do so throughout this chapter.

other.) From your vantage-point, a PVC can be thought of as a network pipe running between two **DLCI**s. PVCs are not directional, nor are they strictly associated with bandwidth, although many like to talk about the "speed of the PVC"—they should be talking about the CIR associated with that PVC.

CIR—Committed Information Rate (expressed in bits per second) is the maximum rate at which your provider guarantees that you can transmit packets over your PVC without any packet loss. (Actually, this guarantee is often a "best efforts" type of service.) **CIR**s, unlike **PVC**s, *are* directional, which means that the guaranteed bandwidth from router$_A$ to router$_B$ does not have to equal the guaranteed flow in the reverse direction. Not all providers allow you to specify this sort of **asymmetrical CIR** for a PVC. If they are available, they are a good way to save costs while still providing adequate bandwidth for your application.

LMI—Local Management Interface is the method by which Frame Relay routers keep each other notified regarding the status of the network. This involves the exchange of status messages between your node and the router at the POP. These messages may be one of three different standards: **LMI**, **ANSI** (also known as **Annex D**), and **Q.933** (also known as **Annex A**).

NNI—Network to Network Interface is a term used by providers when they connect two disparate networks. This enables them to provide a PVC between routers located on different Frame Relay networks. (If you need a PVC between one of your nodes and a business partner who uses a different provider, ask your provider if he/she has an **NNI** with the other provider.)

5.1.1 Frame Relay Bandwidth

One thing that confuses first-time Frame Relay administrators is the question, *How much bandwidth do I have?* The question is important because ordering Frame Relay services can get complicated (and expensive), and you want to know what to expect. There are different parameters in a Frame Relay network which dictate the end-to-end bandwidth. Some scenarios which affect this bandwidth are:

1. You may be saving telco costs by multiplexing applications on a single piece of digital access. In this case, your access is necessarily larger than your port.

2. If access is inexpensive, you may choose a port smaller than your access to avoid paying for a port which fills up the access.

3. Once your data enter your provider's network, they become subject to the CIRs you have selected for your PVCs. Different providers may enforce the CIR upon ingress (entering the network) or egress (exiting the network). Still others never enforce the CIR at all, in which case link speed equates to the lower of the two associated port speeds.

4. You may have different port sizes at each end of a PVC, which limits through-put to the lesser of the two. (However, depending upon how your provider's

network performs buffering, you might not notice this limitation until the differences in port speed are pronounced.)

5. Some nodes in your network might be **oversubscribed**, a situation where the sum of the ports attached to a node via PVCs exceeds the port speed at this node. If you are oversubscribed, and all of the nodes on the other ends of your PVCs burst (send data at their full port speed) to you simultaneously, things may slow down and/or get lost.

In the case of a simple two-node network, your average throughput in a given direction will be the smallest value found between points A and B. Figure 5.2 illustrates this. Note, however, that this is the **guaranteed rate**. The **burst rate**, the maximum speed at which an interface can transmit data, is equal to the port speed for that interface. The **burst throughput** for a PVC, assuming that your provider does not enforce the CIRs, is the lesser of the two port speeds for that PVC.

Figure 5.2 Frame Relay Bandwidth

Exceeding Your CIR   When you exceed your CIR, the ugly truth is that your provider may discard some of your packets. Whether or not it does so is determined as follows. The upstream switch (at your provider's POP) continuously monitors how much bandwidth you are using. If you exceed your CIR, the packets are marked by setting a bit in the packet header. If any other node in the cloud is heavily congested, it can discard packets with this bit set. So, while exceeding your CIR can squeeze more bandwidth out of your link for a lower cost, doing so also puts you at risk for packet loss. Of course, TCP-based applications will notice the missing packet and correct the situation, but at the expense of retransmitting the packet, which wastes time and bandwidth. The situation can be particularly bad for geographically remote locations which already experience high packet latency. If you habitually exceed your CIR, your provider may request or force you to increase the CIR for which you are subscribed.

5.1.2 Reviewing Frame Relay Concepts

Let's review what we've covered so far and add a few finishing details.

- Each **node** is connected via a piece of **access** to a **port** at your provider's **POP**. Your *node* is a **CPE** router.

- A **node** (or **CPE**) is designated by its **DLCI**, which is an integer used as an address.

- A **PVC** builds a path through your provider's network (the **cloud**) between two **nodes**.
- A **PVC** has a **CIR** associated with it. **CIR**s may be used to discard data being sent over the **PVC** when it exceeds predefined bandwidth limitations.
- **CIR**s are directional. If your provider indicates that they are not, ask whether a 64kbps **CIR** is 64kbps in *each* direction, or 32kbps in each direction. Different providers sell bandwidth differently.
- A **PVC** with the same **CIR** in each direction is said to have a **symmetrical CIR**. An **asymmetrical CIR** has a different data rate in each direction. This can be useful for sites which pull more traffic than they push, as is the case for sites which do a lot of Internet browsing.
- A node can **burst** at the **port speed**.
- A node is **oversubscribed** if it cannot satisfy the potential bandwidth requirements of the nodes attached to it.

For those of you who would like to know more about Frame Relay, there are numerous tutorials available on the Web. As a starting point, visit *http://www.frforum.com/*. This is the home of *Frame Relay Forum*, an association of assorted commercial members who have an interest in promoting Frame Relay. They have a document for download called *The Basic Guide to Frame Relay Networking*. The 86-page document of general information is a bit cutesy, but useful nonetheless.

5.2 LINUX WAN ADAPTERS

For our purposes, a **WAN adapter** is an add-on card that is essentially the equivalent of an "async" port on a traditional router. These cards support WAN protocols such as Frame Relay, synchronous PPP, X.25, Bisync, HSSI, and others. They typically have their own processor to run the link-layer protocol on the card. This offloads this task from your system's CPU and simplifies the device drivers needed. When the card has a decoded frame available for the operating system, it triggers it via an interrupt and passes it to the device driver in the same way that an Ethernet card would. These WAN adapters connect to the outside world through a high-speed serial port (usually V.35 or RS–232), suitable to connecting a CSU/DSU and then to a digital telco access circuit. Some cards are available with an integrated CSU/DSU so that they can be connected directly to a digital access circuit. The cards available now have between one and four ports and support speeds from 56kbps to 52Mbps.

Interfaces of this type offer several advantages over a simple data pump or modem. The first I've already mentioned: Since the link-layer protocol is being executed on the card itself, the host processor is free to do other things. (Because of this, zinc was able to handle a T1 running Frame Relay on a 66Mhz 486-based system.) Second, the code run by the card's processor (the adapter's firmware) is stored on a EEPROM or similar device which is downloaded to the card when it is initialized. The upswing of this is that the link-layer protocol can be changed or upgraded simply by re-initializing the adapter with new firmware (and take effect without ever rebooting the router). Finally, in an emergency, almost anything can host these adapters, even your workstation.

This section lists manufacturers of cards who have Linux driver support (at the time of writing). Of these, I only have experience with the Sangoma products. When you start research to the card for your application, use these manufacturers as a starting point; they have solid reputations for providing Linux solutions.

5.2.1 Sangoma—the S508 and S514

Sangoma offers two WAN interface cards: the PCI-based S514 and its ISA-based predecessor, the S508. Currently, there is protocol support for running IP over Frame Relay, PPP, X.25 and Cisco HDLC. In the event that you do not want to be hindered by the limitations of TCP/IP, you can use the Bisync and HDLC LAPB API interfaces to develop your own protocol specific to your application. All of these protocols and cards are supported by their freely-available *WANPIPE* software. As I mentioned, I have been a longtime user of Sangoma cards, and enjoyed working with them so much that I took over the Debian package of their driver utility software (called **wanpipe**). A brief rundown of the cards follows. For more information, visit *http://www.sangoma.com*.

- The S508 comes with two ports: a high-speed (up to E1 speeds, 2Mbps) port, and a second port which can run CHDLC (only) at up to 256kbps. The high-speed port uses a DB–25 connector and a special cable to connect it to RS–232, V.35, EIA530, or X.21 external devices. The low-speed port uses a DB–9 to connect to a RS–232 device. Internally, the card connects to a 16-bit ISA bus.
- The S5141 is the single CPU version of the S514. Like the S508, it is a dual port card. In this case, the high-speed port can handle link speeds up to 4Mbps, while the second port is limited to 512kbps.
- The S5142 is a quad-port, dual CPU version of the S514. It is equivalent to two S5141 cards (i.e., two high-speed ports and two low-speed ports), but occupies a single slot.
- The S514/FT1 and S508/FT1 are variants of their respective cards with an integrated fractional T1 CSU/DSU. These cards come with a single port which connects to the digital access directly.

HINT: INTEGRATED CSU/DSUs SAVE MONEY, SPACE, AND TIME

You should consider cards with integrated CSU/DSUs when ordering your router cards. The additional cost is less than the least expensive external CSU/DSU on the market. Because the integrated card connects directly to the demarc provided with your leased-line, your installation is neater—fewer boxes, fewer cables, fewer power outlets. This allows for a tidy rack-mounted installation.

5.2.2 ImageStream

ImageStream Internet Solutions offers SDL Communications' adapters in combination with their Linux drivers. They also offer Linux-based routers, firewalls, and servers outfitted with these adapters. These systems run ImageStream's own Linux distribution (*Enterprise Linux*) which includes a full set of standard server daemons, including dynamic routing support for RIP2, OSPF and BGP4. Linux standards such as IP masquerading and firewalling are, of course, accessible. All of their *All-in-One* offerings include redundant RAID disk configurations and some are equipped with hot-pluggable components.

If you would rather build your own router, you can choose from a variety of adapters they offer, ranging from an ISA model with a single 2Mbps port up to PCI adapters with (eight) 8Mbps ports and dual-port HSSI capable cards (52Mpbs per port). If space is an issue, they have another line of 3U format CompactPCI adapters. Most cards are available with integrated CSU/DSUs.

All cards support the following protocols: PPP, HDLC, Frame Relay, X.25, and raw IP. Electrical interfaces are V.35, RS232, RS422 (EIA530 or X.21), and HSSI or T1 or DDS CSU/DSU (as appropriate). X.21 will be a welcome sight if your plans include deployment in areas other than the United States. You can visit ImageStream at *http://www.imagestream-is.com/*.

5.2.3 Gcom

Gcom, Inc. offers an add-on card for ISA and PCI architectures supporting up to four ports. In addition to Linux, they support several other commercial x86 Unix flavors. They also have some heavy-duty protocol support for those who need to interface systems using link protocols other than Frame Relay or PPP. Taken from their website, they support:

- Frame Relay, X.25, and SDLC/HDLC
- SNA LU0, LU2, LU4, LU6.2 over SDLC or QLLC/X.25
- LAPB, LAPD, and LLC
- Available upon request are Bisync and X.3, X.28, X.29 PAD protocols

In addition to producing these boards and driver software, they champion and host the Linux implementation of STREAMS, known as *LiS*. This source is primarily released under the LGPL (the less restrictive library version of the GNU Public License). (Cool!) It is implemented as a Linux kernel module, with drivers for use above or below the IP stack—i.e., it can either use an existing device driver and present a DLPI interface to another STREAMS driver (above the IP stack), or it can interface a STREAMS device driver to the IP stack (below). (Very cool!) For more information on their boards, protocol support, or *LiS*, visit Gcom's website at *http://www.gcom.com/*.

5.2.4 Emerging Technologies

Emerging Technologies produces PCI adapters and drivers and bandwidth management software for Linux and FreeBSD. Like so many others, they have the good taste to release their driver source to the public. Their products include:

- The ET/PCISYNC, a PCI interface card which supports up to four T1 ports running PPP, Frame Relay, or Cisco HDLC.

- The ET/HSSI, also a PCI card which can support two 52Mbps HSSI links on a single card.

- If you would like a complete routers solution, you can purchase one of their ET/R1000 or ET/R1500 systems. These use the cards mentioned above and come preconfigured to dual-boot Linux and FreeBSD.

- They also offer *ET/BWMGR*, their *Bandwidth Manager* software, used to throttle bandwidth used by addresses or interfaces. The software is provided free-of-charge for those who purchase one of the synchronous adapters or pre-packaged solutions, but potentially has applications beyond those in conjunction with their cards.

You can contact them at *http://www.etinc.com/*. As a side note, their Linux routers run *Zebra*, a dynamic routing daemon, which is introduced in Section 8.4.2 in Chapter 8.

ROUTER PHYSICAL INSTALLATION

Once you have your router loaded with a basic Linux install and have installed your interface card(s), you need to find a good place to put it. Physical installation is often a secondary thought, but is important with WAN routers for a few reasons.

- If you have an integrated CSU/DSU, you should be within 40 meters (133 feet) of the demarc installed by your access provider—less if they installed a smartjack which is run over twisted-pair to somewhere else in the building. If you cannot be within this distance, you will need to program your CSU/DSU to compensate for the drop in signal strength (attenuation) due to the distance. This setting is known as **LBO**, Line Build Out.

- If you have an external CSU/DSU, take into consideration the length of the V.35 cables that run between the CSU/DSU and the router. If possible, make sure that you can move the PC without having to reposition the CSU/DSU. (Otherwise, you might find yourself there late at night trying to hold three things at once.)

- Most technicians value "function over form," as do I, but a neat installation is worthwhile. If you ever have problems with your access circuit, you might receive a visit from your local access provider. An accessible, clean installation will make it easier for these people to test the circuit and minimize the chance that they trip over that dangling wire you have been meaning to clean up.

5.3 LINUX AND *WANPIPE* FOR FRAME RELAY

In this section, we build a Frame Relay router using Linux, a Sangoma S508, and Sangoma's *WANPIPE*[3] software. We will assume that the link has been ordered and correctly provisioned by our Frame Relay provider, and that the link on the other side is up and running, waiting for our router to come online and complete the project. (If this is not the case, configuring two Linux routers for Frame Relay is not any more difficult than configuring the first one.) The first time through the configuration is presented as a quickstart. For those who are experienced with Linux and Frame Relay, this should be enough to attach to the cloud and start routing. The sections following the quickstart cover the configuration in more detail, and Section 5.3.3 explains *WANPIPE's* main configuration file line by line.

5.3.1 Frame Relay Router Quickstarts

Here are two recipes for zinc. The first uses Sangoma's *WANPIPE* software as it is distributed from their site and is suitable for all Linux distributions. The second is for Debian users and takes advantage of the **wanpipe** package, a pre-compiled version of the *WANPIPE* software with some path modifications to make it compliant with Debian's filesystem layout. Both versions result in identical functionality.

WANPIPE Quickstart

1. Retrieve the latest *WANPIPE* tarball from *ftp://ftp.sangoma.com/linux/* and extract it in the root directory of your filesystem.
2. Execute the script */usr/lib/wanrouter/Setup*. This script guides you through setting up a default configuration file for your protocol (Frame Relay), installs the kernel patches, and builds the binary tools, if it can.
3. Compile the kernel, selecting the following options in addition to whatever you need to support your NIC and other essential devices.

```
Network options --->
    [*] IP: forwarding/gatewaying
    <M> WAN router
Network Device support --->
   WAN Interfaces --->
        [*] WAN drivers
        <M> Sangoma WANPIPE(tm) multiprotocol cards
        [*] WANPIPE Frame Relay support
```

After you've built the new kernel, reboot. If you received any warnings during the build of the binary tools, execute this phase of the *Setup* again with `/usr/lib/wanrouter/Setup c`.

4. Open up */etc/wanpipe1.conf* with your favorite text editor and edit the `[interfaces]` section to correspond to your PVCs, and the `[wanpipe1]` to match your card and the physical parameters of your link.

---

[3] *WANPIPE*™ is a trademark of Sangoma Technologies, Inc.

5. Run */usr/lib/wanrouter/Configure* to set up IP addresses for your WAN interface(s)—one for each PVC connected to this node.

6. Start your link with `/usr/sbin/wanrouter start`. Add routes as appropriate.

You can check the progress of the startup by looking at the output in */var/log/wanrouter* and */var/log/messages*. You should also be able to `ifconfig wan_interface` to see that your interface is up.

Debian wanpipe Quickstart

1. Load the Debian GNU/Linux package **wanpipe**.

2. Read the release notes in */usr/share/doc/wanpipe/README.debian*; these cover differences between the Sangoma distributed package and the Debian package.

3. Change directory to */usr/share/doc/wanpipe/examples/* and *zcat* one of the compressed *wanpipe1.fr* files to */etc/wanpipe/wanpipe1.conf*.

4. Edit this file for the parameters applicable to your link.

5. Use the */usr/sbin/wanpipeconfig* script to set up your interface files.

6. Reload the new configuration with `/etc/init.d/wanpipe reload`. Check that the link is up, and add routes as needed.

Checking the status of your **wanpipe** link under Debian is largely similar to that with other distributions—only the pathnames for the logfiles have changed. The logfile produced at startup is stored in */var/log/wanpipe.log*; the rest is still logged via *syslog* (probably into */var/log/messages*).

For either package, if your link did not come up immediately and the logfiles do not indicate the problem, you can use *fpipemon* to glean loads of information about the link and what might be wrong (see Section 5.4.3 for more details about using this command). If you're still not up and running, read over the next few sections, especially the detailed configuration information starting with Section 5.3.3, to see if you can spot the problem.

5.3.2 *WANPIPE*, the Linux Kernel, and Debian

You surely noticed the differences between Sangoma's *WANPIPE* and Debian's **wanpipe** in the previous section. As the maintainer of **wanpipe**, I constantly struggle with the trade-offs in trying to strike a balance between maintaining consistency in the Debian version while keeping up with the changes in Sangoma's version. How this came to be warrants an explanation, since it seems as if it's more work for everyone to keep the differences straight. The short answer is that Sangoma's package targets a broad audience of users who run every flavor of Linux out there. In contrast, the Debian package tries to make things easier for the Debian user, as well as conform to Debian guidelines for filesystem layout.

WANPIPE and Kernel Development   During the heyday of the 1.2 and 2.0 kernels, there was a lot more fluctuation in the kernel, and less coordination between the driver authors and the kernel authors/maintainers. When a new patch level of the kernel was released, Sangoma had to test their drivers, make any necessary changes, and release a new set of patches. Because of this, *WANPIPE* was (and still is) distributed including a set of kernel patches and the source code for the utilities (which would need to be compiled by the end-user against their specific version of the kernel).

The direction going forward is to have the patches already integrated into the kernel source so that the drivers can be enabled by simply selecting them during the kernel configuration. (This effort began with the 2.2.x kernel.) During evolution of 2.2.x, there were still releases of Sangoma's code newer than the versions in the upstream kernel source, so there was still a need to distribute patches. As of kernel version 2.2.14, the kernel and Sangoma are in sync. Furthermore, this kernel version became the release candidate for Debian 2.2. *Voilá!* A version of pristine kernel source that will be widely distributed along with a matching set of *WANPIPE* binaries. This gives Debian (and others) the opportunity to offer "out-of-the-box" WAN router support—no compilers or kernel builds required.

Whether or not all of this remains in sync is yet to be seen.[4] The implication is that you may need to check the Sangoma FTP site periodically for new patches that might not be in the upstream kernel. There is even the outside chance that you will have to rebuild the utilities so that they interoperate with the new driver code.

Configuring the 2.2.x Kernel for WANPIPE   Should you have to build a kernel with *WANPIPE* support, configure the kernel with the options listed below. Note that the kernel build scripts will allow you to build the drivers directly into the kernel (i.e., not as modules). Don't do this—the drivers must be modules.

```
Code maturity level options --->
    [*] Prompt for development and/or incomplete code/drivers
Networking options --->
    [*] TCP/IP networking
    [*] IP: advanced router
    <M> WAN router
Network device support --->
    Wan interfaces --->
        [*] WAN drivers
        <M> Sangoma WANPIPE(tm) multiprotocol cards
        (1)    Maximum number of cards
        [ ]    WANPIPE X.25 support
        [*]    WANPIPE Frame Relay support
        [ ]    WANPIPE PPP support
        [ ]    WANPIPE Cisco HDLC support
Filesystems --->
    [*] /proc filesystem support
```

---

[4] Thanks go to Alan Cox for his efforts in this matter.

The Debian wanpipe Package   A few years back, the *WANPIPE* software installed itself as "router," which was a bit too generic and caused some confusion and namespace collisions. Therefore, the Debian package used the name "wanpipe" in place of "router." Now *WANPIPE* likes to call things "wanrouter," but having already gone a long way down the road with **wanpipe**, the Debian package will stick to that name. Aside from trying to shield the user from file changes, the Debian package has the following features:

- It does not require the user to compile the utility programs; they come precompiled for the release kernel. Modular support for *WANPIPE* is in the release kernel. Result: A router needs neither the kernel source nor a compiler.

- Filename consistency—it places all of the configuration files in */etc/wanpipe/*, renames the configuration script */usr/sbin/wanpipeconfig*, renames the startup/shutdown script */etc/init.d/wanpipe*, and places the documentation in */usr/share/doc/wanpipe/*.

- It may provide additional functionality, such as inclusion of the pipemon wrapper script (needed until *WANPIPE* 2.1 was released to monitor a link by its device name) and monitoring and routing hooks into the startup sequence.

If you are running the current stable release of Debian, you have the version from the time that release of Debian was *frozen*.[5] Because upstream (Sangoma) changes are frequent and various improvements are made between major releases of Debian, often there are significant updates which are not available as part of the stable Debian release. There are two different ways to obtain these. First, you can go the Debian homepage and search for newer versions of **wanpipe** in the unstable release. Second, you can get the latest copy from *http://pongo.mancill.com/wanpipe*. Because all of the Debian source is freely available, you can also build a package for an older (or newer) version of Debian, or some other Linux flavor.

5.3.3 Editing *wanpipe1.conf* for Frame Relay

Once you install the Sangoma card, build your system, be it Debian or not, and load the software, you need to configure it to correspond to the settings for your Frame Relay link. The main configuration file is *wanpipeN.conf*, where N is the nth Sangoma card in your system. For our purposes (a single card), this is *wanpipe1.conf*. (If you are familiar with *WANPIPE*, this file was named *router.conf* until the 2.1 release.) On a Debian system, this file is located in the */etc/wanpipe/* directory (samples are in */usr/share/wanpipe/examples*; for non-Debian systems, the file is in */etc/*; samples are in */usr/lib/wanrouter/samples*). The file controls:

- Physical parameters about the Sangoma card, such as the type of interface to the CSU/DSU, the baudrate of the port, and the interrupt of the card.

---

[5] The *frozen* state of the release cycle indicates that the only additional changes which may occur for that release are bug/security fixes.

- The firmware (and therefore the WAN link-layer protocol) to run on the card.
- The name(s) of the interface(s) to be created by the kernel to correspond to the link(s) configured for this card. *wan0,wan1*, and so on. . . .
- Special parameters about those interfaces. For example, do they allow multicast? Should they try to adhere to a provider's CIR?

wanpipe1.conf's Structure   The file might seem a little imposing at first, but it is well commented and easy to follow once you understand the different sections. The format is very similar to a *.ini* file used on other operating systems. The sections are denoted by keywords enclosed in [ ]s. Comments start with the # character and continue to the end of the line.

The file has a hierarchy to it. The two main sections are [devices] and [interfaces]. Both of these sections must appear, and each contains one line for each device or interface you would like to configure, respectively. For each line (i.e., device or interface) in these two sections, there will be a subsection later in the file denoted by the *name* of the device or interface. A brief example of the format should make this clear. In the mock *wanpipe1.conf* file below, there is one **device** and two **interfaces**.

```
[devices]
# this machine contains one device/physical card, wanpipe1
wanpipe1
:

[interfaces]
# there are two interfaces
wan0
wan1

[wanpipe1]
# configuration settings for the physical device wanpipe1
:

[wan0]
# settings for the interface wan0
:

[wan1]
# settings for the interface wan1
:
```

wanpipe1.conf—[devices]   A **device** in this case refers to a physical Sangoma card. That is, the number entries in the [device] section will correspond to the number of S508 cards in your system. (Starting with *WANPIPE* version 2.1, you no longer configure more than one device in this file, but the syntax remains the same.)

If you have multiple cards, you must name the cards (and configuration files) wanpipe*N*, where ($1 \le N \le 8$), and you must number these **consecutively!** On the device line, you also specify the protocol that the card will be running. You may optionally include a comment which will appear in your system logfiles during startup and shutdown. For a system running Frame Relay, the [devices] section looks like:

```
# start the [devices] section
[devices]
wanpipe1 = WAN_FR, myframecircuit - cktid MCI ZAW828360001, DLCI 100
# end [devices]
```

***wanpipe1.conf—*[interfaces]** An **interface** refers to the entity used by the kernel to communicate over the link. This can be a source of confusion, as many people commonly refer to these as **devices**. Just remember that an interface is an entity similar to *eth0*—it can support routes, have different subnet masks, etc.

A single Frame Relay device (or **port**) may have multiple PVCs configured in the provider's network. On your router, each of these PVCs is an **interface** in *wanpipe1.conf.* These interfaces behave like PPP interfaces, except that you address the remote endpoint by specifying the corresponding DLCI in the configuration file. (They are addressed by IP with respect to the rest of the operating system.) For a location with two PVCs, the [interfaces] section looks like this:

```
# wanpipe1.conf for location A
#
# start the [interfaces] section
[interfaces]
#intf = device,   DLCI, WANPIPE, comment
#----   ------    ----  -------  -----------------------------
wan0  = wanpipe1, 200,  WANPIPE, location A <-> location B PVC
wan1  = wanpipe1, 300,  WANPIPE, location A <-> location C PVC
# end [interfaces]
```

In the above file, frames addressed to DLCI 200 will be routed by the Frame Relay switch to location B, while frames addressed to DLCI 300 will go to location C. When the link is up and *WANPIPE* is running, you add routes to location B via interface *wan0*, and routes to location C via interface *wan1*.

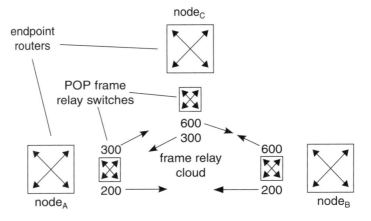

Figure 5.3 A Potentially Confusing Way to Allocate DLCIs

WHOSE **DLCI** IS IT, ANYWAY?

The preceding example configuration indicates that location A needs to address frames to DLCI 200 to get them to location B. From the information given, we cannot tell what the locations B and C will have in their configuration files to send frames to location A. Perhaps they both "call" location A DLCI 100, maybe not. This is because DLCIs only have *local* significance—i.e., your router only sees the DLCIs presented to it by the provider's switch at your POP.

This means the DLCI only has meaning for your router and the switch at your provider's POP, and *not* that DLCI 200 is the "address of the node at location B" in any absolute sense. The concept is simple, but the implications can be confusing. For example, your provider could quite easily setup the switch at location B to use DLCI 200 to refer to the PVC that transmits frames to location A. In this case, both configuration files would list DLCI 200 as the media address to access the remote site. This situation is depicted in Figure 5.3, where site B accesses site C via 600, and site C accesses site B via 600. But site A accesses site B via 200, and vice versa. To make things even more confusing, site A accesses site C via 300.

For this reason, I request that my provider supply a unique DLCI for each router, but to reuse the same DLCI for routers that have more than one PVC. In other words, the switches at locations B and C both refer to location A by the same DLCI. This, in essence, gives each router its own DLCI (or address), and is an intuitive way to approach the matter. (See Figure 5.4.) Now, no matter what node you configure to talk to location A, it uses the same DLCI to get there.

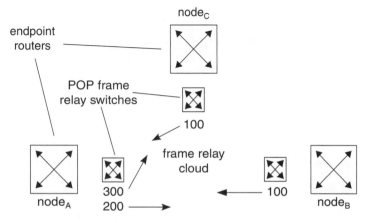

Figure 5.4   A More Intuitive Way to Allocate DLCIs

The [wanpipe1] Device Configuration   Ok, both the top-level sections in *wan-pipe1.conf* are complete. But remember that there is a subsection for every named **device** which details the physical attributes of the Sangoma card and other characteristics of the link which are applicable to the link/port as a whole. An example for a 512kb Frame Relay link on a Sangoma S508 connected to a CSU/DSU with a V.35 follows:

```
[wanpipe1]   ###### Sample Frame Relay Configuration ########
             ### ----- Hardware configuration ------------###
IOPort       = 0x360    # I/O port base                  (S508 only)
IRQ          = 12       # interrupt request level         (S508 only)
#S514CPU     = A        # S514 PCI Card CPU: A or B       (S514 only)
#PCISlot     = 0        # PCI Slot num: 0 for autodetect (S514 only)
#Memaddr     = 0xD0000  # commented out enables auto memory selection

             ### ----- Adapter firmware for Frame Relay --###
Firmware     = /usr/lib/wanpipe/fr514.sfm

             ### ----- Physical interface configuration --###
Interface    = V35      # physical interface type, RS232/V35
Clocking     = External # Tx/Rx clock source, {External|Internal}
BaudRate     = 512000   # data transfer rate in bps, 1200..20480000

             ### ----- Media-specific configuration ------###
MTU          = 1600     # maximum data transfer unit, bytes
UDPPORT      = 9000     # for UDP management

             ### ----- Protocol specific configuration ---###
Station      = CPE      # station type, {CPE|Node}
Signalling   = ANSI     # In-channel signalling {ANSI|LMI|Q933}
#NUMBER_OF_DLCI = 2     # (for "Node" operation only)
T391         = 10       # Link Integrity Verification Timer
T392         = 15       # Polling Verification Timer
N391         = 6        # Full Status Polling Cycle Counter
N392         = 3        # Error Threshold Counter
N393         = 4        # Monitored Events Counter
TTL          = 0x7F     # Time To Live parameter for UDP packets
```

What does it all mean? Let's define each of the keywords, with the keywords grouped as they are in the configuration file.

Hardware Configuration Portion of *wanpipe1.conf*   These values apply to the adapter itself, and how it will interact with the host computer.

IOPort—This is the base address of the S508 adapter. It must be set using the jumpers on the card, and each card must have a unique address. (The default is 0x360.) Be sure to change the jumper setting on the second and subsequent cards if you have multiple cards. If you suspect an ioport conflict, check */proc/ioports* for ports already in use. This parameter is required, but only for S508 cards.

IRQ—This is the interrupt the card will use to notify the device driver that it needs to be serviced. Whatever you specify here is the interrupt that the card will try to use. A listing of interrupts already taken can be found in */proc/interrupts*. (If you ever receive a `interrupt counter test failed` message in *syslog* related to *WANPIPE*, you have selected an interrupt already in use.) This parameter is also required and is applicable only to S508 cards.

S514CPU—This is the CPU to be used—either A or B—applicable only to S514 cards. Unless you purchased an additional CPU, use A.

PCISlot—This is the PCI slot number of the S514 card. For a router with a single Sangoma card, always use 0. For multiple Sangoma cards, the driver needs to know which of these cards corresponds to this configuration file (this wasn't a problem with the S508 because the jumpers set the base address). Refer to Sangoma's documentation for setting this value. (The process is a little complicated and may soon be changed.)

Firmware—This is the absolute path to the software which will be loaded onto the onboard processor at initialization time. For Debian, these files are in */usr/lib/wanpipe/*. For the Sangoma distribution, they can be found in */usr/lib/wanrouter/wanpipe/*.

Memaddr—This is the value of the (dual) memory port that the device driver uses to access adapter memory. The auto-selection performed during driver initialization works well under Linux, and I have never had to use this parameter.

Physical Interface Configuration Portion of `wanpipe1.conf`   This [wanpipe1] section controls how the adapter talks to the outside world (i.e., the CSU/DSU).

Interface—This must either be RS232 or V35 and is dictated by the type of external CSU/DSU you have. Notice that there is no '.' in V35.

Clocking—This determines whether or not the Sangoma card should generate the clocking signal for the CSU/DSU (Internal clocking). It must be either External or Internal. Typically, the CSU/DSU slaves its clock off of the signal on the access line, so this parameter should always be set to External. (The only time that you might want to change this is if you were in a lab environment testing a back-to-back configuration.)

BaudRate—This value is set to your **port speed** (in bps) provided by your Frame Relay provider and corresponds to the CSU/DSU configuration for the number of channels times 56 or 64kbps. (Remember that this might not be equal to the access speed.) The parameter is required.

Media-Specific Configuration Portion of *wanpipe1.conf*   This section specifies link-layer protocol attributes required for negotiation with the port at your Frame Relay provider. Some of these parameters control how often your router will send/expects status information to/from your provider's equipment. Finally, there are a few additional parameters related to the *fpipemon* monitoring utility. Here is a run-down of what they mean.

MTU—This is the maximum data transfer unit in bytes. It is equivalent to the MTU setting for an Ethernet or other network device.

Station—This is your router's station type. This must be set to CPE (Customer Premise Equipment) unless you are running a back-to-back configuration (without a provider), in which case you set it to Node. It is required.

Signalling—In the Frame Relay world, there are several different types of signalling used to communicate between your router and your provider's equipment at the POP. This value can be ANSI, LMI, or Q933. Your provider should specify the type of signalling you should use when you order your link. When in doubt, try ANSI.

T391 [range 5–30, default is 10]—This is the Link Integrity Verification Timer (in seconds). It asks the question, "How often do we check to see if the link is still good?" It applies only to routers with the Station parameter configured to be CPE.

T392 [range 5–30, default is 15]—This is the Polling Verification Timer (in seconds). It is applicable only to routers with the Station parameter set to Node.

N391 [range 1–255, default is 6]—This is the Full Status Polling Cycle Counter, and it is applicable only to **CPE** routers.

N392 [range 1–10, default is 3]—The Error Threshold Counter is the limit of the number of consecutive Status Enquiry Message exchange failures before the link is marked *inactive*. In other words, it controls how many times we'll let something bad happen before we'll start complaining about it. It is applicable to both **CPE** and **Node** Station types.

N393 [range 1–10, default is 4]—This refers to The Monitored Events Counter. When a network becomes active, you need *N393* successful exchanges of Status Enquiry Messages (keepalives) before the link is considered *active*. Like N392, it is applicable to both **CPE** and **Node** Station types.

NUMBER_OF_DLCI [range 0–100, default is 0]—This is the number of DLCIs on the network. This is not necessary for normal CPE links and should not be used for **CPE** Station types. It is useful only for back-to-back configurations.

UDPPORT [range 1–65534, default is 9000]—This is the UDP port used by the various pipemon programs to talk to the drivers. You should change it only if you have already committed to using port 9000 for some other service. Note that if you do not specify this value, the driver will default to using 0, which is probably not what you want. (It would be more correct to say that the "normal" value is 9000.)

TTL [range 0x01–0xFF, default is 0x7F]—This is the Time To Live parameter for the UDP packets being sent to and from the **UDPPORT** in the previous setting. This is a security feature of *WANPIPE*, as it limits the distance (in network hops) from which you can run the monitoring programs. The lower the TTL, the "closer" you need to be in order to be able to access the monitoring port. If you are too far away, you can send to the monitoring port, but replies will be discarded by the network before they reach you.

Logical Interface Configuration Portion of `wanpipe1.conf` Before you heave a sigh of relief, there is still one more section of the file. Remember that each named `[interface]` requires its own section, delimited by the name of the interface. For our example file, we have interfaces *wan0* and *wan1*.

```
[wan0]
# wan0 interface specific information (Frame Relay)
MULTICAST       = NO         # Multicast Enabled?    (YES/NO)
CIR             = 16         # Committed Information Rate   1 - 512 kbps
BC              = 16         # Committed Burst Size         1 - 512 kbits
BE              = 0          # Excess Burst Size            0 - 512 kbits
INARP           = NO         # Inverse ARP Requests?        (YES/NO)
INARPINTERVAL   = 0          # sec. between inverse ARP requests
                            # Default is 10 sec.
[wan1]
# wan1 interface specific information (Frame Relay)
# (nothing to say, since the parameters settings are optional)
# but do not omit the [wan1] part so the file parses correctly
```

The interface-specific section sets up parameters unique to an individual Frame Relay PVC. These parameters apply to either IP configuration.

CIR [range 1–512, default 16]—This is the Committed Information Rate in kbps. It limits how quickly the interface will transmit data when it has a large amount of data to send. If this parameter is used, **BC** and **BE** must be set also. Otherwise, you should comment out all three lines (**CIR**, **BC**, and **BE**). Because your provider may deal with network congestion by discarding packets which exceed your CIR (see the discussion of CIR on page 128), you may want to use this parameter to throttle transmission at your router to prevent packet loss and retransmission.

BC [range 1–512, default 16]—This is the Committed Burst Size in kbits (do not forget to multiply the kB/sec by 8 to get kbits/sec). This is the number of bits that the interface knows will try to send to the CIR before it starts counting using the next parameter, **BE**. When used, this value is nearly always set to the CIR.

BE [range 0–512, default 0]—This is the Excess Burst Size in kbits (once again, watch your bits and bytes). Once **BC** kbits have been sent to the **CIR**, your interface will try to sneak in many more kbits before throttling itself to honor the **CIR**.

MULTICAST [YES or NO, default is NO]—This indicates whether or not to accept packets with a multicast source address. Setting this to **YES** indicates that you allow multicast on your WAN.

INARP [YES or NO, default is NO]—Should this interface periodically send INverse ARP requests? The purpose of inverse ARP is for an interface at one end of

PVC to learn the IP of the interface at the other end of the PVC. (In general, the idea is to learn the **protocol address** of the interface on the other end—it doesn't have to be an IP address.) Inverse ARP is a type of ARP because both sides know the DLCI to reach the other end (analogous to the MAC address for Ethernet). Using Inverse ARP, they can learn of the IP(s) of interfaces at the other end of the PVC[6]

INARPINTERVAL [0–65535, default 10]—If **INARP** is set to **YES**, this parameter indicates the number of seconds between the transmission of these requests. 0 indicates that they should never be sent.

Minimal Frame Relay *wanpipe1.conf*   Let's trim some of the comments and optional parameters and see how our *wanpipe1.conf* looks.

```
# /etc/wanpipe/wanpipe1.conf (for Frame Relay)
###############################################
[devices]
wanpipe1 = WAN_FR, myframecircuit - cktid (my DLCI)

[interfaces]
wan0  = wanpipe1, 200, WANPIPE, loc A <-> loc B PVC
wan1  = wanpipe1, 300, WANPIPE, loc A <-> loc C PVC

[wanpipe1]
IOPort          = 0x360     # I/O port base (jumper setting)
IRQ             = 12        # IRQ (software selectable)
Firmware        = /usr/lib/wanpipe/fr514.sfm
Interface       = V35       # physical interface: RS232/V35
Clocking        = External  # clock source: External/Internal
BaudRate        = 512000    # port speed in bps
Station         = CPE       # station type: CPE/Node
Signalling      = ANSI      # signalling: ANSI/LMI/Q933
UDPPORT         = 9000      # required b/c the default is 0
# interface specific configuration
[wan0]
[wan1]
# end of /etc/wanpipe/wanpipe1.conf
###################################
```

5.3.4 *interface* Files for Frame Relay

Our link is almost completely configured, but there is still the matter of configuring the interfaces with the IP addresses for their point-to-point connection to the other end of the PVC. If you are used to other Frame Relay router configurations, you may think that this step is optional. Theoretically, you do not have to have IP addresses assigned to each of the Frame Relay interfaces—the Frame Relay cloud knows where to route your packets (based on the DLCIs and PVC). However, when you are using *WANPIPE*, you need to assign each end of each PVC an IP address. This is so the kernel can treat these interfaces just like any other point-to-point interface with respect to routing, displaying its properties with *ifconfig*, etc.

---

[6] See RFC 2390 for more information about INARP.

Each end of the PVC is issued an IP address, and the PVC itself can be treated like a network with only two nodes. (In fact, you can configure the point-to-point link to be a network with zero nodes by specifying a subnet mask of 255.255.255.255. See Section 5.3.5 for more information on this method.) For each interface in [interfaces], there is a file bearing its name in */etc/wanpipe/interfaces/* or */usr/lib/router/interfaces/* for non-Debian. For our example file, that means */etc/wanpipe/interfaces/wan0* and */etc/wanpipe/interfaces/wan1*. Looking into this file, you will find:

```
zinc:/root> cat /etc/wanpipe/interfaces/wan0
#!/bin/sh
ONBOOT=yes
IPADDR=202.1.1.1
NETMASK=255.255.255.0
BROADCAST=202.1.1.255
POINTOPOINT=202.1.1.2
NETWORK=
GATEWAY=
```

The file is **sourced** by the startup script (hence the #!/bin/sh, which is really just a reminder that the file must follow Bourne shell syntax). Actually, you do not need to worry much about the syntax because there is a utility which will create the file for you. */usr/sbin/wanpipeconfig* (Debian) or */usr/lib/wanrouter/Configure* (non-Debian) will interactively query you for the values to be placed in this file and into the *[wan]router.rc* file. (Debian uses *router.rc*.) The parameters are:

ONBOOT [yes or no]—This can be used to temporarily disable an interface without having to remove it from *wanpipe1.conf*. Otherwise, it should be **yes**.

IPADDR—The IP address of your side of the point-to-point link representing the PVC.

NETMASK—The netmask of the "network" between the two routers.

BROADCAST—The broadcast address for the "network" between the two routers.

POINTOPOINT—The IP address of the router on the other side of your PVC. Your counterpart should have the same values reversed.

NETWORK—A network address (alternately, a name from */etc/networks*) to be added to the routing table upon starting the interface. There is no way to specify the subnet mask with this, so you are limited to natural class A, B, or C networks, and you may specify only one network. Because of these limitations, I opt for placing my network routes elsewhere. For the Debian version of *WANPIPE*, put them in */etc/wanpipe/wanpipe_routes*.

GATEWAY—A gateway address which will be used for the network route above. Once again, due to the limited functionality, I would ignore this parameter and leave it blank.

5.3.5 Saving Time with Zero-Node Networks

When I first started deploying Frame Relay links, I used subnets carved out of the 172.16.*.* private address space with 255.255.255.252 subnet masks. After setting up and maintaining these links for a while, I found this small IP "network" between the Frame Relay routers to be an annoyance. Let's call these *frnets* for this discussion. Specifically, I encountered these problems.

- First, you have to go to the trouble of assigning some IP address space and noting its usage so that it does not pop up somewhere else in your network. Extra documentation...

- Second, if you want to *traceroute* over a link end-to-end, the traceroute command will want to be able to find the *frnet* (so that it does not print out '*'s). This means that there must be routing table entries for the *frnet* on (almost) every router in your network. If you use static routes, extra routing table entries mean real work.

- You'll need to update your DNS maps—possibly create entirely zones, both forward and reverse (or at a minimum reverse). If you don't, and you forget to specify the -n switch to *traceroute*, then you will have to wait for DNS lookups for the IPs in the *frnet* to timeout.

My solution was to take a pair of IP addresses from the Ethernet subnet on one side of the link. (Which side is an arbitrary choice—I took the addresses from the remote side, since it was typically a smaller office.) The convention is to reserve addresses .2 and .3 for the point-to-point link. For example, if the remote office is subnet 192.168.18.0/24, the hub side of the point-to-point receives 192.168.18.2, and the remote gets 192.168.18.3. To complete the configuration, assign a subnet mask of 255.255.255.255 (/32) to both interfaces when you configure them.

This is where we get the term *zero-node network*, since this includes nothing but the IP address of the interface—not even the interface on the other end of the link. However, the configuration works well. If you are running *WANPIPE* on both ends of your link, try it and see. The situation looks something like that depicted in Figure 5.5. This configuration has these advantages:[7]

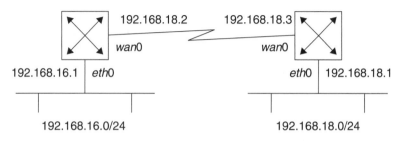

Frame Relay PVC

Figure 5.5 Frame Relay PVC Using a Zero-Node Network

---

[7] Actually, you may be able to get away with even less IPs—you'll see this later on page 277.

1. Configuring DNS maps for location B has either already been done or is on your to-do list. You can quickly modify the reverse DNS zone for location B (18.168.192.in-addr.arpa) to have meaningful names for the ends of the PVC, such as

```
1.18.168.192          IN      PTR          frlocB.yourdomain.com.
2.18.168.192          IN      PTR          pvc100-200.yourdomain.com.
3.18.168.192          IN      PTR          pvc200-100.yourdomain.com.
```

   Having these items in DNS also helps any IP-based authentication mechanism which utilized reverse lookups.

2. Packets to and from the point-to-point IPs will be recognizable to all by their IP addresses.

3. Say that you are logged onto router B and want to talk to a workstation in network A. You know the route to subnet A—it is out over the Frame Relay link. This means that your packets will have a source address of 192.168.18.3 (not 192.168.18.1, as some may assume). When the workstation in network goes to reply, it can easily find 192.168.18.3, since this is just one of the machines in location B. (If you had used a separate network for the link, then the workstation in A might not have been able to find you as quickly, or not at all.)

4. You have potentially saved a routing table entry for every PVC on your network, on every router in your network.

5. You have saved at least 4 IP addresses (one for each node plus the network address and the broadcast address). If IP addresses are in short supply for some reason, this becomes meaningful.

5.3.6 Starting *WANPIPE*

If you are as I am, then you are probably too impatient to read the documentation before trying something. You can test your configuration with `/etc/init.d/wanpipe start` (Debian) or `/usr/sbin/wanrouter start` (non-Debian). If your link comes up, great! If it does not, we'll need to do some troubleshooting. First of all, let's review what the *WANPIPE* startup script does.

1. Reads the contents of *[wan]router.rc* into the environment. This file tells *WANPIPE* where to find certain files and whether or not it should start the router at all.

2. Checks to see if **$ROUTER_LOCK** exists. If it does, then *WANPIPE* is currently running, and should be stopped before restarting.

3. Calls the function `router_up()`, which logs all of its output to **$ROUTER_LOG**. `router_up()` does the following:

   (a) Checks to see if the configuration files for each of the $WAN_DEVICES exist in $WANPIPE_CONF_DIR. Obviously, whatever is not present is not started.

   (b) Checks to see if $ROUTER_BOOT is set to **NO**. If it is, then *WANPIPE* does not start.

   (c) Loads each module in $WAN_DRIVERS, checking first to make sure that the module is not already loaded. The results of the *modprobe* are noted with either "ok" (success) or "fail" (failure) in the logfile. The script will fail automatically if $WAN_DRIVERS is an empty string.

(d) Calls *wanconfig* with *wanpipe1.conf* (and others) as an argument. This is the point where the interfaces listed in [interfaces] are created.

(e) Looks in $IFCONF_DIR to find the IP configuration for each of the interfaces. When *wanconfig* creates an interface and successfully registers it with the kernel, an entry is created in */proc/net/dev*. The script checks each interface file $IFCONF_DIR; when it finds a match, in */proc/net/dev*, it calls the function interface_up for that interface.

(f) interface_up reads the interface file (previously discussed in Section 5.3.4) and uses the values therein to *ifconfig* the interface with the values in $IPADDR, $NETMASK, $BROADCAST, and $POINTOPOINT address.

(g) A host route for the $POINTOPOINT interface is added to the kernel routing table with *route*.[8]

(h) A network route is added for $NETWORK, optionally with $GATEWAY (if it is set). The network route always points to the interface being configured.

Starting *WANPIPE*—Loading Modules   Now that you know what is supposed to happen, we can talk about what can go wrong. The loading of the driver modules must occur. If the modules are not found in */lib/modules/$(uname -r)/net*, or are compiled for the wrong version of the kernel, or if the running kernel does not have *WANPIPE* support built into it, you will have to take some corrective action.

In the first case, perhaps you neglected to perform the last step in kernel compilation, make modules_install. It could be that you have built the kernel, but that *depmod* has not been run since the kernel build. *depmod* normally runs during system startup, so one way to ensure that it occurs is to reboot your system. This should also correct the second problem, as long as you boot from the same place where lilo is writing your kernel (are you using make zlilo during your kernel build?). When the modules are loaded, the output of *lsmod* should look like the output below:

WANPIPE **modules for the 2.2.x kernel**

```
Module          Size  Used by
wanpipe         24176  1
wanrouter       6092   1  [wanpipe]
sdladrv         8064   0  [wanpipe]
```

After the modules load, *syslog* should contain messages like:

```
zinc kernel: WAN Router v1.1 (c) 1995-1999 Sangoma
zinc kernel: SDLA Support Module v3.0 (c) 1995-1999 Sangoma
zinc kernel: WANPIPE(tm) Multiprotocol Driver v5.0 (c) 1995-1999 Sangoma
```

Starting *WANPIPE*—wanconfig   *wanconfig* must read and parse *wanpipe1.conf* and configure the card and drivers with this information. It logs its output in the

---

[8] Kernel 2.0 systems only.

$ROUTER_LOG, so any errors in the format of the file will show up there. If all goes well, you should have the following in */var/log/wanpipe.log* (*/var/log/wanrouter.log* for non-Debian systems):

```
Tue Feb 15 20:57:30 MST 2000: starting WAN router
Loading driver wanpipe ... ok
Starting up device: wanpipe1
WAN Router Configurator.  v2.1.0 (c) 1995-1999 Sangoma Technologies Inc.
 * Parsing configuration file /etc/wanpipe/wanpipe1.conf ...
 * Reading section [devices]...
 * Reading section [wanpipe1]...
 * Reading section [interfaces]...
 * wan0 to used by WANPIPE
 * Reading section [wan0]...
 * wan1 to used by WANPIPE
 * Reading section [wan1]...
 * Configuring device wanpipe1 (Frame Relay link)
 * Setting IOPORT to 0x360
 * Setting IRQ to 12
 * Reading 25084 bytes from /usr/lib/wanpipe/fr514.sfm ...
 * Setting INTERFACE to V35
 * Setting CLOCKING to External
 * Setting BAUDRATE to 512000
 * Setting MTU to 1500
 * Setting UDPPORT to 9000
 * Setting STATION to CPE
 * Setting SIGNALLING to ANSI
 * Reading DLCI(s) Included : 200
 * Reading DLCI(s) Included : 300
 * Configuring channel wan0 (WANPIPE). Media address: 200
 * Configuring channel wan1 (WANPIPE). Media address: 300
```

The activities of *wanconfig* also generate messages in *syslog*. A completely loaded session has information that looks like the following:

```
zinc kernel: SDLA Support Module v3.0 (c) 1995-1999 Sangoma Technologies Inc.
zinc kernel: WAN Router v1.1 (c) 1995-1999 Sangoma Technologies Inc.
zinc kernel: WANPIPE(tm) Multiprotocol Driver v5.0 (c)1995-1999 Sangoma Technologies Inc.
zinc kernel: Processing WAN device wanpipe1...
zinc kernel: sdladrv: found S5080 card at port 0x360.
zinc kernel: sdladrv: assuming CPU clock rate of 16000 kHz.
zinc kernel: sdladrv: dual-port memory window is set at 0xEE000.
zinc kernel: sdladrv: found 128K bytes of on-board memory
zinc kernel: sdladrv: loading Frame Relay for S508 (T1/E1)  (ID=6800)...
zinc kernel: wanpipe1: running Frame Relay firmware vT.00
zinc kernel: wanpipe1: Global CIR enabled by Default
zinc kernel: wanpipe1: Interrupt Test Passed, Counter: 101
zinc kernel: wanpipe1: Running in WANPIPE mode wan0
zinc kernel: wanpipe1: CIR disabled for DLCI 200
zinc kernel: wanpipe1: link connected!
zinc kernel: wanpipe1: Interface wan0: DLCI 200 connected!
zinc kernel: wanpipe1: Running in WANPIPE mode wan1
zinc kernel: wanpipe1: CIR disabled for DLCI 300
zinc kernel: wanpipe1: Interface wan1: DLCI 300 connected!
```

5.3.7 Starting *WANPIPE*—Other Potential Problems

If everything in *syslog* and in the */var/log/wanpipe.log* seems ok, but the connection still doesn't work, then you'll have to dig a little deeper. Although none of these will immediately fix the problem, they are ways to check your work and understand how *WANPIPE* works with your system.

Once *WANPIPE* has started, you can use *ifconfig* to view the interfaces it created for each PVC. If they do not exist (an error message like `wan0: unknown interface`), then review the logfiles carefully. Make sure that you see a message like `wanpipe1: Interrupt Test Passed, Counter: 101`, which indicates that the interrupt you select is available for the S508. If you see `wanpipe1: Interrupt Test Failed`, then you have specified an interrupt which is already in use. **cat /proc/interrupts** works to find an unused interrupt and edit the IRQ setting in *wanpipe1.conf* with your new selection.

```
zinc:/root> ifconfig wan0
wan0      Link encap:Frame Relay DLCI
          inet addr:192.168.20.2  P-t-P:192.168.20.3  Mask:255.255.255.255
          UP POINTOPOINT RUNNING  MTU:1500  Metric:1
          RX packets:743135 errors:0 dropped:0 overruns:0 frame:0
          TX packets:788143 errors:0 dropped:10 overruns:0 carrier:0
          Collisions:0
          Interrupt:12 Base address:0x360 Memory:ee000-effff
zinc:/root> route -n | grep wan0
Destination     Gateway         Genmask         Flags Metric Ref    Use Iface
192.168.20.3    0.0.0.0         255.255.255.255 UH    0      0     4552 wan0
192.168.20.0    0.0.0.0         255.255.255.0   U     0      0    77727 wan0
```

Routers do not live by *ifconfigs* alone; you must also have routes over your link to be able to use it. If you have routes, check to make sure that IP forwarding is enabled in the kernel—see the hint on page 56 if you're not sure.

When *WANPIPE* starts, it creates its own directory in the */proc* filesystem. The directory is */proc/net/wanrouter/* on 2.2.x systems. The files are *config*, *status*, and *wanpipeN* (one for each physical device in the system). Each of these should contain meaningful information—the values of the first two files should jive with what you entered into the configuration files, while the third contains statistics about usage of the card.

```
zinc:/proc/net/wanrouter> pwd
/proc/net/wanrouter
zinc:/proc/net/wanrouter> cat config
Device name    | port |IRQ|DMA|mem.addr|mem.size|option1|option2|option3|option4
wanpipe1       |0x360 | 12|  0|0xEE000 |0x2000  |  5080| 16000| 131072|   6800
zinc:/proc/net/wanrouter> cat status
STATUS FOR PORT 0

Device name    |station|interface|clocking|baud rate| MTU |ndev|link state
wanpipe1       | DTE   | V.35    |external|   512000| 1600|  4 |connected
```

```
zinc:/proc/net/wanrouter> cat wanpipe1
            total packets received:        81010211
        total packets transmitted:        86599548
            total bytes received:        56464117067
        total bytes transmitted:        21996285192
            bad packets received:               0
        packet transmit problems:             902
        received frames dropped:                0
        transmit frames dropped:              412
       multicast packets received:              0
            transmit collisions:                0
            receive length errors:            138
        receiver overrun errors:                0
                    CRC errors:                 0
    frame format errors (aborts):              45
            receiver fifo overrun:              0
            receiver missed packet:             0
        aborted frames transmitted:             0
```

If you are still stuck, do not despair! This section was about configuration and system problems. There are many factors which contribute to the functioning of your Frame Relay circuit. Please review the information in Section 5.4, which covers other scenarios which can result in your link being down.

If your link is up, congratulations. (I always find bringing up new links exciting.) You add routes simply by listing the interface at the end of the route statement—no **gw** *gateway* required—as we did with Ethernet devices in Chapter 3. With a few exceptions, you can do anything with your *WANPIPE* Frame Relay interfaces that you can do with an Ethernet or PPP interface. The next section covers most of the exceptions.

5.3.8 TCP/IP Tools That Do Not Work with Frame Relay

The interfaces created by *WANPIPE* are just like any other interfaces on your system, right? Unfortunately, the answer is "almost, but not quite." You may be tempted to use a couple of your familiar TCP/IP tools to watch traffic flow and help with trouble-shooting, only to find that they do not work for Frame Relay interfaces. The first of these I encountered was *tcpdump*, but I later learned that it extended to all tools based on the *libpcap* library. You may be unfamiliar with *libpcap*, so here is an excerpt from the *README* file accompanying the distribution.

> *libpcap* provides a portable framework for low-level network monitoring. . . . Since almost every system vendor provides a different interface for packet capture, and since we've developed several tools that require this functionality, we've created this system-independent API to ease in porting and to alleviate the need for several system-dependent packet capture modules in each application.

libpcap has been widely accepted. Because *libpcap* reads the raw packets, not just the TCP/IP payloads, it needs to understand the link-layer protocol being used. To date, no one has added support for Frame Relay packet formats.[9]

---

[9] This is potentially my next project; anyone interested in helping should contact me.

Other monitoring and trouble-shooting tools based on *libpcap* which work for Ethernet devices but not for Frame Relay, are listed by their Debian package names: **arpwatch**, **epan**, **ethereal**, **ipgrab**, **karpski**, **libnet-rawip-perl** (this is not a tool per se, but another library), **sniffit**, and last but not least, **tcpdump**.

5.4 Trouble-Shooting Frame Relay with *WANPIPE*

Problems with Frame Relay links can occur at many points along the path between your routers at locations A and B. Effective trouble-shooting involves using (often limited) information to deduce the root cause of a problem. Once the problem has been located, you devise a strategy to repair the problem, and then test the repair. Because WANs span large distances by their very definition, your strategy is to first determine *where* the problem is occurring. I use the following list:

- your router at location A
- the access between location A and your provider's POP near A
- your provider's router at POP A
- the network between your provider's POPs
- your provider's router at POP B
- the access between your provider's POP near B and location B
- your router at location B

Because there are a lot of steps, the first thing to do is to reduce the possibilities. The following sections list items you can check at each of these locations. They also mention some uses of the *fpipemon* utility, which is more fully introduced in Section 5.4.3.

5.4.1 Frame Relay Trouble-Shooting—Your Router

- Did your router recently reboot? Use *uptime* to see. Because of the number of nodes along the way between locations A and B, it can take 30–40 seconds before an interrupted link starts passing traffic again. If you router has just rebooted, it could be negotiating link parameters and waiting for its peer to notice that it is back on the network.
- Have you recently genned a new kernel which perhaps does not have *WAN-PIPE* support? Have you done this accidently and then rebooted?
- Is *WANPIPE* started? After stopping and restarting it, are there error messages in */var/log/wanpipe.log* or *syslog*? Most *syslog* messages are lines containing the string "wanpipe," so you can look at them all with `grep -i wanpipe /var/log/messages | more`.

  Use *last* and *lastb* to determine who has logged into the router and *whom* to see if someone else may be logged in performing maintenance.

- Does an *ifconfig* show the interface(s) as up?
- Does `route -n` show a routing table entry for the point-to-point link?
- Does `route -n` show the route(s) for the remote subnet?

- Is there a network admin in another location performing maintenance? Sometimes you cannot determine whether the problem is in the provider's network or on the other side—you will just be able to say for certain that it is not between you and the provider's POP for your location. In this case, check with your counterpart in the remote location, or use analog dial-in to check the status of the router there. (If you always immediately open a trouble ticket with your provider and release the circuit for testing, your provider may bring the circuit down as part of his problem determination procedure. If it turns out that the problem is on the other end of the link and could be quickly resolved, you have, in effect, created two outages from one.)

- Have you recently made changes to *wanpipeN.conf* or upgraded the *WANPIPE* software? Is this the first time that you have restarted *WANPIPE* since either of those activities?

- Have you (very) recently added another device to the system? A second S508 card (without remembering to change the base address)? An ISA card that wants the IRQ of your *WANPIPE* card? An ISA PnP device? There should be a message about `Interrupt Test Passed` in */var/log/messages*—otherwise, you probably have an interrupt conflict.

- Is your system otherwise sick? Out of disk space? Did the kernel panic? (Word to the wise: If you have panics that make no sense whatsoever, fall back to a kernel that you know has worked in the past. If that doesn't help, change out all of the memory in the system.)

- Last but not least, the dreaded: Did you check the cables? Unfortunately, this is often the case for server rooms and telecom closets which experience a lot of foot traffic.

O.K., I admit that none of those was rocket science, but you have to start somewhere. Spending a few seconds reflecting upon what changes you might have recently made to the system and performing a quick sanity check can save much time barking up the wrong tree. The fact is, once your Linux/*WANPIPE* router is up and running, there are very few things to trouble-shoot with the router configuration itself. Still, it makes sense to check out the router first. Now we move on to the next potential point of failure: the digital circuit between you and the POP.

5.4.2 Frame Relay Trouble-Shooting—Access Problems

Without the local loop (so aptly known as **access**) functioning properly, you are not going to be able to get your traffic to your provider and into the cloud. Access is simple and tricky at the same time. While it may be easy enough to locate access problems, it can take quite a while to get them solved. For one, they are telco circuits, so you are at the mercy of your local access provider. The issue is more complicated when your Frame Relay provider does not provide the access circuit. In that situation, your Frame Relay provider leases the **last mile** from the local access provider, which makes your Frame Relay provider the *customer* as far as the local access provider is concerned. To trouble-shoot the access circuit, even if you *know* that the access is down, you normally have to contact your Frame Relay provider, wait for him to go through his preliminary testing, and have him call the access provider. The problem can exist the other way around, too. In either case, all of this takes time, during which you have a link down. Ways to detect access problems are:

- Does `fpipemon -i interface -u 9000 -c xm` show the circuit up? (Note: *interface* is either the name of the interface of the IP address or the IP address of the *other* end of the point-to-point link.) Good output looks like that below.

```
zinc:/root> fpipemon -i wan0 -u 9000 -c xm

         ---------------------------
                 MODEM STATUS
         ---------------------------

DCD is HIGH
CTS is HIGH
```

Bad output lists either of the signals as LOW. If you get an error from *fpipemon* about checking the IP address and the port, then either you are not specifying the correct IP address or interface, or *WANPIPE* is not running.

- If *fpipemon* thinks that the circuit is down, is there any problem indicated on the CSU/DSU or on the circuit's demarc? If there is, contact your Frame Relay provider. You will need to have your circuit ID when you call, which is why I put this information directly into *wanpipe1.conf*.

- If the circuit looks fine at your end, maybe the problem is not the access. You should be able to use *fpipemon* in trace mode to see some traffic between your node and the switch at the POP. At a minimum, you should see the status messages (keep alives), full status enquiries, and possibly data packets being traded.

fpipemon **Tracing Status Messages, FSEs and Data Payloads**

```
zinc:/root> fpipemon -i wan0 -u 9000 -c ti

Starting trace...(Press ENTER to exit)
OUTGOING   16    19821   Link Verification      Request Sx 7C   Rx 06
INCOMING   16    19823   Link Verification      Reply   Sx 07   Rx 7C
OUTGOING   16    7727    Full Status            Request Sx 1D   Rx 1B
INCOMING   21    7730    Full Status            Reply   Sx 1C   Rx 1D  \
                                                DLCI 600 PRS 600ACT
INCOMING  293    49726   Data Frame on DLCI 600
INCOMING   52    30939   Data Frame on DLCI 600
```

If you see outgoing traffic, but no incoming traffic, then the card thinks that the access is O.K. Perhaps the problem is with your provider's equipment, or with the access on their side. When it cannot talk to the provider's router, *WANPIPE* marks the circuit as down in */var/log/messages* because it does not receive any replies to its keep-alives and status enquiries. It will continue to generate OUTGOING LMI messages, in the hopes that the circuit will come back up, but it will not try to transmit TCP/IP data.

- If you call in a problem and there is not something else obviously wrong, your provider will probably want to perform a **loopback test**, or "loop up the CSU/DSU." If the provider cannot loop up your CSU/DSU, he or she will surely ask you if your equipment is powered-up and connected. As demeaning as it is, you should check all of your cables, and, if you have an external CSU/DSU, check to make sure that it is on and properly connected. If your side looks good, then there is a problem with the access circuit.

WHAT'S A LOOPBACK?

A **loopback** refers to a provision for automated testing built into all T1 interface equipment. What happens is that the provider sends a special sequence of bipolar violations down to your equipment that instructs it to complete the circuit between the transmit and receive pairs. Now that he has a "loop," the provider can send test patterns down the circuit and see them. This is done to determine how much noise there may be on a circuit, and that the circuit is complete.

Don't confuse this with the local loopback network interface found on every Unix system—interface *lo* with IP address 127.0.0.1.

Problems in the Cloud   The **cloud** refers to the portion of your provider's network that lies beyond your routers and access. Once packets make the trip from your router along your access to your port on the provider's equipment, you basically have no control over them until they egress on the other side. This means that it is difficult to actually detect a problem in cloud. The more likely scenario is that you will exhaust all of the other possibilities and deduce that the problem is there.

The "symptom" is that routers on both ends are up and sending and receiving keep-alive messages (so that you know that LMI is up and your ports are active) but you cannot pass packets end-to-end. If both sides believe that the remote DLCI is active, then the problem could be with buffering in the provider's network. If one side cannot see its partner DLCI, then the provider has probably built the PVC incorrectly (or not built it at all).

In either case, there is nothing you can do except to open a trouble ticket with your provider. Because most Frame Relay networks have multiple redundant paths, problems in the cloud often mean something bad is afoot. Alternately, the problem could be with the switch or PVC configuration within the provider's network.

Problems with Access at Location B and Router B   Any problems on the other side can be evaluated in the same manner that you did on the A-side of the link. The only sticky point might be that you cannot get to router B (because the link is down!), or that router B is not a Linux router. If you are responsible for problem resolution on the B-side of the link, you should make provisions for emergency access.

5.4.3 Using *fpipemon*

The *fpipemon* utility is the "window into your router"—it displays card status and acts
as a general-purpose sniffer for link-layer packets (known to *fpipemon* as **protocol**
packets). Several common uses of *fpipemon* were introduced in Section 5.4.2. In
this section, we'll cover all of the options of the utility. First, let's look at the general
command form:

```
fpipemon -i interface -u port -c command [-d dlci]
```

When invoking *fpipemon*, you must list an interface, the UDP monitoring
port,[10] and a command. Optionally, you can specify a DLCI modifier for the command. The *interface* can be the (local) interface name (as it shows up in *ifconfig* on
this router) or the IP address of far-end of your point-to-point interface in decimal
format. Because the monitor uses UDP to communicate with the driver, the device
you are monitoring does not have to be local to your system. As long as the IP
address is routable, you can run *fpipemon* against a remote machine.

fpipemon Commands   After you specify the interface and the monitoring port,
you have to tell *fpipemon* what you'd like for it to do. The command follows the -c
switch, and is either two or three characters. The first character specifies the type of
command and can be one of the following:

fpipemon **Command Types**

command type	meaning
x	card status
c	card configuration
s	card statistics
d	driver statistics
T	FT1 configuration and statistics
f	flush (statistics)
t	interactive trace

Now we will introduce all of the commands for each of these command types, grouped
into tables. The flush command forms are presented alongside the parameters they
affect. Note that there is no space between the command type character and the
command specifier(s). A valid command looks like `fpipemon -i wan0 -u 9000
-c trp`, which is command form "t" (for trace) with specifier "rp" (for raw protocol).

---

[10] The Debian version of the command doesn't require the UDP port. It assumes the default of
9000.

fpipemon **Commands–Card Status Forms (**x**)**

specifier	meaning
xm	modem status—This shows the status of the DCD (Data Carrier Detect) and CTS (Clear To Send) pins of the S508's interface to the CSU/DSU. These should both be HIGH. If one of these is LOW, then there is a problem with either the access circuit or the CSU/DSU.
xl	link status—This shows the driver's opinion of the status of the link. It should say OPERATIVE.
xru	router uptime—This returns the time elapsed since you last started *WANPIPE*. (Note that this does not always equal the uptime of the machine.)

fpipemon **Commands–Card Configuration (**c**)**

specifier	meaning
cl	active DLCIs for this adapter—This lists all active DLCIs as reported in your provider's reply to the last FSE (Full Status Enquiry). If there are DLCIs missing, then either you have a problem on the other side of your link or there is a configuration problem with your provider.

fpipemon **Commands—Card Statistics (**s**)**

specifier	meaning
sg	global statistics—This displays the data regarding the link management (LMI) taking place on your link. You might use this to trouble-shoot an incompatibility or settings mismatch between your router and the switch at your provider's POP. CRC errors indicate errors during packet transmission, while ABORT refers to errors detected while the line was idle.
sc	communications error statistics—This will list the number of times that CSU/DSU dropped out or otherwise told the Sangoma card to hush. It is useful for noting packet loss/bandwidth loss due to communications errors (potentially noisy access or otherwise).
se	error statistics—This displays counts of the instances when sends or receives failed due to problems with the Frame Relay headers (e.g., invalid sequence numbers, frames with invalid lengths or other formatting errors).
sd	DLCI-specific statistics—For the DLCI specified on the command line, statistics about frames sent to or received from that DLCI are displayed. You must use the -d *dlci* switch to indicate which DLCI you would like see.

You can use the "f" command form to flush (reset) each of these statistics individually. Use the same specifier (g, c, or e) to zero the corresponding statistic. To zero a DLCI's stats, use i for the specifier, as in -c fi -d *dlci*.

Example *fpipemon* **Statistics Output**

```
zinc:/root> fpipemon -i wan0 -u 9000 -csd -d 200

                                Information frames transmitted: 837911
                                 Information bytes transmitted: 354079392
                                  Information frames received: 810404
                                   Information bytes received: 118737889
                  Received I-frames discarded due to inactive DLCI: 4
     I-frames received with Discard Eligibility (DE) indicator set: 5480
                     I-frames received with the FECN bit set: 0
                     I-frames received with the BECN bit set: 12223
```

The frames and bytes counters are self-explanatory. `Received I-frames discarded due to inactive DLCI` are packets which come from a DLCI that this router did not know (in our case, not from DLCI 200). `I-frames received with Discard Eligibility (DE) indicator set` is a count of the number of frames that we *received*, although they were eligible to be thrown away in the cloud if they had encountered sufficient congestion—in other words, how many of the received frames sent by the indicated DLCI were done so while that router was exceeding the CIR for the link. In the case above, 5480 out of 810404, or about 0.7%. (Not bad.) FECN stands for Forward Explicit Congestion Notification. The FECN bit is sent to the next hop in the Frame Relay network (the cloud) when a router there is experiencing congestion. It makes sense that this counter would be zero, since our router is leaf node and is not situated so that it could be the forward router in the cloud. The BECN count is more interesting, as it indicates the number of times that the provider's switch told our router that it was congested and asked it if it could possibly throttle what it was sending onto the network. If you know that you are never exceeding your CIR, yet you received packets with the BECN bit set, then there is a possibility that your provider has oversold its network.

fpipemon **Commands–Driver Statistics** (d)	
specifier	meaning
ds	`If_Send` driver statistics—This option gives you access to the statistical variables in the driver related to sends. It can tell you some interesting things about what is happening to your packets, especially if you suspect packet loss or other foul play.
di	interrupt driver statistics—This displays more statistics like those shown with `ds`, but these are related to interrupts (which are packet receives).
dg	general driver statistics—This shows even more driver statistics.

Don't be alarmed if these don't make a lot of sense to you. They are normally used by Sangoma's technical staff for support and driver debuggings. Still, it's nice to access to the interesting bits.

Use the `fd` command form to flush (reset) all of the driver statistics.

fpipemon **Commands–FT1 (**T**)**

specifier	meaning
Tv	view status
Ts	self test
Tl	line loop test
Td	digital loop test
Tr	remote test
To	operational mode

Note that these commands are valid only if you have a FT1 version of a Sangoma card with an integrated CSU/DSU. Better descriptions of the output are available in the documentation that comes with *WANPIPE*, and are therefore not presented here. A warning: If you loop up your CSU/DSU while your router is running, you will undoubtedly bring down your link, at least for a short while. Except for Tv (view status), you should use these commands only when *WANPIPE* is stopped.

fpipemon **Commands–Traces (**t**)**

specifier	meaning
i	interpret/all—This shows both data (IP) and protocol (link-layer) frames in an easy-to-read "cooked" format.
ip	interpret/protocol—This shows protocol frames only in an easy-to-read "cooked" format.
id	interpret/data—This shows data payloads only in the easy-to-read "cooked" format.
r	raw/all—This shows the contents of all data (IP) and protocol (link-layer) frames in hexadecimal.
rp	raw/protocol—This displays the raw link-layer frames. This might be useful as a learning aid. (Sit down with the applicable RFC— probably RFC 1490—and decode the values in the frame headers.) You should do the same if you suspect some sort of incompatibility with your provider's equipment.
rd	raw/data—This displays the frame payloads in hexadecimal format.

For all of the trace modes, you toggle tracing on when you issue the command with *fpipemon*, at which point it starts tracing to *stdout*. To turn off the trace, hit **ENTER**. Depending upon the options used to invoke *fpipemon*, the output is Link Verifications or Status Requests (protocol), various replies to these (also protocol), or INBOUND or OUTGOING data.

The interpreted protocol trace is an excellent source of trouble-shooting information. The output is the **LMI** (Local Management Interface) information being exchanged between your router and the equipment at the POP. Once you learn how to decipher the output, you can tell from the **FSE** (Full Status Enquiry) messages which DLCIs are active, available, and missing. The exact format of the messages depends upon which of the status polling (LMI) protocols you are running. The original LMI is known simply as **LMI**. This protocol has the limitation of being uni-directional (your node router had to ask the questions, and the POP router would answer them). After some updating, the newer choices are Q.933 (Annex A) and ANSI (Annex D).

Your router will periodically send out an **enquiry** to the effect of *Are you alive?* The upstream router should reply within a certain timeout period (T391). Your node may send a Full Status Enquiry to the POP router, requesting more information about the status of the network. The POP should reply within the timeout period specified by T392. The POP router may also originate messages. These messages may be things like *DLCI 600 is no longer active* or *DLCI 400 has become active*.

HINT: SANGOMA'S *SNOOPER* UTILITY

Sometimes so many things have gone wrong, or documentation is so scarce, that you just want to establish some confidence that your access circuit is functioning. For these situations, you can use Sangoma's *SNOOPER* utility. (If you do not have the floppy disks that came with your card, you can get a copy of it at *ftp://www.sangoma.com/snooper/*. Note that it operates only with Sangoma ISA cards, such as the S508.)

SNOOPER is a DOS executable. To use it, place it on a bootable DOS floppy diskette and boot your router from this floppy. It will diagnose many problems with a T1 link, including a noisy T1. It can also tell you if the router on the other side is talking PPP or Frame Relay. When you're stumped as to why things aren't working, it's a convenient way to establish the validity of your CSU/DSU configuration and eliminate the access circuit from suspicion.

That concludes the discussion of *fpipemon* and Frame Relay trouble-shooting. Documenting trouble-shooting procedures and strategies is difficult when you consider the range of different situations one may encounter. I have tried to emphasize the knowledge gained during my experiences with *WANPIPE* Frame Relay links. You may come across completely new and mind-bogglingly difficult issues to solve. If this happens, you should not be discouraged or assume that the problem is automatically on your side. I've seen providers make mistakes configuring a circuit where I had to all but solve the problem for them before they finally corrected it. This is one of the advantages of Linux and *WANPIPE*—you are armed with information and tools. A lot of this information may be available on Sangoma's trouble-shooting webpage. The URL is *http://www.sangoma.com/linedebug.htm*.

Once you are up and running, you'll want some way to determine how much and how effectively you are using your link. The next section covers a web-based tool to monitor bandwidth.

5.5 *MRTG*—MONITORING LINK UTILIZATION

MRTG is short for *Multi Router Traffic Grapher*. It is a network monitoring tool which specializes in presentation of traffic data graphically, both in real-time and over intervals, such as hourly, daily, weekly, monthly, and yearly. It uses the **SNMP** protocol[11] as its data collection mechanism, so it can be used with more than just Linux routers. **SNMP** is an acronym for Simple Network Management Protocol which can be used to gather statistics and perform configuration changes. It is the basis upon which many embedded systems routers' management tools are built, plus some enterprise management tools, such as HP's *OpenView*—Linux is willing to play along with any open standard.

In this instance, you will need to load the **snmpd** Debian package (or equivalent for your distribution) to any system which you would like *MRTG* to monitor. You can think of the *snmpd* as a server (listening on port 161), willing to serve up information about the system to any SNMP client who connects and has the required credentials to get the information it requests. *MRTG* can be configured to produce graphs for anything that will respond to an *snmpget*. It presents its traffic summaries via GIF images in HTML pages, so they may be viewed by any standard web-browser that supports images. An example of the output is shown in Figure 5.6.

Traffic Analysis for wan0

System:	zinc
Maintainer:	tony@mancill.com
Interface:	wan0 (3)
IP:	atl-sfo-pvc.mydomain.com (172.16.1.9)
Max Speed:	192.0 kBytes/s (frame-relay)

The statistics were last updated **Sunday, 18 July 1999 at 15:40** at which time **zinc** had been up for **12:17:23**.

Daily Graph (5 Minute Average)

| Max In: | 20.5 kB/s (10.7%) | Average In: | 5377.0 B/s (2.8%) | Current In: | 2982.0 B/s (1.6%) |
| Max Out: | 19.5 kB/s (10.2%) | Average Out: | 5350.0 B/s (2.8%) | Current Out: | 2992.0 B/s (1.6%) |

GREEN ### Incoming Traffic in Bytes per Second
BLUE ### Outgoing Traffic in Bytes per Second

MRTG MULTI ROUTER TRAFFIC GRAPHER

2.5.4-1998/10/13 Tobias Oetiker <oetiker@ee.ethz.ch> and Dave Rand <dlr@bungi.com>

Figure 5.6 MRTG Sample Output

---

[11] Note that the SNMP code is built into *MRTG*, so there is no need for an external SNMP collection mechanism on the server.

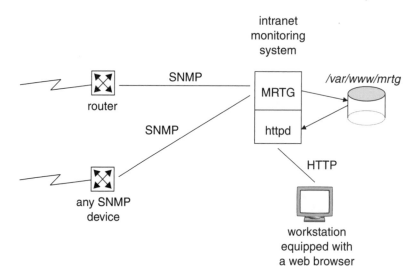

Figure 5.7 MRTG Architecture

To view the graphs via a browser, you also need to load some sort of HTTP daemon. I suggest *Apache*, since it is readily available and has excellent documentation and support. It will also allow you to configure some security around your *MRTG* statistics pages by using *.htaccess* files. Figure 5.7 gives an overview of the architecture. Note that *MRTG* and the web server need not be loaded on your router, but can be put on an intranet server or on your workstation. In this way, you spare your router the overhead of calculating statistics, drawing graphs, and serving up webpages.

5.5.1 Configuring *MRTG*

It takes only about an hour to set everything up, including loading the software, and the system needs practically no ongoing maintenance. The log file format used by *MRTG* is efficient and self-pruning. Let's walk through a sample configuration to monitor one or more of our routers. Remember that *MRTG* is useful for more than just Frame Relay routers.

1. On the system that will be performing statistics collection, the **support system**, you will need to load *MRTG* and *Apache* (Debian packages **mrtg** and **apache**). If this system will also be monitored, add to this the SNMP daemon (**snmpd** for Debian).

2. On each of the routers to be monitored, load and configure the SNMP daemon. Most Linux distributions now come with the *UCB SNMP* daemon, but a few may run *CMU SNMP*:

   - For *CMU SNMP*, the configuration file is */etc/snmpd.conf*. You'll need to add an `interface:` line for your Frame Relay interfaces along with their type (from Section 3.5 of RFC 1213—also known as MIB-II) and speed. For a 512kbps interface named *wan0*, I use:

```
interface:     wan0    32         512000
```

Once you restart the daemon, the SNMP agent programs should recognize your interface and *MRTG* will be able to judge its speed correctly.

- For *UCB SNMP* (at least on Debian), you need to open up the default security a little bit to be able to use it. You need to add read-only access for hosts other than *localhost* so that your *MRTG* server has access to read the statistics. This is all in the */etc/snmp/snmpd.conf* (or better yet, in the */etc/snmp/snmpd.local.conf*) file. Refer to your system's documentation for more information about the options in this file.

  After changing either of these, you'll need to restart the daemon to read the new configuration file: **/etc/init.d/snmpd reload**.

3. Go back to the support system and configure *Apache* to suit your tastes. The out of the box configuration will work fine, and the remaining steps assume that your `DocumentRoot` is */var/www* and that you have created */var/www/mrtg* for your *MRTG* data. When you create this directory, make it group-readable by at least `www-data` so that Apache can get to it. It should be writable by the user you will run the *mrtg* executable as.

4. Now you need to create the *MRTG* configuration file, which is located in */etc/mrtg.cfg*. The configuration file syntax is not difficult, but the *MRTG* authors decided to make the process even easier by providing *cfgmaker* and *indexmaker* utilities. You invoke *cfgmaker* once for each router you would like to monitor. It goes out and queries the router about how many interfaces it has and of what type and speed. (This is why we needed to configure *snmpd* to know the speed of our *wan0* interface.) Do this with `cfgmaker public@`*router* `»/etc/mrtg.cfg` for each *router* you would like to monitor.

  The configuration file format is easy enough to decipher, and you can read the *MRTG* documentation if you need to fine-tune the configuration for a particular router or interface. You will also need to review the documentation if you want to monitor MIB values not included by *cfgmaker*. The only other value required in *mrtg.cfg* is the `WorkDir:`, which you should set to */var/www/mrtg*.

5. Once you have the configuration file, you have to configure a way to invoke *mrtg* periodically with the path to the configuration file as the argument. Note that *MRTG* is not a daemon.[12] Every time that it runs, it reads its configuration file to know which systems to query and where to write the results. The Debian package comes with a cronjob already set up for this in */etc/cron.d/mrtg*. You can see that it executes once every five minutes.

6. At this point, you could point your browser at your support system and access the HTML pages created for each router. You would do this with a

---

[12] This is a good example of keeping the code focused on the task at hand. Leave the coding of *cron* to *cron*.

URL like *http://support/mrtg/*ipofrouter.intf.*html*. Look at the contents of */var/www/mrtg* to see what I mean.

Just so that you cannot complain about having to type all of this into your browser, the authors of *MRTG* included an easy way to generate an index to the routers you have configured—*indexmaker*. Review its manpage, and run it every time you make changes to *mrtg.cfg*. Now you can point your browser at *http://support/mrtg* to see an overview, and click on the links provided to view details of each router and interface.

If you followed along with the example, I hope that your configuration went smoothly. It is not a difficult package to configure and well worth the effort once you see the nice graphs of router traffic. By default, *MRTG* produces daily, weekly, monthly, and yearly graphs, so it is immediately useful for watching trends in network traffic develop. Because it is based on SNMP (and you have the source code!), it can become the backbone of your monitoring infrastructure. There are many potential "next steps" with *MRTG*. One possibility I find interesting is making IP accounting counters available via SNMP. With this and a little time spent configuring *MRTG*, you could produce traffic graphs for certain protocols, or certain subnets—anything you can configure with IP accounting. Cool, eh?

5.6 LRP WITH *WANPIPE*

If you are a fan of LRP and need the functionality of *WANPIPE*, you are in luck. The LRP maintainers have already packaged a version of Sangoma's driver software like the Debian **wanpipe** package. The package is available at the LRP site, *ftp://ftp.linuxrouter.org*, and can be added to your LRP root disk as explained in the following section. Note that there are a few differences between the LRP and Debian **wanpipe** packages, in the interest of saving space. The trimmings include documentation, the verbose startup and shutdown script, the kernel patches, etc. If you plan to use the LRP *wanpipe*, you should obtain the documentation from elsewhere (e.g., Sangoma's FTP site). From a configuration perspective, here are the major differences:

- The *router.conf* is called */etc/wanpipe/wanpipe.conf*.
- There is no */etc/wanpipe/interfaces/* nor any interface files. You will need to configure your *WANPIPE* interfaces with *ifconfig* after *wanconfig* parses the configuration file.
- There is an additional command called *wanstat*, which displays some status information from the */proc* filesystem.
- The *cfgft1* is not included. If you want to have it on your LRP root disk, do not copy the binary from the Debian wanpipe package or Sangoma's tarball. Because these are dynamically linked, they are not likely to run on the LRP system with its pared-down libraries. Instead, either compile a statically-linked version (edit the makefile to use the `-static` switch) or configure your S508-FT1 on another system before installing it in your LRP system. Because the configuration is stored in non-volatile memory, it will remain intact while you transfer the board.

5.6.1 Adding LRP Packages to Your LRP Root Disk

Adding a package to LRP is straightforward; the steps are listed below. If you have any problems with the command syntax for any of these, refer back to Section 3.4 in Chapter 3.

1. Make any changes you require to the *.lrp* tarball, e.g., for *WANPIPE*, you can provide your specific *WANPIPE* configuration file, and then reassemble the tarball.

2. Mount the LRP root floppy on your workstation (remember that it is a DOS formatted floppy) and copy the *.lrp* file into the root directory of the floppy. Use a command such as `mount -t msdos /dev/fd0 /floppy` to mount the disk as */floppy*.

3. Edit */floppy/syslinux.cfg* and modify the `LRP=` portion of the *append=* line to reflect the package(s) you added. For the base packages plus *WANPIPE*, the list looks like `LRP=etc,log,local,modules,wanpipe`.

4. Unmount the floppy with `umount /floppy` and re-run *syslinux* against it to update the configuration.

USING **mtools** TO WORK WITH **MS-DOS** FILESYSTEMS

Alternately, you can use *mcopy* (part of the **mtools** package) to copy files to and from the LRP floppy. These tools allow you to work with MS-DOS formatted filesystems without explicitly mounting and unmounting them as part of your filesystem. The tools include most of the basic DOS file manipulation commands and use */etc/mtools.conf* to assign "drive letters" to devices and partitions on your system.

For example, in */etc/mtools.conf*, I have:

```
drive a: file="/dev/fd0" exclusive
```

This allows me to use commands like:

```
# copy the file over so that I can edit it
zinc:/root> mcopy a:syslinux.cfg /tmp/syslinux.cfg
zinc:/root> vi /tmp/syslinux.cfg
zinc:/root> mcopy /tmp/syslinux.cfg a:syslinux.cfg
# check the new configuration file
zinc:/root> mtype a:syslinux.cfg
```

5.7 SUMMARY

When I configured my first Linux Frame Relay router with *WANPIPE*, I immediately felt as if I were better off with Linux than with the traditional Frame Relay routers we had in production at the time. My comfort level with using a Unix shell as the command interface, the accessibility of information, and the ease of configuration were all factors. It was this experience that really brought me onto the Linux router bandwagon. This chapter covers a lot of ground regarding Linux Frame Relay routers:

- Basics of Frame Relay for a CPE (endpoint) router. There is a lot more to Frame Relay if you are a provider or want to run voice-over-IP applications alongside your data. The material presented is geared towards basic WAN applications—you don't have to be a Frame Relay expert to deploy it effectively for your organization.

- Various WAN adapters available for Linux. These range from single-port ISA cards running 56kbps to quad-port HSSI boards at 52Mbps. Protocol support also covers the spectrum, from LU6.2 to Cisco HDLC.

- Configuration of *WANPIPE* Frame Relay, both using the Debian **wanpipe** package and Sangoma's general version of the software. Depending upon the current version of the kernel and *WANPIPE*, you may get into patching your kernel with new driver code. Once you have the necessary support, you configure *wanpipe1.conf* and the appropriate *interface* files to match your link parameters.

- Trouble-shooting a Frame Relay link running *WANPIPE* using *fpipemon* can be a pleasurable experience, especially when you use the information from the utility to quickly isolate the location and cause of the outage.

- Configuring *MRTG* to monitor link performance and establish a web-based reporting engine—free software keeps looking better and better.

## CHAPTER 6

Oxygen—Internet Router

Once upon a time, our Internet link was connected with a BigName router. One day, this router decided to die in a very poetic "it just will not boot" sort of way. In total, it took about an hour to get a technician from BigName on the phone; we whiled away the time scrambling around looking for our support ID, wading through the "press six if you'd like to use our fax-back server" menus, waiting on hold, and fending off frantic users. After a short discussion about my abilities to configure a terminal program (peppered with a few curt remarks of my own about what sort of idiot cable was needed to access the BigName router console), the technician decided that we needed a new motherboard.

Since we had paid dearly for our support contract, a new board was to arrive the next day. We informed our users of the situation and eagerly awaited our package. A package did arrive promptly the next day by the promised time. However, much to our dismay, we had received a new power-supply and case—no motherboard. Now we were in trouble. BigName was going to send us our part, but that meant at least another 24 hours of downtime. Based on our experience with our Linux Frame Relay router, we decided to bring up the T1 link with our spare Sangoma S508 card. We were loaded and configured in about an hour. Everyone took a deep breath and let out a sigh of relief—for now we had oxygen.

Because there is a lot of territory to cover when connecting a system to the Internet, the topic is spread across two chapters.[1] This chapter begins by getting our access router up and running using Sangoma's *WANPIPE*, this time for synchronous PPP. Then we review general network security for Linux (and Unix in general). Once the system no longer has any gaping security holes due to services running on it, we'll

---

[1] The second chapter which relates to Internet routers is Chapter 8.

turn to IP firewalling to protect our networks and our router even further. There are two basic ways to use IP firewalling: by preventing forwarding of traffic across the router or blocking it altogether from entering (or exiting) the router. We will cover both of them. They are the kernel facilities which form the basis of **packet-filtering** and all of the tools which can help you configure it. Finally, we'll talk about notification tools available for Linux so that you can monitor your environment and receive notification when something is wrong.

6.1 CONNECTING TO THE INTERNET

Unlike some networks, which may have only a few different types of access media and corresponding link-layer protocols, you can connect to the Internet in literally dozens of ways. (You might recall the discussion of access and protocols back in Chapter 2.) This section presents a Linux-based router which uses synchronous PPP over a fractional T1 to connect to an ISP and the Internet.

Synchronous PPP, as a protocol, is not actually any different from vanilla PPP. The name qualifier is an abridged way of saying " I'm running PPP over a dedicated digital access circuit to my ISP." Running over a leased-line simplifies some aspects of the protocol. First, you don't have to dial anything. When your router is running and your ISP's router is running, you're on the Internet. Second, the security of the PPP link itself is less of an issue, because the access circuit is terminated at your site and at your ISP. They know who you are, and you know who they are. Thus, most connections dismiss the familiar PAP or CHAP-based authentication and just start routing traffic. The third difference is that you shouldn't need to run *pppd*. I say "shouldn't" because there are scenarios where you might run *pppd*, for example, if your synchronous data pump was merely that—a data pump. In this case, the device driver would present itself to the Linux kernel as a tty instead of a network device. To my knowledge, this is rarely the case, and for the Sangoma S508 card, it's definitely not so. It runs the protocol on the board itself and presents itself to the system as a network interface. As you will see, it is very similar to the Frame Relay router from Chapter 5.

6.1.1 A SPPP Router with *WANPIPE*

Ingredients:

- (1) x86-based PC, 486/66 or faster with 16MB RAM
- (1) 1GB IDE hard drive
- (1) Sangoma S508/FT–1 adapter card
- (1) Ethernet adapter
- (2) CAT5 cables
- set Debian GNU/Linux version 2.x rescue and driver floppies

Once you have installed the S508/FT–1 adapter card and the Ethernet adapter and performed a base load of the operating system, you're ready to configure the *WANPIPE* software. This section assumes that you are using Debian and the **wanpipe** package (but the differences between this and the Sangoma release are purely aesthetic). When loading Debian, you want to install just the "Basic" installation plus some networking tools and the **wanpipe** package. Once installation is complete:

1. Use */usr/sbin/wanpipeconifig* to create an interface named *sppp0*; use the IP configuration given to you by your service provider.

2. Use `zcat /usr/share/doc/wanpipe/examples/wanpipe1.ppp.gz > /etc /wanpipe/wanpipe1.conf` to seed the configuration file. Then edit */etc/ wanpipe/wanpipe1.conf* to suit your particular configuration.

3. Use the */usr/sbin/cfgft1* utility to configure the integrated CSU/DSU on the Sangoma card. (For those not using Debian's **wanpipe**, this package is available as a separate tarball from Sangoma's FTP site.)

4. Connect the S508/FT–1 to the T1 smart-jack (or demarc) installed by your provider using a CAT5 cable.

5. Execute the script **/etc/init.d/wanpipe reload**.

6. Use *ifconfig* to verify that the *sppp0* interface is up and operational.

7. Add a default route to the Internet with **route add -net default sppp0**.

8. Take the rest of the day off!

Once you return to the office (or, if you're so equipped, while dialed-in from home), add your default route statement to */etc/wanpipe/wanpipe_routes*. If you are the paranoid type, you should break into a cold sweat at this point. You're on the Internet without any security in place! (We'll address this later.) The configuration process for *WANPIPE* and PPP is very much like it is for Frame Relay. Procedurely, they are identical, so you can review Chapter 5 for more detailed instructions. In a nutshell, PPP has the following differences:

- There are different parameters in *wanpipe1.conf*, which are covered below in Section 6.1.2.
- You will not be inventing IP addresses for your */etc/wanpipe/interfaces/sppp0* file. The IP address and network will be given to you by your ISP.
- Later on, there is more emphasis on security for the router in general.

6.1.2 Configuring *wanpipe1.conf* for Synchronous PPP

The *wanpipeN.conf* file for PPP follows the same format as for Frame Relay (covered in Section 5.3.3), except for some new parameters which are applicable to PPP. A sample configuration file is listed below and contains a summary of the new parameters and changes after each section.

```
#
# /etc/wanpipe/router.conf
#
# ==========================================================
# wanpipe S508 sample router configuration for PPP
# ==========================================================
#
# ----------------------------------------------------------
```

```
# The [devices] section
#  device = config_id,description
# --------------------------------------------------------
[devices]
wanpipe1 = WAN_PPP, **edit router.conf with your ckt id/vendor info**
```

Devices which will run the PPP firmware modules need **WAN_PPP** as their **config_id**. You should edit the comment field to contain your circuit id, and perhaps even the telephone number for support at your ISP.

SPPP [interfaces] Configuration in *wanpipe1.conf*

```
# --------------------------------------------------------
# The [interfaces] section defines logical channels and
# corresponding network interfaces created by the router.
#
# name=device,media_addr,description
#
# --------------------------------------------------------
[interfaces]
sppp0 = wanpipe1, , WANPIPE, ** edit router.conf - sppp link **
```

sppp0 is the interface name I use for synchronous PPP WAN interfaces, but the choice is arbitrary. If you would like to change it, do not forget to change it in the interface-level configuration section that follows. The *device* is any device you have already defined in the [devices] section that has a config_id of **WAN_PPP**. PPP links do not have media addresses[2], so media_addr remains blank. This is because there will only be one [interface] per [device] for PPP. The PPP is not designed to share the line with any other protocol or link—it wants to use all of the link for itself. The comment field can be used as you see fit. I recommend placing the IP addresses of your PPP configuration or more contact info for your ISP.

SPPP Device-Level Configuration in *wanpipe1.conf*

```
# --------------------------------------------------------
# device-level link configuration section.
# --------------------------------------------------------
[wanpipe1]                      ### WAN_PPP interface ###
IOPort          = 0x360         # I/O port base
IRQ             = 12            # IRQ
Firmware        = /usr/lib/wanpipe/ppp508.sfm     # adapter firmware
Interface       = V35           # physical interface type, RS232/V35
Clocking        = External      # Tx/Rx clock source: External/Internal
BaudRate        = 512000        # data transfer rate in bps
IP_MODE         = STATIC        # PEER/STATIC: do/not request address
MTU             = 1500          # maximum data transfer unit, bytes
UDPPORT         = 9000          # for UDP management
AUTHENTICATOR   = NO            # initiate PAP or CHAP authentication?
TTL             = 0x7F          # TTL for UDP monitoring packets
```

---

[2] apart from the IP addresses of the PPP interfaces themselves.

The device-level configuration prepares the driver for PPP. It is largely the same as the device-level configuration for Frame Relay. The `Memaddr` has been omitted since we want the driver to auto-select the memory range to use. Note that the `Firmware` path has changed from the Frame Relay configuration to reflect the fact that this is a PPP link. (If you remember back to the general discussion of the S508 card in Section 5.2.1, you will recall that this card runs the WAN protocol on the card itself, offloading much of the work from the CPU of your router.) The two new parameters for PPP device-level configuration are:

IP_MODE [STATIC or PEER, default is STATIC]—When set to `STATIC`, the IP addresses in the */etc/wanpipe/interfaces/sppp0* file are used to configure the link. `PEER` indicates that the peer on the link, i.e., your ISP's router, should provide the IP addresses for the link.

AUTHENTICATOR [YES or NO, default is NO]—If set to `YES`, your router will request authentication information from the peer router. This is configured in the interface-level configuration for this interface. For most digital access (leased-line) circuits, this is set to NO (or simply omitted from the configuration), since the physical termination of the link at your facility is enough to convince the ISP that you are the party using the link and will therefore pay the bill. There may be, however, security applications where this option is useful.

SPPP Interface-Level Configuration in *wanpipe1.conf*

```
# --------------------------------------------------------
# interface-level configuration section
# --------------------------------------------------------
[sppp0]
MULTICAST  = NO    # Multicast Enabled?
PAP        = NO    # Enable PAP?    (YES/NO)
CHAP       = NO    # Enable CHAP?   (YES/NO)
#USERID    =       # If not the authenticator then enter your login name
                   # If you are the authenticator then provide a list of
                   # all login names.  (USER1 / USER2.../ USER10...)
                   # The login name are separated by "/"
#PASSWD    =       # if not the authenticator then enter your passwd for
                   # your login name.  If you are the authenticator then
                   # provide a list of all the passwd for all the login
                   # names in the SAME ORDER. For eg.  (PASS1 / PASS2.../
                   # PASS10...)
#SYSNAME   =       # If you are the authenticator then enter your local
                   # system name.  Otherwise keep it commented out
```

The only things new in the interface-level configuration for PPP interfaces are related to authentication. A caution about authentication—if you find that you need to be able to authenticate yourself to the peer, then make sure that the peer speaks either PAP or CHAP. Otherwise, you could be out of luck or requesting a special patch from Sangoma... If you are the authenticator (i.e., you set **AUTHENTICATOR=YES**), then you can specify *one* of the protocols. You must also set the name of your system with **SYSNAME**.

USERID=*username* [*/ username* [*/ username*. . .]]—If you are asked to authenticate yourself, then you should supply a single *username*. If acting as an authenticator, you can list the usernames to be used by your peer(s).

PASSWD=*password* [*/ password* [*/ password*. . .]]—Use this in the same manner as **USERID**.

SYSNAME=*sysname*—Use this only if you are the authenticator. This is the same as the second field in a *pppd pap-secrets* or *chap-secrets* file.

Configuring the `default` Route on Your Internet Router   The final step to configuring *WANPIPE* is to tune your interface file created by *wanpipeconfig*. You can edit the file directly: */etc/wanpipe/interfaces/sppp0*. Your ISP should provide you with IP addresses, network address, and subnet mask for the point-to-point link. If the ISP indicates that its router will supply yours with the IP information, then you need to make sure that you set `IP_MODE=PEER` in */etc/wanpipe/wanpipe1.conf*.

In the case of an Internet router, you want the default route to point to the *sppp0* interface—i.e., out to the Internet. For this application, it does make sense to configure the `NETWORK` and `GATEWAY` parameters in the interface file, since once you have a default route pointing to an interface (not the same as a gateway), any other routes over that interface are redundant. `NETWORK` should be set to `0.0.0.0`, and the `GATEWAY` is the IP address of your ISP's side of the point-to-point interface (the **peer**). If your IP address is being set by the peer, you can just as easily add the statement `route add -net default sppp0` to */etc/wanpipe/wanpipe_routes*.

HINT: ADDING A DEFAULT ROUTE TO *WANPIPE*

> *WANPIPE* supports an easy way to add a default route over an interface. Set `NETWORK=0` in the interface file, and leave `GATEWAY` blank. When *WANPIPE* starts and configures the interface up, the route will be added automatically. (Regardless of how you add a route, the kernel will remove it automatically as soon as the interface for that route is configured down. Therefore, be careful when you're logged in from a remote location.)

Trouble-Shooting SPPP—*ppipemon*   If your link doesn't work right off the bat, then you'll need to do some trouble-shooting. Fortunately, *WANPIPE* provides a monitor program for each of the WAN protocols it supports. For synchronous PPP, that command is *ppipemon*, and its operation is very similar to the *fpipemon* utility in Chapter 5. You can use the monitor to determine a range of information about your link, from the status of the modem to statistics about the interface, to the contents of the IP data packets themselves. Invoke the command without any options to see the usage statement.

6.1.3 Internal Routes on Your Internet Router

The way you configure the remaining routes on your system depends upon your firewall topology, what sort of address space you have and how much of it, and whether or not you will be using a dynamic routing daemon. I've included Figures 6.1–6.4 (all

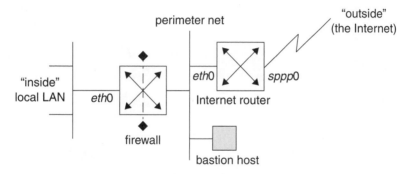

Figure 6.1 Perimeter Net Internet Router Topology

explained below), which cover a few of the possibilities for topologies, but really only begin to scratch the surface. This book is not the right forum for a detailed analysis of firewall topologies; I heartily recommend *Building Internet Firewalls* by Chapman and Zwicky (see the Bibliography for the complete reference) if you require this sort of information.

My idea of configuring routes on an Internet router is to make it the ultimate authority on what networks exist inside your network, but to not necessarily advertise that information to the world (aside from what the world already knows because of your presence on the net). This way, everyone on the inside can use the router (indirectly as a gateway), and trouble-shooting is easy. If you intend to proxy all services you provide your users, allowing no masquerading (of users) or direct outbound connections (perhaps with a topology like that in Figure 6.1), then you'll want to do something else. For a few ideas, briefly review each of the topologies in this section, starting with Figure 6.1, which we will call the **perimeter net topology**.

This topology logically separates the functions of the Internet router and the firewall (although you may also perform firewalling on the Internet router, too), which makes the configuration of both easier. The **perimeter net** is the network between the Internet router and your firewall, on the *perimeter* of your network. This is a good place to place your external DNS server, SMTP gateways, and external web servers. The firewall can function as a packet-filter, perform masquerading, or both. You may want to place proxy servers on the perimeter net (so that users may access the proxies only through the firewall).

The Chapman and Zwicky book refers to these external hosts as **bastion hosts**. The idea is that if someone were to hack into them, they are located outside of the firewall, so crackers[3] would still be limited in the network attack they might launch against your corporation, although much better off than they were before.... For this reason, you shouldn't be storing the secret formula or any other trade secrets on the perimeter net. You should be prepared for the worst case, that these systems will be completely destroyed by an attack from the outside. (You always have your backups, right?)

---

[3] The term *hacker* means *good programmer*, and *cracker* refers to a person of malicious intent.

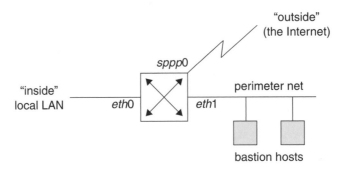

Figure 6.2 Combination Firewall/Router with Perimeter Net

Maybe this isn't as bad as it sounds after all. Linux boxes are great at doing lots of things at once. If a system is compromised, you can configure another system to act like it until you get it back online. In the not-so-bad case, you can spend some time beforehand configuring packet-filtering rules on the Internet router itself. Remember that the distinction between firewall and Internet router is more for the users and network diagrams than a statement about which systems have security measures installed. Your Internet router can have strict policies, just like your firewall; they simply have different policies.

Combination Firewall and Internet Router   Another way of having a perimeter net, without having a separate firewall is to use a topology like that in Figure 6.2. This results in one less system to maintain and protect, but is more demanding in terms of configuration. To make this configuration work, you will definitely want to use both **forwarding** and **input/output** firewalling rules to control the flow of traffic through your firewall. This sort of configuration is complicated, so you should test it thoroughly after you're up and running from a shell account on the outside, or by using a security tool such as *Firewalk* or *Satan*.

If you do not have the need for a perimeter net and want to run your site with a single Internet firewall router, you have something that looks like Figure 6.3, which is a degenerate case of the previous example. Because you do not have to control forwarding between three different networks, this is much simpler to configure.

Isolating the Router from the Perimeter Net   Finally, if you really want to do something different, you can isolate your router from your perimeter net with a private network, as depicted in Figure 6.4. The idea here is configure the subnet

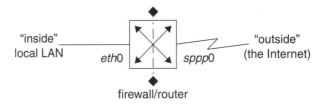

Figure 6.3 Combination Firewall/Internet Router

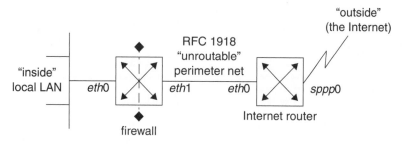

Figure 6.4 Isolation of Internet Router with an Unroutable Network

between the Internet router and the firewall to be a private network, and completely unroutable on the LAN (inside of the firewall).

You should also configure the firewall to reject any traffic with source IP address of the Internet router. The effect is that even if someone compromised the Internet router, he would be no better off than he was from the outside. This works because the packet-filtering code on the firewall will be blocking traffic from the Internet router's IP address (i.e., traffic which originated there), and not which was forwarded by the Internet router (and bears only its MAC address). The firewall's default gateway is the Internet router, and the Internet router knows to forward packets for the inside to the IP address on the external interface on the firewall. The cost for this extra protection is that managing the Internet router remotely is not possible without introducing some sort of hole in the firewall between the management workstation and the Internet router. This might be O.K., but an attacker will quickly see the portal to the management system and start attacking there. A better idea would be to perform all management of the Internet router on the console of the router itself. To keep management tasks to a minimum, you could use the LRP distribution, or some other mini Linux distribution where you can prepare the configuration with the relative comfort of your workstation, and then *hand-lib* it over to the router. Because the security depends upon there being no way to communicate directly between the Internet router and the inside, you will have to think about how you want to perform logging and system problem notification.

That concludes our short tour of Internet router topologies. Remember that they are not meant to be inclusive, or even representative, of the most common configurations. The first three are probably pretty common, and I've used the first two. The fourth is meant to serve as an example of how a little creative thought on your part can add security to this vital portion of your network (however non-intuitive your topology may be). A stable Internet router is not worth much if your network is easily compromised. Nor is a secure network useful if you cannot maintain it. Choosing your configuration is really just a bunch of trade-offs, with security and ease of administration often being diametrically opposed to each other.

Internet Routes—the "Inside" Versus the "Outside" As I stated before, how you configure your routes will depend on your topology. It will, however, consist of at least three components: the *loopback*, the *inside*, and *everything else*. *Everything else* is the default route that points out towards the Internet over your *sppp0* interface.

The *inside* includes everything that is *behind* the Internet router—the portion of the Internet that is yours. At the very minimum, it should include the networks alloted to the private address space,[4] as shown in Table 6.1. You should also configure packet-filtering rules to not allow these IP addresses to originate from outside your network, in case your router advertises them and somebody nearby (in terms of netspace—say, at the same ISP) notices and decides to see just how open your network is. These will be one of the examples later in this chapter.

What you will configure in your routing tables also includes the Internet address space which has been allocated to you by your ISP, since it will not automagically be known to your Internet router. This is obvious, but I didn't want you to forget in your excitement of bringing up the link. Note that the IPs for the point-to-point connection normally do not need to be routed by your internal network. Unless this is the only Internet-valid address space you have (which is problematic, as will be explained in Chapter 8), you can forget that they exist, since you should not have to contact either of the routers on the network directly via those IPs. Finally, your routing table might include any *other* address space, e.g., IPv6 address space or Internet-valid address space, which is not allocated to you, but which you somehow know is not being used or will never be accessed from your site. If you're going to configure a dynamic routing daemon, now's the time to do so.

Otherwise, put your default route in */etc/wanpipe/wanpipe_routes* (if you didn't configure it in */etc/wanpipe/interfaces/sppp0*) and the others routes into */etc/init.d/ networks*. Once everything is up and working, you're probably about 20% done (although it might feel like 80%); you still have to configure your security. Much of the remainder of this chapter contains discussions about security. First comes a section on general network host security which will hopefully help you prevent people on the outside from hijacking your router for their own personal (ab)use. The section following that deals with how to configure two variants of firewalling (really, packet-filtering) for Linux, limiting IP forwarding and blocking packets from entering or exiting the system.

Table 6.1 Private Routes

network	dotted netmask	abbreviated netmask
10.0.0.0	255.0.0.0	/8
172.16.0.0	255.240.0.0	/12
192.168.0.0	255.255.0.0	/16

6.2 GENERAL NETWORK SECURITY MEASURES

Security is no light matter on a system exposed to the Internet today. If you think that your system will be safe, either because your organization is benevolent or no one knows that your link exists, you may be in for a rude awakening to life on the Internet. Even if no one targets your site, a cracker might like to use it as a convenient launching

---

[4] See Section 2.1.5.

point for attacks on others. People may want to use your systems to generate spam. Or they may just want to destroy something. As for people not knowing about your presence on the Net, don't count on it. I set up a cable modem at a non-commercial location one afternoon and was quite surprised to see a port scan (originating from a university on another continent!) being run against the system only three hours after it first came online.

You will have to form your own philosophy about how to deal with such incidents. My personal reaction was to make sure that the port scan did not result in anything useful and to review *syslog* log files more carefully than normal for the next few weeks. In my opinion, there was no need to actively confront the scanner until a more intrusive attempt to access the system was made. Of course, this was a private system and the consequences of a security breach would have been inconvenient, but not devastating to my livelihood. In general, I recommend that you consider your reaction carefully unless you know that you have the resources and know-how to lock horns with a wily cracker. Depending upon your workload or your organization's policies, you may not have a choice. . . .

The remainder of this section is divided into a subsection which deals with general network host security, i.e., how to keep people from hacking services which run on your router, and a somewhat longer subsection on how to configure packet-filtering with Linux. Although the sample router configuration in this chapter is for an Internet router, the security measures apply to all routers. Attacks from the inside are just as likely, and typically more devastating because the attacker already knows something about your network and what they would like to target.

6.2.1 Generic Host Security

Developing a comprehensive security model is not the purpose of the book, nor do I believe that I would be the right person to present it. My recommendations are colored by my experiences. Host security for Unix is an exceedingly complex topic and the subject of several books much thicker than this one. One of the best ways to mitigate the risk of this complexity, and the unnerving fact that crackers trying to break into your systems will invariably be better equipped with tools and have more time than you do, is to eliminate it whenever possible. Simply put, any services which are not required to be running on your router should be disabled. Because Unix has a history of being exposed to the Internet, university campuses, and corporate data centers, there are some good measures which have already been taken, e.g., logging, *tcpd*, etc. I'll introduce those as appropriate. Consider these few points as food for thought. If you do not already have a security strategy, you should do these things at the very minimum. More would be better.

1. Be aware that network security is meaningless if you do not have any physical security for your systems. Why would a **social engineer**, sent to do some corporate raiding, go to great lengths to break into your system over the network when she could casually walk by with a floppy disk, quickly bounce the system and add herself to */etc/passwd* and */etc/shadow*? You'll notice the reboot, but nothing in *syslog* is going to tell you what happened. *Your* instance of the operating system isn't the one that made the change. It just knows that it went down

and came back up. This was mentioned in Section 1.2, but it bears repeating: Physically isolate your routers from the general public whenever possible. If you cannot do that, then use power-on (BIOS) passwords, case locks, and any other method you can think of to prevent unauthorized access to your machine.

2. Do not be naive about the dangers of sending passwords in cleartext over the network. The Linux version of *login* prohibits you from logging in as a super-user via *telnet* or *rlogin*, but by default it does not go so far as to prevent you from logging in as a normal user and then performing a *su* to root. If you do this, you will be sending the root password in cleartext via the telnet session. Your login mechanism should be such that you are able to login to your router(s) from any location securely (unless you are restricting access to the console only, which is not a bad idea). In any event, do not fall into the trap of believing that network access to your systems is safe if there is not some form of session encryption taking place at every step along the way. Otherwise, your password could traverse one link encrypted, only to be unencrypted and sent in cleartext over the next hop. I am referring to the situation when you are using machine A to access machine B via a secure mechanism, and then login to machine C from the shell you have running on machine B. Even though A $\rightarrow$ B is secure, B $\rightarrow$ C is not necessarily so.

   ssh can help you out of the predicament immensely because it encrypts the entire session, allows *rexec*-style execution of commands, and also comes with *scp* (a secure form of *rcp*). Note that the original *ssh*'s license (for version 1) is not compatible with all forms of use or philosophies. You should read the license carefully if you are in the business of supplying turn-key systems or intend to otherwise integrate *ssh* into a commercial product. The license accompanying version 2 is much more restrictive, so do not neglect to review it and comply with it. Fortunately, there is now an *OpenSSH* which is "free."

   Because ITAR[5] considers *ssh* (and many other programs which include cryptography) a dangerous encryption-based weapon when it is transmitted in electronic format, it is not publicly available for download from sites within the United States and certain other countries. You can find it and other encryption-based software on FTP sites in the "free world." For Debian packages, see *http://www.debian.org/misc/README.non-US*. Alternatives to the **ssh** package are **telnet98** and **telnet-ssl**.

3. Equally as dangerous as sending passwords in cleartext over the network is storing them anywhere where they can be retrieved or sending them via email. But it can be tough to remember a long list of passwords, especially passwords which you use only rarely. For example, you may need to exchange a set of passwords with another administrator in the company in case something happens to you.

---

[5] See **ITAR** in the glossary.

PGP—Pretty Good Privacy

PGP, *Pretty Good Privacy*, is a public-key encryption mechanism which has been embroiled in legal issues surrounding export restrictions from the United States and multiple patent holders in different locations. I use it by name because it is probably the best known of this type of software. There are several alternatives, including *GNU Privacy Guard*, known as *gpg* or *GnuPG* (get the **gnupg** package for Debian or visit http://www.gnupg.org/) and OpenPGP (described in RFC 2440).

The best system I have come up with is to use a *PGP*-like mechanism. I sign the email containing the password(s) with my public key, which I have already exchanged with the other admin in a secure manner, and then encrypt the email with the other admin's public key, so that it is for his eyes only. This way, she can store the email in her email system, but not access it without using her PGP key. If she cannot be trusted with the security of her own PGP key, then you have bigger problems. You can add a layer of security to this by encrypting the contents of the email with a conventional (single password) mechanism, sending the email, and then disclosing the password when you talk to the valid recipient of the email. The step confirms that the email was received by the right person. Public-key cryptography is also a handy way to send things to yourself, i.e., to store them securely on your workstation. Even if someone were to physically remove the hard drive, take it somewhere else and mount it, he wouldn't get the passwords, because he doesn't know how to unlock your private key.

If you need to leave the passwords in a safe place in case something happens to you, you should either use a PGP mechanism, or, to get computers out of the loop altogether, put them in a sealed envelope in a fireproof safe with your signature on the outside. If someone opens the envelope, you'll notice, and if someone steals it, you'll notice, and if someone steals it and tries to replace it with a forgery, you'll notice. Of course, you have to check the status of the envelope regularly, say, once a week.

Password choice is also important, but you *already* know this. Still, I'm amazed at the passwords that some people, even system administrators, use. At one environment I worked in, you could get into most of the back office systems by guessing from a list of three or four passwords which we had *retired* from use in the Linux environment over a year prior. Maybe they're still valid. If you're completely at a loss for picking passwords, try either the **pwgen** or **makepasswd** packages, which include binaries of the same name. These will produce passwords which are not based on dictionary words and contain sufficient variation to be considered non-trivial by */bin/passwd*. They are also a good method of automatically generating passwords for users.

4. Be careful about which packages you load on your Internet router. If you load **samba**, you will have the *smbd* daemon listening on port 139, and the *nmbd* daemon broadcasting your existence to the world. This does not say that I

am aware of any problems with the Samba daemons. There are many server packages which run as root, open ports, and have potential security exploits. Basically, anything that is not needed should not be loaded. If there are servers which you would like to have loaded on the system, but do not want to be executed upon startup, you should script these not to be started. Every service on your system should be started either from *inetd*, or from the system startup directories, e.g., */etc/init.d/* for Debian systems. One way to quickly disable a service is to edit its startup script and add `exit 0` as the first executable statement. This leaves the software and startup script intact, and can be easily reversed. Two notes of caution about this, though. First, you should stop the service with `/etc/init.d/`*servicename* `stop` before editing the script. This way, you won't have to try to stop the process(es) by hand. Second, for Linux distributions which support the concept of local configuration files, you may have to take manual intervention when upgrading the packages which own these startup files. This is a mixed blessing. On the downside, it requires manual intervention when upgrading the package. On the upside, this reminds you about customizations you have made to your system, allowing you to revisit them as necessary.

5. Subscribe to, read, and participate in a security mailing list or newsgroup, either for your distribution or for Linux/Unix in general. Security is a moving target, and keeping abreast is not easy to do when you have other duties to perform. When working with management, it is often the sort of topic that receives a lot of verbiage, but little support when it comes down to requesting the time, training, or money to perform security enhancements. It is also the sort of thing where the technology is complex enough that it may preclude meaningful decision-making on the part of your management and they will lean upon you to set the direction (and maybe the policy, too). For all of these reasons, it is good to stay in touch with others who have similar interests. For Debian, see *http://www.debian.org/security/*.

6. Get into the habit of using the *last* and *lastb* commands regularly to determine when and from where people have been logging into your system, or failing to log into your system. If it appears that no one ever logs into your systems, then attackers could be removing these logs to cover their tracks. There is plenty of information created by *syslog* (in */var/log/*)—learn what is there and how to read it so that if you suspect something has occurred, you can quickly spot something unusual in the log files. I like to configure *syslog* to dump everything into a single file, */var/log/messages*, so that I do not have to keep going from file to file. I can also watch this one file, either interactively with `tail -f`, the "old-fashioned way" with *grep*, using custom perl scripts, or one of the Debian packages listed below. The security conscious will consider using the built-in facility in syslog to log both locally and to a remote system.

   xlogmaster is a GUI logfile viewer which is customizable to support triggers and even audible alerts.

   gnome-admin contains *logview*, which is a nice GUI logfile viewer that contains descriptions of many common *syslog* messages (see the **zoom** feature).

since is a *stateful* version of *tail*. It adds useful functionality for scanning low-volume logfiles by displaying the logfile *since* the last time it was viewed.

syslog-summary incorporates similar functionality to that described above with *since* (with the `--state` switch), has a filtering mechanism (with `--ignore`), and delivers on its name by summarizing the occurrences of a message in the logfile.

xwatch can color-code a logfile being watched to make more important events easier to notice.

7. Read *Practical UNIX and Internet Security* from cover to cover. This book is filled with valuable information based on extensive experience. A reference is available in the Bibliography, which starts on page 337.

8. If you become paranoid that someone within your group (another administrator, perhaps) is doing Not Good Things, you can use the **ttysnoop** (and **ttylog** if your system is accessible via a serial interface) to record every telnet and login session.

6.2.2 Network Service Security

You want your systems to be secure. You have made sure that the passwords are secure. You never send your password over the network unencrypted. Better yet, you login only to the console. The system is physically secure. You have taken every measure possible to make sure that nothing logged by *syslog* eludes you. What about network-based attacks? Unfortunately, you cannot completely hide your router from the network—it is the network. To limit your exposure, you should disable any (network) services.[6] To check to see which network ports are open on your system, use the *netstat* command with various options.

- Review */etc/inetd.conf* and turn off any services which are not needed. These are security holes waiting to happen. Decide between *telnet* and *rlogin*, or even better yet, if you are compatible with the license, use *ssh*. You turn off a service by commenting out the appropriate line in *inetd.conf* and then stopping and restarting *inetd*. The same applies for *xinetd*, a more configurable replacement for *inetd*, should you choose to run it. You can ask *inetd* to re-read the configuration file with either `/etc/init.d/netbase reload` (Debian), `kill -HUP $(pidof inetd)`, or go for the gusto and `kill $(pidof inetd) ; /usr/sbin/inetd`.

- `netstat -a | more` is the old standby that will be familiar to most Unix hacks. It displays all `family inet` (i.e., TCP/IP) sockets in use, in addition to `family unix` sockets (which are not of concern to us here). It resolves service names using */etc/services* (or whatever mechanism is indicated in */etc/nsswitch.conf*.

---

[6] Network services are often referred to as just **services**, due to their connection with the */etc/services* file.

Use -n to prevent the lookups from occurring. (This is more commonly done as part of `netstat -rn`, which displays the kernel's routing table.)

- `netstat --inet -a` will display just the TCP and UDP ports and the ICMP services to which our machine will respond. This is better-suited to our task of finding potential weaknesses.

- Linux, in keeping with the ideal that providing information about the functioning of the system is a better policy than hiding it, has made some nice improvements to *netstat*. They include:

    — -p—lists the PID/process name associated with the socket, a la *lsof* functionality.

    — -e—creates extended output. For network sockets, it lists the UID associated with the socket.

    — -v—is the obligatory verbose switch. Oddly enough, it does not result in any additional output.

netstat looks like:

```
### active TCP connections between this system and other systems
oxygen:root> netstat --inet -n
Active Internet connections (w/o servers)
Proto Recv-Q Send-Q Local Address      Foreign Address      State
tcp        0      0 192.168.18.1:2089  192.168.18.2:113     TIME_WAIT
tcp        0      0 192.168.16.1:23    192.168.18.2:1107    ESTABLISHED
tcp        0      0 192.168.18.1:2086  192.168.18.2:23      ESTABLISHED
tcp        0      0 192.168.101.2:23   192.168.16.2:1026    ESTABLISHED
tcp        1      1 38.29.61.100:1995  209.81.8.242:80      LAST_ACK
tcp       57      0 38.29.61.100:1809  207.179.18.134:21    CLOSE_WAIT

### active TCP connections AND
### all "server" processes listening for connections on this system
### just look at all those potential security holes...
oxygen:root> netstat --inet -a
Active Internet connections (including servers)
Proto Recv-Q Send-Q Local Address        Foreign Address    State
tcp       57      0 oxy.mancill.com:1809 ftp.kde.org:ftp    CLOSE_WAIT
tcp        0      0 *:auth               *:*                LISTEN
tcp        0      0 *:exec               *:*                LISTEN
tcp        0      0 *:login              *:*                LISTEN
tcp        0      0 *:shell              *:*                LISTEN
tcp        0      0 *:telnet             *:*                LISTEN
tcp        0      0 *:ftp                *:*                LISTEN
tcp        0      0 *:time               *:*                LISTEN
tcp        0      0 *:daytime            *:*                LISTEN
tcp        0      0 *:discard            *:*                LISTEN
tcp        0      0 *:sunrpc             *:*                LISTEN
tcp        0      0 *:ssh                *:*                LISTEN
tcp        0      0 *:printer            *:*                LISTEN
tcp        0      0 *:snpp               *:*                LISTEN
udp        0      0 *:bootps             *:*
udp        0      0 *:791                *:*
udp        0      0 *:2049               *:*
udp        0      0 *:talk               *:*
```

```
udp       0      0 *:ntalk            *.*
udp       0      0 *:time             *.*
udp       0      0 *:daytime          *.*
udp       0      0 *:discard          *.*
udp       0      0 *:sunrpc           *.*
raw       0      0 *:1                *.*
raw       0      0 *:1                *.*
raw       0      0 *:6                *.*
raw       0      0 *:1                *.*
raw       0      0 *:6                *.*
```

- Get acquainted with *lsof*, which, among other things, is a more capable version of *netstat*. It walks the kernel's list of open file descriptors, collecting detailed information about how that file descriptor is being used. If you're wondering what good that does you, you should realize that many things in the Unix kernel are represented internally as file descriptors. Taken from the *lsof* manpage:

  > An open file may be a regular file, a directory, a block special file, a character special file, an executing text reference, a library, a stream or a network file (Internet socket, NFS file or UNIX domain socket.)

  Although many Unices have their own methods for obtaining this information (with Linux, you can get this info by walking the individual file descriptor files in */proc/*pid/fd/filedes), *lsof* uses the same switches and formats it consistently across the different flavors. It also supports dumping its output in a format easily read by scripts. See the **-F** option.

  It is available for virtually every Unix dialect around (currently 18 different dialects, often two or three different kernel versions per dialect). It is extremely useful for debugging client-server problems and network application performance problems, especially when you do not have access to the source code. (I've often used it on HP-UX because their version of *netstat* does not show the port number on the other end of a socket, only the IP address). With nothing sensible coming from *inetd* or the application, how else are you going to find out what's connected to you? You're better off with the basic networking tools that come with Linux, but you still might like some of the features of *lsof*.

    — When using the **-i** to list `inet` sockets, you can filter the output by specifying a particular `[protocol][@host][:port]`. There is also limited AND and OR functionality—see the manpage for details.

    — *lsof* has a **r**epeat mode (**-r**), where it will run itself iteratively. When used in conjunction with **-i**, it is an easy way to watch for a connection to start or die.

    — You can list file descriptors based on PID with **-p**, UID with **-u**, and PGRP (Process GRouP ID) with **-g**. The PGRP is the set of all child processes of parent. Just specify the PID of the parent as the argument to **-g**. Note that you'll probably want to use the **-a** (AND) option to see the intersection of the file descriptors matched by the options (as opposed to the union). For example, to see all of the `inet` file descriptors open for processes spawned by *inetd* on your system, you can use:

```
oxygen:/root> lsof -a -g $(pidof inetd) -i
COMMAND        PID PGRP USER     FD    TYPE DEVICE NODE NAME
inetd          241  241 root     4u    inet    162  TCP *:discard (LISTEN)
inetd          241  241 root     5u    inet    163  UDP *:discard
inetd          241  241 root     6u    inet    164  TCP *:daytime (LISTEN)
inetd          241  241 root     7u    inet    165  UDP *:daytime
inetd          241  241 root     8u    inet    166  TCP *:time (LISTEN)
inetd          241  241 root     9u    inet    167  UDP *:time
inetd          241  241 root    10u    inet    168  TCP *:ftp (LISTEN)
inetd          241  241 root    11u    inet    169  TCP *:telnet (LISTEN)
inetd          241  241 root    12u    inet    170  UDP *:talk
inetd          241  241 root    13u    inet    171  UDP *:ntalk
inetd          241  241 root    14u    inet    172  TCP *:shell (LISTEN)
inetd          241  241 root    15u    inet    173  TCP *:login (LISTEN)
inetd          241  241 root    16u    inet    174  TCP *:exec (LISTEN)
inetd          241  241 root    17u    inet    175  TCP *:smtp (LISTEN)
inetd          241  241 root    18u    inet    176  TCP *:finger (LISTEN)
inetd          241  241 root    19u    inet    177  TCP *:auth (LISTEN)
in.telnet     6528  241 root     0u    inet  27557  TCP 10.1.1.2:telnet->10.1.1.1:2013 (EST)
in.telnet     6528  241 root     1u    inet  27557  TCP 10.1.1.2:telnet->10.1.1.1:2013 (EST)
in.telnet     6528  241 root     2u    inet  27557  TCP 10.1.1.2:telnet->10.1.1.1:2013 (EST)
in.telnet    26341  241 root     0u    inet 132753  TCP 10.1.1.2:telnet->10.1.1.1:3824 (EST)
in.telnet    26341  241 root     1u    inet 132753  TCP 10.1.1.2:telnet->10.1.1.1:3824 (EST)
in.telnet    26341  241 root     2u    inet 132753  TCP 10.1.1.2:telnet->10.1.1.1:3824 (EST)
```

— Use the **-t** option to get (very) terse output, i.e., just the PIDs which match the criteria given. If you want to kill not only *inetd*, but every process it might have spawned (say, to get **everybody** off of the box), you can specify the command above along with **-t**. (Take care that you don't kill your own connection to the router.)

You should understand the function of every service running on your router. If you are not familiar with a service, you should do some research about the service and its security configuration, and disable it until you are certain that you can provide it securely or that you need it so badly that you are willing to take the risk of serving it as is.

***tcpd*—Access Control Wrappers**   The *tcpd* program monitors incoming network requests via *inetd* and determines whether the requestor may access that service. If it is allowed, it spawns the normal network daemon to deal with the service requested. Otherwise, the connection attempt is rejected, and in either case the attempt is logged via *syslog*. It uses the files */etc/hosts.allow* and */etc/hosts.deny* as configuration files to filter requests on one or more of the following criteria:

1. pattern-based access control (such as IP address ranges, DNS names, and net-groups)
2. client username lookups with the RFC 931 (*authd*) protocol
3. forward and reverse lookups for hostname/IP correlation
4. source-routed clients, systems that are using source routing and therefore possibly address spoofing (i.e., pretending to be a different IP address).

Many *inetd* services make use of the *tcpd* wrappers by default. This allows you to configure your security once and have it apply to multiple services. This satisfies the principle of letting the application programmer focus on the programming of the application (in this case, say, a telnet daemon), and letting the network security guru concentrate on designing network security. *tcpd* should be part of the base network installation of any full-sized Linux distribution.

An Alternative to *inetd—xinetd* Often you are not able to escape using some of these standard services, but you need more protection than they provide, or than can be had using *tcpd*. After all, what good is a network computer which cannot interact with the network safely? Rewriting all of them would be a lot of work, and any time a new service becomes available, you have to modify it to comply with your security architecture. Why not cut them off at the source, before the service starts? You can do this to a certain extent with the kernel's packet-filtering, but the kernel code should remain lean and fast, and the problem predates GPLed kernels which come with source anyway. (Imagine being responsible for this big Unix system with no source code available anywhere. Feel the bugs! <shudder>) Panagiotis Tsirigotis had the same ideas you have and came up with *xinetd* back in 1992. Since that time, it's been ported and maintained by Charles Murcko and Jan Wedekind. *xinetd* is a drop-in replacement for *inetd* that offers a very complete network access control mechanism to be executed before a network service even starts. This list of features is taken from the Debian package notes:

1. Access control on all services based on:
   (a) address of remote host
   (b) time of access
   Access control works on all services, whether multi-threaded or single-threaded and for both the TCP and UDP protocols. All UDP packets can be checked, as well as all TCP connections.
2. Hard reconfiguration:
   (a) kills servers for services that are no longer in the configuration file
   (b) kills servers that no longer meet the access control criteria
3. Prevents denial-of-access attacks by
   (a) placing limits on the number of servers for each service (avoids process table overflows)
   (b) placing an upper bound on the number of processes it will fork
   (c) placing limits on the size of log files it creates
4. Extensive logging abilities:
   (a) for every server started it can log:
      i. the time when the server was started (*)
      ii. the remote host address (*)
      iii. who was the remote user (if the other end runs an RFC 931/RFC 1413 server) (*)

   iv. how long the server was running
       (*) each of these can be logged for failed attempts, too).
   (b) for some services, if the access control fails, it can log informa-
       tion about the attempted access (for example, it can log the user
       name and command for the rsh service)

These features are quite useful for a production environment, and impressive compared to the normal *inetd*. The distribution also contains *itox*, which can convert
your existing */etc/inetd.conf* to a format suitable for */etc/xinetd.conf*.

6.2.3 IP Event Loggers

Sometimes you like to monitor services which are not started via *[x]inetd* at a level
similar to what *xinetd* offers. You are once again faced with the same issue: needing
to perform your own logging hacks on several system daemons. Even if the servers
provide adequate logging, suppose you would like for *all* connections to the system
to be logged in the same format, regardless of whether they were made through *inetd*
or directly to the daemon running on the service port. For this situation, you can
employ one of the IP event loggers described below. None of them provides access
control or extensive amounts of logging. For one, they do not pretend to understand
the protocol being used, they simply watch incoming connections. Each of these is
denoted by its Debian package name, but you can use the URLs listed to visit their
home sites.

iplogger provides two separate daemons, one to log TCP and the other to log ICMP
   events. It performs its logging through *syslog*. Of note is its ability to detect
   the FTP server *bounce attack*, for which a white paper is included in the documentation. Its source code is available from several Linux mirrors, including
   Sunsite as *iplogger-ident–1.1.tar.gz*.

jail (Just Another IP Logger) is also for logging TCP and ICMP events, and is originally based on *iplogger*. It performs its logging via *syslog*, and is configurable
   to log different types of events at different *syslog* levels. You might find it
   interesting that *jail* is distributed under the *Artistic License*, which is different
   from the GPL, but not extensively different in its effect. A copy of this license
   is included with the distribution. (See *http://www.wiw.org/ ams/jail/*.)

ippl is the IP Protocols Logger, and is capable of logging TCP, ICMP, and UDP.
   It is similar to *iplogger* and is based upon it, but provides some additional
   features such as being configurable with *Apache-like* rules and having a built-
   in DNS cache. Instead of logging through *syslog*, it writes to its own logfiles
   (configurable). Its home site is *http://www.via.ecp.fr/~hugo/ippl/*.

net-acctd advertises itself as a "usermode IP accounting daemon..., similar to what
   tcpdump does." While I worked with the package, I found it more similar to the
   IP event loggers, but offering more information (much more, in some cases).
   The output fields it generates are configurable, and output is to filenames listed
   in the configuration files, as with *ippl*. It is also the only program listed which

will associate traffic to a particular local user (e.g., for slip or PPP connections).
http://www.bladesinger.com/net-acct

If any of these event loggers detects anything interesting on a regular basis, say an excessive amount of telnet requests from an external system to a system which does not support external user accounts, or a great number of connection attempts in a short interval, you will want to find out more about the packets triggering the event logger. You might need a better tool to do this—I suggest that you use one of the packet sniffers described in Section 4.5. You might find that someone is using one of the programs described in the next section, a **port scanner**, to detect a way to infiltrate your network.

6.2.4 Port Scanners

The goal of a **port scanner** is a program which looks for holes in a server or firewall. It is called a port scanner because it walks through the entire list of TCP and UDP ports (ICMP, too) trying to find available services or types of traffic which are allowed to pass. It also tests the system for known vulnerabilities of services and TCP/IP itself. The most famous of these is *Satan*, which received a large amount of media attention because it was publicly released and effective. At that time, people were afraid that releasing such a tool to the public instead of only to the network administration community would result in a rash of cracked sites. The problem with this logic is that there isn't a very good way to release software only to system administrators except by making it very expensive, which means that only large/rich corporations will be able to afford it—this is regressive. It also assumes that the hacker community doesn't already have tools this sophisticated or more, which is a poor assumption. Since that time, people (seem to) have come to understand that the only way to make things more secure is to expose their problems, and not cover them up, hoping that you'll get a patch before a *script kiddie* ruins your day.

You can (and should) employ port scanners to periodically check your configuration and services for weaknesses. If possible, you should try to run them from the *complete* outside of your network. If you have a good source for access on the outside, like a cable modem, then you're in luck. Another alternative is to strike up a rapport with a system administrator at another organization and work out a deal wherein the admin sets up a Linux box outside their firewall with a shell account for you, and vice-versa. This sort of configuration could be used for more than just testing your network security. Examples include testing your SMTP gateway configuration (as a place to originate external messages), checking your external DNS configuration, and verifying that Internet services are functioning as they should.[7]

If you cannot find a system completely external to your site, then a system on the perimeter net is acceptable (if you have one). Whatever you do, you should consider using one. If you worry that it will detect holes in your configuration and then mail them off to some hacker organization, pull down a copy of the sources and review it for code which might do something like that. This is part of the beauty of

---

[7] If I had a dime for every time an employee at a client site would call up and ask me why the FTP server was down, only to find out that they were behind a firewall on their end. . . .

free software. *Use the Source, Luke.* I introduce three such port scanners which are freely available. Sorry, I'm not going to tell you any more about how to use them. I live in a very litigious country and would hate to have to recall all of the printed copies of this book to plaster a *warning: contents discuss networking* sticker on them.

HINT: PACKAGE SOURCES WITH DEBIAN

Debian's *apt* package manager provides a way to pull the complete sources of a package with a single command (once you set it up properly). All you need to do to set it up is to add a `deb-src` line to */etc/apt/sources.list* for each source repository you would like to access. For the packages included with the base distribution, this line looks like:

```
deb-src http://http.us.debian.org/debian stable main contrib non-free
```

Once you add this line, you need to run `apt-get update` so that *apt* can refresh the list of packages. Then, any time you want to retrieve a set of sources (for any package in the archive category for which you set up a `deb-src` line—there can be multiple `deb-src` lines in your */etc/apt/sources.list*), you can do so with a command such as `apt-get source` *packagename*. This retrieves the original source and the `.diff.gz` file which contains the *debianizations*, and extracts them into the current directory. (Debaianizations are those things which were done to make the package compatible with Debian, and everything required to compile your own version of the package by using the Debian developer tools, also available in the standard archive.)

- *Satan* is the original. It is written largely in Perl and uses a browser for its user interface (preferably a graphical one). It is likely the best tool to try first, because it comes with HTML-based documentation and a tutorial. It is available as a Debian package **satan** (which is part of the *non-free* of the archive because of Satan's license) or *http://www.fish.com/satan*.

- *SAINT*, the Security Administrator's Integrated Network Tool is the follow-up to *Satan* and is released under the same license. The program focuses on security, but generates a significant amount of general network information in the process. According to its webpage, it aims to be "the best investigative security network tool available, at any price." (*SAINT's* license is similar to the GPL except that neither it nor derivative works can be sold.) See *http://www.wwdsi.com/saint/* for more information. Even if you are not interested in the software, you should spend some time working through the vulnerability tutorials available at this website.

- *nmap* is a command line port scanner which supports a wide variety of scanning techniques. It is available from *http://www.insecure.org/nmap*. You should retrieve this package even if you have no intention of using the binary just so that you can read the manpage and the documentation in */usr/doc/nmap/*.

The current version supports these scanning techniques:

— Vanilla TCP connect() scanning,
— TCP SYN (half open) scanning,
— TCP FIN (stealth) scanning,
— TCP FTP proxy (bounce attack) scanning,
— SYN/FIN scanning using IP fragments (bypasses packet filters),
— UDP recvfrom() scanning,
— UDP raw ICMP port unreachable scanning,
— ICMP scanning (ping-sweep), and
— Reverse-ident scanning.

- *Firewalk* scans for open ports in a firewall, and is based on a modification of the behavior of *traceroute*. It can be used via the command line, and the latest version sports a GTK interface. At the time of writing, it is not available as a Debian package, but you can retrieve the source and the white paper describing the technique at *http://www.packetfactory.net/firewalk/*.

6.3 IP FIREWALLING

IP firewalling takes many forms and is a topic which covers many facets of TCP/IP networking. For our purposes, I will associate IP firewalling directly with mechanisms which are used to restrict the flow of packets into or out of a host, or through a router. The first of these can be termed **packet-filtering** and the second **conditional forwarding**. The term **conditional forwarding** has been coined only to separate it from input/output ruled-based packet-filtering. In the Real World, people interchange the terms **packet-filtering** and **firewalling** freely to mean both of the functions listed above, and several others, such as **proxying** and **masquerading**. And more often than not, **conditional forwarding** is lumped in with **packet-filtering**. This is because they do the same thing, but under different circumstances, which is why I present them separately.

Before we get started with our discussions of forwarding and packet-filtering, remember that they are not the only game in town for firewalls. Depending upon your application(s) and firewall topology, you can have a firewall or Internet router which does not route or forward at all (*/proc/sys/net/ipv4/ip_forward* = 0). Instead, your users will use proxies to access what they need. This type of topology can be very secure and will work for smaller organizations where a single system can function as the router, firewall, and proxy server. If you implement this type of firewall, you will still use packet-filtering to protect the proxy daemons and the host itself, but you will not need to specify any restrictions on forwarding, since none is taking place.

What you do with the rules can be logically separated from *how* you do it. This section concentrates on *how*. *What* varies wildly from application to application, and is left as a topic for a book on firewalls, although some examples will be scattered throughout this section and Chapter 8. Both packet-filtering and conditional forwarding are supported in the Linux kernel and is an application of our friend *ipchains*.[8]

---

[8] For the 2.2.x kernels.

Instead of just counting packets, as with IP accounting, or modifying packet source headers with IP masquerading, you now decide the fate of a packet by allowing it to pass, throwing it away, replying to the sender that the packet is not allowed to pass, or redirecting the packet to a port on the local system.[9]

One more note: Unlike IP accounting, the order in which the firewalling rules are encountered is significant. If the first rule blocks all packets, there is no point in even having the following rules. Similarly, if there is a rule which forwards all packets before any of the **reject** or **deny** rules, why bother with packet-filtering at all?

6.3.1 Conditional IP Forwarding for Firewalls

Conditional IP forwarding is a fancy term for configuring a router to reject the forwarding of certain packets, or vice-versa, to allow only certain packets to be forwarded. It operates like IP masquerading, evaluating packets which are to be forwarded, to see if they meet the criteria specified in the rule(s). When a match occurs, the policy (or target) of the rule is invoked. We cannot predict the final fate of the packet at this point, because we do not know if the default action—the action taken when no rules match—is to forward the packet or to reject it. In any case, your system must be configured with IP: forwarding/gatewaying set to **yes** in the kernel for 2.0 kernels; */proc/sys/net/ipv4/ip_forward* = 1 for 2.2 kernels and later. Otherwise, the packet will never be examined by the forwarding chain at all.

In the case that forwarding is enabled, there will be a default policy associated with it. The default policy, when no firewalling rules have been specified whatsoever, is **ACCEPT**. If the router can forward the packet, it will. The default policy can be set using *ipchains* to one of these three values: **ACCEPT**, **REJECT**, or **DENY**. The second two are equivalent in that the packet is discarded. REJECT notifies the sender that the packet could not be forwarded via an ICMP host unreachable message. For denied packets, no such message is sent. Typically, you use **DENY** for packets originating outside of your network (so the sender is not sure what happened to the packet), and **REJECT** for internally rejected packets as a polite way of saying "no." As you can easily surmise, there are two basic ways to go about configuring your rules.

1. You can expressly list the types of traffic which should not be allowed to traverse the system by using the default policy of **ACCEPT** and then specifying the traffic to be blocked with either **REJECT** or **DENY** rules.

2. The other way is to alter the default policy to be either **REJECT** or **DENY** and then explicitly list the types of traffic which are allowed to pass with **ACCEPT** rules.

Which of these you choose will depend upon the desired effect and your skill level. The more secure of the two is undoubtedly refusing all traffic by default, and then listing traffic which may pass in **ACCEPT** rules. However, this can be

---

[9] Covered in Section 8.2.

difficult (read: *maddening*) until you are familiar with the types of traffic you expect and understand all of the protocols which will be in use in your network. It is a time-consuming process to get the rules right the first time, and if you are in a time-critical situation, you might have to defer this type of configuration until later. Still, I recommend it, as it provides more protection and is an excellent way to earn your IP protocol "wings." If the default policy is to accept traffic, then you must explicitly block everything which should not be allowed to pass, which may be quite a lot. It also means that you have to test to make sure that services are blocked.

An example for 2.2.x systems using *ipchains* is presented below—configuring the default policy to reject all traffic and to allow two services, HTTP and telnet. You use the same syntax to specify packet-matching criteria to build rules as you did while configuring IP masquerading. You should recall the definition of **forwarding interface** from the discussion of IP masquerading (Section 4.4). When specifying an interface with any type of forwarding rule, the **forwarding interface** is the interface via which the packet leaves the router, not the one that received it.

The example refers to Figure 6.5. As you see from the diagram, it represents one basic configuration of the oxygen router. For our forwarding example, we will use a system with three interfaces. (Forwarding rules with only two interfaces are not very different from input/output rules.) Our system is a combination firewall and Internet router with a perimeter net to boot. The *sppp0* interface is our point-to-point connection to our ISP, and is configured as the default route in the kernel. The perimeter net (*eth1*) hosts our site's proxy servers. The inside (*eth0*) should have access only to the perimeter net, and for now, we will allow the perimeter net to speak freely to the Internet.

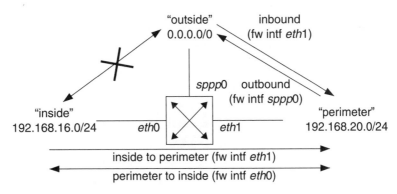

Figure 6.5 Conditional Packet Forwarding Example

Conditional IP Forwarding with *ipchains* If you are accustomed to working with *ipfwadm* and the 2.0.x kernel, *ipchains* provides a more powerful interface than *ipfwadm* for rule specification. The only thing you have to keep in mind when working with forwarding rules is that they must be part of either the built-in **forward** chain, or on a user-defined chain which is the target of that chain. For our example, we add rules to the built-in chain. But first, let's review the syntax of *ipchains* (Tables 6.2–6.6).

Table 6.2 *ipchains* General Forms

General usage:

```
ipchains -[ADC] chain rule [options]
ipchains -[RI] chain rule [options]
ipchains -D chain rulenum [options]
ipchains -[LFZNX] [chain] [options]
ipchains -P chain target [options]
ipchains -M [-L|-S] [options]
ipchains -h [icmp]
```

Table 6.3 *ipchains* Commands

command	description
-A chain	append to *chain*
-D chain rule	delete rule matching *rule* from *chain*
-D chain rulenum	delete rule *rulenum* from *chain* (rules are numbered starting at 1)
-I chain [rulenum]	insert rule into *chain*, optionally at position *rulenum* from the start (rules are numbered starting at 1)
-R chain [rulenum]	replace rule *rulenum* in *chain* (rules are numbered starting at 1)
-L [chain]	list all rules, or, if a chain is specified, list all rules in chain *chain*
-F [chain]	flush all rules, or, if a chain is specified, flush all rules in chain *chain*
-Z [chain]	zero counters for all rules, or, if a chain is specified, zero counters for all rules in chain *chain*
-C chain rule	test the packet defined by *rule* in chain *chain*
-N chain	create a new user-defined chain *chain*
-X chain	delete a user-defined chain *chain*
-P chain target	change the policy (default target) for chain *chain* to *target*, which must be one of the built-in targets: • ACCEPT—allow the packet to pass • DENY—swallow the packet • REJECT—swallow the packet but notify the sender with an ICMP host-unreachable message • MASQ—masquerade the packet • REDIR—redirect the packet to a local port • RETURN—return to the calling chain (not valid for built-in chains)
-M -L	list current masquerading connections
-M -S tcp tcpfin udp	set masquerading timeout values (in seconds—all three must be specified, use a value of 0 to indicate no change)

Table 6.4 *ipchains* Options Which Affect Packet Matching Specifications

option	description
`-p [!]proto`	match protocol *proto*, which is one of **tcp**, **udp**, **icmp**, **all** or an IP protocol number
`-s [!]addr[/mask] [!][port(s)]`	the IP source specification. The address can be a dotted-IP address or a hostname, the mask can be in dotted format or / format, and the ports can be a range *low:high*, or a space delimited list. The '!' reverses the sense of the comparison.
`-d [!]addr[/mask] [!][port(s)]`	the IP destination specification
`-i [!]  intf[+]`	the name of the network interface, which may end in '+' which acts as a wildcard. The sense may be reversed with '!.'
`[!]  -f`	match second or further fragments only (or not)
`[!]  -y`	match TCP packets only when SYN set (or not)

Table 6.5 *ipchains* Options Which Affect Chains and Rules

option	description
`-b`	insert two rules: one with -s & -d reversed
`-j target [port]`	specify a target rule of *target* for this rule should it match. Valid targets are other user-defined rules, **ACCEPT**, **DENY**, **REJECT**, **MASQ**, **REDIR**, or **RETURN**. When using **REDIR**, you must specify a *port*, which can be 0 (which indicates that the destination port in the packet header will be used to determine the local port), or any other port.

2.2.x Kernel Support for IP Firewalling   Before you start building rule chains, you will need to make sure that your kernel has support for IP firewalling built into it. The support is enabled by using the following options and recompiling the kernel:

```
Networking options --->
    <*> Packet socket
@   [*] Kernel/User netlink socket
@   <*> Netlink device emulation
+   [*] Network firewalls
    <*> Unix domain sockets
    [*] TCP/IP networking
    [*] IP: advanced router
+   [*] IP: firewalling
@   [*] IP: firewall packet netlink device
+   [*] IP: always defragment (required for masquerading)
```

The options denoted by the '@' character are not required, but are highlighted to talk about features in progress in the Linux kernel. The `Kernel/User netlink socket` is a mechanism by which user-space programs can interact with the kernel

Table 6.6 *ipchains* Options Which Affect Output and Misc.

option	description
-n	numeric output of addresses and ports
-v	verbose mode
-x	expand numbers (display exact values)

other options

option	description
-l	enable kernel logging (via *syslog*) for matching packets
-o *[maxsize]*	Copy matching packets to the user-space device. This is currently mainly for developers who want to play with firewalling effects in user-space. The optional `maxsize` argument can be used to limit the maximum number of bytes from the packet which are to be copied. This option is valid only if the kernel has been compiled with CONFIG_IP_FIREWALL_NETLINK set.
-m *[+-]markvalue*	Mark matching packets. Packets can be marked with a 32-bit unsigned value which may (one day) change how they are handled internally. If you are not a kernel hacker you are unlikely to care about this. If the string `markvalue` begins with a + or -, then this value will be added or subtracted from the current marked value of the packet (which starts at zero).
-t *andmask xormask*	Masks used for modifying the TOS field in the IP header. When a packet matches a rule, its TOS field is first bitwise AND'ed with first mask and the result of this will be bitwise XOR'ed with the second mask. The masks should be specified as hexadecimal 8-bit values. As the LSB of the TOS field must be unaltered (RFC 1349), TOS values which would cause it to be altered are rejected, as are any rules which always set more than TOS bit. Rules which might set multiple TOS bits for certain packets result in warnings (sent to *stdout*) which can be ignored if you know that packets with those TOS values will never reach that rule. Obviously, manipulating the TOS is a meaningless gesture if the rule's target is DENY or REJECT.

via a device file. Among other things, it provides an alternative to logging kernel packet headers via *klogd*, which is one of the options available when a firewalling rule makes a match. In the case of IP firewalling, the netlink copies the entire packet to a character special file under */dev* with major number 36 and minor number 3. The upshot is that this can be used to detect attacks in real-time, and possibly even take some form of action against the attack (or the attacker!). By creating device file with different minor numbers, other types of packets, e.g., raw Ethernet (as an alternative to using *libpcap*) and routing messages can be monitored. At the time of writing, there is only minimal application support available for this, so we're going to stick to the mainstream features, such as selectively forwarding packets with *ipchains*.

An Example of Conditional Forwarding with *ipchains*   We will now configure our three-way router, depicted in Figure 6.5. We want to prevent traffic from flowing between the *inside* and the *outside* in either direction, but wish to allow traffic to flow between the *perimeter* and the *inside* and between the *perimeter* and the *outside*.

```
### (1)
### flush any existing rules on the "forward" chain
oxygen:root> ipchains -X forward
### (2)
### our default forwarding policy is "deny"
### after this, nothing works
oxygen:root> ipchains -P forward DENY
### (3)
### expressly prohibit those on the inside from reaching
### the outside, but be polite about it ("reject")
oxygen:root> ipchains -A forward -j REJECT -i sppp0            \
                  -s 192.168.16.0/24
### (4)
### allow anyone to send TCP to the perimeter net
oxygen:root> ipchains -A forward -j ACCEPT -p tcp -i eth1 \
                  -d 192.168.20.0/24
### (5)
### allow the perimeter net to send to the inside
### when responding to TCP connections
oxygen:root> ipchains -A forward -j ACCEPT ! -y -p tcp -i eth0 \
                  -s 192.168.20.0/24                           \
                  -d 192.168.16.0/24
### (6)
### allow the perimeter net to forward to the outside
oxygen:root> ipchains -A forward -j ACCEPT -i sppp0 \
                  -s 192.168.20.0/24
```

1. This rule initializes us in a known state. All rules in the built-in **forward** chain are flushed.

2. Configure the default policy for forwarded packets to be REJECT.

3. Prohibit any direct communication between the inside and the outside. The forwarding rules will be executed in order until a match occurs, so even though the default policy already excludes this communication, a misplaced rule could "open up" the firewall again.

4. Allow both the outside and the inside to send TCP packets (from any port to any port) to the perimeter net. This gives the inside access to the proxies and allows the outside to deliver mail, etc.

5. Allow the perimeter net to respond to TCP connections when talking to the inside.

6. Allow the perimeter net to send freely to the outside. Note that this doesn't mean that everything can be answered. In other words, you're not done yet. Although you can send out all protocols, only TCP replies will be forwarded back to the perimeter net (as per rule #4).

So that's all there is to forwarding. Forwarding rules are more useful when you have three or more interfaces. In many cases, you will find that input (for systems which only route) and output rules (if there are services running on the system too) are sufficient to configure your packet-filtering needs. Still, conditional forwarding can quickly realize configurations which would be more complicated using only input rules. One example which comes to mind is to prevent forwarding of ICMP, but to still allow the internal interface(s) to respond to pings. You can disable ICMP forwarding with a single rule, and all interfaces will still be able to respond to pings. If you want to prevent external interfaces from responding to pings and traceroutes, you could use an input rule on that interface to block ICMP. Even better, use an output rule on that interface, so that the sender never sees a reply, but any IP event logging occurring on the system will still take place.

Anyway, keep conditional forwarding in your little bag of magic tricks. When you need it, sometimes nothing else will do. If I'm allowed one complaint, it's that the default listing format does not show the interface (nor did it for *ipfwadm*). For this reason, you should get into the habit of opening wide windows into any system which will be using any of the kernel firewalling features and using the -v switch for *ipchains* (and -e for those who use *ipfwadm*).

6.3.2 IP Packet-Filtering

Packet-filtering is a term that often goes hand-in-hand with firewalls, although that is only one application of its usefulness. But before it can be used, we should answer the question, "What is packet-filtering?" Everything that enters and exits our routers via the network is in the form of a packet. Normally, there are no restrictions on which hosts may use a system as a gateway. If the system can forward the packet, it will. Aside from systems with *tcpd*, there are few restrictions as to which hosts may attempt to contact a system on any given port via any particular protocol. If the system can answer, i.e., it has a daemon or service ready to answer on that port, it will. **Packet-filtering** allows us to restrict the flow of packets entering and exiting our system, based on the properties of the packets themselves. It differs from IP masquerading and conditional forwarding in that it only operates on input and output from the system, not packets selected for forwarding by the kernel's routing table. This is not to say that rules cannot match packets which are being forwarded; they can. The difference is that the matching occurs when the packet enters (or exits) the system. As you've come to expect, the rules are specified using *ipchains* with its usual syntax.

For simple routers, we talk primarily about **input** rules; **output** rules are equally valid, but I find it conceptually easier to think about blocking things on the way into the machine rather than on the way out of it. This also seems like it would result in less work for the machine. If you reject packets on the way in, you can potentially short-circuit a lot of the filtering rules. That is, you do not have to compare the packet to the remainder of the input chain, the forward chain, and then the output chain before finally rejecting the packet with the output rule.

The situation changes on a system with services, e.g., proxies, and/or users. In this case, output rules may be the only way to prevent certain traffic from originat-

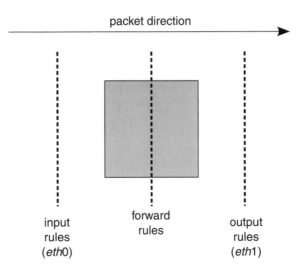

Figure 6.6 Packet-Filtering for Two Interfaces

ing from your system. (Packets originating from a system are never considered to be forwarded.) Keep this in mind when configuring proxies. In either case, input or output, you can alter the default policy of the **input/output** rules chain, just as with forwarding. Once again, specifying a default policy of **REJECT** or **DENY** is recommended.

I find it very helpful to draw pictures of what's going on when working with packet-filtering. One reason for this is that the definitions of **input** and **output** are relative to your position. Input with respect to an external interface means a packet from the outside of your network, while input rules on an internal interface apply to outbound packets. Figure 6.6 illustrates the difference. I often refer to your perspective on packet flow as "where you stand." For example, if you are "standing" outside of the firewall, all input rules apply to *eth1*.

Realize that the picture becomes more complicated when you have more than two interfaces, so keep this in mind when designing your network topology around your firewall and Internet router. To give you an idea, take a look at Figure 6.7.

Packet-filtering is just another example of how there are many ways to accomplish a given task with Linux. I believe this to be part of its Unix heritage—part of the toolbox philosophy. Your solution to a problem depends upon how you look at it. In the case of packet-filtering and firewalling, there are many "correct" answers; use the one that you understand.

6.3.3 Packet-Filtering with *ipchains*

ipchains provides a very powerful mechanism for limiting traffic into or out of a system or between networks. (Later, it is also the tool used to take advantage of some of the kernel functionality like port forwarding.) This section provides a short introduction to using *ipchains* to configure input and output firewall rules. You can refer back to Tables 6.2–6.6 for help with the syntax or run `ipchains -h` to see all of the options available. Let's work through a couple of examples.

Packet-Filtering Example #1   First, we need to prevent the training workstations in the training department from browsing the Internet. The instructors have complained that the users are browsing instead of paying attention to the course material. Fortunately, you planned for this when designing the company network, and the training workstations are all located on a separate (possibly virtual) subnet. That subnet is 192.168.36.0/24.

```
# ipchains input/output firewalling example #1
############################################################
# set up a few variables
INSIDE="192.168.0.0/16"        # all of our internal address space
TRAINING="192.168.36.0/24"     # training workstations

                               # eth0 is the "inside"
                               # eth1 is the "outside"
# setup default policies for the chains
#   by default, no input is allowed
#-----------------------------------------------------------
   ipchains -P input REJECT
# allow _our_ address space to access the outside
#-----------------------------------------------------------
   ipchains -A input -i eth0 -j ALLOW -s $INSIDE
# prevent the training workstations access to the outside
# (have to "Insert" this before the previous rule
#-----------------------------------------------------------
   ipchains -I input -j REJECT -s $TRAINING
```

This will prevent workstations in that subnet from accessing the outside. But because this has been such a problem for the instructors, they would also like to know which workstations are trying to access the outside during class. We can easily fulfill this

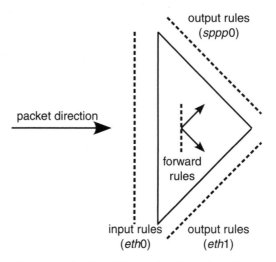

Figure 6.7 Packet-Filtering for Three Interfaces

request by enabling packet logging for matching packets. We do this by adding the -l (for "logging") switch to our REJECT rule above. When someone on a training workstation tries to access an external website, we'll see an entry like this in */var/adm/messages*:

```
Jun 30 12:00:19 oxygen kernel: Packet log: input REJECT eth0 PROTO=6
        192.168.36.21:4306 207.200.75.204:80
        L=60 S=0x00 I=28632 F=0x4000 T=64 SYN (#1)
```

That first line tells us when and what happened. At the time given, a packet trying to enter *eth0* of protocol "6" (which is TCP) was rejected. The second line lists the source IP:port and destination IP:port of the packet. The third line contains more information about the packet. It is produced by the code in */usr/src/linux/net/ipv4/ip_fw.c*. The fields have the following meanings:

- L=n is the length of the packet (in bytes).
- S=0xnn is the value of the TOS (Type Of Service) field in the packet.
- I=n is the identification field of the packet.
- F=0x$nnnn$ is the fragment offset.
- T=nn is the value in the TTL (Time To Live) field of the packet—the number of hops the packet can take before being discarded.
- The presence of SYN indicates that this bit is set; the (#1) is the absolute sequence number for the TCP sequence.

With this information logged via *syslog*, we can quickly scan for any attempts, all attempts made by each individual IP, and the times of those attempts.

Packet-Filtering Example #2   Our second example is to use packet-filtering to prevent direct access to FTP sites. Instead, we want to force users to use a FTP proxy client. The motivation is management wants us to keep a log of all transfers in case a disgruntled employee decides to FTP a copy of our trade secrets to a competitor.

We are going to load a FTP proxy directly on the firewall and instruct the users to connect to the proxy when they need to access external sites. We will not cover configuring the FTP proxy itself, which is simple enough, but will focus on the rules needed to allow the proxy to get outside of the firewall, but not any internal systems. Drawing a picture helps—see Figure 6.8. From this, we can write out the high-level rules required.

- Allow FTP access from the inside to the FTP proxy service running on oxygen.
- Prevent direct FTP access to the outside for any clients on the inside.
- Prevent external clients from connecting to the FTP proxy.
- Allow FTP access to the outside from the FTP proxy service.
- Prevent any other traffic from traversing the firewall.

Figure 6.8 Providing a Secure Environment for an FTP Proxy

But before we can write the packet-filtering rules to block direct FTP (or any protocol), we need to understand how the protocol works:

- FTP in "normal" mode

  1. The client uses a client port (a port in the range between 1024 and 65534) to contact the FTP server on port 21. This is called a **control connection**.

  2. Authentication occurs over the control connection, as do any client-issued commands and server acknowledgements of those commands.

  3. However, if one of those commands results in a data transfer (including getting a directory listing), then the client prepares for it by opening a second client port and sending this port number to the FTP server over the control connection.

  4. The FTP server opens a connection from port 20 on the server to the second client port on the client system. This port is used to transmit the data.

  Because you do not know the port to allow for the data transfer beforehand, you have to allow all external sites to use port 20 to connect to your internal clients. Thus anybody on the outside can probe your network by sending packets from port 20 on their system.

- FTP in passive mode

  Because of the dangers of normal FTP, some bright people came up with the idea of passive mode FTP, which works as follows:

  1. The control connection works as before. However, when a data transfer is initiated, the client asks the server to open an additional port on the server for use by the data transfer.

  2. The server finds a free port and sends this value back to the client over the control connection.

  3. The client then makes an outbound connection to the port the server just gave it, and the data transfer takes place over this connection.

The server thinks that this is cool because it already authenticated the client (as much as it wanted to), so it does not mind the inbound connection—it has to allow these anyway to offer the FTP service. The firewall likes the idea because it doesn't have to accept inbound connections from the outside. The client likes the idea because it gets its file.

Back to the problem at hand: Aside from the obvious requirement that we need to protect our network, we have the management mandate to log all transfers. A FTP proxy can help us do this and more. (Several proxies for Linux are covered in Section 8.1.) The idea of a proxy is to have a process running which handles conection requests and data transfers to the outside on behalf of the client. This offers the following advantages:

1. They run on a single system, which means that if you do have to allow normal mode FTP, it is only to a single system.

2. They log all transfers, connection attempts, etc.

3. Most of them have access control mechanisms to prevent just anybody from using the proxy.

4. They provide "application" level protection. Because they are proxying the FTP commands (i.e., they converse with the client, and then turn around and converse with the FTP server, in such a manner that the client believes that the FTP proxy is the FTP server, and the FTP server believes that the FTP proxy is the client), the proxy can examine the commands for illegal commands, buffer overflow attempts, and other assorted unscrupulous actions a FTP server (or client) might attempt.

For our rules, we will NOT assume that the FTP proxy always operates in passive mode on the client side (client-proxy), because a user may neglect to configure their FTP client to automatically request passive mode transfers. The proxy will use passive mode data transfers between it and the server. A sample set of rules is listed below. The section before each rule documents its role in preventing (or allowing) access through the firewall system.

```
#
# ipchains input/output firewalling example
##############################################################
# set up a few variables
INSIDE="192.168.0.0/16"          # all of our internal address space
ETH0=192.168.16.1/32        # fw intf on the inside
ETH1=192.168.20.1/32        # fw intf on the outside
ANY=0.0.0.0/0

# create new user-defined chains, "eth0in" and "eth1in"
# these get first dibs on anything that enters the system
ipchains -N eth0in
ipchains -N eth1in
ipchains -I input -i eth0 -j eth0in
ipchains -I input -i eth1 -j eth1in
```

```
# also create output chains, eth0out and eth1out
ipchains -N eth0out
ipchains -N eth1out
ipchains -I output -i eth0 -j eth0out
ipchains -I output -i eth1 -j eth1out

# setup default policies for the chains
#   by default, no input is allowed
#   by default, no output from eth1 is allowed
#      (note, this rule should remain the LAST rule on
#       the eth1out chain, so insert all other eth1out rules)
#-----------------------------------------------------------
   ipchains -P input REJECT
   ipchains -A eth1out -j REJECT

# turn off any forwarding of FTP
#   nothing on the inside may forward to port 21 on the outside
#   not allow anyone to forward traffic to ports 20 or 21
#-----------------------------------------------------------
   ipchains -I forward -j DENY -p tcp -s $INSIDE -d $ANY 21
   ipchains -I forward -j DENY -p tcp -s $ANY 20 21

# now that we know that FTP traffic cannot bridge the gulf
# of the forwarding code in the kernel, we can
# be a little bit more relaxed with our rules

# CLIENT <-> PROXY, control connection
#   client * -> proxy 21
#   proxy 21 -> client * (ACK set)
#-----------------------------------------------------------
# allow the internal machines to connect from a client
# port to port 21 of the proxy service

   # client -> proxy
   ipchains -A eth0in -p tcp -s $INSIDE 1024: -d $ETH0 21

   # proxy -> client
   # none needed - the proxy can answer because there is no
   # output rule restricting flow on the output of eth0

# CLIENT <-> PROXY, data connection (normal mode)
#    proxy 20 -> client *
#    client * -> proxy 20 (ACK set)
#-----------------------------------------------------------
   # proxy -> client, none needed,
   # the proxy is free to speak with the client

   # client -> proxy
   ipchains -A eth0in -p tcp ! -y -s $INSIDE 1024: -d $ETH0 20

# CLIENT <-> PROXY, data connection (passive mode)
#    client * -> proxy *
#    proxy * -> client * (ACK set)
#-----------------------------------------------------------
   ipchains -A eth0in -p tcp -s $INSIDE 1024: -d $ETH0 1024:
   # the proxy is open to talk to the client
   # (if it were not, we would use a bi-directional (-b) rule)

# PROXY <-> SERVER, control connection
#   proxy * -> server 21
#   server 21 -> proxy * (ACK set)
```

```
#------------------------------------------------------------
    # proxy -> server
    ipchains -I eth1out -p tcp -d $ANY 21

    # server -> proxy
    ipchains -I eth1in -p tcp ! -y -s $ANY 21
    # there's no need to specify a destination, since the
    # forwarding code will discard anything not for the proxy
    # "! -y" means the packet must be an ACK
# PROXY <-> SERVER, data connection (always passive mode)
#    proxy * -> server *
#    server * -> proxy * (ACK set)
#------------------------------------------------------------
    # proxy -> server
    ipchains -I eth1out -p tcp -d $ANY 1024:

    # server -> proxy
    ipchains -I eth1in -p tcp -k -s $ANY 1024:
```

Whew! FTP is relatively difficult to provide with a packet-filter and a proxy together. If you look at the connections we allow between the proxy and the server, you should understand why we want to use a proxy. Fortunately, most protocols are much easier to block and proxy. For example, a protocol such as telnet uses only a single server port, similar to FTP's control connection. (A notable exception is DNS when you have to deal with servers and clients, which points out a caveat about the example above. It won't work in most situations as written. The FTP part will work, but you will need DNS name resolution available to the proxy before it will be useful.)

Before you throw up your hands, there is a lot of help available out there. To start, most protocols are well-documented, so you can get the details of the protocol and use that to write your own rules. There are several packages out there where someone has already come along and written most of the rules for you. Some of these were already introduced along with the section on masquerading (Section 4.3.3). A few more available are: **mason**, **gfcc**, **fwctl**, and **ipmasq**. If you use one of these tools, you leverage all of their experience with a few keystrokes (or mouse clicks).

The point in the painful example is to show you what went into rules and what the automated tools need to go through. No amount of slick GUI should replace understanding what is happening at the system level. You should "take the rules apart" and look at what each of them does individually, and then start piecing them together to see how the entire chain works. This knowledge will help you during configuration of firewall tools, and it is the basis of any trouble-shooting you may have to do when these tools don't work as expected. For additional information, refer to the *LDP* for several appropriate HOWTOs. But we're not out of the firewalling forest yet. The next section covers a little necessary housekeeping when configuring your own rules.

6.3.4 Scripting Firewalling Rules

As you play with IP firewalling, you may be tempted to enter rules one by one on the command line to build up your configuration and test ideas. You may quickly find out that this is a frustrating method of working. For one, there is no easy way to list

out your rules in a format that is easy to enter into a script to reproduce the same
environment. Say you spend a few hours testing various rules and have them just
the way you like them. Now you want to save them into the script that will be run at
boot time to configure your packet-filter. There is no easy way to list the rules with
ipchains so that you can reproduce the switches used in the commands to configure
the rules. (A shell with a history file might help here, but because the process involves
adding rules and then deleting them again to enter a slightly different variant of the
same rule, you will have to spend a while pouring over the history to find out which
commands negated each other.)

Finally, and definitely most significantly, packet-filtering rules function as a set
and are adequately tested only when they are tested as a single unit. Therefore
you should get used to the idea of working with them as a set. For these reasons, I
recommend that you enter all rules into a shell script and then edit $\rightarrow$ run $\rightarrow$ test $\rightarrow$
edit . . . this shell script until you have what you want. In this way, you can document
your rules and design trade-offs as you go along and will have a script ready to add
to your system startup. If you use a script like the skeleton below, you can edit the
script, `stop` it, and then `start` it again so that you are always testing the rules as a
group.

```
############################################################
#!/usr/bin/ksh
#
# firewall_rules.sh
#
# modification history:
# 19990524/tm              initial release
# 19990624/tm              added rule 1 to combat HackerX, who
#  attacks from RFC1918 private IP addresses
# kernel version check
if [[ $(uname -r) == 2.0* ]] ; then
   USE_IPFWADM=1
else
   USE_IPFWADM=0
fi

# specify interfaces in rules as either $I or $E
I=eth0                     # Internal interface (inside the firewall)
E=eth1                     # External interface (outside the firewall)

############################################################
# Install_input_rules configures input packet-filters
###########################################################
Install_input_rules()
{
   # rule 1
   # disallow IP spoofing of private subnets
   # (i.e. they must not originate from the outside)
   ###############################################
   for subnet in   192.168.0.0/16 \
                   172.16.0.0/12  \
                   10.0.0.0/8
```

```
        do
            # ksh shorthand for mask=$(echo $subnet | cut -f2 -d'/')
            mask=${subnet#*/}
            network=${subnet%/*}
            if (( $USE_IPFWADM == 1 ))
            then
                ipfwadm -I -a deny -S ${subnet}/${mask} -W $E
            else
                ipchains -A input -j DENY -s ${subnet}/${mask} -i $E
            fi
        done

        ########
        # rule 0
        # default rule is to prevent any packet from flowing
        # any packet into the firewall
        # not specifying a src or dest is the same as using
        # -S 0.0.0.0/0 and -D 0.0.0.0/0
        ###################################################

        if (( $USE_IPFWADM == 1 ))
        then
            # default reject (internal client receives ICMP failure)
            ipfwadm -I -a reject -W $I

            # default deny (no ICMP error sent)
            ipfwadm -I -a deny -W $E
        else
            ipchains -A input -j REJECT -i $I
            ipchains -A input -j DENY -i $E
        fi
} ### end Install_Rules()

###########################
# main script starts here
###########################
case "$1" in
    start)
        # load any modules required for IP masquerading rules
        modprobe ip_masq_ftp
        modprobe ip_masq_irc
        Install_input_rules
        #Install_forward_rules
        #Install_output_rules
        ;;
    stop)
        # unload IP-masquerading modules
        modprobe -r ip_masq_ftp
        modprobe -r ip_masq_irc
```

```
        # flush all input rules
        ipfwadm -I -f && echo "INPUT RULES FLUSHED - FIREWALL INACTIVE"
        #ipfwadm -F -f
        #ipfwadm -O -f
        ;;
    reload|restart)
        echo "$1 of $0"
        $0 stop
        $0 start
        ;;
    *)
        echo "Usage: $0 {start|stop|reload|restart}"
        exit 1
        ;;
esac
exit 0
```

6.3.5 Testing Packet-Filtering Rules

What do you do if you want to test your packet-filter before placing it in production? There are a few alternatives. Perhaps the most thorough is to set up an identical environment and test. The problem with this, as when testing any sort of Internet service, is that it is difficult to simulate the Internet without really having the Internet. If you have perimeter net topology, this is still an option. You can configure a test firewall and add a route to your Internet router for your test workstation via the test firewall. The test workstation will use the test firewall for its default gateway. See Figure 6.9 for the topology. This will work, but you should be careful not to weaken your security by allowing another way into your network via the test firewall. It is also a lot of work. The pros are that it is an accurate test of many client-server type connections and that your method of testing/problem detection is identical to your day-to-day firewall activities.

Figure 6.9 Test Firewall Network Topology

If this is too time-consuming, or if you would like to quickly test a rule, there is an easier option. *ipchains* has the ability to generate test packets which will be checked against the rules configured in the kernel. Creating a test packet looks very much like any other command used to enter, edit, or remove a rule. Because the Linux kernel is not known for its ability to invent information, you need to specify a source, a destination, each with a port, a protocol, and the interface which *receives* the virtual packet (for **input** and **forward** rules) or the interface which should send the virtual packet (for an **output** rule).

For *ipchains* use the -C *chain* (or --check *chain*) switch in addition to:

argument	comments
-s *address port*	a regular dotted IP + port
-d *address port*	a regular dotted IP + port
-p *protocol*	**tcp**, **udp**, or **icmp**
-i *interface*	interface to receive/send the packet

	Results from **check**ing include:
accepted	The packet matched a rule with a policy of **accept** and would have been forwarded, allowed to enter (input rule) or exit (output rule) the firewall.
denied	The packet matched a rule with a policy of **deny** and would have resulted in an ICMP denied being sent to the sender.
rejected	The packet matched a rule with a policy of **reject**, and would have been thrown into the bit bucket.
masqueraded	The packet matched a forward rule with a policy of **accept** and with the -m switch, and would have been forwarded and masqueraded.
redirected	The packet matched an input rule which indicated that it should be redirected to a local port.
caught in loop	The packet matched a rule with a *target* which consequently resulted in the packet returning to that same rule. This will result in nothing but wasted CPU cycles in production, and is therefore a good example of how checking rules can be helpful.
passed thru chain	The packet passed through the chain without jumping to another chain.

Checking rules in this manner is a good way to review new configurations and configurations where you have reordered the rules for some reason—perhaps for performance reasons as described later in this chapter. My recommendation is to develop a script which contains a comprehensive list of rules and compare the output of this script against the output of a control run which you know generates the correct results. The reason that I suggest using only the check functionality for testing changes in sets of rules is because I think that there are several drawbacks to testing firewall rules using *ipchains*. For one, there is no *virtual reply* to the packet, which is important for any realistic network communication.

The second reason is related to the first. Assume that you do code your set of check rules to include replies. Furthermore, assume that you have a test case (a **check** command) for each rule of your packet-filter. Because you wrote the packet-filtering rules, chances are likely that *your* rules will pass *your* checks. Most of the errors I have encountered when specifying rules for blocking or allowing a given protocol came from a lack of understanding of the protocol (or from a lack of adequate documentation of the protocol). For this reason, I recommend that you test using a real environment whenever possible. When you run into problems, you can use a combination of *tcpdump* and reviewing the packet and byte counters for each of your rules to determine why something is passing or not passing. Thorough testing can be quite difficult and time-consuming. Refer to Appendix C for a general discussion of the topic.

Firewall Performance Tune-Up   After running your packet-filter for a while, you might want to take a close look at the output of `ipchains -L -nxv`. It will be handy to print this out so that you can take a good look at it.

HINT: PRINTOUTS OF WIDE-COLUMN TEXT

If you work in an environment where the usefulness of a wide-carriage dotmatix printer is undervalued, you can get a reasonably good 132-column printout of an ASCII textfile using *a2ps* (in the **a2ps** Debian package). `a2ps −1 --font-size=9.5 --landscape --output=outfile.ps infile`. If you need more columns, just adjust the `font-size` to be smaller.

The byte counts will show you which rules are being used most often. Some (not all!) rules will be interchangeable with respect to position in the list without affecting the security of the firewall. You can highlight all rules of an equivalent ordering priority, and then shuffle these rules around in your *firewall_rules* script so that the most frequently utilized rules appear further up in the list. The result is that the packet either blocked or allowed to pass earlier, before unnecessary checking is done.

Another way to tune is to check for rules which encompass other rules, or a set of rules which can be expressed by a single rule. An example is separate rules which are identical except for the source or destination specifications, and these specifications are consecutive subnets which can be aggregated into a CIDR subnet. Another example is rule X which allows passive mode FTP transfers and rule Y which allows connecting to a well-known port for streaming audio. Rule X implies that your internal clients are able to initiate outgoing TCP connections from ports 1024–65535 to ports 1024–65535. Rule Y implies that your internal clients may initiate outgoing TCP connections from ports 1024–65535 to port 1070. Rule X already supports Rule Y, so Rule Y can be removed. These methods will admittedly result in only small performance gains, but they can help, and are part of the philosophy, "waste not, want not." They also increase your understanding of what your system spends its time doing.

A quite popular guide to this topic is the LDP's *Firewall-HOWTO*. I would not consider it an alternative to what has been presented here so much as required additional reading. The more input, theory, and advice you receive about firewalling with Linux, the better able you are to critically analyze what's out there and decide what works best for your environment.

6.4 NOTIFICATION SYSTEMS

Pop quiz: Which is more inconvenient, being paged at 3AM in the morning because your organization's Internet link is down, or coming into the office at 8:30 to deal with hordes of angry users, a thousand bounced emails, and another 500 or so in the outbound queue? The answer, of course, depends upon your particular situation, but, as uncomfortable as it is, I prefer the former. The more quickly a problem is addressed, the fewer negative repercussions to deal with later. This section is for those of you who need to know when your network is not well. As such, it is not only applicable to Internet routers. Your instincts may be able to whip up something clever to signal you when there is a problem, but before you get started designing your notification system, spend a moment and reflect on the following questions:

1. *What sort of failures should result in notification?* We will call this **detection**.

2. *How would you like to be notified? Are different methods of notification required for different types of failures?*

3. *How much money and time are you willing to spend to incorporate redundancy into your notification system?*

4. *What software and hardware are needed to implement the system you require? Are they available? Is there a current system in place with which you need to integrate?*

Since all of these questions are interrelated, you may find that your answers to one change the answers to another. There are several ways to go about notification, ranging from simplistic to quite elaborate. Which you choose will be dictated by your needs and individual tastes. A word of caution, however, to those who would implement a grand sophisticated notification system: How will you know if your system fails? For that reason, the simpler and more robust a notification system is, the better. Each of the questions above is discussed briefly in this section, the last of which reviews some monitoring and notification software for Linux.

6.4.1 Failure Detection

Before we even worry about how we're going to send the message, we need to know what the message is. Here's a list of "Bad Things" for our Internet environment and certain requirements in order to be able to detect them:

power failure—To be able to detect power failures, you will need a UPS which can be connected to your notification system. That system, including its modem, must also be on protected power. As was mentioned in Chapter 1, there are several UPS manufacturers who have Linux support. You can get pre-packaged Debian packages for many of these.

catastrophic router failure—If your router suffers a hardware failure, or if the kernel panics, it will no longer be capable of alerting you to its condition. For this reason, you should consider having a notification system in your environment separate from the resources being monitored. (See Section 6.4.2.)

Internet link down—If the link itself fails, but not the router, then your router will be able to detect this. It is probably sufficient to use *ping* in this instance (not so with other hosts, as we will see shortly), and your ISP should be OK with this, since you are paying for the service. However, it is bad etiquette to ping some other well-known Internet site at any regular interval. Pings generate *syslog* entries and use up bandwidth that is not yours. It's not a good idea anyway, since the well-known site could be down. If you're using *WANPIPE*, you can watch *syslog* for disconnect messages.

system under attack—This is a more difficult situation to accurately detect. There are, however, a few things which might signal a possible break-in: someone logging into the system or attempting to login during non-business hours or excessive pings or other connection attempts from an external or internal source—many attacks are launched from the inside source. A reboot is a sure sign of a problem. For this reason, you might want to have the startup scripts on the router send notification whenever the system restarts.

In any event, you are going to have to put on your coding cap to be able to detect that your system is under attack. To my knowledge, there are few packages readily available which will notify you of attacks in real-time while they occur. (One exception is *iplogger*, discussed later, which can detect the FTP-bounce attack.)

excessive system load—This seems easy to detect because the system is up and able to communicate its status, but it's not always easy to tell when load becomes too high. What you monitor will depend upon the application(s) running on your router, but here are some ideas:

- **free disk space**—If you don't already know, do not let the root filesystem of a Unix system fill up—ever. You should also be concerned about the integrity of your logs; for this reason, make */var* its own filesystem.

- **memory/swapspace usage**—Don't let your system run out of virtual memory, either. For systems functioning strictly as routers, this should not be a problem because the system should be sized so that it does not normally swap. The system may occasionally swap, but it should be only during system maintenance functions, like loading packages, compiling a kernel, etc. You can get the information you need from */proc/meminfo* and */proc/swaps*.

- **number of users**—If your system allows users, there might be a limit to the number of simultaneous users allowed, e.g., some FTP daemons place a limit on the number of certain types of connections allowed.

- **number of free file descriptors**—Running out of file descriptors can ruin your whole day (even though the Linux kernel is suprisingly resilient and the problem can be fixed on the fly). Even if the kernel does not suffer, applications and daemons may not handle it as gracefully.

HINT: INCREASING FILE DESCRIPTORS ON A RUNNING SYSTEM

You can easily increase the number of file descriptors available to the system without having to recompile the kernel. Just write the number of file descriptors you would like to have to */proc/sys/fs/file-max*, with a command like `echo "8192" >/proc/sys/fs/file-max`. You can check the current usage with `cat /proc/sys/fs/file-nr`. The fields are: the current number of file descriptors in use, the number of unused file descriptors already allocated by the kernel, and the maximum number for file descriptors available. (The second value is not overly important; it merely indicates how many requests for file descriptors the kernel can service without having to stop and allocate more—up to the limit of *file-max*).

Another interesting place to check is the `filp` field of */proc/slabinfo* (Linux kernel version 2.2). The first column indicates the current number of file descriptors in use, while the second is the high watermark (the maximum number of filedescriptors used at any time since the system was started).

If you do run out of file descriptors, you can expect the following code to spit a message into *syslog*.

```
printk("VFS: file-max limit %d reached\n", max_files);
```

Note that there is also a parameter set in */usr/src/linux/include/limits.h*, OPEN_MAX, which controls how many processes a single process can open. (If you change this, you'll probably need to recompile your applications.)

- **number of free ports**—Running out of ports is less likely, but possible. See the information on page 105 about checking the number of ports available for masquerading.

- **number of processes**—When the kernel is unable to fork additional processes, processing will end as we know it. The pertinent variable is NR_TASKS, found in */usr/src/linux/include/linux/tasks.h*. Modifying it will require a kernel rebuild. The default value with the 2.2.x version of the kernel is 512. (Note that the x86 limits the maximum number of processes to 4096.)

- **system load**—This should be evident. You don't need to use either *top* or *uptime* to get this value, just `cat /proc/loadavg`.

Most of these parameters can be easily read at regular intervals, perhaps as part of an SNMP monitoring system. If your mechanism supports it, you can record the values for trend analysis and system sizing. Of more immediate concern, set thresholds, and have your monitoring system either take corrective action or notify you (or both).

6.4.2 Methods of Detection

Most of the scripts you write to monitor the things listed above will run on the system being monitored, but you will probably need more for a complete solution. We have already mentioned the need for a monitoring system separate from the systems being monitored. This is not entirely true; the monitoring system can be configured to perform other tasks too, but you should try to relegate some lesser duties to it. The principle here is that a production outage may ripple through your network—a router failing on one end of a link may result in two or more failures—so the monitoring system's function should be orthogonal to that which is being monitored.

You may be quick to point out that the notification system might also fail. Although possible, what is the likelihood of both systems failing simultaneously? (And if the notification system goes down, but the router stays up, then you do not have an outage.) Nevertheless, this system should be minimally configured so that software failures are unlikely. If you have the resources, monitor this one system with another system.

There are different ways of monitoring your router just to make sure that it is alive. One way which is **not** safe is to use *ping*. The reason for this is that once a NIC has been configured with its IP address, the card has the ability to respond to ICMP pings without the help of the host operating system, as long as the card is physically powered on.

For this reason, a better, and yet still very simple test, is to *telnet* one of the kernel services, e.g., time. `telnet` *inetrouter-ip* `13` should respond with the current date and time, as long as you haven't disabled this service in */etc/inetd.conf*. You can script this as follows, although your production version should have more error-checking in case the call to *qpage* does not work, among other things:

```ksh
#!/usr/bin/ksh
#
# check_router.sh [<targetip>]
#
# modification history:
# 19990714/tm                initial release
##################################################################
INTERVAL=60
LONGINTERVAL=3600
TARGET=${1:=192.168.22.13}
DATE=$(date '+%Y/%m/%d-%H:%M')

while (( 1 == 1 ))
```

```
do
    # the test
    telnet $TARGET 13 2>/dev/null
    retval=$?
    if (( $retval != 0 ))
    then
        # problems! - notify via QuickPage
        qpage dutypager "something is WRONG at $DATE"
        sleep $LONGINTERVAL
    fi
    sleep $INTERVAL
done
# not reached
```

Of course, there are ways to do this without writing your own scripts. Several packages which perform such monitoring are introduced on page 215.

6.4.3 Methods of Notification

How you are notified of a (potential) problem will depend upon how you like to work, your budget, and how quickly you need to know about the problems. Different problems may have different priorities and may generate different forms of notification. Here are some ideas to get you started:

- **pager**—Alphanumeric pagers can be pretty useful, and many providers have email gateways making notification as simple as sending an email. Of course, if your Internet link is down, you need to do something else. (The easiest thing might be to dial an alternate ISP and send your mail that way....) If you are going to be doing a lot of paging, you need to learn about SNPP, and you can use the *QuickPage* package introduced later in this chapter. This software uses a dial-up gateway provided by your paging service to page out. With the advent of two-way pagers, you can take corrective action from your pager. See the information about *mon*, also later in this section.

- **email**—For many types of problems, an email notification is sufficient, and it has the added bonus of being able to include information about the problem. Since we've all been trained that reading our email is slightly more important than bathing or eating, the notification should not go unread for long.

- **logfile**—Since you will probably want to record the incident and some information about it, you can use *syslog* as a basis for your notification system. If you condense the amount of data written to the logfile sufficiently, you can review the data manually. Otherwise, use a logfile scanner to look for problems, and have it use another form of notification (e.g., emailing you an URL to access the logfile or paging you).

- **remote logfile**—As was already mentioned in the section on general host security, remote logging enhances security by forcing a hacker to compromise two systems to hide the evidence of an intrusion. It also means that you can perform archiving without adding a lot of disk space to your routers.

- **printout**—For certain systems, e.g., your firewall and other systems located outside of the firewall, hardcopy printouts are priceless. If someone hacks into your system and deletes your logfiles, you will be an Unhappy Camper. Using the *syslog* facility to log certain things to a locally attached printer may provide the only clue after a successful break-in. (A wide-carriage dot matrix printer with a nice box of fan-fold green-bar paper is perfect. A laser printer much less so. . . .)

- **window popup program**—If you are typically glued to the screen, you can throw an X client to your workstation. If for some reason you do not have an X-server, you can use *linpopup*, a utility which will generate popup messages on Windows machines.

- **system management console**—An extension of the previous method, a system management console assumes that you have staff members who are on duty watching a status screen, ready to take action should one of the green lights turn red. This can be any sort of UI, but the trend is towards web-based interfaces. *Big Brother* and *mon* both provide this sort of interface. Most network management systems provide some sort of management console, so you might be able to use the next method instead of deploying your own.

- **integration with another system**—Why recreate the wheel? And why separate yourself from other OS support groups in your organization? Part of making Linux work for you might include making it work in the data center, alongside the other production systems, and using the same tools. Of primary importance is the availability of SNMP for Linux. This software package is fully configurable and supports status queries through *snmpd*, generating exception conditions with *snmptrap*, and acting as the data acquisition workstation with *snmpget* and *snmpwalk*. You can also set values using *snmpset*.

You will probably be happier with a system which is configurable to use more than one of these methods. How far you go with this is up to you, but don't forget that the more complicated the system, the more opportunities there are for bugs and failure within the system itself.

6.4.4 Notification Software

Monitoring and notification tools are often thrown together, since they share such a close relationship. For Linux, the strong monitoring players seem to be *mon* and *Big Brother*, both of which support HTML interfaces and are detailed in their own sections below. In addition, there are several *Big Brother* spin-offs which you might like to use as they are or as a starting point for your own modifications.

- *angel*—The Angel Network Monitor (*http://www.paganini.net/angel/*) is similar to *Big Brother* and produces a very nice-looking status screen. The plugins are written in *Perl*, so you are invited to extend the system. Currently available are plugins for TCP port services, low disk space, high system load, and ping roundtrip times.

- *BSB-Monitor* is a very light-weight system which can be used for simple monitoring purposes. It has hooks for alerts so that it can page you when something is wrong. See *http://www.bsb-software.com/download/bsb-monitor/* for more information.

- *Spong* is another *Big Brother-esque* monitoring package written in Perl which supports histories for machines. Check it out at *http://strobe.weeg.uiowa.edu/ed-hill/public/spong/*.

- *snmptraplogd*, available as a Debian package of the same name, is an SNMP trap daemon, but is configurable. As such, it is not a monitoring system by itself, but could be a useful component if you decide to develop your own SNMP-based system or simply want to use the *snmptrap* client on different Unix systems to notify one central system that something is wrong. (Compare this to *snmptrapd*, which performs the same task, but does not support configurable output.)

Paging Software The software packages in the previous section will detect system problems and display the results via HTML, but they won't necessarily track you down and find you. For that, you will need to use a package like *yaps*, *Yet Another Pager Package* (don't ask me why it's not *Yet Another Pager Software*). *yaps* includes support for several standard paging protocols, including **SMS**, **UCP**, and **TAP**. It is not currently available as a Debian package, but is part of the S.u.S.E. distribution. The last upstream update was done in June of 1997, so it must be pretty stable by now (although the author calls it alpha software). You can find the sources at *ftp://ftp.sta.com/pub/fk/yaps/*. Other paging software is available by looking at one of the Sunsite mirrors in */pub/Linux/apps/serialcomm/machines/*, including:

- *sms_client* for sending messages to cellphones and pagers. Unlike some of the other clients, it appears to be currently maintained.

- *danpage* will send alphanumeric pages via a paging service provider (i.e., such as *QuickPage* or *yaps*).

- *npager* is the utmost in simplicity, which can be beautiful. It uses the modem to dial the number and send the digits for the message, so it can handle only numeric pages. It hasn't been modified since 1995, but it compiled fine on my system.

If you are using Debian, you're not left out in the cold. Another popular paging system called *QuickPage* is available in the **qpage** package. You will find it in the *non-free* section of the archive (merely due to the wording of the license). *QuickPage* can act as both a paging client and as a server. It uses the standard SNPP protocol (RFC 1861), so that it can be integrated with other paging software solutions for other systems in your environment. You define one or more *QuickPage* servers, which are systems equipped with modems so that they can send pages. These systems also have detailed configuration files about how to get in touch with whom (and even when certain "whoms" are available for paging and when they are not). You can then load the *QuickPage* client everywhere you might want to initiate a page. The client will contact one of the server machines and get the message out to you.

If you really need something custom, you can write your own paging software—the **libnet-perl** includes the `Net::SNPP` modules for integration of notification directly into *Perl* scripts. But before you start coding, you should take a look at the two packages described below. They represent a lot of work and contain a lot of functionality. They both have some advanced features such as web-based output, grouping of machines, configurable error levels, pager and email notification, and come equipped with a nice collection of monitors. They also have support for system histories, reducing the amount of work required to maintain event logs on each system. They are also different enough from each other, not only in design, but in look and feel, to warrant your trying both of them.

Big Brother as a System Monitoring Tool   *Big Brother* provides a web-based *matrix* of servers and services, updated continuously, and accessible from almost any graphical web browser. It does not use SNMP, but instead has its own client/server (monitoree/monitor) protocol and a collection of scripts. It has support for notification via email and paging; it uses *kermit* to send SMS messages to pagers and cellphones and to page numeric pagers. One interesting thing about *Big Brother* is that binaries are available for Novell and Windows NT, so it should cover most of what's in your data center. It can monitor the following without modification:

- DNS, NNTP, FTP, SMTP, HTTP, and POP–3
- network connectivity (ping)
- disk space usage, cpu usage, and uptime
- the status of processes and daemons you define
- messages logged via *syslog* containing a given string

Configuration is different from some other packages and may be taxing. Some people jive well with *Big Brother* from the start, while others wrestle with it continually. If you intend to use it, you should review the license at BB's homepage, *http://www.maclawran.ca/bb-dnld/*. (Redistribution as part of the Debian distribution (package **bigbrother**) is possible only with written permission from the author.) I mention these things because free software is about respecting licenses, not breaking them. If you want to use *Big Brother*, there should be no problem. If you want to make it part of a service offering or commercial product, contact the author.

Mon as a System Monitoring Tool   *mon* uses a combination of its own service monitors and SNMP (where it's applicable) to perform the task of system monitoring. It is very capable, and therefore very popular (or perhaps it's the other way around). It comes with a variety of interfaces, so it should please both web-browser jockeys and command-line diehards, and even those who aren't in the office. The descriptions are taken from the *README* which accompanies the distribution.

- *moncmd* is a command-line client which supports the full functionality of the client/server interface.
- *monshow* displays nicely-formatted column output of the current operational status, groups, and the failure log.

- *skymon* is a SkyTel 2-Way paging interface, allowing you to query the server's state and to manipulate it in the same manner as *moncmd*, right from your pager. Access is controlled via a simple password and an access control file.
- *opstatus.cgi* is a simple operational status webpage which highlights failures and shows things which are disabled. It is meant to be quick to use and to display the most critical information at the top.
- *mon.cgi* is the interactive web interface, allowing you to not only view status information, but to change parameters in the server while it is running.

mon includes alert scripts for sending alerts via email, alphanumeric paging via email, and *QuickPage*, although extending the system to support other forms of alerts is easy. It has a thorough collection of monitors, known as **service monitors**, ready for use. You should be able to cover most of your needs with these, but because *mon* is written 100% in *Perl*, extending it is relatively easy, and porting issues are all but non-existent. Should *mon* not be available for your Linux distribution, you can find it at *http://www.kernel.org/software/mon/*. The current version includes the following service monitors:

- ICMP echo (ping), SMTP, telnet, FTP, NNTP, HTTP, POP–3, IMAP, LDAP, and DNS
- HPNP (for monitoring HP network printers)
- system disk space, uptime, and processes
- any (other) simple TCP-based service
- network appliance free space and quota trees
- dial-in terminal servers

mon even comes with a script that will convert a *Big Brother* configuration file for use by *mon*. See the file *README.Big-Brother* in the program documentation directory.

How you configure your notification system depends largely on your organization's needs and individual preferences. The larger the organization, typically the more advanced the notification systems need to be, including elements such as exception reporting (i.e., formally noting anything system outage) and escalation procedures. Because different admins have different ideas about the right way to do notification, you may find that much of the available GPL code is "almost" what you want. (The same is true for many expensive commerical systems.) Be prepared to strike out on your own to get the system that you want.

6.5 SUMMARY

This chapter started out simply enough—using a Linux router to connect to an ISP via synchronous PPP over a dedicated access circuit. Linux makes a very inexpensive and capable access router. Unfortunately, connecting to the Internet is not so simple. Security is a primary concern that has to be taken into consideration just to decide where to place our Internet access router. In other words, we need to choose a network topology for the area outside of our firewall. Once we have an idea where the sytem will be, we need to secure it. Because Linux is capable of acting as a server, we must take some precautions to ensure that we do not leave services running which can be used to launch attacks against our system—some tips were presented in Section 6.2. Even after we've locked down our router, we'd like to know when others are trying to access it and if they can. Tools to detect this—IP event loggers—were the topic of Section 6.2.3, while tools to detect weaknesses—port scanners—were discussed in Section 6.2.4.

The next section covered IP firewalling, along with two different methods to go about it. The first is to control what can be forwarded by the firewall, also known as **conditional forwarding**. This is often appropriate for systems with more than two interfaces, such as a combination firewall/access router that supports a perimeter net via a second Ethernet interface. It is applicable only to routers. The next method of firewalling is **IP packet-filtering**, where we limit what can enter or exit the system. This form of firewalling is appropriate for any Linux system. In practice, both types of firewalling are used together to achieve the desired goal. The final section introduced some concepts about notification systems and what is available for Linux. Depending upon the organization, the importance of an Internet link ranges from a convenience to the lifeblood of the company (say, for e-commerce). Having a stable system is crucial—being able to detect a problem and notify the necessary personnel is important, too. This final section gives some ideas about how detect an outage and send notification.

Before we move on to the next chapter, which discusses a flexible WAN router, I would like to reiterate the importance of physical security as it relates to your routers and any system(s) you use to manage them. If you lock down your routers tight and never allow a password to traverse the network in cleartext, you've made a good start. But if the management station (the computer where you're typing that encrypted password) is not physically secure, you might not be helping yourself much. All it takes a floppy and a few minutes to break into a desktop, and the attacker can use a tool such as *ttysnoop* to quickly ferret out every password you use as you type it into the keyboard. Therefore, you should treat your management workstations to the same (or higher) level of scrutiny when it comes to security matters, especially if it is not physically secure.

Californium—Satellite Office Router

```
californium:/root> uptime
2:36pm  up 244 days,  1:14h,  1 user,  load average: 0.05, 0.00, 0.00
```

Californium is the first Linux router I deployed which was remote to the headquarters office. The small project office had no IT staff on site and the router was its lifeline to the corporate source code revision system, the intranet, and through the firewall out to the Internet. I have to admit that I did have some angst about the router's being so distant. Should anything happen to it, it would have been costly and time-consuming to make a service call. There was a bit of pride at stake here, too—a professional rivalry with a colleague who was deploying traditional routers remotely. The argument goes that because the traditional router has no hard drive and runs more stable code, it is less likely to fail, easier, and therefore less expensive to support. My counter-argument is that the risk of hard drive failure can be managed, and that the Linux code is plenty stable. Furthermore, the flexibility of the Linux platform warrants any additional administrative overhead.

Californium was also the first WAN router I configured to do more than just route. Because the remote office was lightly populated (and scarcely funded), the strategy was to try to do more with less—much less. To keep costs low, californium took over some duties normally relegated to non-Linux systems at my organizations, and some duties that a traditional router typically cannot handle. Additionally (no matter what the users believe), a WAN administrator always takes pity on the less bandwidth-fortunate. To this end, californium is configured to help make their plight more bearable by adding services which helped conserve bandwidth on the WAN connection back to the main office.

219

This chapter devotes a section to each of the capabilities and concerns surrounding californium. First, it reviews the configuration of a WAN link running CHDLC using Sangoma's *WANPIPE* software. CHDLC (Cisco High-level Data Link Control) is another protocol used for WAN links, similar to synchronous PPP. The next four topics cover the ways Linux routers can save hardware and bandwidth:

- Californium acts as the DHCP server for the site, issuing IP addresses and other network info to local clients.

- It runs a copy of the DNS daemon *named* (part of *Bind*) as a slave. In this configuration, it fetches copies of internal zones and caches any external name lookups made by its clients.

- Californium is configured with *Samba* to act as a local print spooler for a network attached printer.

- Californium provides a caching HTTP proxy so that frequently accessed pages are kept locally.

These sections about adding functions to the router are followed by discussions about monitoring system load and supporting Linux systems remotely. The section on remote support goes into methods of accessing the router when the primary connection is down as well as a few tricks for sites with redundant links. It concludes with a few backup strategies for remote systems.

7.1 CHDLC ROUTER TOPOLOGY

After getting bogged down in CIRs, PVCs, ports, and DLCIs with Frame Relay, CHDLC will be a welcome surprise. It is simple to configure, and as such, it supports basic configurations. Hardware-wise, the router is configured much like Frame Relay or synchronous PPP. The main difference is how you use the access. CHDLC is a protocol useful when you have a digital access circuit connecting two sites directly. From this access, you allocate a subset of channels to be used for data, and run CHDLC routers on both ends of the link. A typical scenario is a small office, which needs to have telephone service and data, and perhaps access to the company voicemail system. If the point-to-point access circuit costs are reasonable, there is no need to pay for each of these services individually at the remote location. You can order a single digital circuit which connects the remote site to the main office. With a couple of fancy CSU/DSUs, multiplex the T1 by allocating some of the channels to the PBX (for voice), and others to your data circuit. The hardware costs may be higher up front, but you'll end up saving money in the long run because:

- There are no port or PVC charges, and no CIRs. The full bandwidth of the trunks allocated to data is available to the connection.

- You can reconfigure the allocation on the access circuit as you see fit. If data bandwidth becomes less important over time and you need more voice capacity, you can change the channel allocation yourself with no reconfiguration costs.

- Apart from your telco provider, there is no other vendor or service provider. This saves time during contract negotiations and reduces finger-pointing during an outage.

- You will not have to pay for toll charges for calls between the offices (if your telephone equipment supports it).

- Rerouting voice calls to/from the smaller location leverages the capacity at the main office, which is purchased in larger quantities and therefore costs less per channel or minute. For example, a toll-free support line which may re-route calls to a specialist at the remote office.

- Even if you have no need for voice circuits, a point-to-point access circuit may be less expensive than paying for two shorter access runs, ports, and CIRs, especially if you need a high CIR.

A typical topology is like that depicted in Figure 7.1. Because it is designed for point-to-point operation, configuring CHDLC is very similar to the synchronous PPP link as described in Chapter 6. The only real difference is that you own both ends of the link, and have to configure both routers. The hardware setup is the same as what has been presented previously for the Frame Relay and Internet routers running *WANPIPE*.

If you are intending to multiplex a T1 in the manner described, you shouldn't order WAN interface cards with the integrated CSU/DSUs. The integrated units are not designed for multiplexing. The type of CSU/DSU which supports this operation is refered to as **drop-and-add**, and will have ports for both your router and the PBX. If you already have a Sangoma card (S508) in operation, you might be able to spare purchasing another card for the home office. These cards have a second port, a DB9 connector underneath the DB25, which can be used to run CHDLC at up to 256kbps. Note that you MUST have a CSU/DSU with a RS–232 interface to use this port, or use a V.35 to RS–232 converter. (Many CSU/DSUs come with a V.35 data port.) This port may be used only to run CHDLC, and you will need to order a cable from Sangoma to use it. Once you have a card in each router, and have the routers connected to their respective CSU/DSUs, it's time to configure the *wanpipe1.conf* file and the *interfaces* file. If you are using the Debian **wanpipe** package, keep the following pathname translations in the back of you mind.

Figure 7.1   Satellite Office with CHDLC Router Topology

Sangoma *WANPIPE* tarball	Debian **wanpipe**
/etc/wanpipe1.conf	*/etc/wanpipe/wanpipe1.conf*
/etc/wanrouter.rc	*/etc/wanpipe/router.rc*
/usr/lib/wanrouter/interfaces/	*/etc/wanpipe/interfaces/*
/usr/lib/wanrouter/wanpipe/	*/usr/lib/wanpipe/*
/var/log/wanrouter	*/var/log/wanpipe.log*
/var/lock/wanrouter	*/var/lock/wanpipe*
/usr/lib/wanrouter/Configure	*/usr/sbin/wanpipeconfig*
/usr/lib/wanrouter/samples/	*/usr/share/doc/wanpipe/examples/*

7.1.1 Configuring *wanpipe1.conf* for CHDLC

Save yourself some time by copying a sample configuration (*wanpipe1.cpri*) from the appropriate directory over the default *wanpipe1.conf* (as long as you do not already have a working configuration!). The configuration presented here assumes that you are using the card solely for CHDLC, although it is not difficult to configure a card to run CHDLC on the secondary port (or a second card). If you would like to do this, refer to Sangoma's documentation.

Open up *wanpipe1.conf* in your favorite editor and get to work. I've prepared a configuration file with the non-essentials removed. The file is an example of a configuration where the IP address will be assigned to this node explicitly through the use of the an interface file, which is dictated by SLARP_TIMER=0. The parameters in the example file are discussed in Section 7.1.2.

```
# /etc/wanpipe/wanpipe1.conf
# Protocol: Cisco HDLC   (CHDLC)
# ---------------------------------------------------------

#*****************************************
# Device Definition Section             *
#*****************************************
[devices]
wanpipe1 = WAN_CHDLC, Cisco HDLC

#*****************************************
# Network Interfaces Definitions         *
#*****************************************
#
# The [interfaces] section defines logical channels and corresponding
# network interfaces created by the router.  Each statement in this
# section has the following format:
#
#      {interface name} = {device}, {media_addr}, {function}, Comment
#
[interfaces]
chdlc0 = wanpipe1, WANPIPE, cisco hdlc connection on Port 0 (PRI)
#chdlc1 = wanpipe1, WANPIPE, cisco hdlc connection on Port 1 (SEC)

#*********************************************
# Link configuration section                 *
#*********************************************
```

```
[wanpipe1]
IOPort    = 0x360                # I/O port base
IRQ       = 11                   # IRQ
Firmware  = /usr/lib/wanpipe/cdual514.sfm  # adapter firmware
CommPort  = PRI                  # primary port (DB25 on the S508)
                                 # use "SEC" for the DB9 port on the S508

#*************************************************************
# Logical channel (interface) configuration sections.       *
#*************************************************************
# To turn OFF Dynamic IP addressing set SLARP_TIMER to 0.

[chdlc0]
Interface           = RS232    # physical interface type, RS232/V35
Clocking            = External # external clocking
BaudRate            = 256000   # 256k link
MTU                 = 1500     # for CHDLC, this can be 300 - 15354
HDLC_STREAMING      = NO       # use CHDLC
                               # (YES == raw frames and no polling)
KEEPALIVE_TX_TIMER  = 10000    # interval to send keepalives
KEEPALIVE_RX_TIMER  = 11000    # interval to expect keepalives
KEEPALIVE_ERR_MARGIN = 5       # keepalive timeouts allowed
SLARP_TIMER         = 0        # (disable SLARP/dynamic addressing)
                               # and use IPADDR and POINTOPOINT values
                               # from /etc/wanpipe/interfaces/chdlc0
```

7.1.2 CHDLC Configuration Parameters for *WANPIPE* Explained

Now let's go over each of the parameters in more detail. The file is broken up into four logical sections: devices, network interfaces, link configuration (detailed device configuration), and logical channels (detailed interface configuration). Each of these is addressed separately.

CHDLC *wanpipe1.conf*—Device Definition Section   This section is the first in the file, and begins with [devices] appearing on a line by itself. In previous releases of *WANPIPE*, this section may have consisted of multiple lines, but now that each device (really, each port for the dual port cards) has its own *wanpipe.conf* file, there is only one "device" line. Aside from the comment text, there are no options.

$$\text{wanpipe1} = \text{WAN\_CHDLC, } comment$$

CHDLC *wanpipe1.conf*—Network Interface Definition   This section begins with [interfaces] appearing on a line by itself. The section defines the interface name which is used by the kernel to access the link, and associates it with a device. Although most any interface name will do, you should stick to a name no longer than six characters—most networking commands do not expect a longer interface name than that. I recommend *chdlc0*. The line has the following format:

$$intf = device, \ port, \ function, \ comment$$

intf—whatever you want to name your interface (within reason)

device—the physical device name used above—normally `wanpipe1`

port—(no longer used). Don't forget to leave a blank here. Otherwise, your configuration file will have a syntax error.

function—use `WANPIPE` unless you're using the raw socket interface to the board, in which case you will use `API`.

comment—for your own use. Because this will show up in log files, you should make it descriptive.

CHDLC *wanpipe1.conf*—Link Configuration Section   The section begins with the device defined at the beginning of the file; for a single adapter, this is `[wanpipe1]`. Each of the allowable parameters is listed along with the possible values. If there is a default value, it is in bold.

IOPort = *0xNNN*—the I/O port address for the ISA board (S508 and S508/FT–1). The default is **0x360** unless you have modified the I/O port base jumper on the board. This parameter is required for the S508, and is not allowed for the S514.

IRQ = *irq* [3,4,5,7,9,10,11,12]—a free IRQ on your system. Required for the S508; not applicable for the S514.

Firmware = *pathname*—the pathname to the adapter firmware binary. This value should be set correctly in the sample configuration file. For Debian's **wanpipe** package, it is */usr/lib/wanpipe/cdual514.sfm*. This parameter is required.

Memaddr = *0xNNNN*—the dual port memory address used to read and write to the card. This value is detected by the OS automatically, and is not needed unless you suspect some sort of memory conflict. See Sangoma's documentation for possible values.

UDPPORT = *port* [1–65534, default **9000**]—the UDP port used by the *WANPIPE* utilities for status information. There is no need to modify the default.

Interface = **RS232** or **V35**, depending upon the physical interface type on your CSU/DSU. For an integrated CSU/DSU, use **RS232**. (Required)

Clocking = **Internal** or **External**—always **External** unless you know better. For the Port 1 (secondary) interface on S508 cards, you set this via a hardware jumper as well as for any S514 device running RS232—see the *WANPIPE_USER_MANUAL* for details. (Required)

BaudRate = [2048--2048000] for Port 0 interfaces, [2048--256000] for Port 1 interfaces. This should jive with CSU/DSU setting for the link. This parameter has no default value and is required.

MTU = [300--15354] for Port 0 interfaces, **[300–2048]** for Port 1 interfaces. Initially, you should leave it at the default of **1500** if you are using Ethernet on the other router interface. This prevents fragmentation of packets traversing the router.

TTL = [0x00--0xFF]. This is used only for the monitoring system, and can be left at its default of **0x7F** (127) or omitted.

CHDLC *wanpipe1.conf*—Logical Channel Section(s)   This section consists of an interface-specific section for each interface specified earlier in the file. Starting with *WANPIPE* 2.1, this is typically a single interface, such as [chdlc0].

MULTICAST = **YES** or **NO**; used to enable multicasting via this interface.

IGNORE_DCD = **YES** or **NO**; the default is **NO**. This parameter decides whether DCD will be ignored or not when determining active link status for CHDLC.

IGNORE_CTS = **YES** or **NO**; the default is **NO**. This parameter decides whether CTS will be ignored or not when determining active link status for CHDLC.

IGNORE_KEEPALIVE = **YES** or **NO**; the default is **NO**. (Are you beginning to notice a pattern?) This parameter decides whether keepalive packets will be ignored or not when determining active link status for CHDLC.

KEEPALIVE_TX_TIMER = [0--60000]; the default is **10000** (milliseconds). This sets the interval between keepalive packet transmissions. If you are set to ignore keepalives, then this value is meaningless.

KEEPALIVE_RX_TIMER = [10--60000]; the default is **10000** (milliseconds). This tells the router how often to expect keepalive packets from the other router. If **IGNORE_KEEPALIVE=YES**, then this is of little use.

KEEPALIVE_ERR_MARGIN = [1--20]; the default is **3**. If you are not ignoring keepalives, and there are KEEPALIVE_ERR_MARGIN consecutive timeouts, the driver will bring down the link assuming that something is wrong.

HDLC_STREAMING = **YES** or **NO**; the default is **NO**. If set to **YES**, this turns off CHDLC and uses raw HDLC frames.

SLARP_TIMER = [0--60000]. The interval between sending SLARP packages in milliseconds. SLARP packets are the mechanism by which the IP address of one side of the link can be dynamically assigned. The default value is **5000**; a value of 0 disables dynamic IP assignment. See Section 7.1.3 for related configuration information.

7.1.3 Configuring the Interfaces File for CHDLC

Just as with PPP and Frame Relay links running *WANPIPE*, both ends of the link need to be assigned an IP address in order to talk to one another. Unlike those protocols, CHDLC offers a mechanism to assign one end of the link automatically. To use this feature, decide which side will be the **master** and configure its IP address (IPADDR) in the *interfaces/chdlc0* file. Set POINTOPOINT to be value of IPADDR incremented by one. You should also configure SLARP_TIMER=0 in the *wanpipe1.conf* on this system.

On the remote router, the **slave**, you should set IPADDR=0.0.0.0 (otherwise, you will have problems when *WANPIPE* starts) and leave POINTOPOINT blank.

Make sure that you set SLARP_TIMER in the [interfaces] section of the configuration file on the slave. (If you do this, it will never ask the local router for its IP address.) Assuming that the timer value is non-zero, after the SLARP_TIMER expires, the slave sends an **inquiry** which says, "Please tell me your IP address." When the master router replies, the slave takes the given IP address and increments its last octet by one, and assigns this to its CHDLC interface.

NOTE: SLARP-ASSIGNED IP ADDRESSES

When using automatic assignment of the IP address for a pair of CHDLC routers, the IP address that you assign to the master must have a host address of .1—for example, 192.168.64.1. The slave will be assigned the .2 address in the same network. Since this is so rigid, I prefer to set the IP addresses explicitly. Note that with explicit assignment, you may also use a subnet mask of 255.255.255.255 and a "0 node network" like the one described in Section 5.3.5.

If you want to assign an IP to both ends of the link explicitly, then set the SLARP_TIMER on both sides to be zero, and set the IPADDR and POINTOPOINT fields accordingly. In case you are wondering, besides being so phonetically pleasing, SLARP stands for Serial Line Reverse Address Resolution Protocol, and is often used in conjunction with ISDN links.

As you have seen, by virtue of the limited number of parameters, CHDLC is uncomplicated to configure and well-suited for point-to-point links. Where you have access running directly between two of your locations, you can use any protocol you'd like. CHDLC should be considered along with PPP in this scenario. Frame Relay would work, too, but its DLCI overhead does not buy you anything when you have a 2-node network. The CHDLC support in *WANPIPE* is also handy when you actually need to interface a Cisco (or some other CHDLC router). When you do interface a Cisco, be sure to configure the Cisco to "generate IETF packets only." This disables proprietary extensions such as CDP (Cisco Discovery Protocol). If you do not, the Cisco will generate non-IP packets that are logged in *syslog* as unintelligible by *WANPIPE*.

Another option you need to disable when interfacing a non-Linux router is any sort of packet compression. Although this sort of thing is theoretically possible, not all of the vendors' compression protocols are open, and therefore not implemented. To save bandwidth with Linux (until there are open standards for compression), you have to do more than set a parameter in a configuration file. You need to use your head. The next section talks about a couple of ideas to save bandwidth over your low bandwidth links.

7.2 CONSERVING BANDWIDTH—CACHES AND SLAVES

There is a group which calls itself the *Bandwidth Conservation Society*. As I understand it, its charter boils down to educating people to designing web pages without ridiculously large graphics so that browsing is comfortable for users without lots of bandwidth. They provide documentation on how to produce graphics which look good without being monstrous. Even if the techniques described there result in a modest 15% reduction in graphics size (and I suspect that you could do far better than that), you've saved 15%. Sometimes I get the feeling that people expect improvements in the computer field to be exponential in nature or else they are not worth the effort. Processor technology may follow Moore's Law,[1] but the bandwidth available to the average user has not. A 33.6k modem is only 100 times faster than the 300 baud modem I had in 1984, and a DSL circuit averages 10x again. (By Moore's Law, the increase in speed should have been a factor of 2^{16}!) You can visit the BCS at *http://www.infohiway.com/faster/index.html*.

Deep down, every WAN administrator is a latent member of a private mini-Bandwidth Conservation Society—depending upon how loud the users' cries for more bandwidth are, sometimes a very active contributor. This section covers two things I did for the users on the far side of californium. The first of these is to deploy a DNS slave server for their site, and the second is an HTTP caching proxy. Both of these can be used to save bandwidth without modifying your users' habits. (The best way to save bandwidth is to train your users to use it wisely. It's probably also the toughest. Good luck....)

7.2.1 Slave DNS Server

Name resolution is part of almost every network transaction conceivable, anywhere, yet IMHO remains widely misunderstood by users (and sometimes administrators too). For the administrator, the only excuse is ignorance. If you fall into this category, stop guessing and *throroughly* read the manpage for `gethostbyname()` and whatever pages it may refer you to. On any flavor of Unix, this should get you on the right track to enlightenment.

For the user, a DNS outage means "the network's down" and DNS performance problems equate to "the network's slow today." If you are lucky, the problem is a local configuration problem, such as a nonsensical domain search order, or a bogus DNS server entry. Oftentimes, however, poor performance is related to the time required for the DNS service to locate the requested information. The performance problems can be particularly acute for external (Internet) domains, where you have limited control over the latency and choice of server. The easiest way to alleviate the problem is to provide a caching DNS server close to the clients. (Any good ISP will do this; the lesser ones do not.) A properly configured DNS server can handle the client load and caches any successful lookups it performs. In that way, only the first time a name is resolved is expensive (until the TTL associated with the lookup expires). One reason that the emphasis is placed on the server is that most DNS clients do not cache any information. If you open three windows and type `telnet foo` in each of them, your machine will issue three DNS queries for the name *foo*, provided that it is not available in */etc/hosts* or via some other mechanism. This is one of the reasons that you will see some popular web browsers start *dns-helper* processes, which basically act as caching resolvers. (Solaris even provides a daemon for this: *nscd*.)

---

[1] See the glossary.

The System Impact of a DNS Server   Providing a DNS server on the local LAN, instead of expecting our clients to access a DNS server across the WAN, is a big performance win that can realized with little effort on your part. A DNS server is a relatively low-impact process to add to your router. It requires almost no disk space (unless you are acting as a secondary server for some massive zones), and not much processing power. The only thing you will need is some memory, and typically not much of that. I checked the memory footprint of the primary DNS server and mail exchanger for a site with over 1000 users—the daemon had be running for 110 days— and it was about 19MB. A satellite office will use considerably less than this, probably on the order of 2–4MB. If you are concerned about impacting the performance of your router, check the size of the process from time to time to make sure that it's not consuming too much of the system's resources. An easy way to check the memory footprint, especially from within a script, is look at the status file corresponding to the pid of the daemon in */proc*. An example on a system running *Bind* (*named*) looks like:

```
californium:/root> cat /proc/$(cat /var/run/named.pid)/status
Name:    named
State:   S (sleeping)
Pid:     128
PPid:    1
Uid:     0        0        0        0
Gid:     0        0        0        0
Groups:
VmSize:     2488 kB
VmLck:         0 kB
VmRSS:       852 kB
VmData:     1040 kB
VmStk:        64 kB
VmExe:       436 kB
VmLib:       920 kB
SigPnd: 0000000000000000
SigBlk: 0000000000000000
SigIgn: 0000000000000000
SigCgt: 0000000009015a0b
CapInh: 00000000fffffeff
CapPrm: 00000000fffffeff
CapEff: 00000000fffffeff
```

The field of interest is VmSize. Should it get out of hand, you can simply stop and restart the daemon. (Note, don't just *reload* it, because this will reread the configuration file but not release any memory.)

DNS Daemons for Linux   For DNS daemons for Linux, I am aware of two choices. You can stick with the old standby, *Bind*, which is heavily documented and used, yet considered by many to be antiquated. Some of those people decided to roll their own and create another RFC 1035-compliant DNS server dubbed *Dents*.

    Dents is licensed under the GPL and boasts some nice features, such as a modular interface allowing you to store your configuration in whatever format you see fit. Currently, a SQL module is provided with the package, but documentation is included on how to extend it. It comes from some clever folks who just happen to work at an ISP that does a *lot* of DNS. You can retrieve the source, review the white paper, and subscribe to the mailing-list at *http://www.dents.org*. One side note: the *Dents* development team uses Linux as their primary development platform, which means that new features work under Linux first. (The software runs on many different Unix flavors.) Because I haven't worked with *Dents*, I won't pretend that I know how to configure it. The webpage touts that it's a drop-in replacement for *Bind*, so it shouldn't be that difficult.

If you're still interested in using *Bind*, a sample configuration file for the slave server I use for californium follows. It is for versions of Bind $\geq$ 8.1. All it does is configure Bind to act as the master for the localhost (which is a convention) and to not try to perform resolution on its own, but to forward requests to the forwarders listed. Once it performs a lookup, it caches the value for future reference.

```
//   /etc/named.conf
// "forward only" indicates that we are a slave
// "forwarders" are DNS servers "in the know"
options {
    directory "/var/named";
    forward only;
    forwarders {
       192.168.16.1;
       192.168.18.2;
    };
};
// local zone information
zone "localhost" {
    type master;
    file "named.local";
};
zone "127.in-addr.arpa" {
    type master;
    file "named.rev-local";
};
```

After you reload *named* (with /etc/init.d/bind reload), you should update your DHCP configuration to reflect the new DNS server. For added protection against failures, configure your clients to use one of the forwarders as their secondary DNS server. (Make sure to list the caching DNS server first because it is your clients' first preference.) Assuming a 30–100ms response time for DNS queries over the WAN, your users should see a noticeable improvement.

7.2.2 Caching HTTP SERVER

HTML and its underlying transport mechanism, HTTP, have changed almost every desktop everywhere. This has changed your job as a network administrator almost as much as it has changed the thin-client client/server world. Now, it is your job— no, your duty—to bring the World Wide Web to those desktops, and to make it quick, although you may find the statistics concerning how much of your precious bandwidth is clogged with Internet HTTP downright appalling. We would like to help our bandwidth-impoverished users on the end of a skinny network pipe in any way possible (so that they can accomplish real work while their colleagues are browsing the Internet).

A common approach is to deploy HTTP proxy servers which cache successfully retrieved pages. A proxy can be very effective for increasing browsing performance for your users, especially when they frequently access a particular page, or many users use common pages, such as search engines. Because you locate the proxy "netographically" near to the clients, cache hits are serviced at LAN speeds (almost as quickly as a webpage designer sees!). Misses cost the client only slightly more than the original lookup. Aha! The catch, you say. How *much* more is *slightly more*? The lookup and caching operations, when viewed from the vantage point of the user, are free. They take place at least an order of magnitude faster than any actual HTTP GET could be completed, regardless of how small, but certainly several orders of magnitude faster for a GET of any considerable size. Many browsers support user-level caches, which results in similar savings. The added benefits of a caching proxy are:

- The first miss for one user results in subsequent hits for all other users. This improves throughput for commonly accessed pages like intranet pages substantially. If you make a file accessible via a HTTP URL, the proxy will cache it, too, which is invaluable when you need to update dozens of client machines with a virus definition file or new piece of software.

- Caching provides a useful excuse for simultaneously logging user activities. While you shouldn't use these data improperly, logging can be useful for studying bandwidth usage and to have an audit trail in case a user does something improper on the web.

- Caching can be run in conjunction with *Apache*, making the additional overhead for web server minimal. Although you might not want to deploy a large website on your router, you can provide a general information page for the office, a telephone directory, or something similar quite easily.

There are several caching proxies available for Linux. I have used *Squid* and *Apache*, which are both available as Debian packages, **squid** and **apache**. Either one of them will serve your need; which you choose is a matter of preference. I tend to use *Apache* because I am more familiar with its configuration, but am beginning to suspect that *Squid* has more options. Below are some general notes on using them:

Apache   *Apache* is best known as a web server, but it is also quite capable as a proxy. If you already have it installed, you need to do the following to modify it to act as a proxy:

- Modify */etc/apache/httpd.conf* to load the proxy module and enable proxying, with statements like:

```
LoadModule      proxy_module /usr/lib/apache/1.3/libproxy.so
ProxyRequests   On
CacheRoot       /var/spool/apache_cache
CacheSize       2000000                 # cache size in kb (2GB)
CacheGcInterval 4
```

After these changes, you need to stop and restart *Apache* with */etc/init.d/apache restart*. The parameters you added do the following:

— `LoadModule` tells *Apache* to include certain code/functionality, in this case, the proxy module. The first argument is the name of the module, `proxy_module`, and the second argument is the path to the object file containing the code for the modules. (The path may vary on your system, depending upon your Linux distro and version of Apache.)

— `ProxyRequests On` enables proxying of requests. (Having the module loaded gives you the potential to proxy requests.) This statement cannot appear in the configuration file before `LoadModule proxy_proxy` or else it will not be understood.

— `CacheRoot` *pathname* tells the module where to cache successful proxy requests.

— `CacheSize` *sizekB* sets the maximum size of proxy's cache. You will feel sheepish if your router runs out of disk space because the proxy cache filled an important system partition. If possible, you should have a separate partition for the cache. If you're worried about performance, then a separate spindle (drive), preferably on a different controller from the OS, would help, too.

— `CacheGcInterval` *hours* tells the daemon how often to run its Garbage collection routines on the contents of the cache. If you're clever about when you start the daemon, you can ensure that this takes place only once a day in the evening, or something like that. (Hopefully, future versions will let you indicate *when* to perform garbage collection.) There is no default, so if you do not have this enabled, garbage collection will never occur. This is Not Good, because it means that there is no way to enforce the limit set by `CacheSize`. On a high-load system with limited cache space, you need to tune this parameter to make sure that it runs often enough, but not continuously.

- Optionally, you can add the `NoProxy` and `ProxyBlock` statements to *httpd.conf*. The first of these tells the proxy to not proxy requests to the listed IP addresses or hostnames; instead, the client should contact the server directly. The second says not to allow connections to certain sites.

```
# no proxying for internal webservers
NoProxy         192.168.0.0/16 172.16.0.0/12 10.0.0.0/8
ProxyBlock      .dontgothere.com
```

- You can also adjust `MaxClients` *value* to the maximum number of clients. *Apache* considers proxy users to be web server users, and thus may limit the number of simultaneous connections. You can use this to either allow more concurrent sessions, or to purposefully limit the number of sessions to a reasonable number.

- If you would like to run your proxy server on a port other than port 80, you can use the `Listen` parameter in *httpd.conf* to do so. 8080 is a popular choice.

- Access control works just as it does for *Apache* configured as a web server. You should refer to the Apache documentation at *http://www.apache.org* for the different options available to you.

Trouble-shooting is easy, because logging is performed for proxy requests just as it is for web server requests. This has the added benefit that any existing scripts and procedures you already have in place to analyze your *Apache* log files will work on the proxy. Take a look at *analog* (Debian package **analog**); its main site is *http://www.statslab.cam.ac.uk/ sret1/analog/*. It is a very configurable logfile analyzer and report generator. It might take a few minutes to wade through the myriad of options, but once you have it set up, it will produces nice-looking detailed reports.

If you are not already familiar with *Apache*, or if the overhead of running a full-blown web server to perform proxying is too much for you, there are other options. The *Squid* daemon introduced in the next section has been designed from the beginning to be a caching proxy server.

Squid   With a name like *Squid*, it's gotta be good. At least if you're talking about the high-performance caching HTTP proxy, it is![2] Unlike *Apache*, which offers proxying as an add-on, *Squid's* prime directive is to proxy and cache lookups. As such, it provides some advanced features not available elsewhere.

- It supports deploying a hierarchy of caching servers. Server A may not have the document cached, but it can ask Servers B, C, and D if they have a copy. In californium's case, it may refer to the other servers before going to the Internet to retrieve the requested document. This is not limited to a hierarchy within your site. You may apply to connect to an upstream NLANR (National Laboratory for Applied Network Research) cache using the ICP (Internet Cache Protocol).

- It supports a variety of authentication mechanisms, enabling you to limit access to the proxy. You can define ACLs (Access Control Lists) and then use them to dis/allow access to certain functions. You can also use one of the security modules (an **auth_module**) to identify proxy users. This is fantastic if you need security and do not have fixed IP addresses (or do not want to have to keep up with who has what IP address). These include:

  1. Authenticating against an SMB source (a Windows NT domain server) with the *smb_auth* module.

  2. Authenticating using the OS's `getpwnam()` routines. In short, this means that whatever authentication mechanism you are using for */bin/login* can be used. On Linux, this may include NIS(+), LDAP, PAM, or the contents of */etc/passwd* (or */etc/shadow*). This uses the *auth_getpwname* module.

  3. Authenticating against a NCSA httpd-style password file, perhaps prompting reuse of an already developed system.

---

[2] Apologies to those of you who enjoy eating squid.

- Runtime parameters, such as how much memory *Squid* is allowed to allocate, are tunable.

- *Squid* can act as an **httpd-accelerator**, a mode in which it caches outgoing data from your HTTP servers. These data would normally be sent directly from your servers, but *Squid* acts on their behalf, potentially improving response time and adding resilience to your configuration (because you can have multiple *Squid* caching communicating with each other via ICP).

- *Squid* provides CGI scripts for management of the cache through a web interface, getting you off the command-line. For this to work, you will have to have a HTTP server with CGI support, e.g., *Apache*.

- URL **redirectors** are supported. A redirector rewrites a URL according to some rules defined by you. Many of these redirectors (they are implemented externally to *Squid*) support using regular expressions. For example, you can tell the redirector to rewrite any URL containing the string "donotgothere" to be *http://company-policy.yourcompany.com*. One of these is *Squirm*, available at *http://www.senet.com.au/squirm/*. Debian offers one of these already packaged and ready to go in the **urlredir** package.

- Commercial support is available! (Apache has this, too.) See the package documentation for details.

For Debian users, the package name is **squid**; if *Squid* is not included in your distribution, you can find it at *http://squid.nlanr.net/*. It is offered under the GPL. *Squid* also has its own logfile analyzer, named aptly enough, *Calamaris*. Its Debian package is **calamaris**, and the upstream source can be obtained from *http://Calamaris.Cord.de/*

7.3 REPLACING SERVERS—MULTIFUNCTION ROUTERS

You cannot always to limit bandwidth used by a remote site. There is a certain amount of bandwidth that it will always use; typically, this value seems to be "all of it." If your router cannot cut down on the amount of traffic, perhaps it can save you money and effort in other ways. Maybe it can reduce the number of network infrastructure systems you need to support at the remote site. The next two subsections are about little ways in which you can squeeze more value out of your technology investment dollar. System administration costs your company money—money as real as commercial software licenses or floppy disks. When Linux flaunts its flexibility and saves more than others, it ingratiates itself (and you, by association!) even more to management and the bean-counters.

7.3.1 DHCP Server

Acting as a DHCP server is nothing new for either Linux or traditional routers. But at my organization, the task was traditionally assigned to the Windows NT domain controllers. Californium was a good chance to show that Linux can easily do the job. If it couldn't, there would have to be another system deployed at the site. Configuring a DHCP server for Linux is even easier than configuring Linux to act as a DHCP client. If you have Windows workstations in your network, don't worry, the Linux

DHCP daemon supports a slew of options so that your clients will not know the difference.

A router is the right place to have the DHCP server anyway. With non-routers, issues crop up when you have more than a single subnet—you need to start configuring BOOTP relay agents (daemons which listen for DHCP requests on a given subnet and forward them to a different subnet where the DHCP server is located). Because this requires a reconfiguration on the router anyway, why not configure it as the DHCP server? Such a relay agent is available for Linux. It is packaged in Debian as **dhcp-relay**. The original source is available from the *Internet Software Consortium* at *ftp://ftp.isc.org/isc/dhcp/*.

To get started, load the Debian package **dhcp** or get the source from the same site listed for **dhcp-relay**. Before using the package, you have to configure a few options into your 2.2.x version of the kernel.[3] You need:

```
Networking options--->
   <*> Packet socket
   [*] Socket Filtering
```

Configuring the DHCP Daemon   The default configuration is completely worthless to you, so the Debian package comes configured to not start *dhcpd* until you edit */etc/init.d/dhcp* and set run_dhcpd to 1. After you edit the configuration file (*/etc/dhcpd.conf*), you can start the DHCP server with /etc/init.d/dhcp start. Editing the configuration file is simpler than it looks, even though the sample file reads like part of a Douglas Hofstaedter book. If you get stuck, there is a manpage for *dhcpd.conf*. (It reads like a Douglas Hofstaedter book, too.)

> The *dhcpd.conf* file is a free-form ASCII text file. It is parsed by the recursive-descent parser built into *dhcpd*. The file may contain extra tabs and newlines for formatting purposes. Keywords in the file are case-insensitive. Comments may be placed anywhere within the file (except within quotes). Comments begin with the # character and end at the end of the line.

Instead of drilling into the configuration in all of its complexity (and capability), I summarize what you need to configure to get started. For a small office like the one californium is in, we have only a single interface on the router (not including the WAN interface). Still, *dhcpd* wants to know about *all* of the interfaces. One way to skirt around the issue is to use a zero-node subnet like that described on page 146 in Chapter 5. By doing this, you trick the DHCP daemon into thinking that it's taking care of all of the interfaces when it takes care of the LAN subnet. If you have multiple subnets for your interfaces, you must declare each of them.[4] A sample configuration file looks like:

---

[3] This does not apply to the 2.0.x versions.

[4] The 1.x version of the DHCP software does not get along with Linux on systems with multiple interfaces (except in the case I describe here). Make sure you use a version $\geq$ 2.0.

```
# a name by which we may identify this DHCP server
# you should set this to the DNS canonical name of the box
server-identifier californium.mancill.com;

# options for all subnets connected to this server
option domain-name "mancill.com";
option domain-name-servers 192.168.34.1, 192.168.16.1;
option time-servers 192.168.16.1;

# windoze stuff - see "man dhcp-options" for the full list
option netbios-name-servers 192.168.16.4;

# subnet definition
subnet 192.168.34.0 netmask 255.255.255.0 {
    range 192.168.34.128 192.168.34.254; # the actual scope
    option routers 192.168.34.1;
    option subnet-mask 255.255.255.0;
    option broadcast-address 192.168.34.255;
    default-lease-time 36000;              # 10 hours
    max-lease-time 72000;                  # 20 hours
}
```

The preceding example will dole out IP addresses and assign the WINS server, but it scratches only the surface of what you can do with the DHCP daemon. Other possibilities are:

- Assigning fixed IP addresses, using the BOOTP or DHCP. This can be handy for things like network printers and Xterminals.
- Assigning other NetBIOS specific settings, such as **netbios-node-type**, **netbios-scope**, and the **netbios-dd-server**.
- Assigning values for the following server types: NTP, NNTP, SMTP, IRC, POP3, WWW, finger, NIS, lpr, syslog, and others.
- You can assign DHCP addresses for clients of multinets such as those described in Section 3.2. This is known as a **shared-network** in DHCP parlance.

The DHCP daemon will log information about requests via *syslog* using the LOG_DAEMON facility. You can have it log directly to *stderr* by using the -d switch when starting the daemon. If the daemon detects configuration file errors, it will show them immediately. (This is unlike many other daemons which expect you to look in *syslog*, e.g., *bind*.) Let's see... software source, kernel configuration, software configuration, and logging—that about wraps it up for DHCP. Keep in mind the DHCP-relay for situations where you want to use the existing DHCP server for remote subnets.

7.3.2 *Samba* Print Spooler

The next thing we are going to do with our router is definitely *not* something that you can do with a traditional router. Before we dive right in to setting up a print spooler on our router, the matter bears a little consideration. First of all, you are adding processing overhead to your router. If you believe that it is already heavily loaded, then you should pass on the idea. Above all, you will need more memory and more disk space. (*Samba* recommends about 1MB of real memory per active session.) You also need disk space for print spooling. The partitioning scheme recommended throughout the book fits well with this, because your print jobs will be spooled on the */var* partition. If you intend to run a heavy-weight protocol conversion filter such as *Ghostscript* (the **gs** package) and the spooler will be busy, plan to have some additional processing power, too.

One last thing to consider: Samba has several different security models, some of which require that user IDs and passwords are stored on the local system (i.e. these users must exist). If you require this security, you should really start asking yourself whether your router should be your print server as well. In most organizations, printing is a basic user right, so there is little need to protect it with authorization mechanisms. If a user monopolizes the printer or otherwise takes advantage of it, he runs the risk of being pummelled by his co-workers. So for a small office, I would recommend that you forego the complexity of named user accounts for printing and allow all printing to be performed by single UID on the router. Why use *Samba* at all? In a small office with a network printer, you can configure each system to print to the printer directly. In my case, it was an issue of configuration uniformity. Other offices used SMB print queues service user requests, so why not this one, too?

Now we need to choose a spooler. Actually, depending upon your printer, a spooler may not be necessary. You can use the *netcat* toolkit to print directly to port 9000 of HP printers with JetDirect interfaces. But we are going to use old-fashioned LPR queues, since JetDirect supports this also. (LPR refers to either the **lpr** or the **lprng** software packages available for Linux.) Remember that you want to keep things simple, as in the example files shown below.

```
;
; /etc/samba/smb.conf
;
; simple configuration to allow anonymous
[global]
    ; printing
    printing = bsd
    printcap name = /etc/printcap

    ; logging
    log file = /var/log/samba/log.%m
    debug level = 2

    ; security (or the lack thereof)
    guest account = nobody
; a printer definition
[itprinter]
    printer name = itprinter
    comment = printer in IT area on 3rd floor
    printer driver = HP LaserJet 5N
    path = /var/tmp
    printable = yes
    browsable = yes
    public = yes
    valid users =
```

```
### LPR configuration
#
# excerpt from /etc/printcap for an LPR system
# the "rm" parameter is the IP address of the JetDirect card
mailroom27|mailroom27:\
        :lp=:\
        :rm=192.168.16.82:\
        :rp=raw:\
        :sd=/var/spool/lpd/mailroom27:\
        :mx#0:\
        :sh:
```

HINT: TROUBLE-SHOOTING SAMBA/LPR SPOOLS

> If this were a book on *Samba*, LPR, or network printing, I might go into some detail about trouble-shooting. Here's a quick hint anyway. If you can print from the router to the printer, then the problem is with *Samba*. If the problem is with *Samba*, then you should look in the `log file` (defined in the *smb.conf* file) to see what is happening—nine times out of ten it will have to do with either security (insufficient permissions) or the interface to the spooler (**cooking** the job—not passing the spool job in raw binary is often the culprit here). For more information, turn up the `debug level` parameter in *smb.conf* and restart *Samba*.

Once you restart *Samba* and LPR, you should be able to print through the SMB print queue on your router to the network printer. Small installations notwithstanding, print spooler configuration can be very involved, and is a function generally better left to systems other than your routers. That is not meant to scare you away from such a configuration—only to remind you to keep system load in mind.

7.3.3 How Much Additional Load Is Too Much?

You need not be overly paranoid about breaking your router by extending its capabilities beyond those traditionally attributed to a router. In the print spooler case, the performance issue is more likely to come from memory use by Samba than anything with LPR. Routers tend to not use their drives much when then are just routing. Most of the disk access will come from the host operating system maintaining itself. (For example, the Debian distribution needs to update the database used by the *locate* command daily. The cron job which does this (*/etc/cron.daily/find*) invokes *updatedb* and generates a substantial amount of disk access.) Many of these system management features can be trimmed or cut out entirely, if you see the need.[5] The point is that disk I/O contention is rarely an issue for routers that only route, so you should

---

[5] I never have.

be able to add some I/O without worry of bringing the system to its knees. I/O bus contention is another matter for heavily-loaded LAN routers, but unlikely for a typical WAN router. When you are debating whether or not to add some functionality to a router, you should take into account these potential system bottlenecks:

- **Memory**—Insufficient memory leads to swapping, which leads to disk I/O, which takes time. Time leads to packet latency. The kernel is **locked** into memory, as are its buffers, and the routing table. (Locked memory pages cannot be swapped out to disk.) When the kernel receives packets, it needs some (real) memory for them so that it can take a look at them and then forward them. If you have other processes consuming all of the available memory, then the kernel will choose to swap out a few pages from one of those processes. This is neither Good nor Bad, it just takes time. If there is already contention for the disk due to other activity on the system, then it will take some time to swap the page.

- **Disk I/O**—Swap is just one of the system's uses for the disk. You may be performing heavy logging, or print spooling, or logfile analysis. (Of the three of these, you can move all but the first to a different system.) Tools which measure disk I/O interactively have been somewhat scarce for Linux when compared to proprietary Unix releases. Only relatively recently has the Linux community turned an eye towards benchmarks and tuning. At the time of writing, there are several harddrive benchmarking programs available, and a few programs designed to flag performance problems during normal system operation. Some of these are listed below with other performance tuning tools.

- **CPU**—If you are **CPU-bound** on your router, then you need to spend time investigating what is using so much CPU. CPU-bound is a term used for systems which have processes being repeatedly put to sleep by the kernel because their timeslice has expired. Normally, a process will relinquish the CPU by some other natural cause, such as blocking on an I/O request or waiting for input.

  A simple check for this is to use either *uptime* or *top* (or go to the source, */proc/loadavg*). If the load average is consistently ≥ 1.0, then there is more happening on the system than can be successfully scheduled and completed. The system will continue to route, but other things will have to wait. Normally, you can locate the problem quickly using *top* or by repeatedly looking as process listing with *ps* to determine which processes are quickly accumulating CPU time, as seen in the TIME field of `ps fax`.

- **Interrupts and DMA**—Interrupts are a bit different because they span different types of devices, and are more related to the design of the device; i.e., how much buffer space it has, and how sensitive it is to variations in the time it takes to service the device after it raises the IRQ line. If you load the Debian **hwtools** package and read the documentation for *irqtune*, you will see that sometime relatively low-speed devices are very sensitive to IRQ latency. (You can get *irqtune* at *http://www.best.com/~cae/irqtune/*.)

DMA is the anti-IRQ. It is a Good Thing, and should be used whenever you have a choice to use it, because it allows data to move between devices and memory without having to shuffle through the processor using `inb()` and `outb()` calls.

- **PCI, and Other Bus-related Issues**—There are a few ways to tune PCI, typically via settings in the driver. Because there are so many different PCI devices, the tuning may improve performance for any type of device. Recently announced is *Powertweak*, which has been available for Microsoft Windows for a while, but is now ported to Linux and free software (for Linux only). See *http://linux.powertweak.com/* for more information.

  When performance tuning, you should consider the system bus(ses) to be a resource just like any other device. Most of the proprietary Unix architectures go to great lengths to insure that the bus-architectures on their systems are capable of moving large amounts of information quickly. When a bus becomes overloaded, it is often possible to add another bus interface to the backbone bus (the **backplane**), and partition I/O channels by redistributing the load across multiple busses. The PC platform does this to a certain extent with things like the AGP bus, a separate memory bus, and having both PCI and ISA busses. Unfortunately, there is no magic way to know everything that is happening on your bus without purchasing a logic analyzer and spending months learning how to use it and what to look for. For the PC, the bus implementation depends upon the motherboard chipset used. If you intend to use disk-intensive or graphics-intensive operations you should do some research on the different chipsets themselves. Not all chipsets (or their features) are supported equally under Linux; you'll have to do even more homework to find out what works best.

- **Network**—Network performance is a separate animal from the other topics listed here because it depends largely on what is happening outside of the system. If you want tune the machine itself, then you should focus on things like drivers and busses. The IP stack is also tunable via the */proc* filesystem. See */usr/src/linux/Documentation/networking/Configurable* (in the kernel source tree) for pointers to the lists of tunable parameters. Sometimes network performance of an individual link is important, in which case you may tune the MTU of the interfaces on each end to correspond to the most frequently used packet size. Chatty protocols normally prefer smaller packets, while large data transfers like larger packets.

  Once you are outside of your system or a single link, you will have to look at the networking environment itself. If you are retrieving software from a mirror site, use tools like *netselect, traceroute, bing,* and *pathchar*[6] to find the best path—a function of both the number of hops and the bandwidth between the hops.

---

[6] See the hint on *pathchar* later in this chapter.

HINT: LOCATING `pathchar` FOR LINUX

pathchar is a great tool for very easily determining the characteristics of the various network hops between two points. It was developed by Van Jacobson, who is also responsible for *traceroute*, one form of PPP compression, and others. Unfortunately, the command is not available in source form, nor is its license clear, which is why you won't find it in Debian. A statically linked binary for Linux (in ELF format) can be found at *ftp://ftp.ee.lbl.gov/pathchar*. The tarball comes with a short *README*, but the tool is so widely used that others have taken the time to document it. One such site is: *http://www.caida.org/Pathchar/ pathcharnotes.html*. When you first use the tool, be sure to use the -m MTU switch to disable MTU detection. Otherwise, the command will produce no output while it determines the MTU, making you think that it's not doing anything.

General Performance Tuning Tools   I will offer a few pointers to commonly available tools not mentioned above. As the experienced can attest, performance tuning is as much of an art as a science. (Really, it's an art based on a science.) I caution you to not blindly follow every recommendation made by these utilities, but to take them in the context they were intended, which may be very different from your configuration. Nor would I start tuning systems with acceptable performance unless you foresee considerable system growth or change in functionality. There is surely a wealth of information available just from the */proc* filesystem alone, but I am not aware of a comprehensive resource for how to interpret it. In the meantime, you can use the extremely useful information at *TuneLinux.COM*, a site dedicated to sharing Linux performance tuning information, as well as *http://tuneup.linux.com*.

- To get a basic idea of what your system is spending time doing, invoke the *vmstat* command, which is available on all flavors of Unix. The different fields are covered in the manpage. They will show you the number of processes which are waiting to run, and virtual memory statistics (including the si and so fields, which indicate whether your system is swapping). Also of interest is the amount of I/O performed by the kernel and the number of interrupts and context switches per second.

- *systune* and its companion program *systunedump* are used to examine the current state of kernel parameters tunable via the */proc* filesystem, as well as provide a convenient way of setting these parameters to desired values at boot time (without having to go and edit the kernel Makefiles or includes to modify the defaults). It is a "native" Debian package—**systune**—but as always the source is freely available and it should work under any distribution. You might want to note the sample configuration files in */usr/share/doc/systune/examples/*, particularly *systune.router.conf* for some ideas.

- *hdparm* (part of the Debian package **hdparm** or freely available from one of the Sunsite archive sites) performs some benchmarking on drive performance and allows you to modify settings in the driver to greatly increase performance of the disk system. It will also let you slightly decrease filesystem performance while improving interactive performance by changing how interrupts are processed. It is of little use for SCSI users, but very valuable for IDE systems.

- *tune2fs* can be used to modify the tunable parameters of ext2 filesystems. Although the parameters are necessarily related to raw performance, they can be quite useful for tweaking your production environment. They are part of the **e2fsprogs** package.

- *latencytest* was used by its author to determine the amount of latency introduced by different types of heavy system load with respect to the maximum amount of time which could elapse before the sound driver in the kernel could be serviced. The intent is to try to keep the sound uninterrupted, but the idea extends to any sorts of real-time or pseudo-real-time kernel activity (especially copying and writing bytes to your WAN port—which, when under-utilized, represents a cost to your company and users. See the homepage at *http://www.gardena.net/benno/linux/audio/*.

- *VTad* is a rule-based performance monitoring package which can be used to collect statistics during normal system operation. It is written in *Perl*, and, according to its author, is similar to the *SE Performance Toolkit* distributed by Sun Microsystems for use under Solaris. It gets its information from */proc* and comes with a sample ruleset which should get you started. It would be a flexible framework for use in many different types of tuning situations. It even offers suggestions based on tuning principles. See *http://www.blakeley.com/resources/vtad/*.

One of the biggest problems for the performance tuner can be correlating what is happening in the system to what is happening in user-space for multitasking operating systems. Good luck!

7.4 REMOTE SYSTEM SUPPORT

Unless you have very special security considerations, technically speaking almost all of your support will be remote support, meaning that it is not performed on the system console. This section is not about remote system support when everything is working, but about planning for problems at remote locations. It is roughly divided into two topics: strategies to quickly restore functionality when links fail, and methods to minimize restore times after harddrive failure.

7.4.1 Redundant WAN Links

What to do when your WAN link fails is a problem for anyone, regardless of the router platform. Your service provider may have internal network outages which cannot be rerouted, your access provider(s) may have problems, or it may just be a case of bad weather. In any event, despite any SLA (Service Level Agreement) you may have with your provider, you need to be prepared for a link outage. Redundant links are one of the most common solutions; if you have the economic means, they protect against provider outages and hardware failures at the same time.

In a typical scenario, there are two routers, each connected to different circuits, ideally from different service providers. With some creative routing, you can even use both of the circuits normally, and then operate in a degraded mode when a link is unavailable. While this looks good on paper, there are some potential pitfalls. For one, there might not be multiple (economically feasible) service providers at a given location. Ordering redundant links from a single provider does nothing in the case of a provider outage (and there have been a few *significant* provider Frame Relay outages in the past few years). The second concern is that although there might be different service providers, they may use the same access provider to deliver service to your site. In this case, a construction crew up the road cutting a piece of fiber-optic might render both of your circuits useless. (If you have a large enough installation, you should be able to impress upon your service provider the need to ensure that the access circuits are sufficiently redundant. But if you are dealing with smaller sites, good luck.) Before you leap for the panacea of redundant links, you may want to do some homework about available options at your different sites.

It may be that different locations call for different strategies. One way to mix things up is to have redundant links which use different types of access, in hopes that partial access providers' outages will not affect both types of circuits. If you had digital access for normal conditions, and ISDN or analog access as a backup mechanism, then you might be spared when a backhoe misses its intended target. Most sites with redundant access have dial-in access as an additional line of defense.

Multipathing over Redundant Links   It may be that using an analog or ISDN circuit as the only form of redundant access is simply too uncomfortable for your users or detrimental to your organization's business model. If you have a second link, you should use a second router (it might be a system which normally serves another function) to protect against hardware failures, too. If you are paying for a second link (with the associated access and port costs), you certainly want to use it 100% of the time, and then have your site operate in a degraded mode when one of the links/routers fails. (Don't forget the prior discussion of adequate redundancy for access circuits, and don't forget about redundancy on the other end.)

If you are running an dynamic interior routing protocol more capable than RIP, such as OSPF, then you can design the redundant paths into your routing topology. This is a very "traditional" way of doing things. Since Linux is about choice, there is another way. There is functionality in the 2.2.x kernel called `IP: equal cost multipath` which will forward packets over multiple pathways in a *non-deterministic* manner. To enable it, you need to compile your kernel with:

```
Networking Options --->
+   [*] IP: advanced router
+   [*] IP: equal cost multipath
```

You also need to load the **iproute** Debian package or visit *ftp://ftp.inr.ac.ru/ip-routing/* and get the sources for the *iproute2* package. The command used to configure the routing is *ip*. You can add a multipath route with:

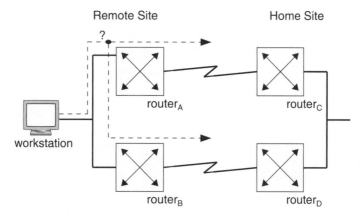

Figure 7.2   Redundant Routing with Multipath

```
ip route add  net netmask  mask      \
   nexthop dev  wan0 nexthop via  ip_of_router(B)
```

At the time of writing, the documentation for *ip* and friends is still a little patchy,[7] but the idea is to look at the route as having two parts, *nexthop dev wan0* and `nexthop via ip_of_routerB`. If you like, use `nexthop via gateway` for both the local and redundant routes, as in:

```
ip route add  net netmask  mask      \
   nexthop via  ip_of_wan0 nexthop via  ip_of_router(B)
```

For both of the statements, every time this router receives a packet that matches *net*, it rolls the dice. Depending upon the outcome, it forwards the packet directly over its interface, or forwards it to the secondary router as the gateway. The secondary router does not need to know that this is happening. It just forwards any packets it receives, which will statistically (hopefully) be about 50% of the load. You perform the same routine on the other end of the link. I've included Figure 7.2.

Configuring Your Environment for Multipath   To complete your system, you need to have both routers (on both sides) watching their peers using a script somewhat like the one introduced in Section 6.4.1. If router$_A$ fails, router$_B$ will need to configure an IP aliased interface with router$_A$'s IP address so that the clients do not need to be reconfigured. (The converse is not true, because the clients expect router$_A$ to be the gateway.)

The configuration at the home office (router$_C$ and router$_D$) is similar. The multipath configuration will randomize which link is used. Alternately, you can configure the remote office routers to perform masquerading. Because the homebound packets will be marked with the IP address of the WAN interface on the sending

---

[7] If you go in search of documentation at the *LDP* and don't find anything, try *http://www.compendium.com.ar/policy-routing.txt.*

router, they will be returned over the same link to that router. (You need to configure host routes for each of the WAN interfaces for this to work correctly.) Another alternative is to masquerade inbound traffic at router$_C$ and router$_D$. In any case, you'll want to have scripts at the home office which monitor their link peers so that they can take the appropriate action—essentially the same action you took at the remote site—should a link fail.

Another method, possibly easier to conceptualize and debug, is to have a single monitoring system with the ability to *rexec* (or preferably, *ssh*) routing changes on the systems it monitors. It would be located at the home office, and would have host routes to each of the IPs of the WAN interfaces so that it would not get caught up in any multipath configuration you may have. (The kernel always services the other end of a point-to-point link using the host route registered when the interface is configured up. This host route has a more restrictive subnet mask than the general network route for the remote site, so it will match the destination first.) When the monitoring system notices a link down, it takes appropriate action on the required routers for a re-route. If it sounds like a mess, just consider what you would do manually to re-route traffic, and script it on these machines.

Configuring for Redundant Links without Multipath   You can use the above strategy without the multipath routing by dividing your clients into two groups and assigning one group of the clients on the remote site to use router$_A$ as a gateway, and the other group to use router$_B$. It may be easiest to do the assignments with DHCP. You will not really divide the traffic in half or perform any sort of load balancing, but the approximation should be sufficient. Using the same sort of monitoring scripts, you can take sensible actions depending upon the situation, similar to what you would do with multipath. Examples include:

- If the WAN link fails, but the router is still up, have it add the route using the other router as a gateway. Then have it mail you a message that the remote site is running in a degraded state. This covers both situations where the link itself dies (for whatever reason) or when the router on the other side is unexpectedly offline. Because this router is still running, as soon as it detects that the WAN link is once again useful, it can reconfigure its routes back to the normal state.

- If one router fails entirely, the other router should notice and assume its IP address.

- If both links fail, the scripts will configure both routers to use the other as a gateway. For this reason it may be preferable to do something to the packets as they are forwarded to the other router for gatewaying so that you can detect this situation. Modifying the TOS of a packet is perfect for this. The scenario works like this:

    1. A client sends a packet to router$_A$, its gateway, for forwarding.

    2. Router$_A$ knows that its link to the home office is down, so it forwards the packet using router$_B$ as a gateway. But before it does this, it modifies the TOS field to some magic number.

3. Router$_B$ receives the packet, but its link is also down, so it forwards the packet using router$_A$ as a gateway (*deja vu!*).

4. Router$_A$ receives the packet, but notices the magic number in the TOS field. Using the *ip* command, you can configure a route which will respond to the sender with an ICMP host unreachable message. (This is done by adding an *unreachable* route type entry to the table.) In this way, you tell your clients that things are bad without generating a storm of packets being bounced between router$_A$ and router$_B$.

If one of the routers has an alternate form of access to connect back to the home office, you can add the route over this alternate form of access, using the TOS strategy described above.

Making the Most of a Little Bandwidth   Should your WAN link(s) fail, you need to establish some sort of connectivity during the interim. If this is an analog modem-based connection, you may want to take some measures to prioritize the traffic to and from the remote site. One idea is to configure a few IP firewalling rules to prevent surfing and FTP and other non-critical functions (what these are will depend upon your office).

How you use the analog bandwidth depends upon your needs. If the remote site is primarily interested in browsing, then you can have the modem dial a local ISP (and avoid toll charges back to the main office). Users can access the Internet over that link (be sure to configure masquerading on the router). Users can use PPTP or some other VPN software to connect back to the main office as if they were on the road. Since VPN is easy to set up for Linux, the router itself could establish this link, too. This has the added bonus that VPN software typically compresses its payload, which will squeeze a more out of the limited bandwidth.

The multipathing code can, of course, be used with PPP route running on analog modems. If you have multiple modems, have them both dial into ISPs, configure the kernel to masquerade over both links, and then to multipath over both links. Now you're really talking. So that mail (and other things) will function properly, don't forget about changes to the DNS server configuration when you're running in a degraded mode. In any event, have the remote router send you an email after it's connected to the ISP so that you know where to find it in the Internet.

All this is well and good, but failover scripting can be complicated, so there is always the chance that something with it will also fail. For this case, and the general case of gaining access to your remote systems without opening them up to the Internet, configure a way *into* your remote site, which is the next topic.

Gettys—Another Way In   Assuming that your normal link is down but the router is still running, you can connect back into your system if you have a modem and a **getty** running. A **getty** is a process which allows login to the system via a tty (serial port) or via the console. Before networking was a big thing, this was the only way to access the system. Since then, however, the arcane arts have been maintained and advanced by the diligent few. There are gettys available now which can handle dial-up (with ringback), virtual consoles, fax, and voicemail. If you intend to be dialing into your system, you will probably want to exchange the system's default getty with one sporting more features.

HINT: GETTYS ARE SPAWNED FROM `init`

If you are not used to working with gettys, you need to know that they are not started where most of your system services are started—that is, they do not start as standalone daemons out of the */etc/init.d/* startup scripts or via *inetd*.

Instead, they are started by *init*, which reads its configuration out of */etc/inittab*. If you look at *inittab*, you will see that it has four colon-delimited fields: `<id>:<runlevels>:<action>:<process>`. When you add lines for the dial-in getty process, select a unique `<id>`, choose the runlevels in which it should run (probably two and three), and configure it with an action of `respawn` (so that the process is restarted once it dies and exits). The `<process>` field contains the program to execute along with any options. Therefore, it depends upon the getty, and should be described in the getty's documentation.

To signal *init* to reread the contents of *inittab*, issue the command:
```
telinit q
```

Linux Getty Replacements

- **getty_ps**—The gettyps package contains two versions of a serial capable getty. The first is *gettyps*, and the second is *uugettyps*. You should use the latter, as it supports UUCP-style lockfiles for serial devices. This is important if you want to be able to use the same modem for dial-out. In this configuration, you are able to use a single modem for dial-in (in a support scenario) and automatic dial-out (in a link failure scenario). *getty_ps* is available in the Debian package named **gettyps** or from Sunsite. There is ample documentation included with the package to get things running.

- **mgetty** is another full-featured getty replacement that even comes preconfigured to allow dial-up from PAP clients. The source is available at

  ftp://alpha.greenie.net/pub/mgetty/source/

  or you can load the Debian package **mgetty**. There are also add-on Debian packages available, **mgetty-voice** (voicemail support) and **mgetty-fax**.

- **mingetty** is *not* for use with modems or serial lines. It is only for running your console from virtual consoles, which is sufficient for most applications where the console is not on a serial port. It is a lightweight alternative to the default getty shipped with most distributions.

- **fbgetty** is also not useful for modems, but it can be used with frame-buffer consoles. The Debian package is **fbgetty**; the upstream source is

  http://www.multimania.com/lch/fbgetty.

HINT: RUNNING THE SYSTEM CONSOLE ON A SERIAL PORT

There is a kernel setting in the 2.2.x and later kernels to enable your console on a serial port. Select the following during kernel configuration and regen the kernel:

```
Character devices --->
   <*> Standard/generic (dumb) serial support
      [*]    Support for console on serial port
```

You also need to add a line such as `"console=ttyS1"` to your bootloader configuration (probably the `append=` line in *etc/lilo.conf*). When you boot with the new kernel with this setting, you'll be able to use a dumb-terminal or terminal communication program to access the system console. No more expensive KVM switches or monitors!

After you have configured your replacement getty, test the configuration. And then test it again. Getty configuration can be unkind to the uninitiated and fat-fingers (typos). The following is taken from the README that accompanies *getty_ps*.

> After the sources are compiled, MAKE A BACKUP COPY OF YOUR EXISTING WORKING GETTY PROGRAM! I cannot stress this enough. There is a good chance that you will not have things configured correctly the first time around, and will not be able to log into your machine. This is also probably a good time to get one of those bootable rootdisks. In any case, be sure you can boot your system in single user mode before you install anything.

Automatic Dial-Out by the Remote Router   Dial-out via either an analog or an ISDN piece of access is not covered in depth because of the great deal of general experience with PPP and information about it. On the remote system, which should dial back into the home office, you can use any of the PPP configuration tools mentioned in Chapter 4, Section 4.1.3. On the home office side, you'll be using whatever normal dial-in solution you have implemented, which brings up a few issues:

- The access password must scripted into the remote router, so pick a secure password (it doesn't need to be easy to remember if it's stored in a script) and change it periodically.
- Most dial-in solutions issue IPs from a pool of addresses (unless you are connecting to a separate dial-in solution from that normally used for remote access). Because you need to know the IP address assigned to the remote router's PPP interface to log into it, you should have the router send an email to your account as soon as the link is up with the IP address of the PPP interface.
- The home office doesn't expect that the remote office will be connected via the dial-in solution, so configure the remote router to masquerade the traffic that it sends back to the home office. Although this is not a 100% solution, it takes care of most protocols.

As you can see from the examples given, things can get esoteric quickly when you are trying to strike a balance between efficient use of resources and flexibility. The *iproute2* has some very advanced features which will aid you. My point in this section is not to feign to provide you with a comprehensive solution, but to stress the idea that creativity and planning will serve you better during a system outage than mountains of hardware and circuit redundancy. The previous discussion dealt with what to do when network paths fail. What about when hard drives and entire machines fail? You will need a backup and recovery plan for your production environment. Otherwise, it's just a matter of time. The next section has some pointers.

7.4.2 Backups and Restores

Backups are a part of life, not unlike taxes or the inevitable demise of hard drives. One day (hopefully soon) there will be a breakthrough in non-volatile memory density and price which will make disk drives a thing of the past. Most traditional routers already operate with flash-able ROMs and NVRAM or flash cards. LRP (Section 3.4) nicely circumvents this issue, but leaves most admins wanting for more disk space. Instead of launching into a discussion about the relative merits of backup software and media formats, I will propose some alternate ways to approach the issue. First of all, let's list some reasons why we wouldn't want to use full backups to tape:

1. Restoral times are typically long, especially when users/systems are down.

2. Backup media and equipment are expensive, as is correct handling of them. Even the bare minimums, such as keeping tapes offsite and manually changing a tape every day (or weekly) are expensive in terms of time.

3. Backups are worthless unless they and their procedures are regularly tested. This is also time-consuming and prone to operator error (or sloth).

4. For a router, there is very little *data* which are not easily reproducible.

5. There is something about Murphy's Law and backups. . . they have this affinity for each other that defies the laws of probability. (Call me paranoid, but the potential for weirdness seems to increase drastically when you actually insert a backup tape in the drive for restoral.)

For the reasons above, and because downtime is expensive, I propose some entirely different methods for backup and restoral. Routers are admittedly easier to back up than other types of machines because they do not have user accounts or user data on them. They should consist of the OS software plus configuration files, and nothing more.

Brute-Force Backups   For the price of DAT drive and a handful of DAT tapes, you can buy half a dozen 1GB disks. For remote sites like californium, you can add a second hard drive on the secondary controller. You should use the same partition layout you did on the primary disk (although the sizes do not need to match exactly). Every so often (only after configuration changes), you can run a script such as:

```
###########################################################
# brute-force backup
###########################################################
# this really only needs to happen the first time
# separate this out into another script if you'd like
mkfs.ext2 -c /dev/hdc1
mkswap -c /dev/hdc2
mkfs.ext2 -c /dev/hdc3

# mount the hot spare
mkdir /tmp/root 2>/dev/null
mount /dev/hdc1 /tmp/root || {echo "abend!" && exit 1}
mkdir /tmp/root/var
mount /dev/hdc3 /tmp/root/var || {echo "abend!" && exit 1}

# copy the entire contents
cd /var
find . | cpio -pdmv /tmp/root/var
cd /
find . -mount | cpio -pdmv /tmp/root

# fix fstab
cat /etc/fstab | sed 's/\/dev\/hda/\/dev\/hdc/' >/tmp/root/etc/fstab

# leave a trace of our actions
touch /tmp/root/root/$(hostname)_clone_on_$(date '+%y%m%d')

# unmount
umount /tmp/root/var
umount /tmp/root
```

Sure, it's overkill, but it is almost foolproof. *cpio* will not bother to overwrite files with identical timestamps, so subsequent backups will run very quickly. To make our new disk usable, leave the floppy in the drive which will boot off of the backup drive. When things go south with the primary drive, ask one of the employees onsite to pop the floppy disk into the drive and reset the hardware. Because the backup partitions are not mounted, the abrupt reset will not damage their filesystems. The floppy is required to keep LILO from trying to boot from */dev/hda*. There are several different ways to generate such a floppy:

1. You can write a kernel image to it with `make zdisk`, and then use *rdev* to set the root and swap devices with `rdev /dev/fd0 /dev/hdc1` and `swapdev /dev/fd0 /dev/hdc2`.

2. You can use *loadlin* to build your boot disk on a DOS foundation. This is a simple way to leave the disk in the drive (so that you can mount it as a FAT partition and write new versions of the kernel to it), and then have a short batch script which will *loadlin* and point the root to */dev/hda1* after some timeout, but if someone interrupts the boot sequence, then boot from */dev/hdc1*. Or, reverse the defaults to suit your tastes.

3. Use one of the other half-dozen ways there are to boot Linux from a floppy. *syslinux* is an example.

Backups Based upon Filesystem Orthoganality   If you do not want the heat or cost of a second drive inside your router, then we can take a more civilized approach to the matter. There are only a handful of files which separate one Unix machine from another. If you load two machines from the same sources using the same package selections, they have the same software on them. The only differences are the things which you configured. Because the software load is readily reproducible to a very high degree of accuracy, you need to back up only those configuration files. This is not always as easy as it sounds.

The first idea is to touch a file just after the OS is loaded, and then back up any files modified after that timestamp (using `find -type f -newer touchfile`). The problem is that most of the current distributions ask you questions while they install files, so it may not be so easy to differentiate between what is part of the OS and what is part of your configuration. Still, it is better to err on the side of too much than too little. You can note the system time when you start your load and use this to create your *touchfile*. What you back up will probably be too much, including some directories created during the install and other various things, like logfiles, but it is much better than everything. It will NOT include all of the binaries. You can create a compressed tarball of these newer files and store it on another system.

You can take a more conventional approach than the one used above and back up everything under */etc/* and */usr/local/*. If you are diligent about where you place your site specific customizations (preferably under */usr/local/etc/*), this should not cause any harm. If you have the habit of dropping things in your home directory, you'll need to get */home/* and */root/*. But... if you built your own kernel, you might have special modules under */lib/modules/*. (I wouldn't back up the kernel source, just the file */usr/src/linux/.config*.)

Restoral consists of taking a spare drive which already has the base image of your OS install on it, and uncompressing the backup tarball on top of it. Creating this image can be as simple as using the brute-force script mentioned previously. You might also place the image on a CD and then distribute the CD with a bootable floppy which loads it onto the hard drive. For this to be useful at a remote site, you'll need to have the spare drive and image already there! This is also a way to save time when loading systems; you don't need to always install from the source media. If you have time, learn where *all* of the configuration files are for your distribution.

No backup strategy will work if you are not diligent about backing up the system after changes take place. You should also be prepared in case that you lose your image. You can build another image, but only you know what was on it. You can do this by using your distribution's package maintenance program to print out a list of everything that you loaded on the system. For Debian, `dpkg -l` will produce this list. Be sure to note any other items which you may have compiled and installed by hand.

Until Unix installations can be completely orthogonal with respect to configuration files and OS files, this will result in some extra files being backed up, but that's not (too) bad. I created such backups for several of my systems, and they averaged between 300 and 400kb when stored as a gzipped tarball, an easily manageable size. Just keep in mind the concept of orthogonality when adding things to the system. It goes without saying that you should have spare IDE disks and cables on hand, suitable mailers in case both drives in a router fail, and possibly some of those itty bitty jumpers used to configure the drive for the controller. You should also back up the tarballs and images using a "real" backup system.

Other Backup Tools Should you desire to generate a "real" backup, there are literally dozens of choices of tools and equipment, with constantly more options becoming available.[8] I recommend that whatever you choose, you become familiar with it to the point that you have a high degree of confidence in it, and then stick with it. This means that you need to do more than just back things up—you must also rigorously test restores in as many distinct scenarios as possible, as well as at scheduled intervals (to account for system configuration changes and to test media integrity).

If you're not sure where to start, you should shy away from solutions that are tied to a particular type of particular backup medium. Backup technologies change often and come in several different scales. By this I mean that is what is inexpensive per MB for 2GB backup solutions may be prohibitively expensive to back up 100GB, but at the same time you cannot justify the cost of a 100GB solution if you never back up more than 1GB. Your needs will change over time (either growing due to environment growth or shrinking due to things such as better filesystem orthagonality), and you don't want to be using backup software tied to a certain type of device. (For example, sometimes you'll want to speed to back up directly to another disk.) In any event, take a look at the traditional standbys as a starting point and assess your needs from there.

- *tar* and *cpio* are your basic system primitives for backup and restore. Because they are so general-purpose, they may fall short of your needs, but they are typically utilized far short of their capabilities. As an example, they can be used together with *rmt* to manipulate a remote tape device for either reading or writing.
- The BSD *dump* and *restore* utilities are more inline with what people think of when they imagine a backup tool. They support incremental backups via levels and use of a remote tape device through *rmt* like *tar* and *cpio*.
- *taper* gets you off of the command-line and into using an *ncurses*-based user interface, while supporting the same generic functionality as *dump*.
- If none of these suits your tastes, there are several good commercial products available for Linux. These typically provide the added features of verifying backups after they occur, counting the number of times a piece of media has been used, a GUI interface, and so on. You may also find some of the big-name companies offering Linux clients that interoperate with their backup server code.

7.5 SUMMARY

How often does your naming scheme work out to describe the physical location of a system? (Californium happened to be located in northern California.) It performed

---

[8] For example, when I started writing this book, there were no writable-DVD drives on the market.

its tasks so well and so quietly—as if it belonged there—that it was the sort of router that made you feel good about Linux. This is exactly the ease of maintainability that the traditional routers brag about, and with extra functionality, too. I consider the entire project to be a complete success, and this chapter documents what californium brought to its office, and what I did to allay my fears of a support nightmare.

This chapter covered a new WAN protocol, CHDLC, useful for point-to-point access links; configuring a slave DNS server, a caching HTTP proxy, DHCP, and a Samba print spooler; how to get back into your systems when links fail (with a modem and a *getty*); a few strategies for routing over redundant links; and a different way to think about backups. It's the first of the router chapters which had fewer details about commands and more concepts and ideas about running Linux routers. Hopefully, you will have a californium somewhere in your fleet of systems—a system where things work better than planned, and are configured once and then forgotten.

## CHAPTER 8

Hafnium—Internet Services Router

W ith its impressive uptimes, ease of adminis-
tration, and meager hardware appetite, Linux sometimes leads one to boastfulness—
the origin of hafnium's name. In this case, a co-worker was loading a web server using a popular commericial web server and operating system and was adding copious
amounts of memory to the system so that it would be "usable." I snidely remarked
that Linux could provide the same functionality using "half the hardware." Thus,
hafnium was born. In Chapter 6, we focused on connecting to the Internet, security,
and keeping our routers running. Now we're going to do more with our routers. Because one strategy to reduce the TCO (Total Cost of Ownership) of an environment
is to reduce the overall number of systems, there is economic merit to such efforts.
For this chapter, you could almost say that we're building network servers and adding
routing as an after-thought.

There are a few issues to keep in mind when you start mixing routing with
network services; this chapter addresses some of the more common problems. For
small environments (say, a website run from a cable modem in your house), these
techniques will help you get by with less equipment. For larger installations, they
increase potential for high availability by allowing network servers to act as backup
routers and routers to act as backup network servers. Beyond combining services, the
chapter shows methods for sites with limited amounts of Internet-routable address
space, either for your clients or servers which provide Internet services. It goes on
to introduce dynamic routing daemons for Linux, and finally, it explains what to do
when your system is down. The chapter is divided into the following sections:

- proxies—making external resources available to users on the inside
- redirecting Internet services from one host to another
- general Internet services which may co-exist with routers

- dynamic routing daemons
- emergency down procedures

8.1 ALLOWING ACCESS TO THE OUTSIDE—PROXYING

We've already discussed the caching HTTP proxy in Chapter 7. This type of proxy can increase HTTP performance for your users by saving bandwidth. Although this is one reason to deploy proxies, it is neither the only reason nor the original reason for proxies. The impetus for the development of proxies was the need for security and control. Let's call these **firewall proxies**. Like a caching proxy, these proxies accept HTTP requests and performs them on behalf of the user. Additionally, they perform authentication and access control, limit who may access what sites, and log all transactions in (configurable) detail. Firewall proxies are also useful for environments where IP masquerading is not possible.

As you might guess, there are proxies for protocols other than HTTP; almost any TCP protocol can be proxied. To eliminate having to write a proxy for every protocol, there are generic proxy servers available. (We will talk about the difference between generic proxies and protocol-specific proxies later in this section.) UDP can also be proxied, but presents its own challenges. Because it is connectionless, you might have to perform authentication for every packet to make sure that the same person who initiated packet exchange is the same one sending the nth packet. A reasonable compromise is to specify a timeout for the valid session, as is done with ticket-granting security models, such as Kerberos. For UDP application protocols—common ones include IRC, ICQ, DNS, and some RealAudio applications—there is another form of server which is like a generic proxy, called a SOCKS server. SOCKS, covered in Section 8.1.3 requires a **SOCKsified** client (these are common), and offers the possibility of encrypting the internal session (between the client and the proxy).[1]

Any of these proxies may coexist on your Linux router, although those which require local user accounts, significant disk space, or considerable CPU cycles are candidates for their own server. Be forewarned that some network security purists will be abhorred by the idea of mixing proxies and packet-filtering. In a perfect security-minded world, you would have either a firewall that is purely a packet-filter, or a dual-homed non-routing machine with only proxies. In either case, the idea is to keep you focused on the concept of forwarding packets *or* proxying services, without worrying about the other. Of course, the proxies described here are not limited to use on routers, but you will often find the functions combined. Furthermore, I believe that benefits outweigh the security risks, as long as you keep your mind on what you're doing. With that word of caution, let's look at some different protocol proxies.

8.1.1 The TIS Firewall Toolkit—FWTK

The *TIS FWTK* (Trusted Information Systems FireWall ToolKit) seems to be the one that started it all. (If there were others before it, there were not as widely used

---

[1] SOCKS V5 only.

and distributed.) It is a collection of proxy programs which work together and focus on firewall security. Note that the software is not free, in the sense that GPL or BSD software is free, but you may retrieve the sources if you agree to comply with the license. See *http://www.tis.com/* for more details. Even if you do not want to take a look at the source, there is a very good document about the design and use of the "toolkit" available at that same website entitled *TIS Internet Firewall Toolkit Overview*. If the concept of firewalling and proxying is new to you, then this will be good reading.

TIS Toolkit Concepts The toolkit consists of a set of servers and clients which all use a common permissions file or authentication mechanism. These clients and servers are proxies for different network services you may provide to your internal users. Think of a proxy as a ferry, which transports users' requests from the internal interface (where the proxy is bound and listening) to the services they are requesting on the remote servers. Introducing this step allows you to control and log all access attempts to the ferry. Furthermore, because you have control of the packets, you may inspect their contents, as well as the contents of replies. This is where firewall proxies can set themselves apart from generic proxies (whose main focus is acting as an alternative to masquerading). You wouldn't want someone transporting contraband using your ferry, nor should you allow someone to sneak a bomb in via one of the reply packets. (In this case, a bomb is anything which the sender's client is not expecting and therefore may not handle gracefully.) For protocol-specific proxies, this is done by making sure that the response follows the state machine of the application protocol. Any commands which are not known by the proxy can be discarded (or at least logged), since there is no way to know whether or not it is safe to "transport" them to the inside. There are also ways to make the ferry itself safer, should someone attack it directly. It can be run in a chroot()'ed environment so that a vulnerability in the proxy or the application protocol provided by the proxy does not endanger the proxy host.

At what cost, security? Operating a ferry obviously requires more overhead than just routing or filtering the packets. The packets must be copied into user-space and dissected by the proxy, the proxies themselves are statically linked (not necessarily detrimental to execution speed, but expensive in terms of memory), and you will need a separate proxy process for each connection. The proxies also like to perform logging—perhaps a great deal of it—which further increases the overhead. As a firewall administrator, you have to make this sort of tradeoff, depending upon the needs of your environment. Slow response times might be preferable to less security in some situations, in others not. Where you draw the line is a difficult decision, and this is what differentiates you from other firewall administrators. No defense is 100% complete; remember that you're connecting your network to a network which is filled with potential attackers who, relative to you, are infinite in number, have infinite time, and typically have superior knowledge and tools. (Try telling your management that!) Instead of waxing philosophical about security for any longer—that topic is better left to a security book—let's review the tools available to you in the FWTK.

TIS FWTK Modules

auth—the authentication server and libraries. These allow you to develop a database of proxy users and provide support for authentication mechanisms based on several popular schemes in addition to plain old (insecure) passwords. This database is also useful if you have external users whom you would like to allow into your network. Authentication against the server is available to the user-based proxies in the toolkit.

ftp-gw—the FTP proxy server.

http-gw—the HTTP and gopher proxy. (No caching here!)

netacl—the TCP/IP access control wrapper, similar in function to the *tcpd* package, but with a different file format. You can use this to integrate additional application proxies into your existing configuration without a lot of rework.

plug-gw—the "plug-board" proxy server. It is a generic TCP protocol proxy, which allows you to ferry traffic across your firewall for application protocols which do not have their own proxy. It doesn't provide the level of protection that the application-specific proxies do because it doesn't know how to detect that there is a "bomb" in the boat. It does integrate with the rest of the access control and authentication information available in the toolkit. Viewed this way, at its worst, it is still as secure or better than any other generic TCP proxy.

rlogin-gw—the rlogin proxy server.

smap—the SMTP proxy, used in conjunction with **smapd** (the sendmail wrapper daemon) to provide a way to shield SMTP daemons on the inside from SMTP daemons on the outside.

tn-gw—a telnet proxy server.

x-gw—a proxy for X11 traffic.

There are additional tools and patches which are not officially part of the FWTK, but have been contributed by users and are available along with the source distributed by TIS. TIS is also kind enough to provide a mailing list for FWTK users. You can see their website for details. If you are considering using the FWTK, you should also visit *http://www.fwtk.org/*, which is a good source of information about the toolkit, FAQs, patches, and more.

8.1.2 Other Proxies for FTP, Telnet, and HTTP

Although you can configure packet-filtering and/or masquerading to allow user access to the outside, you lose the logging and ease of trouble-shooting user problems offered by a proxy server. If your mode of operation is incompatible with the TIS FWTK license and you need proxying, then you will need to look elsewhere. However, when you go searching for a generic proxy server for Linux (SOCKS withstanding, which is covered in the next section), you might come to the same conclusion that I did: Most corporate cultures which require detailed logging of client accesses to the Internet either do not use free software, or do not share their developments with the free world. When searching for a telnet proxy on *freshmeat.net*, I was able to find only one with a free license. Of course, the one I found is capable of doing everything I was looking for and more. It built "right out of the box" and starting proxying telnet sessions for me five minutes later. It is called *DeleGate*; its homepage is *http://wall.etl.go.jp/delegate/*.

> DeleGate is a multi-purpose application level gateway, or a proxy server which runs on multiple platforms (Unix, Windows and OS/2). DeleGate mediates communication of various protocols (HTTP, FTP, NNTP, POP, Telnet, etc.), applying cache and conversion for mediated data, controlling access from clients and routing toward servers. It translates protocols between clients and servers, merging several servers into a single server view with aliasing and filtering.

If you don't need the *emacs* of proxy servers and telnet is not your worry, there are several different special purpose proxies available. Keep in mind that another term for **proxy** in this context is **application level gateway**. Many application level gateways concentrate on proxying a single application, just as the individual proxies in the TIS FWTK do. Because masquerading and package filters are so widely used, you are most likely to find application level gateways for protocols which cannot be provided easily using those methods. Here is a partial listing by protocol:

IRC—This is UDP-based which requires inbound as well as outbound connections. One such proxy is *tircproxy*, whose homepage is *http://www.mmedia.is/~bre/tircproxy/*:

> tircproxy is a full featured IRC proxy. It can proxy DCC CHAT, DCC SEND and other DCC requests transparently to the user, block common trojans (such as script.ini), hide the user's identity and more. It can be used with the Linux kernel or IPF transparent proxy features to transparently proxy IRC sessions.

ICQ—I am not aware of an ICQ proxy, but many clients support use of a SOCKS server, covered in the next section.

NNTP—Because most newsfeeds are not open, news is not something you really proxy all of the time. Still, there may be a need to allow access to a vendor's news server. You can use a package like *DeleGate* or *plug-gw* (in the TIS FWTK). Otherwise, look into a lightweight NNTP server such as *NewsCache* (*http://www.infosys.tuwien.ac.at/NewsCache/*).

FTP—This can be a problem. Apart from the FWTK (or *DeleGate* again), I am not aware of a stand alone FTP proxy server. Fortunately, many HTTP proxy daemons support use of *ftp://* URLs implicitly.

HTTP—These proxies are wildly abundant. In addition to the TIS FWTK and the caching proxies described in Section 7.2.2, there are literally dozens of others. Some are very lightweight and simple, while others provide features not available in many clients. For example:

Junkbuster is an instrumentable proxy that filters the HTTP stream between web-servers and browsers. It can prevent ads and other unwanted junk from appearing in your web browser.

Junkbuster's homepage is *http://internet.junkbuster.com/*. It is available as a Debian package of the same name.

POP—*pop3gwd*[2] is available, along with the support built into *DeleGate*.

RealAudio—This has an application gateway which is made available by RealNet-works. It is disguised on their website under a section for firewall developers. See *http://service.real.com/firewall/fdev.html*.

There are many other application gateways for these and other protocols. The list above is only a starting point for your search. If you cannot locate a suitable proxy, then you may be able to use a SOCKS server. If SOCKS, masquerading, and proxying are out of the question, then you might be breaking new ground on the protocol field. In a vast majority of cases, however, someone has run across the problem before you and has been generous enough to make his or her tools available. If the application is one under development, so that a specific user needs access to a specific site or short list of sites, see Section 8.2 for information about redirecting that traffic.

8.1.3 A SOCKS Server

Another way to approach proxies is to use a SOCKS server. Unlike other proxy mechanisms, SOCKS does not try to make the presence of the proxy server transparent to the user. To use the proxy, you need SOCKS-capable (or **SOCKsified**) clients. In other words, you cannot use a standard telnet client to connect to the SOCKS proxy server and then continue out to your Internet destination. This is not as bad as it sounds, since many popular clients have SOCKS support built into them, including browsers and most modern Internet clients (e.g., ICQ, IRC, FTP GUIs, etc.) On the command line, use one of the *rclients*, such as *rtelnet*, *rftp*, *rfinger*, and *rwhois*. There is library support for building your own clients on a variety of platforms.

The need for special clients can be viewed in a positive light, as it requires your users to understand the difference between connecting to an internal machine directly and using resources on the Internet. In the case of command-line clients, you can hide this from the user completely by aliasing the SOCKsified clients to the names of the standard clients and configuring the location about the SOCKS server(s) in */etc/socks.conf*. The SOCKS clients will revert to direct (normal) connections for their application protocol if no SOCKS server is available for the service you are using. You can also use the *runsocks* scripts (available for both SOCKS V4 and V5—part of the **socks4-clients** Debian package). The description below is taken from the manpage for the Linux version of *runsocks*:

---

[2] *http://caristudenti.cs.unibo.it/~borgia/homepage/Software/Software.html*

runsocks is a shell script that initializes environment variables to ensure that the linker uses the SOCKS shared library when you link at runtime. Use *runsocks* to SOCKSify an application without recompiling. *runsocks* only works if you dynamically link and the operating system supports all the runsocks features.

SOCKS V4 vs. SOCKS V5   There are two versions of the protocol in circulation: SOCKS V4 and SOCKS V5. Both have the following advantages:

- SOCKS alleviates the need for any sort of masquerading or NAT for outgoing connections and provides the logging available with other proxies.

- Even if you don't need any sort of address translation, using a SOCKS daemon protects the (IP) identity your clients (as any other proxy would).

- SOCKS is not application protocol-dependent, and includes extensions for more complicated TCP protocols, such as FTP.

Whether or not you decide to deploy SOCKS V4 or V5 depends upon your needs (and license issues). Here are the primary differences between the versions:

SOCKS V4	SOCKS V5
• Supports client authenticated only through *ident*, or via the itself to the proxy. You can check the client's IP address against an access control list similar to most proxy servers.	• Provides for strong client authentication through the GSS-API (Generic Security Service Application Programming Interface) in addition to *ident* and IP-based access. The GSS-API specification as it relates to SOCKS V5 (RFC 1961) also allows for encryption between the client and the proxy server.
• Supports TCP connections only.	• Supports both TCP and UDP connections.
• Has a free license, as in the definition of free software. You can retrieve the sources from *ftp://ftp.nec.com/pub/socks/socks4/*, or use the Debian package **socks4-server**.	• Source code is available free of charge, but the license restricts certain types of use. (Because of this, you will not find a Debian package for it.) If your use is compatible with the license, it is easily retrieved and built. See *http://www.socks.nec.com/* to retrieve the sources.
• Is compatible only with SOCKS V4 clients.	• Depending upon the implementation, can be backwards compatible with SOCKS V4. The NEC implementation is. • Has extensions which support ICMP applications like ping and traceroute.

SOCKS is well-supported for Linux. You can retrieve the sources listed above and be up and running in less than a half hour. If you run into problems, NEC hosts FAQs and mailing lists and in general has a well-designed site with lots of information about using SOCKS. If you choose it for your primary method of providing user access to the outside, you will not be alone.

Dante—a Free SOCKS Implementation   If you are not partial to NEC's implementation or license, then there are alternatives. Check out *Dante*, which has a BSD-style license. You can visit its homepage at *http://http.inet.no/dante/*. The following description is taken from *freshmeat.net*:

> Dante is a free implementation of the proxy protocols socks version 4, socks version 5 (rfc1928) and msproxy. It can be used as a firewall between networks. It is being developed by Inferno Nettverk A/S, a Norwegian consulting company. Commercial support is available.

In summary, SOCKS is a good way of providing proxies if you do not mind dealing with modified clients. If you use a dual-homed SOCKS server with routing disabled and properly configured access control lists, it is an effective firewall, and can alleviate the need for masquerading (as long as the external interface on the SOCKS server has a Internet-valid IP address).

8.2 Redirection of IP Traffic—Smoke and Mirrors

This section is about methods to take traffic headed to one destination and point it towards a different destination without the sender (and sometimes the receiver) ever being aware that any such activity is taking place. The action does not necessarily have to be covert; it may be the only way to allow access from the outside to systems inside a masquerading firewall. Redirection is like the Perl slogan in the Camel book,[3] TMTOWTDI (*There's More Than One Way To Do It*). The options run the gamut from simple user-space processes to kernel firewalling rules, a combination of these two, and then finally some more complex kernel rules which perform reverse-masquerading. We cover each of these with an example.

8.2.1 User-Space Redirection—The Illusion of the Facade

The first, and likely the most common, method of redirection is to use a user-space process to listen to networking requests on the desired interface and port, and then to forward these unaltered to the destination system and port. To a large extent, these processes are like the proxies discussed in Section 8.1. In fact, these processes are often referred to as **proxies**, although I think that **redirector** is more precise. If all goes well with the redirection, the user cannot tell the difference between connecting to the redirecting and the true destination. (Note, however, the destination sees the connection attempt come from the redirecting server.) One positive upswing of all this is that servers with private IP addresses can still be used to provide services to Internet clients. The topology is depicted in Figure 8.1.

---

[3] See *Programming Perl* in the Bibliography.

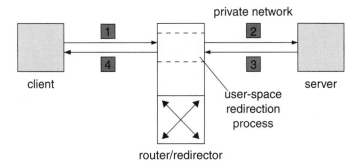

Figure 8.1 User-Space Redirection of Traffic

Because this type of topology is frequently used (or at least frequently desired), and in many cases admins do not choose to run HTTP daemons on their firewall or external routers, people have invested some time in developing redirection solutions. There are several popular redirection packages available, some of which are listed here.

Transproxy *transproxy* provides a daemon, *tproxy*, which is easy to set up and use. It has no configuration file—all options are passed as command-line arguments. It is very simple to configure after you take a look at the manpage, so I won't go into detail. But since I've used it a lot, here are a few notes on things that may not be immediately obvious.

- It can be run either from *inetd* or as a stand alone server (the absence of -s *port* indicates that it should run from *inetd*).
- You need to specify -t when you are not proxying HTTP—the default mode is for *HTTP translate*, which is for use when connecting to HTTP proxy servers *Squid* or *Apache*.
- Use -r *username* to have the proxy run as a non-root user. This is valid even if the listening port is ≤ 1023.
- You can use *-b ipadress* to force the daemon to bind to a particular interface or IP address.

transproxy is available from the upstream source *ftp://ftp.nlc.net.au/pub/ linux/www/*. (There may be a Debian package, too.) There are some instructions floating around out there that incorrectly note that you need to have transparent proxying enabled in the kernel to be able to use the daemon; you can safely ignore this. Note that *transproxy* is for "simple" TCP connections, so it will not work for every application protocol. You will have to use something like the next tool for FTP.

redir *redir*, like *transproxy*, is only for TCP connections. It does everything that the *transproxy* does, and adds some nice capabilities. You can download the sources from *http://users.qual.net/‾sammy/hacks* or use the Debian package **redir**. The additional functionality above *transproxy* is listed here by the command-line switches used to invoke it:

- —`ftp` will handle passive mode FTP connections.

- —`timeout=`*n* will close the connection after *n* seconds of inactivity.

- —`syslog` enables logging via *syslog*. It's not in the manpage, but it will log to the facility *daemon* at the level *notice*.

- —`name=`*string* or —`ident=`*string*[4] will use *string* instead of *redir* in the *syslog* entries.

- —`debug` will write debugging information to *stderr*, or to *syslog* if you are using the `--syslog` switch.

- —`transproxy` – This option, in conjunction with a kernel running transparent proxying,[5] will report the original sender's address and port to the proxied destination.

Here is an example. When machine$_A$ connects to the redirector running on router$_B$ which forwards the traffic to machine$_C$, machine$_C$ will see the packet as having originated from machine$_A$. When machine$_C$ goes to reply to machine$_A$, the packet will be intercepted by router$_B$, which bound itself to the sender's interface IP and port. This is possible only if *redir* is running as root and `IP: transparent proxy support` is compiled into the kernel. Furthermore, it will work correctly only for connections which are symmetrically routed (i.e., in both directions) by the system running *redir*. Lastly, there is always the chance that the sender's port is already in use on the firewall, and will not be available for use. Nonetheless, it's a neat and useful trick. One benefit is that things like web-server logs will contain the correct source address for generating access statistics. See the *transproxy.txt* file accompanying the distribution for more information.

rinetd   *rinetd* is a multi-headed (and multi-threaded) server which acts like *redir* and *transproxy*. Like these, it redirects only TCP connections (but not FTP, so keep a copy of *redir* around!). *rinetd* sets itself apart with its configuration file. Unlike the previous two, it can listen to an arbitrary number of ports simultaneously, each of which may be bound to a (possibly different) interface address on the router. These port/address tuples are specified in the configuration file with lines in the format of `bindaddress bindport connectaddress connectport`. The addresses may be hostnames, and the ports may be service names. *rinetd*'s configuration file may also include global and service-specific "allow" and "deny" lines, reminiscent of the configuration file used by the *TIS FWTK*. Any connection from a source which is explicitly denied or is not found in a global allow will be immediately rejected. The next feature is a choice of logfile formats. You may choose to have no logfile whatsoever, use *rinetd*'s format, or use a common web-server format. Like *inetd*, *rinetd* can be caused to reload its configuration by sending it a SIGHUP.

---

[4] Not noted in the manpage for the version I have, but it works fine.

[5] Transparent proxying is covered in Section 8.2.2.

If you would like to try *rinetd*, it can be found at *http://www.boutell.com/rinetd/*. There is also a Debian package of the same name. The following is an excerpt from the manpage which provides a good synopsis.

> *rinetd* redirects TCP connections from one IP address and port to another. *rinetd* is a single-process server which handles any number of connections to the address/port pairs specified in the file */etc/rinetd.conf*. Since *rinetd* runs as a single process using nonblocking I/O, it is able to redirect a large number of connections without a severe impact on the machine. This makes it practical to run services on machines inside an IP masquerading firewall.

If none of the packages listed above fits your needs, you can always roll your own. If the nitty-gritty network programming scares you, use one of the general-purpose socket utilities such as *socket* or *netcat*. They should be available anywhere, but if you have problems finding them, refer to the **socket** and **nc** Debian packages. The next section is about using the kernel to do some of the work of redirection, nomally in conjuction with a user-space redirector.

8.2.2 Transparent Proxy Support—Slight of Hand

This form of redirection augments the kernel with the ability to redirect traffic encountered by the router to a local port. The redirection code is integrated with the firewalling code for input filters. As with any other firewall rules, you have to specify some packet-matching criteria, in addition to the local port to receive these packets. On any router located along the flow of traffic, you can take traffic headed for a particular host or subnet, from a particular subnet—anything which can be specified as an input firewall rule—and redirect it to a local port. A process server capable of dealing with the packet should be running on that port (otherwise the client will get a `Connection refused` message). This is depicted in Figure 8.2.

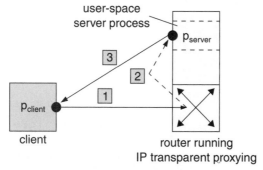

Figure 8.2 Kernel Redirection Using IP Transparent Proxy

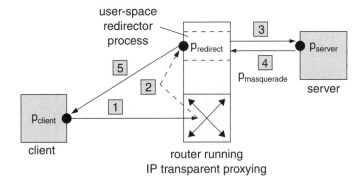

Figure 8.3 Kernel + User-Space Redirection of Traffic

Instead of a service process, you might have a user-space redirector running on the local port, which then forwards the traffic to some remote *system:port*, such as *transproxy* (introduced in Section 8.2.1). If you would like to enforce the policy of using proxy servers, you can use transparent proxying to forward all outbound requests for direct connections to the internal proxy server. Figure 8.3 is an illustration of this.

Strictly speaking, the system does not need to be a router because the firewalling rule must be specified as part of an input rule. In that case, you would redirect traffic from certain sources (the destination will be you, since you're not anybody's gateway) to a particular port, and traffic from other sources to a different port. This is the poor admin's (easy) way to enforce IP-based security (useful for things like inside vs. outside) on an ident or finger server by running two separate daemons on different ports, but on the same server.

IP Transparent Proxy Support with the 2.2.x Kernel   The drill for the 2.2 kernel is similar to configuring any of the firewalling rules, and is done with *ipchains*. Similar to the MASQ target used for masquerading, *ipchains* allows you to specify REDIR as a target of a rule. You may optionally specify a port, and no port means to use whatever port was in the original packet's destination field. Before configuring rules, you will need support in the kernel:

```
Networking options --->
    <*> Packet socket
    [*] Network firewalls
    [*] TCP/IP networking
    [*] IP: advanced router
+   [*] IP: firewalling
+   [*] IP: transparent proxy support (EXPERIMENTAL)
```

For our example, we want to let everyone know that a server is down, should anyone try to access it. Note that you can use the flexibility of *ipchains* to redirect traffic from different sources to different destinations.

```
### redirect all traffic headed for port 80 on moose.mancill.com
### to local port 12970, where a user-space proxy will send the traffic
### to another web server while moose gets a brain transplant
ipchains -A input -p tcp -j REDIR 12970   \
        -s 0.0.0.0/0 -d moose.mancill.com/32 80

### configure transproxy to listen on port 12970 as user "nobody"
### anything received by the proxy is is sent to port 80
### on cow.mancill.com, which has get-well message about moose
### when people access it with an http://moose... URL
tproxy -s 12970 -r nobody cow.mancill.com 80

### management says that the message is too casual for the external
### customers who use moose, and that it would be better if the
### server were just down with no error message
### (?!? - I'll never understand mgt)
# assuming that our internal addresses are 192.168.0.0/16
ipchains -I 1 input -p tcp -j REJECT          \
        ! -s 192.168.0.0/16 -d moose.mancill.com/32 80
```

The above example works well for "onesy-twosy" situations, when there are only a
few ports to redirect. However, when the server process is not local to the router,
you incur the overhead of user-space redirection. For high-bandwidth applications, it
seems like a lot of work to ask the router to review all of the packets with firewalling
rules and then to copy them into user-space to be redirected. Is there a better way?
The next section covers pure user-space redirection, and the following presents a
kernel-only solution.

8.2.3 Kernel Port Forwarding—High Wizardry

Now we are about to come full circle on TCP/IP stack tricks. Some clever kernel folks decided that the functionality being performed by the user-level processes
we've discussed could also be implemented completely in the kernel. In review of
the previous two sections, **IP transparent proxying** could have been named **firewall
port redirection**. Its purpose is to redirect traffic to a local port, regardless of its destination. In contrast, the user-space redirectors take traffic bound for a local port,
and forward it to a pre-determined destination. This section covers extensions to the
IP masquerading code in the kernel which can perform a mixture of these functions.
But before we dive in, there are a few things you should know about kernel port
forwarding.

1. This functionality is available only in the 2.2 kernel or later. (This is not
   entirely true. There are patches for the 2.0 kernel available which support
   IPPORTFW, one of the functionalities discussed here. If you want to use this
   on the 2.0 kernel, retrieve the Debian packages **ipportfw** and **kernel-patch-
   ipportfw** to get started. You may also want to refer to the documentation at
   http://www.monmouth.demon.co.uk/ipsubs/portforwarding.html. This section
   will not cover the 2.0 kernel.)

2. You will need the *ipmasqadm* package if your distribution does not include this
   binary. The source is *http://juanjox.linuxhq.com/*. Debian users already have
   it; it is included in the **netbase** package.

3. This code is still considered experimental. This means that YMMV, and in some places the documentation, is still a little spotty. The 2.3 kernel coders are working on an entirely new functionality called *netfilter*,[6] which will replace this code and *ipchains*. I mention this because you may not see a lot of additional development for these modules.

To use kernel port forwarding, you must compile support for it into your kernel. Each of the IP masquerading special modules may be compiled as a module or directly into the kernel. The options required are:

Compiling Support for Kernel Port Forwarding into the 2.2.x Kernel

```
Code maturity level options --->
    [*] Prompt for development and/or incomplete code/drivers
Networking options --->
    <*> Packet socket
    [*] Network firewalls
    [*] TCP/IP networking
    [*] IP: advanced router
    [*] IP: firewalling
    [*] IP: always defragment (required for masquerading)
    [*] IP: masquerading
    [*] IP: masquerading special modules support
    <*> IP: ipautofw masq support (EXPERIMENTAL)
    <*> IP: ipportfw masq support (EXPERIMENTAL)
    <*> IP: ip fwmark masq-forwarding support (EXPERIMENTAL)
Filesystems --->
    [*] /proc filesystem support
```

The last three options are the ones of interest—they are actual "special modules." To differentiate among them through the end of this section, I will refer to them as **AUTOFW**, **PORTFW**, and **FWMARK**, respectively.

Kernel Port Forwarding—AUTOFW   The first of these, AUTOFW, allows for the masquerading of protocols which do not have their own protocol helpers. The list of masquerading protocol helpers (i.e., protocols which already have support in the kernel) can be found on page 100. The idea is that sometimes an internal (masqueraded) client will connect to an external resource via a control connection (typically TCP), but the external resource returns data on a range of ports, possibly UDP ports. This is often the case for streaming media protocols, such as RealAudio and Netmeeting. When the router masquerades the outgoing connection, it expects traffic to return only from the server port to which the client sent. The situation is depicted in Figure 8.4.

---

[6] Those of you who like to be on the bleeding edge (and who can tolerate a kernel panic or two) can check out the new development at *http://netfilter.kernelnotes.org/netfilter-hacking-HOWTO.html*.

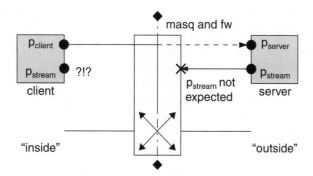

Figure 8.4   An Application for AUTOFW

AUTOFW attempts to mend this situation by allowing a range of ports to be forwarded to the internal system, also known as the **hidden system**. There are two ways to specify which internal system should receive the packets. The first is to explicitly define the IP address of this system (using the `-h hiddenhost` option). The second is to use an auto-detection technique which watches for traffic to traverse a specified control port. The (internal) sender of that traffic is then noted as the correct recipient of the inbound data destined for the range of ports. If you take a moment to consider either of these two options, you'll notice (at least) one serious problem. Namely, the functionality is not designed for use by multiple internal clients connecting to a single external server simultaneously. Any single client can use the service, and as soon as it is finished, a different client (assuming that you're using the auto-detection mechanism) will be able to use the service. By specifying the hidden host explicitly, only one client can ever use the service (until you reconfigure the AUTOFW rule). When it does its thing, port forwarding looks like Figure 8.5.

Its limitations aside, the AUTOFW functionality may have usefulness, and it is a handy thing to have in your bag-o-tricks. In order to use it, make sure that you have support for it in your kernel, and that you've loaded the `ip_masq_autofw` module if you compiled it as a module. Next, you need to masquerade the outgoing (control) connection as you normally would with *ipchains*. Now you need to add your auto-forwarding rule with `ipmasqadm autofw -A`. Documentation on this is a

Figure 8.5   AUTOFW at Work

little sparse. If you invoke `ipmasqadm autofw` (with no arguments), then you will evoke a usage statement. (Note that the option syntax is the same as for the *ipautofw* which was used for the AUTOFW patches running on the 2.0 kernel.)

```
hafnium:/root> ipmasqadm autofw
Usage:
    ipautofw <command> <options>
Valid commands:
    -A                          add new autoforward entry
    -D                          delete an autoforward entry
    -F                          flush the autoforward table
    .
    .
    .
```

It supports three basic commands, similar to *ipchains*, plus options that specify how you want the auto-forwarding to work. Remember that there are two ways to use auto-forwarding. The first specifies the hidden host explicitly; the second infers it from activity on the control connection.

```
    ipmasqadm autofw -A -r proto lport hport -h ipaddr -u
```

The first syntax always names the hidden host with `-h`. `-A` indicates that a rule should be added. The `-r` specifies the protocol (either `udp` or `tcp`) and the range of ports to be auto-forwarded to the hidden host. The `-u` tells the kernel to allow timeouts longer than the default of 15 seconds.

```
    ipmasqadm autofw -A -r proto lport hport -c proto port -u
```

The second command is the same as the first, except that instead of specifying a hidden host, `-c` indicates the control connection of protocol *proto* and port *port*. Once you establish rules, look at */proc/net/ip_masq/autofw* to get an idea of what is happening.

A BETTER WAY TO AUTOFW—NAT

Another way to handle the auto-forwarding situation is to use a NAT (Network Address Translator). The idea is to allocate a set of Internet-valid IP addresses to the router for use when masquerading these special (or all) types of protocols. The router then binds on of these addresses on the external interface before it sends (masquerades) the outgoing packet. This is the method used by most commercial NATs; unfortunately, Linux does not have this sort of functionality in the kernel yet, nor am I aware of a user-space daemon that does this.

Kernel Port Forwarding—PORTFW   The PORTFW feature has a different focus (and is less complicated!) than AUTOFW. Its aim is to replace user-space redirectors by performing the same task in kernel-space. If done correctly, it should have lower resource requirements than the user-space equivalents. The drawback is that some features, such as configurable logging formats and access control lists[7] are not implemented to prevent bloating the kernel code. (The developers did manage to include support for preferences and load-balancing.) There is much less to discuss about using this option because you should already be familiar with the concepts from the discussion on user-space redirectors. PORTFW has the added feature of preserving the original sender's IP address when forwarding the connection (like *redir* using the `--transproxy` option).

There are a couple of details you should keep in mind when using PORTFW. First, because this code is an extension to the masquerading code in the kernel, it may occur only during the forwarding of a packet. This means that you cannot use PORTFW on a firewall to redirect an internal to a local port on that firewall. Because the packet remains on the "inside" of the firewall, no forwarding occurs. In practice, this is not the sort of thing you would want to do with PORTFW anyway, but it might cause some confusion when you test your port forwarding from an internal address. (You can achieve the desired effect with transparent proxying anyway.) The second point is that the PORTFW rules, by themselves, do not masquerade the outgoing (internal) server → (external) client replies. This means that if you port forward inbound requests (from an external client to an internal server), you may want to masquerade the outbound reply. Otherwise, the client will see the reply from a different server (the internal address) than the one it sent the request to (the external firewall address). This may or may not pose a problem. If it does, add a masquerading rule for these packets, similar to one you would use for connections in the other direction.

To make use of PORTFW in production, you advertise the IP address of your webserver to the world via DNS as the IP address of the external interface on the firewall. If internal users are to use the same resource, you can overload this name on the internal DNS server with the internal IP address. Then configure the PORTFW rule to redirect inbound connections to the IP address(es) of the web server. You set up your forwarding rules using the following syntax:

```
hafnium:/root> ipmasqadm portfw -h
Usage: portfw -a -P PROTO -L LADDR LPORT -R RADDR RPORT [-p PREF] add entry
       portfw -d -P PROTO -L LADDR LPORT [-R RADDR RPORT]        delete entry
       portfw -f                                                 clear table
       portfw -l                                                 list table
       portfw <args> -n                                          no names

PROTO is the protocol, can be "tcp" or "udp"
LADDR is the local interface receiving packets to be forwarded.
LPORT is the port being redirected.
RADDR is the remote address.
RPORT is the port being redirected to.
PREF  is the preference level (load balancing, default=10)
```

Notice that the -a (add), -d (delete), and -f (flush) options are in lowercase, unlike for AUTOFW (<frown>), and that you always precede these options ipmasqadm portfw. The usage is straightforward, but there are a few additional tips in Table 8.1.

---

[7] Which is not a distinct limitation since only the connections specified by the masquerading rule will be matched.

Table 8.1 *ipmasqadm* PORTFW Options

option	description
`-l`	lists not only the rules but also the `pcnt` and `pref` fields, which are explained along with the `-p` option.
`-n`	suppresses name resolution, as it normally does. It makes sense to specify this is in conjunction with `-l`.
`-p` *preference*	load-balancing is implemented via a simple counter. The rules are stored in the kernel as a linked-list, and by default, each rule is initialized with a preference count (pcnt) of 10. Each time the rule is used, the preference count is decremented. When the counter reaches 0, the rule is moved to the end of the list. In the degenerate case of a single rule, this doesn't change anything. But if there are multiple rules for a given `LADDR:LPORT` pair, then shuffling the list will result in the next entry (with a different `RADDR:RPORT` value) being used on the next request. Use `-p 1` to implement a simple round-robin scheme. If one server is more capable than another, you can weight your preference values according.

The following sequence of commands is a simple example of usage:

```
# kernel PORTFW for inbound requests
### set up the port forwarding
# the .27 system gets the bulk of the requests because it
# has the new UltraPANTHEON 4692 HTTP co-processor chip
ipmasqadm portfw -a -P tcp -L extip 80 -R 192.168.16.27 80 -p 15
ipmasqadm portfw -a -P tcp -L extip 80 -R 192.168.16.28 80 -p 5
### need masquerading rules too!
ipchains -A -p tcp -s 192.168.16.27/32 80 -j MASQ
ipchains -A -p tcp -s 192.168.16.28/32 80 -j MASQ
```

Remember that you can perform a sort of load-balancing by specifying preferences for your rules. Test your setup by telnetting to an external machine and then trying to telnet to the firewall at port 80. You should connect to the internal system. Issue the command `quit` to disconnect. As with most things in the kernel, you do not have to use the commands provided to get an idea of what is going on. In this case, you can view the contents of */proc/net/ip_masq/portfw*.

Kernel Port Forwarding—FWMARK   FWMARK basically accomplishes the same goal as PORTFW—to redirect traffic to an internal host using private address space—but adds a more powerful way to specify which inbound connections are to be forwarded. It does this by operating in conjunction with *ipchains*, which is used to **mark** packets with a label (actually, an integer). A FWMARK rule can then act upon a packet bearing a certain mark, with different rules operating on each type of mark.

Consider the case where you would like a certain set of users to be redirected to one web server (perhaps with privileged information) while the rest always use another server. With PORTFW, there is no way to specify any sort of source criteria; this also goes for transparent proxying. So you would have to publish a second IP address (and therefore DNS record, etc.) and use PORTFW or a redirector bound to the second interface and then perform some sort of filtering to make sure that unprivileged machines could not connect to the restricted redirector. As long as you can differentiate between clients based on IP address, FWMARK allows you to do this sort of selection without leaving clues as to the different forms of access.

The command syntax is similar to that for PORTFW (except that most of the options have changed from lowercase to uppercase and vice versa). There is no need to specify the local address or port because *ipchains* syntax takes care of that with the criteria it uses to mark the packet.

```
hafnium:/root> ipmasqadm mfw
Usage: mfw -A -m FWMARK -r RADDR RPORT [-p PREF] add entry
       mfw -D -m FWMARK [-r RADDR RPORT]         delete entry
       mfw -E -m FWMARK [-r RADDR RPORT]         edit entry
       mfw -S -m FWMARK                          force scheduling
       mfw -F                                    clear table
       mfw -L                                    list table
       mfw <args> -n                             no names
```

The syntax is straightforward, but the option -s does bear explanation. The round-robin scheduling mechanism used in PORTFW is also available for FWMARK, but with an extension. If a rule's preference is set to 0, no scheduling is performed and that rule retains its position in the linked-list of rules. If there are other rules with non-zero preferences, the zero-preference rule will eventually become the first rule in the list for that mark, and will stay there. This will remain so until you force scheduling to occur by invoking ipmasqadm mfw -s. At this time, whatever rule is at the head of the linked-list will be moved to the back, promoting the next rule. An application of this is to perform failover from one RADDR to another—set all preferences to 0 and if the primary server is detected to be down, force scheduling of the rules to select the next in line.

Marking packets with *ipchains* is not difficult either. You mark them with an integer value using -m *markvalue*. Below is a sequence of commands which will enforce a policy like the one we described at the beginning of this subsection.

```
# kernel firewall mark forwarding for web access
#
# use these symbolic names to keep everything straight
MARK_FRIEND=1
MARK_NEUTRAL=3
FRIEND=209.81.8.0/24
FRIEND_SVR=192.168.17.3/32
NEUTRAL_SVR=192.168.15.46/32

# mark packets as they enter the system
ipchains -I input -s ${FRIEND} -m ${MARK_FRIEND}
ipchains -I input -s ! ${FRIEND} -m ${MARK_NEUTRAL}

# establish forward/redir rules based on marks
ipmasqadm mfw -I -m ${MARK_NEUTRAL} -r ${NEUTRAL_SVR}
ipmasqadm mfw -I -m ${MARK_FRIEND} -r ${FRIEND_SVR}

# make sure that the replies are masqueraded too
ipchains -I forward -d ${FRIEND} -s ${FRIEND_SVR} -j MASQ
ipchains -I forward -s ${NEUTRAL_SVR} -j MASQ
```

The script is a pretty simple case, but not so trivial that it cannot have interesting uses. Note the lack of `-p protocol` and port specifications in the *ipchains* commands and the lack of a `rport` in the *ipmasqadm* statements. Because they are not specified, the commands will forward traffic for all ports (TCP, UDP and ICMP) to the corresponding internal server. The same is true for the masquerading rules on the return trip. You could have just as easily added specific ports—it is up to you.

That concludes our tour of some of the redirection facilities available for Linux. You will undoubtably find other methods to perform no end of TCP/IP acrobatics. The change in the amount of capability between Linux 2.0 and 2.2 is significant, primarily due to the addition of *ipchains*. You can expect that much change (again) with the 2.4 kernel which uses new firewalling and masquerading code known as *netfilter*. *netfilter* is a complete rewrite and rethink of how to provide the range of features found in the current Linux kernel in a consistent manner, plus making it easy to add more features. Part of this is making it easy (and quick) to pass packets from kernel-space into user-space and back down. This should give birth to a whole new breed of network management daemons which can perform complex and arbitrary manipulations of packet headers, and which potentially have the ability to detect network-based attacks and take defensive measures in real-time. Visit *http://netfilter.kernelnotes.org/* to get the full story. The next section takes us up a level to talk about Internet services. After all, what good is a fancy TCP/IP stack if you cannot do anything with it?

8.3 GENERAL INTERNET SERVICES ON ROUTERS

This book has intentionally tried not to get overly-involved with how to run a particular type of router. The topics were chosen, for the most part, because they are applicable to many router applications. If you need to run an Internet shop and have questions, you should refer to the *LDP* documentation or one of the books already published about using Linux as an Internet system. However, I would be remiss not to share some knowledge I have gained about running Internet services on Linux routers. The section is divided into different services which are likely to co-exist with a router, and it includes points I learned during my encounters with these.

8.3.1 Internet DNS on a Router

We have to cover this one first, because it can be the main sticking point concerning the other services. DNS daemons run fine on routers; we covered this in Section 7.2.1. The potential issue has to do with how packets are formed by the IP stack. Remember that when Linux originates a packet, it populates the IP source address field of the packet to be the IP address of the sending interface. The point to remember when planning to use DNS is that which you run your daemon on your Internet router, the default route points out over that router interface on the Internet link. This is worth mentioning because this address space may not be part of the address space allocated to you by your ISP. Consider the following situations:

- The Internet link runs PPP. The point-to-point IP addresses may or may not belong to you—"belong" meaning that you may not have authority to register them with the InterNIC. If this is the case, and your ISP will not cooperate with you on registering the IP address to correspond to your domain name, you need to work around the problem. The easiest solutions are either to run DNS on a different system or configure the DNS daemon on the router to bind to a specific interface which *is* part of your address space. (Most DNS daemons support this; see the following hint.)

  If you do not own any IP address space of your own whatsoever, you have issues. (This is the case for many sites operated using cable modems or non-commercial DSL providers.) The issue is, when you go to register your IP address with the InterNIC as the primary nameserver for your domain, you'll have to give them the (Internet-valid) IP address of the system, i.e., the PPP or cable modem interface. When they perform a reverse lookup on this (i.e., resolve the IP address into a name), they will see that the name is already registered with the InterNIC, and it belongs to a zone which is not yours. You will not have authority to register that IP address as a nameserver for your domain without permission from the IP's owner (your ISP). Your ISP may be helpful and submit the nameserver request on your behalf. However, the ISP may refuse, or charge you a handsome sum.

- The Internet link runs Frame Relay. In this case, the address at both ends of the Frame Relay PVC may not be intended to be Internet-routable (and you must have some Internet address space). This does not have any affect on traffic which flows through the point-to-point, but has serious consequences for traffic which may originate from your router. If you run DNS on this system, people will be able to send you queries because they will be using the Internet-valid IP address of the router (most likely on the *eth0* interface). They will receive your replies, even if the Frame Relay interface does not have an Internet-valid IP address, because it has the right destination address and is headed in the right direction. When your machine makes queries, however, they will be from your unroutable address. They will go out into the Internet with bogus source addresses, never to be heard from again. The same fate would befall any masqueraded internal traffic bound for the Internet. If the address is Internet-routable but does not belongs to you, then the situation is the same as described above for PPP.

It all seems like a rip-off, eh? Not only do you have to purchase your domain name, pay for a port at the ISP, pay for access, buy the router, pay a bunch of setup fees, but now you can't even do anything without buying some address space! (And registering it... and waiting...) If you truly have a single IP address, or an address (or addresses) which belongs to your ISP, you are going to have to find someone else to host your DNS, do without, or break down and get some IP addresses.

TCP/IP allows you to use the `bind()` system call to bind the socket to a particular interface (really, an IP address); you can force the outgoing packets to contain your source IP of choice, provided that it belongs to an interface directly attached to that machine. (BTW, do not confuse `bind()` the system call with *Bind* the DNS daemon.) Properly coded Unix network applications should allow this to be configured, and default to binding to address *0.0.0.0* if no address is specified. (Binding to address is done by binding to `INADDR_ANY`.) Still, many do not.

The *Bind* daemon does, which is extremely useful in situations like those described previously in this section. Refer to the documentation; the keywords you need are `query-source listen-on`, which are part of the `options` statement. After editing the configuration file and restarting the daemon, take a look at *syslog* to make sure that the configuration does what you want it to.

If you would like more information on the topic, or are coding your own Internet-capable daemons, see the manpages for `bind()`, `accept()`, `listen()`, and `connect()` (all in Section 2 of the man database), or pick up a copy of the classic and authoritative work on the subject by W. Richard Stevens, *Unix Network Programming: Networking Apis: Sockets and Xti (Volume 1)*.

8.3.2 HTTP and NNTP on a Router

The issues you may have with running a web server on your Internet router are, in essence, the same as those for DNS, but they are, for the most part, not as severe. For one, many HTTP daemons also allow you to specify the IP address(es) they should bind to. Even if yours does not, people accessing an HTTP server rarely perform a reverse lookup on the IP address of the web server to make sure that it matches the forward name lookup.

This may not be the case for other services though, such as NNTP (used for a Usenet news feed). Let's say that you have only the single fixed IP address that your ADSL provider issued you, and you have found someone else with an established nameserver to provide forward resolution for your domain. Therefore, when people connect to *www.yourdomain.com*, their system will query DNS for the IP associated with that name. Their DNS system will find your NS and then your A record, and return *w.x.y.z*, the IP address of your ADSL interface. So far, so good... but if an upstream news server were to perform a reverse lookup on this IP address, it would return *someip.at.adsl.provider.com*, which does not match *www.yourdomain.com*. If you connect to an upstream server that uses DNS-based access control, be sure to give them the **canonical** name of your system, i.e., the *someip.at.adsl.provider.com* address.

HTTP daemons also allow you to indicate which server name you would like to use for the server. Although the name should correspond to a valid DNS name (either an A record or a CNAME) for that web-server, it does not need to be the canonical hostname, nor necessarily a name which corresponds to the IP which will be used to service the requests.

8.3.3 FTP on a Router

Serving FTP should be no problem. There is one "gotcha," again with DNS, but this time affecting clients. The FTP daemon may want to perform a successful reverse DNS lookup (IP to FQDN) for all client connections.

TRUE STORY: LOUSY FTP SERVER PERFORMANCE

I once had a call about a performance problem with the FTP server. The client complained that when he tried to connect to the service, it would hang for several minutes and then timeout. I checked the server and there was no load, and no mention of connections from the client's domain in the logfile. As it turns out, the problem was that the client had just switched over to a new Internet link and did not have a IP-to-name mapping for the external IP address their firewall was using to access the FTP server. Before the FTP daemon would do anything with the incoming connection, it would attempt a reverse lookup for the connecting IP to place this in the log. In this case, it took several minutes for the lookup to timeout, and the client would drop the connection before the lookup timed out, so the FTP daemon was not even logging the connection attempt. A couple entries in */etc/hosts* fixed things up until the client's DNS zones were configured correctly. In this situation, being able to take a look at the *ftpd* sources was very useful.

BTW, the requirement that a connecting system have a DNS resolvable IP address, is something that can be enforced by *tcpd* and its configuration files, */etc/hosts.allow* and */etc/hosts.deny*. If you are having trouble connecting to a server which you know is running the service you are requesting, it could be a routing problem, it could be a masquerading problem, but many times it's either DNS or the *tcpd* configuration on the target.

8.3.4 *Sendmail* on a Router

Sendmail (and other MTAs) may be a mixed bag. Let's think about about the functions that they need to perform. First, they have to send mail (prophetic, eh?). Next, they have to be able to receive mail, and forward it as necessary, also known as **relaying**. (I am not addressing the case when mail is to be delivered locally and stored on server; IMO, except for small installations, is not very appropriate for a router.)

Receiving mail should not be a problem. Your DNS configuration needs only an MX record which lists your router as an appropriate Mail eXchanger for your domain. Some senders may be disturbed by the fact that your forward and reverse DNS lookups do not match; they may generate a warning message, but they probably won't refuse to deliver mail to you on these grounds.

Sending mail, however, has issues similar to serving DNS. Furthermore, because of the recent campaigns against spam, there are some other problem situations which may occur. Firstly, you are likely to find mail systems refusing to accept mail from servers which are not properly resolvable in DNS. Secondly, some mail servers may reject your mail based on the sender address (or **domain**), if that domain does not correspond (once again, in DNS) to the domain of the sending system. Finally, you may have problems if your point-to-point link to the Internet is not routable, since not all MTAs allow configuring a bind-to address as we discussed for our DNS daemon.

The DNS and routing issues listed here are applicable to most Internet services. To summarize, some services like to be able to validate that the IP address and hostname are a matching pair in DNS. More specifically, the canonical hostname should match the IP address being used to send traffic to the Internet. This is probably a holdover from earlier times when the predominant security mechanisms were IP-based. The idea still has merit, because it means that the machines on the other end were configured by someone who took the time to configure their DNS properly, and when required, registered their servers with the InterNIC. However, with the explosive growth of the Internet, things have changed. Many people running domains have never even read a RFC. In their defense, they (we) are asked to support an environment with more protocols, less knowledgeable users, and significantly more volume than before. Still, it never hurts to know what you're talking about.

A subtle variation on this theme, not related to DNS, may occur for internal WAN links which use "unroutable" IP addresses for the point-to-point interfaces. An administrator sitting on a router tries to *telnet* to a host on a remote network to test the link. The link seems to be up, but the host never replies. This is because the *telnet* client binds its socket to address INADDR_ANY when trying to connect to the remote host. Instead of using the hostname IP for the source field in the packet, the kernel places the IP address of the interface used to send the packet. The packets reach the intended destination, but that destination may not be able to find a route back to the IP address of the point-to-point interface on the router. The frustrated network admin is confused, because there does not appear to be anything wrong with the link or its routing configuration. For internal links, one solution was offered in Chapter 5 on page 146. Another solution is to ensure that all internal IP addresses, including those part of the point-to-point are routable by getting the right information into the routing tables on all of your routers. Daemons which take care of this are the topic of the next section.

HINT: ZERO-NODE NETWORKS REVISITED

You may recall back in Section 5.3.5 that we said that we could "stretch" a subnet to include a WAN interface on the other end of a point-to-point link. We did this by assigning an address out of that subnet to both the near and far ends of the point-to-point, and using a subnet mask of 255.255.255.255. The motive was to save address space by not assigning a distinct subnet to the link itself.

The Linux kernel will let you take this one step further. Because network interfaces are known to the kernel by their names, and not just by their IPs, two different interfaces on a single system may have the same IP address.[8] This makes the most sense for Internet routers and other WAN routers, where the distinction between the WAN interface and the Ethernet interface is necessary only for the routing table. In other words, users of the system don't care which of the interfaces they are using.

To use this feature, assign the IP address to the Ethernet interface along with its regular subnet mask. Assign the same IP address to the near end of the point-to-point and use a subnet mask of 255.255.255.255. (The far end of the point-to-point can share the IP of its router's Ethernet interface, too.) Presto—no more worries about two IPs in DNS, or IP-based authentication confusion!

8.4 DYNAMIC ROUTING DAEMONS

For some applications, it is not possible to manually configure your routing table with a series of *route add* statements. It may be that the entries will frequently change, or that there are simply so many entries that you cannot enter them all by hand. Or you might simply find typing routing statements into scripts and having to maintain those scripts on all of your systems tedious. There are several alternatives available to set up your Linux router for dynamic routing. They take the form of user-space daemons which read their configuration from local files, listen for routing updates on a network socket, and periodically broadcast their routing table out over their interfaces to their **neighbors**. Machines interested in routing information will receive these broadcasts and update their routing tables accordingly. In this manner, you do not have to type in much of anything, and as long as everything is configured correctly, your network should quickly converge upon a stable routing configuration.

Before you load one of these on your router, understand that they are not for everybody. Certain types of network topologies lend themselves more readily to certain routing protocols; others do not lend themselves to being managed by daemons at all. If you are new to routing protocols, you should do some homework with a book before you crank one up and bring down your network. Also keep in mind that for many topologies, a well-designed internal network can be managed with static routes with less overhead and greater ease than with these daemons. But that is admittedly a manner of opinion.

---

[8] Thanks to David Mandelstam for sharing this tidbit with me. I wish I had known it sooner!

8.4.1 The *routed* Routing Daemon for Linux

Routed is the original, if you will, of routing daemons. It supports **RIP**, the Routing Information Protocol, which was originally designed by Xerox and implemented by the program *GWINFO*. This was renamed *routed* and brought to the mainstream Unix-world via BSD 4.2. It is originally described in RFC 1058 (which is known as **RIPv1**), and has the variants **RIPv2** (RFC 1388 $\rightarrow$ 1723 $\rightarrow$ 2453) and **RIPng** (for use with IPv6, documented in RFC 2080). The version distributed with Linux covers **RIPv1**.

If you want to load it on your system, check to see if it is already there. It is part of the original *NetKit* for Linux and is typically distributed as part of the base installation. Under Debian, it is part of the **netstd** package. By default, it is disabled, but you can enable it by editing */etc/init.d/netstd_init* and then starting the service with /etc/init.d/netstd_init start.

Configuring *routed*   There is no configuration file per se, but there are a few options you might want to modify. You can set these in *netstd_init* so that they will be set to your liking the next time that you stop and start the service.

-d enables debugging, which will log some extra information via *syslog* (by default into */var/log/syslog*).

-g instructs the daemon to advertise routing information about its default route gateway (if it has one). Use this with care, as your topology might not take well to having one default route replaced with another.

-s | -q control whether or not *routed* will generate information about its machine's interfaces and routes. The choice is either to say (-s) or remain quiet (-q). Note that the default is to say for machines with multiple network interfaces (i.e., routers), and to remain quiet on machines with a single interface. Either switch will override the default behavior.

In addition to these switches, you can affect *routed* by configuring the file */etc/gateways*, which is read when *routed* starts. Each line in */etc/gateways* indicates whether a certain gateway should be considered **passive**, **active**, or **external**.

- An **active** gateway is treated like any other active interface on the system, i.e., routing information about it is shared with others, and an entry for it is entered into the running kernel.

- A **passive** gateway will be added to the routing table, but it will not be broadcast as part of the RIP packets.

- An **external** gateway is neither advertised nor added to the kernel's routing table.

A line in */etc/gateways* very closely corresponds to a route add statement, as you can see in the following format (or by reviewing the manpage for *routed*):

<**net|host**> *destIP* **gateway** *gwIP* **metric** *value* <**passive|active|external**>

One final comment about the *routed* process itself. It does not fork and detach itself from the shell where you start it (i.e., it doesn't go daemon). If you start it in the foreground and then want to detach it from your terminal, you can hit **CTRL-Z** and then the command **bg**. Another thing you should know about *routed* is that it will make its own entries into the routing table as it sees fit for anything that isn't marked **external**, regardless of what is currently in your running routing table. If you have static routes already set up, this is an annoyance, so you will either want to adjust */etc/gateways* or quit walking the fence—use either static or dynamic routing, but not both. You may notice that *routed* creates routing entries for net routes for directly attached networks the traditional way, with an explicit gateway IP address. This will look either peculiar or familiar to you, depending upon where you earned your router wings.

ripquery   Say that you would like to know what a router running *routed* is advertising to the world (without running one of the packet sniffers covered in Section 4.5). You can use the *ripquery* command to get the contents of that system's routing table according to *routed*. If you are on the router itself, issue the command `ripquery` `localhost`. For a remote router, use the hostname or IP address of that router in the place of *localhost*. The command also supports a single switch.

-n is the ubiquitous **n**o **n**ame lookups. On my setup, this seemed to be of little use except to prevent `name ???` from being spit out after each line in the results of the query. No amount of prodding of */etc/networks* or */etc/hosts* or their associated configuration files seemed to help. (You should be able to recognize the subnets returned by the query anyway.)

Additional information about *routed* can be found by reviewing the applicable RFCs or the source code itself. Remember that it is part of the *NetKit* when you go to look for it.

8.4.2 The *Zebra* Routing Daemons for Linux

Zebra is the name of the first full-featured routing daemon to gain a popularity and be 100% free (GPL). At the time of writing, it is still beta software, but it is functional. It is being developed by some talented programmers and could surely use the support of the free software community to help test and contribute patches. Taken from the website at *http://www.zebra.org*:

> GNU Zebra is a free software (distributed under GNU Generic Public License) which manages TCP/IP based routing protocols. It supports BGP–4 protocol as described in RFC 1771 (A Border Gateway Protocol 4) and RIPv1, RIPv2 and OSPFv2.
>
> Zebra uses multi-thread technology under multi-thread supported UNIX kernels. However, it can be run under non-multi-thread supported UNIX kernels.

Zebra is intended to be used as a Route Server and a Route Reflector. Zebra is not a toolkit; it provides full routing power under a new architecture. Zebra is unique in design in that it has a process for each protocol.

It also contains support for IPv6, although it's not listed in the description. There is a Debian package (**zebra**) available, but if you have to build it from the sources, don't despair. They are an excellent example of using the GNU tools to their fullest potential. I was able to build the executables and produce the documentation in ten minutes. Note that currently the documentation is in *info* format, not as manpages.

```
### access the documentation
### note: you must have the tetex-bin package installed
$ cd zebra-0.73/doc
$ tex zebra.texi

# to view the documentation
$ xdvi zebra.dvi

# to print it out, assuming that you have
# magicfilter installed properly for your default printer
$ dvips zebra.dvi -o /tmp/zebra.ps
$ lpr /tmp/zebra.ps
```

The configuration of Zebra is covered in the documentation (distributed in TEX format; the `.texi` file). As a bonus for those of you with experience with Cisco, the configuration syntax is similar.

As mentioned on the webpage, Zebra is different from other routing daemons in that it provides a separate daemon for each routing protocol. Also, like other routing daemons and router systems, Zebra supports a telnet session running on a special port which it is known as the **VTY** interface. Each of the protocol daemons has its own port. If you are using the Debian package, this documentation is in */usr/share/doc/zebra/*. A few other points about the Debian package:

- All of the configuration files are in */etc/zebra/*.
- You control which routing daemons start by listed them in */etc/zebra/daemons*.

8.4.3 The Multi-Threaded Routing Toolkit

If zebra doesn't strike your fancy, you can try *MRTd*, the **M***ulti-threaded* **R***outing* **T***oolkit* **d***aemon* which is made possible by grants from the NSF and the Intel Corporation.[9] The presence of money means that everything is organized and there is pretty documentation (which is also pretty good); they even have a release schedule. *MRTd* is not developed natively in Linux, so it does not always compile on the first try. On the other hand, it is available for other platforms.

The latest version at the time of writing includes support for **BGP4+**, **BGP**, **RIPng**, and **RIP2** (which includes support for **RIP1**), with plans to support **OSPF** for IPv4 and IPv6 soon. Like *Zebra* and *GateD*, you can interface the daemon via telnet to a well-known port.

---

[9] Although it *sounds* commercial, this sort of sponsorship is really in the grand tradition of TCP/IP itself, which has its roots in DARPA.

MRTd also comes with a suite of test programs:

- *sbgp*—a utility which can receive BGP4+ messages as well as generate them and inject them into the network.

- *sospf*—a simple OSPF speaker and listener, similar in function to *sbgp*.

- *route_btoa*—a utility to convert binary MRT messages to ASCII.

- *route_atob*—the other direction of *route_btoa*. This is useful because MRT messages can be piped into other MRT utilities.

- *bgpsim*—a BGP4+ traffic generator for performing simulations.

You check out the documentation, mailing lists, and retrieve a copy of the source from *http://www.mrtd.net*.

8.4.4 The GateD Routing Daemon for Linux

Are you multi-homed on the Internet? Do you need more protocol support than what is included with *routed*? Do you crave to be running the same code the people on the Internet backbone are running? If any of these describes your situation, then *GateD* might be for you. *GateD* is a routing daemon for Unix which supports several popular routing protocols. It is produced and supported by the *Merit GateD Consortium*. This group aims be the provider of Internet routing daemons while bridging the gap between industry and academia, among other things.

The first step before running *gated* on your Linux router is not configuring it, but obtaining it. There is a version of the source code available to the public, but it is several revisions behind what members of the *GateD Consortium* have access to, and it is not redistributable without negotiating a license with the GateD Consortium. It is this second point that precludes there being a pre-packaged version of *GateD* available for Debian or any of the other Linux distributions. However, this does not prevent you from legally building your own copy for your own use.

First you will want to visit *http://www.gated.org/* to review the license information and availability information there. You might decide to sign up as an *Academic & Research (A & R) Associate* or some other of membership. You will also be able to find a limited selection of pre-compiled binaries for Linux. Unless you're in a dreadful hurry, you should probably compile from the sources. My test compilations were successful on both glibc2.0 and glibc2.1 systems, both with kernel version 2.2.10. Here are the steps I followed to build my own binaries:

1. Retrieve the public sources by navigating the website until you locate *Public Release for Unicast*.

2. Extract the sources on the workstation where you would like to build them.

3. Configure the sources for the build. My build was of version 3.5.11 and I had to edit the following items in *src/obj/Config*:

    (a) At the very least, remove the '!' comments someone put into the sample config file. On my system, they did not sit well with `make config`.

    (b) If you like, comment out the `options INCLUDE_IOCTL` line, it is not needed and caused a bunch of compiler warnings.

(c) Edit any of the following to match your Linux distribution. Everything was already OK for Debian. You might want to adjust the protocols, since the more you include, the larger the resulting binary, and there is no need to have protocols which you will never use. Look at *./src/configs/README* for information about the protocols available and other options.

```
protocol        bgp icmp ospf rip egp
sbindir         /usr/sbin
bindin          /usr/bin
path_unix       /usr/src/linux/vmlinux
path_pid        /var/run/%s.pid
path_dumpdir    /tmp
path_version    /var/run/%s.version
path_dump       /tmp/gated_dump
path_config     /etc/gated.conf
```

4. Build the sources; this might take several minutes. The process so far looks like:

```
$ tar xzvf gated-3-5-11.tar.gz
$ cd gated-3-5-11
$ mkdir src/obj
$ cd src/configs
$ cp -p linux.inet ../obj/Config
$ cd ..
$ vi ./obj/Config
$ make config
$ make
```

5. Install the binaries and manpages, which are only a few, so you can do it by hand or use `make install` and the `inst-man` script that comes with the distribution. NOTE: Unless you edited the Config file with a different `bindir`, you might want to save a copy of */usr/sbin/ripquery* into another name before installing *gated*, since it has an executable of the same name (and functionality). The same goes for the manpage.

6. READ THE DOCUMENTATION. Besides the manpages, there are manuals online at the *GateD* website.

7. Edit your */etc/gated.conf* configuration file. There are sample configuration files available in *./gated–3–5–11/conf/*. If you are already using *routed*, you can use `rip yes;` as the only line in your configuration file to run in **RIP**.

8. Start *gated* with `gdc start`, and use *gdc* to control other aspects of *gated*.

Fully covering the configuration possibilities of *GateD* would be the topic of several chapters or an entire book, as would thoroughly introducing *Zebra* and *MRTd*. If dynamic routing protocols are new to you, do some research before configuring and deploying routers running these daemon. A good source is *Interconnections* by Radia Perlman, which explains each of the Internet routing protocols along with the protocols they are routing. In any event, don't think that you cannot coexist with *real* routers just because you're running Linux. After all, you can run a *real* routing daemon just like anyone else.

8.5 EMERGENCY DOWN PROCEDURES

Pray to God, but keep rowing to shore.
          — Russian Proverb

So you're running a Linux shop, and everything is peachy. Linux stays up when it's up, and when it fails, there is a logical explanation, and it comes right back up. But what about the one time that it doesn't? The time when your hard disk gets tired of holding heads away from the platters and decides to let them rest for just a few seconds... Or the time when you kick the power cord out of the machine while it's *very* busy? Some planning and advance preparation, coupled with quick thinking and creativity, will keep your environment running when the outside world conspires to make it do otherwise.

This section contains ideas about how to make your Linux production environment more highly available. As with many of the production tips in the book you may find the strategies uninspiring, or you may disagree with them entirely. If you already know better ways, you should use them, and if possible, share them with others. The disclaimer is that they represent what has worked for me in the past. YMMV...

8.5.1 Redundant Services and Servers

Deploying multiple machines, each capable of performing the same task, is the idea behind most of the commercial Unix high-availability suites. Two or more machines perform an orthogonal set of duties when everything is running properly, and share a common data source (typically a dual-ported SCSI RAID array) for the times when $machine_A$ is down and $machine_B$ needs to take over for a while. During this time, $machine_B$ assumes as much of the identity of $machine_A$ as is feasibly possible. Most clustering software operates upon this same principle, but varies in how it tricks the user into thinking that they are still using $machine_A$. Whether they change the DNS record being used to access $machine_A$, or perform some sort of transparent proxying, as we configured earlier in this chapter, the idea is still the same. Most of this software is aimed at applications instead of routers, but, as was discussed in Chapter 7, a few shell scripts and you can roll your own with routers. Now we extend upon this idea and talk about more ways in which you can improve upon the illusion of 100% uptime—the illusion of uptime is far more important than the reality.

Redundant Routers   Because every Linux system can act as a router by using a few simple statements, you can easily have several of your other production machines as potential failovers in times of need. For routers, the key issue is one of connectivity. If you keep this in mind, you will be able to quickly configure one of your other machines to take over the duties of a local network router or a WAN router should a production router go belly-up. Look at the network topology in Figure 8.6 for one way to do this. The idea is very basic—have machines with an extra NIC available to assume the same connectivity displaced by the down router. To be adequately prepared, you should have a script already written which will configure $standby_A$ to *become* $router_A$. During non-peak hours, you can test your configuration by

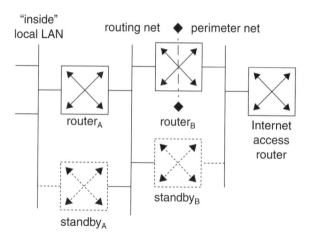

Figure 8.6 Redundant Router Connectivity

configuring the interfaces on router$_A$ down and running the script. Once you trust your script and its ability to make standby$_A$ become router$_A$, you can go ahead and work on ways to automate the failover. Because NICs are inexpensive, and scripts are free, there is no reason not to use Linux servers as standby routers at every point in your network.

Redundant Firewalls   Firewall failover is another story altogether because of security concerns, and what you can do here is largely dependent upon your firewall topology. If you are using proxies, then a second (non-routing) proxy machine should not pose much of a security risk. You're no more susceptible to attack through one than through the other, and having two (or more) machines might be necessary for your amount of client load. In this case, you might want to use an $N + 1$ approach towards allocating backup machines. The configuration of safe packet-filtering rules while allowing ample access to the proxies can get complex. In particular, you will need to forward traffic which traverses the packet filters, but you do not necessarily want to forward traffic which should use only the proxies. If you really need to do this, focus on using forwarding rules to limit traffic instead of input or output filters.

In the case of a packet-filter, you probably do not want to have an extra machine connected to your perimeter net at all times. Because a firewall failure is probably important enough to warrant a personal visit, you can have a standby$_B$ ready to take over, but leave it disconnected from the perimeter network. When you need the machine, you can physically connect it to the perimeter network. If you're less paranoid about internal attacks, you can keep the interface connected but configured down.

To summarize, firewall redundancy is well and good, but you should not compromise your overall security model for it. In my opinion, a good firewall might be one that goes down and stays down until an attack is over, and you've had a chance to verify that the your system was not violated. An automated failover system which pops up in place of the downed firewall will have the same weaknesses, and will suffer the same fate. The issue is that you will not be sure whether the firewall suffered a hardware failure or a software failure except in very special cases. Sometimes a trustworthy human is worth a lot more than clever scripting.

On the other hand, outages are often attributable to human error. Don't cause one because you introduce a shell script syntax error when you make changes to your firewall rules startup script. After any change, you should use `bash -n` *scriptname* or `ksh -n scriptname` to check for typos. Consider what happens if your firewall is restarted with an error in the configuration script. If the script does not configure masquerading, then you have a production outage. If your filters are not in place, then you are running without a firewall...

8.5.2 The Support Server—A "Safe Place"

When you plan for redundancy, do not neglect other important network services. As far as the users are concerned, a DNS or DHCP outage is as tragic and disruptive as a harddrive crash in the router. As you design your network infrastructure, keep in mind that it is handy to be able to copy all of the configuration files around in an automated fashion. If you make changes to the DHCP daemon configuration file, a copy of that file should be transferred to a safe place, as well as to the machine designated to be the standby DHCP server. (DNS takes care of itself with the designation of secondary servers.) Any service crucial to the day-to-day operation of your network should be handled like this. An additional precaution to consider is the habit of saving revisions of these files, if you need to fall back to a previous revision quickly. This might sound like a case for doing away with traditional backups. It almost is. The problem with anything on a tape is that it takes a while to get to it, and you cannot manipulate tapes from a remote location. So where is a good place?

For an environment of any size (more than a couple of machines), I recommend dusting off that old 486/16M machine in the corner, installing a fresh hard drive (and possibly a tape drive), and using this machine as your "Linux environment support server." You can use this server as a software repository; it may be the only machine in your fleet with a CD-ROM drive (so that you can keep a copy of your distribution online and NFS-mountable). It will also have any software you use which is not part of your distribution, kernel source and packages, and the configuration files I mentioned previously. You may also want to copy system logs over to this machine for archiving. In fact, this may be the only machine on your network for which you perform full backups.

In most cases, you can use NFS as your configuration file backup mechanism. If you do this, be sensible about what is backed up and how. For one, you're going to be exporting part of the support machine's filesystem as writable to all of your servers. Export a directory like */usr/local/etc/envbackups*, which may contain a subdirectory for each of the machines in your environment. Your production machines would then mount *carbon:/usr/local/etc/envbackups/$(hostname)* and copy the files while preserving the modification date (*cp* with the `-p` option, *cpio* with `-m`, or *tar* just the way it is). What you copy is up to you, but you could start with the things listed in Section 7.4.2. When you mount the support server, make sure that you use the `-o soft` option to *mount* so that your production boxes will not be unhappy should the mount point be temporarily unavailable. Because the files being copied may contain sensitive configuration information, do not neglect to protect the mount points from prying eyes—to keep your "safe place" truly safe.

8.5.3 Mini-Distributions for a "Warm" Standby

Keep in mind that any machine with a couple of network cards will suffice in a pinch for a LAN router or packet filter. You just need to have a mini distribution which will boot and configure the interfaces, and have the firewalling commands available on it. In the case of a simple router, most distributions' rescue floppies are good enough. In particular, you need IP firewalling (and perhaps IP masquerading) support in the kernel plus the configuration binary which corresponds to particular version of the kernel you are running, i.e., *ipfwadm* or *ipchains*. The *Trinux* and *LRP* mini-distributions come to mind—refer to the list on page 15 for more choices. In all cases, you will want to have the most recent copy of your firewall rules *easily* accessible. Consider incorporating something like the following step into your firewall change control procedures:

> Every time you change your firewalling rules, make a backup of the previous version of the file and document the changes. The *savelog* command (native to Debian) is a handy way of making backup versions of a file. You should also save a copy of the new rules in a safe place, which means not on the firewall itself. You will need the most current ruleset if you have to configure a new router in a hurry. If you're prone to forget to save a copy, set up a cron job to check the file daily for changes, and to mail you the file when it does change. (This is a good idea for the sake of security, too.)

For those of you familiar with change control, you will recognize this as change control in its simplest and most basic form. There is more text on this in Appendix C, Section C.3.

8.5.4 Rescue Disks

Sometimes you will find yourself (stuck) in the position of having to decide between trying repair your primary system or falling back to a standby. Especially if you know that you do not have backups as recent as you might like... Or you may know what the problem is, and just need a way into the system to patch things up. If you decide to operate to try to save the patient, you will have to start with a rescue floppy (or CD-ROM).

Use of rescue disks refers to placing a copy of the Linux kernel along with some common tools as a compressed image on a floppy disk. When you boot from this floppy, it creates a RAM disk, extracts the compressed root image onto the RAM disk, and then boots using this as the root. Once you're booted (you should not have any hardware problems with just memory and your floppy drive—if you do, get your hands on some more hardware quickly), you can take whatever actions are necessary to repair your system. Typically, this involves mounting the root partition (and possibly others) of your hard drive(s) somewhere underneath the root of the RAM disk. You can then edit files, move/rename files, replace a file with another version, unmount the filesystem, and reboot. (Don't forget to unmount the filesystems before the reboot!)

There are a variety of rescue systems out there; which one you use will depend on your tastes and what you happen to have on hand when you need it. I encourage you to experiment with several of these so that you are familiar with their particular capabilities and shortcomings. For the most part, they are all impressive feats of space management, but you will find that some have more of what you need for repairing filesystems, while others have what you need to get back on the network just long enough to copy some files from your backup server. They are useful for more than just hardware outages, too. Here are a few common "whoops, I just shot myself in the foot" situations (not really emergency down) where you might find them useful.

- It is embarrassing, but it happens. Lost password(s) can put you in a precarious situation. The best way I have found to deal with them is to wait for an off-peak period, bounce the box (from the console with **CTRL-ALT-DEL**), and boot using a rescue floppy. Let the rescue floppy boot the system and then execute a shell. In this shell, create a directory */tmp/root* and mount the root partition of the hard drive here. Now just `cd /tmp/root/etc` and use the editor on the rescue disk to remove whatever is in the password field for `root` in *./passwd* and *./shadow*. Now `cd /`, `umount /tmp/root`, eject the floppy, and reboot the system. As soon as it it comes up, login as "root" (just hit **ENTER** for the password) and set the password to something you can remember. If you procrastinate fixing the problem, you may find yourself explaining to a user or manager why you cannot make the requested configuration change in the middle of the day without disrupting normal activity.

- Almost as embarrassing as a lost password is a bad kernel gen. If you generate a kernel which will not boot your machine and do not have a backup kernel image configured in your boot loader, you'll have to boot from something standard to get going again. In this case, boot the system from a different kernel, but mount the root filesystem as itself. For the Debian rescue floppy, you can type `rescue root=/dev/hda1` (substitute your root partition for *hda1*) at the `root:` prompt to boot from the same kernel you used to initially load the machine. Once booted, you can login, clean up the kernel mess, and try again.

- You may encounter a similar situation to the one explained above if you image hard drives from one drive to another. This will confuse your boot manager and prevent it from finding the kernel when you attempt to boot from the newly imaged drive. Once again, boot from rescue media and indicate what the root partition should be. As soon as you're up, issue the command `lilo -v` (or whatever is appropriate for your machine) and then reboot.

Hard Drive Problems   Ok, stupid admin tricks aside, there is another, entirely different class of problems which require rescue disks. Namely, any sort of filesystem corruption which renders the root filesystem unmountable. Filesystem corruption typically takes one of four forms.

1. Filesystem meta-data are inconsistent due to disk buffers not being flushed before the system was halted. This sort of corruption will occur any time that the system reboots unexpectedly. The *fsck* program will usually set things straight again, as long as it is able to execute (i.e., the root filesystem can be mounted read-only).

2. The hard drive detects a bad block and the controller is unable to relocate it to a good block.[10] Any files or inodes with data in that block are now unreadable. In this case, the severity of the problem depends entirely on where the bad block is located. If it is underneath */lib/ld.so* or */etc/inittab* of */bin/mount*, things will get worse before they get better. On the other hand, it could be located in the middle of nowhere, and you may never notice it. It does not necessarily mean that the drive is failing, or that more bad blocks are to be expected.

3. The hard drive is under duress due to any number of physical factors such as failing bearings, excessive heat, etc. This may result in intermittent problems, or it may be the beginning of the very short journey known as "head crash." In this case and in the one above, the best thing to do is to revert to a standby system, try to mount the drive read-only and salvage what you can (if you need to).

4. Incompatibilities may exist between the kernel and the chipset on your disk controller. I used Linux for five years before I ever experienced anything like this. Boy, was I surprised! The problem was easily corrected, but it was costly in terms of lost time. While these types of incompatibilities are not commonplace, they do exist, as I learned when I appealed to others for reasons why my system had suddenly lost its mind.

   The best way to prevent these is to take heed of the configuration help which comes with the kernel, and to be careful when tuning with *hdparm*. If such a failure occurs, you will probably know it right away. What typically happens is that the kernel notices the problem and remounts the root filesystem as read-only (as per `errors=remount-ro` in */etc/fstab*). This will break things such as system logging, being able to edit files and perhaps being able to view man-pages, but will prevent the bug from destroying the filesystem any further. If you notice something odd with your system all of a sudden, if `touch /tmp/moomoo` fails, then you ought to take a close look at */var/log/kern.log* and */var/log/syslog*.

All of these are of varying degrees of badness, depending upon what is affected. The Linux system tools will patch up problems with the meta-data as long as the drive itself is capable of storing and retrieving information accurately. If the drive can boot from itself and clean itself, then you do not have anything to worry about. If the system can mount the root partition read-only but cannot successfully complete a *fsck* run without interaction, then you will be prompted for the root password and

---

[10] A function of IDE drives.

will have to run *fsck* manually. This typically amounts to answering "yes" to a slew of arcane questions. (You can save yourself time by specifying -y on the command line.) Once the run is complete, you can hit **CTRL-D** to continue.

Things get more interesting if the filesystem cannot be cleaned using the copy of *fsck* on the hard drive. Now you bring in the rescue media, boot from it, and try to clean the filesystem. If this is successful, you may be tempted to mount the partition and take a look, just to see if everything seems to be intact. This is reasonable enough. Furthermore, you can use any of the tools provided with the rescue media to move things around, view the contents of the *lost+found* directory, etc.

Rescue Disks and Dynamically Linked Binaries   Less experienced administrators may get into trouble when they try to start using binaries on the mounted root partition. The problem is that those binaries are dynamically linked, and their libraries are not available. If you are not familiar with the difference between dynamically and statically linked binaries, refer to a good text on operating systems concepts. Here is my terse synopsis:

> There are statically linked executables and dynamically linked executables. The static ones are typically much larger, but are wholly independent entities. Dynamic executables have advantages in terms of memory and binary size, but require a functioning linker-loader and libraries in order to be useful. The end.

Rescue disks typically consist either solely of static binaries, or of a pared-down set dynamic libraries. If there are dynamic libraries on the rescue media, they are almost certainly not the versions against which the binaries on the hard disk are linked. This means that you cannot use the binaries on the disk, nor any script which requires an interpreter (or shell) which is not on the rescue media. What's the moral? Don't be fooled into thinking that, once your root filesystem is mounted, you're free and clear to crank up an FTP or *ssh* client. (As a side note, it might not be a bad idea to have printed copies of the *fsck* and *mount* manpages handy. You probably will not be able to access manpages on your crippled system. You should also be aware that the versions of these commands on the rescue media will not always match the versions you are familiar with from everyday use, so be prepared for differences and/or limitations.)

There is another related point to be made about dynamic libraries. For those of you with experience with other Unixen, you may be surprised to discover that for most Linux distributions, even the basic system tools are not statically-linked.

```
hafnium:/root> ldd /sbin/fsck
        libc.so.6 => /lib/libc.so.6 (0x40010000)
        /lib/ld-linux.so.2 => /lib/ld-linux.so.2 (0x40000000)
```

This means that if cruel fate decides to flip a bit in a sector in a block which contains a file, which is called *libc.so.6*, you **will** be using rescue media to work on your system.

Other than these general guidelines, I cannot tell you how to use rescue media to revive your fallen routers. There are simply too many variables to make an "if A, then do B" flowchart feasible. Fortunately, aside from the three "stupid admin tricks," I have had very little use for rescue media. Most situations can be handled more quickly by performing services elsewhere than by trying to repair a badly damaged system.

8.6 SUMMARY

This brings to a close our chapter about routers that do more than just route. Some descriptions of firewalls depict them as non-routing dual-homed hosts running proxy services. Others favor packet-filters, and still others NATs. A Linux system can be all three of these simultaneously, if needed. Like the variety of emergency down situations you will encounter as a network admin, Linux, too, cannot be pigeon-holed into any single role. Hopefully, this chapter conveys the wide range of options you have when using Linux as a network component. Some of the topics covered were:

- Different types of proxy services you can provide to your users, either to heighten security or to provide access for private IP addresses other than by masquerading.
- Deploying Internet-accessible web servers using private address space, making use of port redirectors, such as *rinetd*, just the kernel (AUTOFW), or a combination of the two (transparent proxying plus *redir*).
- Publishing a single set of instructions while using firewall marks (FWMARK) to divert different classes of users to different services.
- Dynamic routing daemons available for Linux.
- Methods to keep your environment available, and what to do when you have system outages.

Conclusion

You've made it this far, and I sincerely hope that *Linux Routers* has given you some ideas, and maybe advanced your knowledge. The scenarios presented in this book are "real-life"—I've used Linux to deploy them in production. As such, I feel confident that they are realistic applications of Linux routers, but am certain that they are merely a small subset of practical Linux production uses. Therefore, the "omission" of an application scenario from this book should not deter you from such a deployment. In fact, I have begun doing some more (different) things with Linux routers recently, such as deploying them as VPN routers within a corporate network to enhance security for groups' special needs. I wish that I had time to include them in this book.

When developing new types of Linux routers, my suggestion is to keep an eye toward fundamentally sound system administration practices. If you recall the first chapter in this book, when we dicussed hardware selection and choice of Linux distribution, the emphasis was not on cutting-edge technology, nor on the distribution with the most bells and whistles. Technology for the sake of technology, has its place, but not in router closets or data centers (IMHO). And stability goes beyond hardware and software—they are merely a foundation. Best practices for system adminstration include good documentation and change management, plus a level head concerning when to deploy what, and how to expeditiously address outages.

I'm not going to review each of the chapters, since they hopefully speak for themselves and you can refer back to them as you like. There were a few comments that surfaced during the technical reviews of this book that I would like to include now. First of all, portions of the text illustrate that I am guilty of an i386 bias with respect to Linux. Actually "bias" isn't really the correct term—at the time of writing, all of my experience had been running Linux on Intel architectures—so "ignorance" is probably more appropriate. Since then I have, much to my delight, worked with Linux on the Alpha, SPARC, and StrongARM platforms. Whether or not one hardware architecture is superior to the other is immaterial. The fact that I can use a common toolset across all of them is simply amazing. It spoiled me, and it also redoubled my complaints about having to work around the abitrary differences that separate the commerical Unices.

Another point which was brought to my attention is this book's lack of emphasis on security. My first instinct is to point the finger back at "traditional" routers that can be booted via *tftp*, have documented back-doors, and have administrative interfaces running on unencrypted protocols. This, however, is merely a defensive parry. The truth is that I believe that any more discussion about security would have clouded the main topic of Linux router configuration. What good is a secure network that doesn't function? That should not lessen the importance of security in your mind. If you do not already have a handle on Unix, network security, and firewalling (the topics of several books), then you should do further research on these topics. There are references in the Bibliography and Appendix A.

Finally, a few people wanted to know why I presented such kooky router scenarios and examples. Once again, all I can say is that the book is very true to life. Unfortunately, this means that the router applications are not designed to most clearly illustrate their functionality and the Linux features they employ. (Chapter 4, "erbium," is certainly a good example of this.) There are some good straightforward NATs and firewalls in the *LDP*. I hope that the information there plus what is in ths book will help you build newer, more advanced configurations than you find in either.

Except for Appendix A, which contains URLs and some support information, the appendices cover topics that are either too general or otherwise do not fit the flow of the main text. I encourage you to thumb through them to see if anything strikes your fancy.

Happy routing!

tony mancill – March, 2000

Helpful Links

Perhaps the greatest challenge facing a network administrator is being able to find the right information in a timely manner. I have listed links which you may find useful.

A.1 GENERAL

- *http://www.linuxdoc.org/* is home to the *Linux Documentation Project*, or *LDP*. This is an excellent resource for up-to-date HOWTOs.

- *http://www.faqs.org/rfcs/* is a good site for retrieving RFCs. RFCs are scattered all over the Internet—so any search should return a long list of hits. But, not all of them are as well-organized or formatted as this site. For Debian users, you can load the RFCs locally by installing the **doc-rfc** package.

- *http://www.linux.org/* and *http://www.linuxlinks.com/* are both good places to start out if you're not sure where you need to go for certain information.

- *http://www.freshmeat.net/* is a wonderfully current directory of software and software development projects for Linux (and other free operating systems). When someone says, "Have you used *X*?" and there isn't a Debian package for *X*, this is the first place I go.

- *http://www.fsf.org/* is the home of the *Free Software Foundation*. Here you can find authorative documentation for the GNU tools both in electronic and hard-copy form. If you appreciate free software, drop in and make a tax-deductible contribution.

A.2 THE LINUX KERNEL

- *http://www.kernel.org/*—the main kernel source repository.
- *http://www.kernelnotes.org/*—this site details the changes available in kernel patches as well as provide other documentation regarding the kernel.
- *http://edge.linuxhq.com/* is another site that posts information about changes in the kernel, patches, etc.
- *http://lwn.net/*—more kernel news, perhaps not as terse or cryptic as the sites listed above. The *Kernel NewsFlash* can be helpful.

A.3 SECURITY

- *http://www.cert.org/*—CERT (Computer Emergency Response Team) provides security bulletins affecting all common operating systems and applications. You can subscribe to CERT's mailing list to keep current on various threats and available patches.
- *http://www.cerias.purdue.edu/*—CERIAS (Center for Education and Research in Information Assurance and Security) is an excellent security site, including news, documentation, and tools. [Some of you may know it from its previous incarnation, COAST (Computer Operations, Audit, and Security Technology), which is famous for its security archive.]
- *http://www.linuxsecurity.org/* is more specific than the previous two sites and focuses on Linux vulnerabilities and security news.
- *http://www.wwdsi.com/saint/*—the *SAINT* (follow-on to *SATAN* website) hosts not only the SAINT network security tools, but also a several vulnerability assessment and awareness tutorials.

A.4 NETWORKING

- *http://www.linuxrouter.org/* is the Linux Router Project's homepage. This site is a must for those who want to use a Linux router on systems without a hard drive.
- *http://www.linuxtelephony.org/* is not strictly a site about Linux routers, but wherever there is a network of any size, telephony integration is not far behind.
- *http://www.sangoma.com/* has some protocol and TCP/IP subnetting tutorials that are useful. Also see the trouble-shooting page (*http://www.sangoma.com/linedebug.htm*).
- *http://www.mancill.com/wanpipe/* is where I keep the latest copy of the Debian version of *WANPIPE*. This version may be substantially newer than what is distributed with the stable version of Debian.
- The 2.0.x kernel-specific passages removed from this book during the rewrite can be found at *http://www.prenhall.com/mancill/linuxrouters.html*.

A.5 DEBIAN GNU/LINUX

- *http://www.debian.org/* can tell you just about anything you want to know about Debian. If it doesn't, try `#debian` on *irc.openprojects.net* for real-time interaction. Alternately, try one of the mailing lists.
- Books on Debian:
  - *Debian GNU/Linux: Guide to Installation and Usage* by John Goerzen and Ossama Othman. ISBN: 0–7357–0914–9 *http://www.newriders.com/*
  - *Debian User's Guide, 2nd Edition* by Dale Scheetz. ISBN: 0–9659575–1–9 *http://www.linuxpress.com/*

Building the Linux Kernel

Many of you are already familiar with Linux and dealing with the kernel. For you, there will be nothing new or interesting in this section. But for those of you who may be reading the book with less exposure to Linux, read on. This section covers the basics of retrieving, building, and patching the Linux kernel.

Although one of the best-scripted and finely-done parts of Linux, compiling the kernel seems to be a very daunting task for a newcomer. Fortunately, it only *seems* that way. Many of the Linux distributions come with their own mechanisms to compile the kernel, and even kernel source as a package. I prefer the "old-fashioned" way of building the kernel, which is the method I will present here. It is a matter of a few easy steps.

1. Prepare your system for the kernel build process.

2. Obtain a copy of the kernel source.

3. Update or patch the kernel source as required.

4. Configure the kernel.

5. Compile and install the kernel.

Preparing Your System to Build the Kernel   To build a kernel, your system needs two things—the tools required to build the kernel and enough disk space underneath

/usr/src to hold the kernel source tree. The disk space required, including the sources and the object files created during the build, is:

version	size
2.0.36	36MB
2.2.9	60MB
2.2.14	93MB
2.3.51	114MB

As you can see, the kernel keeps growing in size as more architectures are supported and more device drivers are added. This is awesome and exciting, although I wonder when you will be able to download architecture-specific versions of the source to cut down on the sheer size.

The tools required are the same as required for a standard C development environment. Because you may not be familiar with this, or did not load a development model when you first loaded the system, here is a list of the bare essentials which may not be part of the base install of your Linux distribution:

bin86 the 16-bit assembler and loader. (Note: This is x86-specific. There are other packages for the other architectures.)

binutils The GNU assembler, linker and binary utilities.

gcc The GNU C compiler.

make The GNU version of the *make* utility.

HINT: WHAT PACKAGES ARE LOADED ON MY DEBIAN SYSTEM?

> To determine what packages are loaded on your Debian system, use `dpkg -l` to generate a listing of all packages loaded. *dpkg* also can also take a package name as an argument to limit the search to a particular package name, e.g., `dpkg -l bin86`, to find out if the **bin86** package is loaded on your system.

One nice thing about the kernel build is that you do not have to fully understand how to use these tools—the commands to invoke them have been scripted for you.

B.1 RETRIEVING THE KERNEL SOURCES

For the first time, you will need to retrieve a full set of kernel sources. These may be packages which are part of your Linux distribution. If this is the case, feel free to use them instead. I normally go to the nearest mirror of *ftp://ftp.kernel.org* and retrieve the latest stable *linux-w.x.y.tar.gz* or *.tar.bz2*.

Keep in mind that the stable versions of the Linux kernel have minor release numbers that are even (e.g., 2.0.x and 2.2.x) and the unstable/development versions have odd minor release numbers (e.g., 2.1.x and 2.3.x). Stick to stable versions of the kernel if at all possible. In fact, you may not even use the most recent major version.

At the time of writing, version 2.2.x is out and stable, but small issues keep popping up. Instead of allowing the 2.0.x series to erode from neglect[1] the kernel developers have extended its useful life by generating patches addressing security holes and new driver needs. Version 2.0.38 is the most recent release of the 2.0.x series, and this is still what I still use in production.

Kernel Versions

The "official" versioning scheme used in the kernel *Makefile* is *Version.Patchlevel.Sublevel*, but I've never heard anyone use this nomenclature. I think that you are more likely to be understood by others if you use *Major.Minor.Patchlevel* or *Major.Minor.Pointrelease*.

So, once you decide upon a kernel version and retrieve the source, you need to extract it. The standard location is */usr/src/linux/*. The kernel source will create the *linux/* directory, so you should extract while */usr/src/* is your current working directory.

```
$ cd /usr/src
$ tar xzvf /path/to/linux-w.x.y.tar.gz
   OR, if you have  bz2 files, use
$ tar xIvf /path/to/linux-w.x.y.tar.bz2
```

To avoid confusion and the version of your current source tree, you can annotate the directory name of the source to contain the current version, and then create a symbolic link so that */usr/src/linux* points to this directory. (If you're not sure what version of the source you have, you can check this quickly by viewing the first few lines of */usr/src/linux/Makefile*.)

```
$ cd /usr/src
$ mv linux linux-w.x.y
$ ln -s linux-w.x.y linux
```

B.2 Patching the Kernel

From time to time and for reasons mentioned previously, you will want to patch the kernel. Either you are upgrading from one point release (also called a **patchlevel**) to the next, or you have patches for a device driver that needs to be loaded.

The kernel source is large, so once you have a full release, it saves time and bandwidth to apply patches to upgrade between the point releases (e.g., from 2.2.1 to 2.2.2). This is done by retrieving the patch files from a kernel archive site and applying them to your source tree. (Don't worry... your kernel configuration will not be overwritten.) These files are named *patch*-w.x.y.[gz|bz2], and are meant to be applied to a *w.x.(y–1)* kernel source tree. If you want to upgrade several by more than one patchlevel, apply the patches sequentially. As an example, let's say that

---

[1] Sometimes referred to as **bit-rot**.

we are running kernel 2.2.1. We need the following files to upgrade to the indicated kernel version:

2.2.2	2.2.4
patch–2.2.2.tar.bz2	patch–2.2.2.tar.bz2
	patch–2.2.3.tar.bz2
	patch–2.2.4.tar.bz2

Apply the patches with the following command:

```
$ cd /usr/src
$ bzcat / path/patch-2.2.2.bz2 | patch -p0 -usEN
```

If you keep your kernel source in a directory containing the version number, remember to update this directory name and point the symbolic link *linux* at it.

```
$ mv linux- w.x.y linux- w.x.y+1
$ ln -f -s linux- w.x.y+1 linux
```

If you are installing patches which are not part of the official upstream kernel source, there should be accompanying instructions. For the most part, they will be similar to the procedure for the point-release patches, except that you might want to rename your kernel source tree something appropriate like *linux-w.x.y_mypatch*. Note that *patch* will create backups (pre-patch versions) of files if you specify the -b option on the command-line. It will also create *.rej* files for any touched hunk(s) of the patch that could not be applied.

B.2.1 To Patch or Not to Patch?

The decision to upgrade to the next patchlevel should be based on a need for either the functionality or protection that it provides. Most patches to the stable kernel tree are bug fixes, security patches, or driver support, and are therefore a Good Idea. There are exceptions, such as one of the 2.2.x releases which had a memory leak in memory management subsystem. Therefore, it is helpful to stay reasonably current with the state of the kernel. You can check out the changes between releases by visiting *http://www.kernelnotes.org* or *http://edge.linuxhq.com*. Other sites offer mailing lists, such as Linux Weekly News (*http://www.lwn.net*).

If these do not have sufficient information here, then install the patch and check out */usr/src/linux/Documentation/Changes*. This file contains pointers to other sources of documentation (and in several different languages). If you really want to see the differences, then download the patch file and zcat it into a text file so that you can review the source itself.

B.3 CONFIGURING THE KERNEL

Decisions, decisions ... Even if you're comfortable with hacking makefiles and applying patches, you still have to deal with the myriad of choices presented by the Linux kernel configuration tools. If at first you find it bewildering, do not fear. Because it amounts to nothing more than software configuration, there's nothing you can break. If you mess up the configuration, `cd /usr/src/linux ; rm .config` and start your configuration over. If you gen a bad kernel, there's nothing you cannot fix by booting off of a rescue floppy and generating a new kernel (or reverting to a previous one).

There are three different ways to specify your kernel configuration; all three are equivalent in terms of result, but vary in terms of user comfort. For all three, you should first `cd /usr/src/linux` so that you will be in the right place to start the configuration.

- `make config` is purely text-based. It goes through the list of configuration questions sequentially, which is a drawback for beginners. If you make a mistake, you must start over from the beginning. On the other hand, you can run it on any type of terminal and easily over low-bandwidth connections. Help for most options is available by answering "?" to a question.

- `make menuconfig` is the menu-based configuration utility. It still runs in text mode, but uses *ncurses* to create menus and dialog boxes. It works on the console and in nearly any type of recognized terminal emulator. It does require that you have the **ncurses** development libraries loaded on your system. The interface seems non-intuitive; note that you use `<Exit>` when you are finished with the menu selections currently on the screen.

- `make xconfig` is the graphical version of the configuration utility. It is based on the **Tcl/Tk** toolset (and therefore requires it to be loaded on your router) and requires that you have an X-server running on your workstation. It is takes a few extra seconds to start up, but is simple to use. Remember to export your DISPLAY to tell the router where to throw the X-client,[2] and to tell the X-server to allow the client connection from the router.[3]

Regardless of the configuration method you choose, you will be presented with a list of questions to which you can answer (Y)es, (N)o, and sometimes (M)odule. "No" means, appropriately enough, that this functionality or driver is not accessible when running this kernel. "Yes" means that the code to support this functionality is compiled directly into the kernel. "Module," however, could be taken to mean "maybe." A module can be loaded into the running kernel at any time after boot-up, and it initializes itself at that time. Modules are a Good Thing—see Section B.5 on page 303 to find out more. My recommendation is to configure any device drivers which are not required to boot the system as modules.

The kernel options are divided into different sections and are hierarchical within each section. Selecting a certain option results in the ability to select suboptions which fall under it. For example, in the section `Networking device support`, you must select the option `3COM cards` to be able to select the suboption `3c509/3c579 support`. Some of the relationships are a bit more complex, but that is the basic gist. You will quickly get the hang of things and learn where drivers and options are found if you play with the *xconfig* version of the configuration utility,

---

[2] `export DISPLAY=`*ip.address.of.workstation*`:0`

[3] `workstation>` **`xhost +`**`ip.address.of.router`

since the effects of your choices can be seen immediately (unavailable options are greyed-out).

Once you select the desired configuration options, all three methods write the results to */usr/src/linux/.config*. If you have a kernel configuration you would like to move to another system, copy this file into */usr/src/linux/*. This is the only file in the kernel source tree which must be backed up to be able to restore your configuration at a later date.

Which options should you choose? For the examples in this book, the required network-related options are spelled out. In addition to those, you need driver support for the other devices on your system. You should not need esoteric filesystem drivers or support for soundcards or joysticks.

B.4 COMPILING THE KERNEL

To compile the kernel, you need a standard build environment loaded on your system. You're going to need this for lots of other stuff anyway, so I'm going to assume that you have it. There are five distinct steps:

1. Build the list of dependencies between the source files.

   ```
   $ make dep
   ```

2. Delete any of the object files from prior kernel builds.

   ```
   $ make clean
   ```

3. Build the kernel and automatically call *lilo* to update the master boot record with the new location of the kernel.

   ```
   $ make bzlilo
   ```

   or to place your kernel on a bootable floppy, use:

   ```
   $ make bzdisk
   ```

   or if you only want to build the new kernel, but not put it into place, you can use:

   ```
   $ make bzImage
   ```

   Actually, there are quite a few variations on this step, but these are the ones I find most useful. If you use LILO as your boot manager, `make bzlilo` will build the kernel, rename your current */vmlinuz* to */vmlinuz.old*, and then invoke *lilo* so that your system will find the new kernel upon bootup. One reason to build the kernel and write to a floppy disk is for a simple fallback when testing a new configuration. Boot from the floppy to test the new kernel. If you do not like what you see, remove the floppy and boot the system from the previous kernel.

4. Build the modules you selected during the configuration process.

   ```
   $ make modules
   ```

5. Install the modules into the */lib/modules/w.x.y/* directory which is where the module utilities *insmod*, *modprobe*, and *depmod* will look for them. Note that *w.x.y* is the release of the kernel being compiled (not the one currently running). The module utilities look in the directory of the *running* kernel when loading modules.

```
$ make modules_install
```

You can combine all of these into a single command line such as **make dep clean bzlilo modules modules_install** or type them into a script that you use every time you build your kernel. However you invoke the commands, you should watch to make sure they do not exit prematurely. For example, if you issue the commands `make bzlilo ; make modules` and `make bzlilo` fails, you may not notice error messages because the output of `make modules` did not result in errors.

B.5 WHY USE MODULES?

Modular device drivers, commonly referred to as **modules**, are part of what sets the Linux apart from other operating systems. Once a kernel is compiled with module support, you can load and unload device drivers at will using the *insmod* and *rmmod* commands, respectively. Aside from illustrating the programming prowess of the kernel developers, they are a fantastic boon for sysadmins. Here is a partial list of the useful properties of modules:

1. Both optional and required arguments are easier to specify when loading the module with *insmod* than when having to specify them as a boot parameter in */etc/lilo.conf* and then rebooting the system to test the new parameter setting. Particularly true when you're trying to configure a device for the first time. . .

2. Modules can be unloaded and then reloaded. Sad but true, every now and then a piece of Linux code has a bug too. (Or maybe the bug is in the firmware on the controller card.) Without modules, reinitializing this device driver requires a reboot of the system. With the driver built into the kernel, it can be accomplished with a simple **rmmod** *module* **; insmod** *module*.

3. Modules can be loaded in any order which you see fit. This is nice for controlling the order in which the kernel creates the network devices (*eth0*, *eth1*, etc.). By dictating the order in which the modules are loaded or by specifying arguments while loading a module, you control the order in which the system detects the interfaces. On systems which have multiple NICs, this helps insure that the physical card which you expect to be *eth0* really is.

4. Kernel builds can take a long time, and they can seem to take forever when your entire network is down. If a NIC fails, it's nice to have a driver for other types of NICs available. I always compile modular support for the most common cards used at a site. This way, you are back up and running in the time it takes to replace a card and reboot.

Modules' advantages go beyond these niceties for the sysadmin. Because the entire kernel must be **locked**[4] into physical memory, a kernel with lots of device driver support is large and consumes RAM which would be available for processes, routing tables, buffers, and so on. Compiling infrequently-used device drivers as modules results in more efficient use of system memory.

They have furthered the cause Linux with more than just their convenience. Currently Linux supports 50+ different Ethernet drivers. If you are developing a Linux distribution, you do not know what type of NIC your potential user has, but you want to accommodate as many of them as possible. This means compiling a kernel with support for all of these (huge!) or the most popular of these (inconveniencing users who own a less popular NIC). They also help device driver development proceed more quickly since consecutive tests of the driver can be made without rebooting the system (usually).

For all of these reasons, the use of modules is assumed for all device drivers throughout this book except where it makes overwhelming sense to have the driver directly in the kernel—e.g., IDE harddrive support so that you can boot your machine. (Remember that you cannot load modules until the kernel has booted and mounted the root filesystem.)

Hopefully you now feel comfortable obtaining kernel sources, upgrading them between point releases, specifying and saving your kernel configuration and compiling it.

B.6 BUILDING SOFTWARE FROM SOURCES

Building software for Linux will come naturally to those who have worked in Unix. For one thing, it is getting easier, thanks to almost everyone standardizing on the FSF tools for configuration of makefiles[5]. Of course, no book can provide instructions for how to compile all of the software available. This section is merely an introduction for non-programmer types who are faced with compiling from sources for the first time.

Let's say that you've just downloaded *coolutil-x.y.tar.gz* and want to try it out. You will need to unpack, configure, compile, install, and then do your testing.

Before you unpack it, take a peek at what is contained in the archive—commonly known as a **tarball**. Do this with `tar tzvf` `coolutil-x.y.tar.gz | more`. The `t` option tells *tar* to look at the contents of the archive, but not to unpack it. Omit the `z` option if the archive is not either gzipped (ends in *.tar.gz* or *.tgz*) or compressed (ends in *.Z*); use `I` if it is bzipped (ends in *.bz2*).

A well-behaved tarball will extract itself into a directory name, including the version of the software. Once you are satisfied that the sources will extract without overwriting something important on your system, extract them by using the `-x` switch in place of `-t` in the example above. You should now change the directory into the source.

---

[4] Locked memory cannot be swapped to disk.

[5] Thank GNU very much! ;)

Configuration prepares the makefile (oftentimes named *Makefile*) for compiling the software in your environment. How it is done depends upon the author of the software. Many authors include a script named *configure* which automates the configuration for you; start it with **./configure**.

If there is not a configure script, or if the configure script bombs out for any reason, you should break down and read the instructions that came with the software. There are typically files named *README* and *INSTALL*. If both exist, the former contains general notes for this current release while the latter has instructions for building and installing the software.

Compiling the software is typically nothing more than typing **make**. Should this complete without errors, you can go on the next step of installing the software. Should it fail, you need to put on your programmer's cap and figure out what went wrong. Often, the software requires the development version of a library or headers which are not loaded on your system. Or it may be looking for the library or a C header file in the wrong location. (You can very quickly find files on your system using the *locate* command). If the build fails due to some problem with the source itself, check the *README* to see if there are any compiler or library version requirements you might have overlooked. If you still require assistance, try to get help locally or via a newsgroup, before contacting the author directly.

Installing the software seems to come in two forms. If the build results in a single executable, you can run it right from where you built it, or you might have to hand-lib it into place yourself. For more complicated software, consisting of multiple binaries or configuration files, you can probably use **make install** to install it. */usr/local/* is a good place to install software you build yourself, as it will not conflict with files in your Linux distribution (but remember to add */usr/local/bin* to your **PATH**).

After satisfactory testing, how do you get the software you built on your workstation installed on the router? I typically take a fresh copy of the tarball, copy it over to the router, and rebuild it from scratch. This ensures that the binaries built are linked against the versions of the libraries on your router, and it's easy. It also alleviates the need to have a compile environment on your workstation that perfectly matches the router, although for large environments, you should consider having such a build system available.

Testing Strategies and VMware

As a network administrator, you have to struggle with devising ways in which to adequately test new configurations, software, and equipment without adversely affecting your user community. The network is an integral part of most computer installations and requires uptimes an order of magnitude better than most applications—most applications use their maintenance windows to perform network-based backups!

Because nothing functions without the network, new routing configurations, new Ethernet drivers, and new versions of the proxy server all need to be right when they are first implemented. If anything breaks in production, it is improbable that it will go unnoticed. Testing network configurations gets complicated because:

- Lab environments which are similar production environments are costly. Resource contention can be very troublesome if you have a limited budget.

- It is difficult to simulate production load on the network.

- Test environments are designed by *you*, and chances are that you have already prepared your system(s) to cover the cases which you anticipate might occur. You may tend to do the same thing when conducting tests—in effect, testing only the cases for which you have already prepared.

- You will often be under pressure to deploy new configurations quickly or in response to problems or bugs. In this scenario, time is more of a resource constraint than money, and testing often takes a secondary role.

- Some parts of the environment are out of your control, and cannot be duplicated. The ultimate example is the Internet itself. Adequately testing new SMTP mailer or DNS configurations is touchy stuff, since mistakes can have disastrous results. (Bouncing mail off of your SMTP gateways for half an hour will require some explaining to your management.)

Dealing with these challenges requires creativity and a thorough understanding of your specific environment. Thus, it is difficult to present any sort of comprehensive test plan, and dangerous to assume that such a plan exists. Therefore, I present a few hints that have helped me in supporting a production environment.

C.1 Basic Testing Guidelines

Given the complex nature of performing comprehensive testing, here are some precepts to keep in mind:

- Don't do anything without having a way to undo it—properly stated, without having a fallback plan. This may be as simple as the backup of a configuration file (so that you can restore the prior configuration quickly). On the other extreme, you may want to load an entirely new system, copy over the pertinent data, and keep the previous system around for a week until you are sure that everything is ok.

- Switchovers which require a series of changes or changes on multiple systems should be "scripted," meaning that you should take the time to write out each required step and in what order. It is annoying to promise your users that you'll be back up in five minutes, forgetting that rebooting the DNS server first will cause daemons on other systems to hang on startup (trying to resolve names). By writing out a sequence, you are more likely to catch this sort of dependency. You can also retrace your steps if you run into problems, or have someone else help you implement the change.

- Testing new DNS functionality, such as load-balancing, is best done with a test domain. (This can be a subdomain of your existing domain.) This is doubly true for *sendmail* and other MTAs.

C.2 Testing: The Buddy System

For the network administrator who works in an Internet environment, there is nothing more useful than having a shell account somewhere on the "outside." Ideally, this system would be a Linux box external to your network and outside your buddy's firewall. If you can establish a rapport with another system administrator whom you can trust and who is willing to trust you, each of you can place a utility machine on the outside and allow the other access to it.

Having a shell account on the outside is almost indispensable for testing configurations as your external clients will see them (and for trouble-shooting too). Examples include testing FTP services, MX records and other associated DNS parameters. If you use *OpenSSH* or have some other means of tunnelling X clients, you can even see what your webpage looks like from the outside, using a graphical browser. Last but not least, you can probe your own systems for security holes—even launch full-blown attacks against your site to assess security risks. The advantages of this type of access are:

- Firewalling rules are generally not designed around preventing internal attacks (although perhaps they should be!), so it is more difficult to design an accurate test of how your systems will perform while under real attack.

- External routing problems are evident only when you're on the outside.

- When you access your own site, you are probably using your own DNS configuration, which works because you control it. Seeing how long it takes for updated DNS maps to propagate out to the rest of the world will give you an idea of how to coordinate changes and minimize client impact.

- You have an external account to which you can send mail *and* view that system's MTA's logs. The ability to view logfiles on both ends of a transaction can be very helpful.

Above and beyond these practical benefits is the fact that you have someone with whom you can discuss configuration problems and security alerts—basically, "talk shop."

USING KERNEL COMPILES TO TEST BASIC SYSTEM HEALTH

The kernel source is a very complicated piece of software, and compiling it requires a great deal of system resources. For this reason, it is good exercise for your system—*make* will spawn multiple copies of itself in addition to *gcc*, *gcc* will use all of the memory it can get its hands on, and requires a lot of CPU, memory, and disk I/O.

For these reasons, I use kernel compiles to test memory chips and as a general benchmark of the CPU/disk/memory subsystem. Compiling the kernel is a good way to test for memory errors because it will consume all of the memory on any reasonably sized system. If your kernel compile ends mysteriously with a SEGV error or signal 11, you should consider replacing the RAM in the system. If you are sure the memory is good and you still receive this error, it is sometimes caused by overclocking your CPU—you should consider setting it to operate within its designed specifications.

As for the benchmark, it provides a relative indication of system speed. For it to be useful, the system should be unloaded during the compile, and you should compare systems with equal amounts of real memory. Use the *time* command to time the entire build process, as in:

```
$ time make dep clean zlilo modules
```

C.3 CHANGE CONTROL

Change control is a large topic that consumes many books on its own. In fact, I've heard of all different types of change control—strong change control, fine change control, coordinated change control, etc. They are all essentially the same thing. When you implement changes, anyone (or anything) affected by those changes should be involved in the process of authorizing them, or at least be aware of them. The goals are to prevent unnecessary outages, ensure that procedures and documentation are updated correctly, and keep everyone in the loop. Your organization may already have some guidelines in place. If they do not, try to implement your own, even if they are nothing more than maintaining detailed documentation about all system changes and notifying your management before you make significant changes.

Change control or not, anything you do is subject to Murphy's Law. As a network administrator, there is the added threat of network-based attacks. After all, you hold the keys to a valuable resource. Because of this, I recommend you deploy a tool to detect the changes you **didn't** apply to the system. (As a side effect, the same software will help keep you honest about normal change management.)

AIDE (Advanced Intrusion Detection Environment) is a follow-on to the very popular intrusion detection tool called *Tripwire*. It has the distinct advantage of being GPL-free. The following description is taken from the software's homepage:

> [AIDE] creates a database from the regular expression rules that it finds from the config file. Once this database is initialized it can be used to verify the integrity of the files. It has several message digest algorithms (md5, sha1, rmd160, tiger, haval, etc.) that are used to check the integrity of the file. More algorithms can be added with relative ease. All of the usual file attributes can also be checked for inconsistencies. It can read databases from older or newer versions.

As you can gather, the software detects any change to a file, and can use several different checksum algorithms to detect changes that might fake-out a single checksum comparison (i.e., modifying a binary file so that its checksum is the same as the unmodified version). The software is straightforward to setup and use. It is, however, almost worthless if you don't really use it. The homepage is: *http://www.cs.tut.fi/rammer/aide.html*

C.4 USING *VMware* TO TEST CONFIGURATIONS

VMware, by VMware, Inc., allows you to create **virtual** machines which run within the environment of your host machine. The emulation of a full-blown PC is impressive, all the way down to the details of a working copy of BIOS which runs inside the virtual machine. A virtual machine runs a copy of the x86 operating system you load on it.[1] Because the emulation is complete, the **virtual** copy of the OS is not aware of the differences. It believes itself to be running on a reasonably well-equipped machine, although it really exists as merely a couple of files and processes running on the host machine.

The upshot for system administrators is an entirely new way to think about testing. Instead of listing all of the product's capabilities, I will talk about a few different ways in which it is useful for testing router configurations, and a few ways in which it is not. Note that I am not suggesting that you run *VMware* on your routers, but that you use it on your workstation or testbed box to help test new software. First, let's cover what you cannot do with *VMware*:

---

[1] This list does not include all x86 operating systems, but includes Linux, Solaris x86, FreeBSD, and several different versions of Microsoft Windows.

Caveats

- Because the emulation provides for a single Ethernet adapter, you cannot test different Ethernet drivers. I cannot see why VMware would want to change this, and I do not know how applicable such a test would be anyway, so I do not expect this to change.

- Similar to the preceding issue, you cannot test any add-on board beyond determining whether or not the driver patch for the kernel (if one is needed) will compile. External modems and ISDN adapters are a different story, as is addressed below under **Capabilities**.

- Because it is emulation and because you are sharing a single set of resources, things can get a little slow, especially if you do not have a lot of memory in your host system.

Capabilities

- You can load a virtual machine with exactly the same configuration as your production router image and use this machine for compiles. This way, you no longer need to compile on your production machines, but you also do not have to have a separate test/compile machine for every router image.

- You can make copies of the virtual machine before testing upgrades, so that there is no need to reload/restore the machine to fall back to a previous version of the image.

- You can use items attached to the host machine as if they exist on the virtual machine. Currently, this list includes the floppy drive, an IDE cdrom drive, a PS–2 mouse port, parallel ports, an OSS compatible sound card, and anything connected to a standard serial port. This last item is of interest when working with external analog modems, ISDN adapters, or anything that connects to a serial port.

- It is trivial to test new kernel versions and patches. It is nice to be able to build kernels and test them without having to reboot your real machine. This functionality is limited in its usefulness only by the fact that most network configurations are heavily dependent upon driver configurations for *real* Ethernet devices, so do not expect to test module parameter settings, etc.

- It is easy to test the mini distributions of Linux, which, due to their nature, have a testing cycle that is Build → Boot → Test → Build → ... This can get annoying if you do not have a second (or third or fourth, depending upon how many hats you wear) workstation at your desk, which is annoying all the same because of the noise, second keyboard, monitor, etc.

- As with mini distributions, you can test full-sized Linux distributions, upgrades between versions, etc., without ever having to reboot your system. You can make copies of a harddrive image before you start an upgrade, or, if you are truly lazy, you can use *VMware's* redo logs and not even worry about what you do to your virtual machine.

- You can test network and router configurations in several different ways. The section below details the different networking configurations available for virtual machines, and how you can use them to test router settings.

C.4.1 *VMware* Virtual Network Configurations

While configuring your VM (Virtual Machine), you are presented with four different options for your VM's network: **no network support**, **host-only networking**, **bridged networking**, and **custom**. Actually, all of them are equivalent to the host machine except for **no network support**—only the conventions of their use differ. When the vmnet module is loaded on the host system, it creates the *vmnet0*, *vmnet1*, *vmnet2*, and *vmnet3* interfaces (on the host system). Each of these is a virtual Ethernet hub and can be configured as you see fit. The only catch is that each of the VMs can be configured to be "attached" to only one of them (at a time), which is specified in that VM's configuration. This means that you can configure your host machine to act as a router between four different (virtual) Ethernet segments plus however many physical Ethernet segments are attached to it. I mention all of this so that you are not afraid to configure the product to suit your needs. Let's review the conventions VMware supports by default.

The first convention is to use *vmnet0* for **bridged-networking**. This is actually accomplished with the *vmnet-bridge* process, which runs on the host machine and bridges *vmnet0* to *eth0* on that machine. You can change this if you must. The command syntax is vmnet-bridge /dev/vmnet$N$ /dev/eth$P$ for $0 \le N \le 3$ and reasonable values for P. **Bridged-neworking**, by default, bridges the VM's *eth0* to the host's *eth0* (via *vmnet0*), which means that everything that the host's *eth0* sees is also visible to the VM's *eth0*, at least from an Ethernet perspective. Therefore, when using this option, you should configure the VM's *eth0* with an (unused!) IP address on the same subnet as the host machine's *eth0*. The end result on the host machine is almost exactly like IP aliasing. Just remember that you can bridge only the vmnet devices with Ethernet devices.

Host-only networking by default uses **vmnet1**, which is normally not bridged to anything on the host machine. The host machine and VM speak to each other through their *vmnet1* and *eth0* devices, respectively. In fact, any VMs running on this host can speak to this device via its virtual *eth0* device, as long as the virtual *eth0* is configured with an IP address and subnet mask compatible with the host machine's *vmnet1*. Because of this, you essentially have an virtual Ethernet segment, to which the host machine (via *vmnet1*) and each of the VMs (via their respective *eth0*s) are connected.

This isolation from your physical network can be used to test various types of attacks (and their patches), test monitoring techniques (things like *tcpdump* and *sniffit* work as well on vmnet interfaces as they do on real interfaces), and test things that you'd prefer not to have on your real network, like beta versions of routing daemons, etc. Note, however, that the isolation exists only as long as you do not configure your host machine for routing. If you have IP forwarding on and have configured IP masquerading, even if you are running in **host-only** mode, your VMs can very effectively communicate with the real world.

The **custom** configuration uses the *vmnet2* and *vmnet3* interfaces as per the convention. These can be used however you would like to use them. If you want to simulate a simple two-segment router topology, like the one described in Chapter 3, you can do the following, which is essentially **host-only** networking for two different

Figure C.1   A *VMware* Network

virtual machines, each on a separate virtual segments:

1. Configure your host system for IP forwarding. Remember the shortcut of `echo "1">/proc/sys/net/ipv4/ip_forward`.
2. Configure *vmnet1* on your host system to be the .1 address on subnet A.
3. Configure *vmnet2* on your host system to be the .1 on subnet B.
4. Configure **host-only** networking for your first VM, and configure it as a client on subnet A.
5. Configure **custom** networking for VM2; specify */dev/vmnet2* when asked for the filename. Once inside VM2, configure it as a client on subnet B.

Now you can route over the routing table, masquerading rules, firewalling rules, etc., of the host machine. Pretty neat, eh? See Figure C.1 for a diagram. You can use this setup to test all sorts of different types of configurations, such as:

- Configure VM_{host} as a sniffer on either $vmnet_A$ or $vnmet_B$.
- Establish services on VM_1 (on $vmnet_A$), like a web server or a SMTP daemon, and then configure packet filters and IP masquerading, to run on VM_{host} to filter and monitor, and alter access for VMs on $vmnet_B$.
- Test routing daemon configurations in an isolated environment by running them on VMs on a single vmnet and turning off IP forwarding on VM_{host}. (Since the VMs are not routers, you will have to configure bogus routing information to be broadcast by their daemons.)
- Launch attacks from VM_{host} against VM on a *vmnet*.

If the idea of having N distinct systems on four separate virtual hubs speaking together via routing on the host system gives you some ideas about system testing, visit VMware's website at *http://www.vmware.com*, for more information about *VMware*.

Ethics and Other Considerations

The sections in this chapter are essentially essays on topics related to being a network administrator with free software. They do not contain information about how to operate Linux routers, but I think that they are important topics for network administrators.

D.1 ETHICAL CONSIDERATIONS OF A NETWORK ADMIN

Being a network administrator is not for everyone. It can be stressful at times. People who do not understand the network tend to blame it for application problems (which they often also do not understand). You may have outages that are out of your control and cause you considerable work, while managers browbeat you and want to know why you did not have a contingency plan—the same managers that denied budget requests for backup links. Performance problems can be difficult to track down. Telcos can be maddening in their carefree attitude when it comes to installing your access circuits in a timely manner. All of this comes with the territory.

Another part of that territory is being in a convenient position to access the personal data of others. There is no need to go into detail about *how* you can do this, Linux comes loaded with enough tools to make anything from sniffing passwords to recording all email transmissions easily accomplished. My purpose is to dissuade you from doing anything like this, regardless of *why* you might decide to do so, and to avoid participating in any such activities asked of you. The ability to see into other people's activities, be they business or personal, may be tempting. We've all seen the sitcoms where people use telescopes to peek into the lives of others. I think the primary question boils down to one of right. Not in the sense of right or wrong, since it is not a question of good or evil—but right in the sense of privilege or permission. Does the ability to do something give you the *right* to do it? Some administrators that

315

I have worked with believed so. The typical rationalizations are, *They are (mis)using company resources* or *The company policy manual states that such monitoring may occur.* While these things may be true, and may even grant any specific authority for the IT staff to engage in such activities, they rarely define sufficient and specific cause to perform such monitoring.

If your management requests such actions from you, I hope that you refuse upon moral grounds. I like to apply Kant's "categorical imperative," but the moral precept has several names, so you may call it what you like. The fundamental question you have to ask yourself is, "Would it be O.K. if everyone were to act as I intend to act?" I think that the answer is a resounding no. Some will maintain that they don't send sensitive person infomatin via email, so they wouldn't mind if someone monitored. But this evades the issue by limiting the principle of monitoring to a single type of monitoring. It would be a simple matter for telephone company technicians to monitor your telephone conversations, for PBX administrators to review your voicemails, and for the U.S. Postal Service to open your mail. Most of this could be done without your ever knowing—the first two without leaving the slightest trace. And it is trivial for your neighbors to point a telescope at your bedroom window, or use a camcorder to record your comings and goings. Society frowns upon these things both legally and socially, although the monitoring could be done with the same rationalization that you might use to watch a user's network activities. The telephone company might be listening to determine if customers are about to commit a crime. The PBX administrator might need to insure that the system is not clogged with personal voicemails. The U.S. Postal Service could maintain that simply trying to make sure that copyrights are not being violated, or enforce other laws concerning materials which may not be sent through the mail. Your neighbors may claim that they have a right to know if you are conducting dangerous activities in your house, since such acts could eventually result in grievous infringement of their rights. In these cases, I believe that most people would scoff at the rationalizations, debunking them as inane, paranoid, and/or intrusive. Is network monitoring (for content) any different?

Of course, not all ideals function flawlessly in the real world. What should you do if your management requests that you monitor the network activities of an individual? You have to be measured in you response, since you do not want to run the risk of being insubordinate. Nor will you always fully know management's reason for asking. Your response certainly should depend upon the severity of the situation, right? I do not believe so. When you are dealing with a corporate network that is owned by your employer and operated for business use, I think you have to draw the line and be willing to perform only certain types of monitoring. Specifically, you should agree to supply information about the source/destination of packets, but not the contents. In other words, if your employer would like to spy on employee 2112, then you might produce a report that includes the fact that employee 2112's workstation transferred packets to and from locations XYZ, YYZ, and XZZ. How is this different? For one, it takes you out of the position of having to peek at the packets themselves, so it is a purely objective assessment of employee 2112's use of the network. Lastly, it is a form of monitoring is generally socially accepted. If management finds the destinations questionable, then may decide to confront employee 2112.

Let's use an analogy. The use of a company's postage machine for business mailings is an example of proper use of a company resource. On the other hand, using the postage machine to mail parcels to your friends in Germany is not the intent. Does it matter what is in the parcels? Perhaps to employee 2112, but not to the company. The policy for the postage machine of business-use-only was violated, and that is the act which should be punished. Employee 2112 does not need to suffer the further disgrace of having the contents (perhaps motive) of the wrong-doing made public. The same should hold for potential network transgressions. Instead of snooping on employee 2112 until this person "digs his own grave," let management confront the employee so that he may a) defend his actions, and b) know that use of the system can be monitored.

I am not so naïve as to believe that every reader of this book has completely honorable intentions with regards to the information available by snooping. Some of you may have plans to generate J. Edgar Hoover files on colleagues or political enemies, since you never know when such evidence might come in handy. Others of you might be jealous of the promotion of a colleague and feel that you were overlooked. And some of you might just want to increase your popularity by being a source of interesting information and gossip. Regardless of your motive, these activities are a misuse of your skills. No one will be able to stop you; there is no one there to remind you of it. And this paragraph may not make much of a difference either, but it's still wrong.

D.2 MANAGEMENT VS. LINUX

Every time I deploy a Linux system or read about Linux being used at places like Cisco (as a print server) or the U.S. Post Office (as a high-speed mail sorter), the phrase "Linux in a production environment? It'll never happen" stills echoes through my head. At a previous employer, this was the pat answer to all of my queries as to when we could try Linux out in our product evaluation lab. Admittedly, that was early on, but some of that mentality remains, and I am as happy to contest that statement now as I was then.

This book has focused on how to get Linux routers running and keep them running. But this is of little use if you never have a chance to test them and deploy them. If you work for an organization where you are the primary decision-maker for technology, then you're fortunate. Many companies manage technical environments by committee, politics, tradition, and treachery. This section contains a few thoughts about why it makes good business sense to have Linux in your production environment.

D.2.1 How Much Does It Really Cost?

For a network infrastructure, everything boils down to the **TCO** (Total Cost of Ownership). A TCP/IP network is in most cases an independent entity from the applications and systems it supports. (The network does not change when you upgrade the operating system revision of your development servers.) This means that the network can be composed of a squirrel-powered adding machine, and your management would not care so long as it is always up and delivers the required performance. Oh yeah, and it should be as inexpensive as possible. Although many technicians may find this philosophy unsavory (it certainly does not appeal to the idealist in me), the truth is that most finance departments are rarely interested in the technical elegance or excellence of their IT departments. In the eyes of those signing the checks, value is more important. Cost includes not just hardware and software, but all related personnel and maintenance costs.

In today's penny-conscious corporate environment, technicians need to be cognizant of the fact that many companies offer routing as a service, which may (at least on paper) look less expensive than your salary and equipment. Wouldn't it be nice if you could just say, "Linux routers are inexpensive, stable, and easy to maintain" and be done with it? This probably will not get you very far unless your management has a high-level of confidence in you. The reason, IMHO, is that many middle-managers today come from one of two backgrounds: **a)** they were active technicians during the reign of Big Blue (IBM) *or* **b)** they were managing during the late 1980s and early 1990s when the idea of a workstation on every desk started to take shape. In both cases, the heritage often contains conservatism. For the Big Blue fans, they know that big is good. For those who helped forge the personal computer revolution, I think many got burned by choosing anything other than Microsoft as their desktop operating system, so they also have a mistrust of the *small guy*. In a way, this sort of scrutiny of alternate technologies is good, or at least understandable. After all, these managers are paid to develop infrastructures usable for several years, sometimes five years or longer. Mistakes can mess up stock options, retirement plans, and entire careers. To them, saving a thousand dollars on a piece of router hardware is hardly a bargain when they cannot hire someone to support it. And paradoxically, they are under constant pressure to keep costs low in the short term. So how do you alleviate their fears that Linux is only a flash in the pan, a strategic snafu waiting to happen? Mount a three-part offensive.

1. Make it well-known how well-known Linux is. Watch for press releases from reputable sources that mention another large company coming out of the Linux closet. These are effective for managers who use a "follow the leader" approach to technology decisions. Watch for articles from very well-known sources, and about large-scale products. Examples that were helpful for me were Oracle announcing the availability of their RDBMS on Linux and IBM, announcing support of the Apache web server. Even better are items from IT consulting firms, such as the Gartner Group, about Linux in production. You might check *http://www.linux.org/business/index.html* for more of this type of news.

2. Make sure that the **total** cost of ownership of the current infrastructure is correctly documented. Don't forget things like:

   - Software licenses
   - Software maintenance
   - Software upgrades
   - Training
   - Downtime
   - Hardware requirements

I have witnessed a shocking amount of piracy and licensing violation occurring in IT departments. Some people claim that the software vendors want it that way; otherwise, they would not make it so easy to do. I'm not sure what this has to do with the issue; it's the same sort of flawed rationalization some people make about network monitoring for content. And if software vendors really do want it that way, then they have their own ethical dilemma to face—they normally are in business to sell software.

The point is that licensing represents a significant portion of many companies' IT budgets (or would, if it were done legally), and this cost (or liability) should be captured. If the industry trend of charging for server software while freely offering client software continues, the free server will have some distinct economical advantages. Not all of this directly applies to the router market, but Linux is not just a competitor of commercial routers. In general, software costs should be easy to capture, but you might find that people are not looking at the cost of the total cycle. For every upgrade, there are purchase negotiation costs, training costs (possibly for both the administrators and the users), and reduced user productivity costs due to server and/or workstation downtime.

3. If your IT shop is already in production with another operating system, you can start developing confidence in Linux by deploying it in non-mission-critical scenarios. After all, cautious managers don't leap without taking a nice long look first. You can ease their anxiety by letting them see Linux do things well over a period of time. Keep a detailed list of your time and cost investment. If it is your first time configuring such an application on Linux, note that reuse of both software and skills will lessen the costs in the future. You should misrepresent your time investment. Remember that an expensive solution for your employer will eventually affect you too. This trial period will also give you time to hone your Linux administration skills, if needed, and will give you time to consider how you would best manage multiple Linux systems on a daily basis. If Linux does what needs to be done either better or more economically, then your management should eventually warm up to it.

D.2.2 Build vs. Buy

Working as a technician, I've seen IT staffs agonize over the "build vs. buy" question. The group has typically polarized into two camps, one that believes that the software can be developed and maintained internally with a lower TCO than purchasing the software from an external vendor, and the other that thinks that purchasing the software will result in lower costs for the company. Those who advocate *buy* cite the salaries of developers, quality problems, and conformance to industry standards as reasons to purchase a product instead of having it developed internally. They will also contend that an 80% fit, available immediately, is better than a 100% fit three to six months down the road. *Builds* take the stance that an 80% fit is generous, that off-the-shelf quality is often subpar and problem resolution takes longer, that planning the proper implementation of a system will take the same time or longer, and that the staff required to support the product internally along with the time spent negotiating contracts will easily outweigh the cost of developing the system in-house. If you cannot guess, I'm a *build* person, as many Linux and Unix people are.

Several stories come to mind where management clearly came to the wrong decision when they decided for *buy*. The one that is strongest in my mind involves software distribution tools in a large-scale Unix environment (3000+ servers). The company had already developed its own internal distribution system, which was very much like the package tools used with today's Linux distributions. It supported versioning, dependencies, verifying the integrity of an installation, and use of scripts before and after the package installation to prepare the system and configure the software. It had some very advanced features, such as hierarchical distribution to reduce bandwidth requirements, the ability to push software to systems (via a nice Motif interface), and to revert to a previous version if something went awry. So what was missing? There were some GUI enhancements that everyone wanted, and it needed to be ported to Microsoft Windows. This was just enough space to allow a vendor to come in and drive a wedge between the build and buy camps. If you detect a note of bitterness, it's not imaginary. A vendor comes in and courts upper management with promises of software that will do everything and more, and will save hundreds of thousands of dollars. There were, of course, a few modifications required to the software to make it fit our needs, and these would be ironed out quickly.

"The Implementation Will Take Six Months." There were a great many stern-faced meetings between the technicians and programmers, who were generally pro-build, and the managers, who were pro-buy. You might think that the technicians were just out to save their jobs, but I can tell you that the issue was much deeper than that. There were other jobs, other things to program. And the in-house system was not newly coded or deployed, but was fully in maintenance mode, so it wasn't an issue of wanting to work on the latest and greatest. When management made it clear that it was seriously considering replacing the in-house system, it was making more than a business decision, no matter it how classifed it. Management was sending two clear messages to the development staff of the software: **a)** what they had produced up to that point was not adequate, and **b)** it had little faith in the team's ability to produce in the future. There was plenty of input from non-programmers who believed that the off-the-shelf product would not be able to do the job.

Within the promised six months, more than $2.5M had been spent on the new software, but its implementatoin strategy was still being developed, and over half of the programming team resigned. This crippled the day-to-day operations of the current software and slowed deployment of the new software. Even so, the Windows port of the in-house software was completed and operational—on time, under budget. I was not part of the programming team, but, I had interaction with them because I used the in-house tool to ship and install my systems software. The morale for the team was terrible, and bad morale was not isolated to the team. It was not just the programmers who voiced their disappointment in the decision to go outside for the software, it was all of the technicians. And when managers do not listen to the advice of their employees about issues central to their jobs (after all, who was running the

3,000 Unix servers here, the managers?), it sends a clear message that either **a)** we did not know what we were doing or **b)** it didn't matter to them whether or not we had the tools we needed to perform our jobs. Is there a happy ending this story? Only if you can take satisfaction in knowing that your instincts were correct. More than three years later, the in-house system is still being used, and despite the money and effort poured into the new system, it still has not been able to replace it. What a waste. . . .

Love's Labor Found   I cannot really think of a situation where it was evident that we had dodged the bullet when we avoided building and decided to buy, but I think that this is nature of *buy*; if it goes well, no one questions it. The point is that people will willingly work harder on solutions in which they take personal pride, and these are often the *build* solutions. It is my opinion that management, the stockholders, and the customers would all be better served if this psychology were better understood and utilized by those making the decisions. (Yes, I'm talking to **you**, all of you who take your minivan to any oil-change place but polish your 1972 MG with a diaper. Don't pretend that you don't understand what it means to take personal pride in your work.) And as a side note, if all of that was not "Dilbertian" enough, the entire decision to go outside for the systems software was made while the new department mission statement was being widely publicized, which was something to the effect of "We will develop a world-class IT organization and set ourselves apart by the utmost quality of our information systems." What, by using the same off-the-shelf software that every other company that doesn't have a world-class IT organization is forced to buy because they cannot build their own? What ever happened to leveraging in-house software as a competitive advantage? Maybe they worked for Big Blue *and* deployed workstations during the late 80s and 90s.

Busy Linux Bees   So where does Linux fit into all of this? Linux has been, and still is to a large extent, a solution for *builders*. I believe that this is what has brought it so far so quickly, and that it needs to be understood by those deploying it and managing it. If you have buyers (and there is no harm in this, I just believe that certain people tend to one or the other) then making them use Linux may have the desired results. Once Linux does reach the point where buyers are advocating its use, I hope that it will retain that "I can do it just as well myself" attitude. It is more important than some people realize. For one, Linux's support structure is heavily based upon people being enthusiastic about it. The same is true for its development. There will always be people interested in programming computers, and hopefully always interested in programming computers running Linux. Finally, it takes builders to find creative ways to use Linux. Innovative buyers are builders at heart.

GNU General Public License

The GNU Public License is one of the basic tenets of the Free Software community. It is included here because most of the programs described in this book, from the kernel to my shell script examples, are covered (i.e., protected) by this license. I use the word "protected" because one of the best things about the GPL is that code licensed by it cannot be arbitrarily taken away from the users. This does not prevent the author from releasing new releases under a different license, but once a revision is released under the GPL, derivatives are allowed, so long as they are also released under the GPL (and distributed with source).

For a given piece of software, this means that a change in marketing strategy won't leave users stranded without source, and with no choice other than to succumb to the terms of the new license. The user always has the option to take the existing version and maintain and improve it for as long as it makes sense to do so. To a certain extent, this make the GPL more important to companies than to individuals–corporations have a lot more to lose from draconian licensing practices than individuals do. In any event, this is why many people insist that all of the software they use be released under the GPL.

If you're relatively new to the Free Software world, this (in addition to the quality of the code itself) is what all the hubbub is about. The text of the license is included here; if you've never read it, here's your chance. If you have questions, there are plenty of netizens who would be happy to help you interpret it. To avoid confusion, I recommend going straight to the source: http://www.fsf.org.

Version 2, June 1991

Copyright (C) 1989, 1991 Free Software Foundation, Inc. 59 Temple Place, Suite 330, Boston, MA 02111–1307 USA Everyone is permitted to copy and distribute verbatim copies of this license document, but changing it is not allowed.

Preamble

The licenses for most software are designed to take away your freedom to share and change it. By contrast, the GNU General Public License is intended to guarantee your freedom to share and change free software–to make sure the software is free for all its users. This General Public License applies to most of the Free Software Foundation's software and to any other program whose authors commit to using it. (Some other Free Software Foundation software is covered by the GNU Library General Public License instead.) You can apply it to your programs, too.

When we speak of free software, we are referring to freedom, not price. Our General Public Licenses are designed to make sure that you have the freedom to distribute copies of free software (and charge for this service if you wish), that you receive source code or can get it if you want it, that you can change the software or use pieces of it in new free programs; and that you know you can do these things.

To protect your rights, we need to make restrictions that forbid anyone to deny you these rights or to ask you to surrender the rights. These restrictions translate to certain responsibilities for you if you distribute copies of the software, or if you modify it.

For example, if you distribute copies of such a program, whether gratis or for a fee, you must give the recipients all the rights that you have. You must make sure that they, too, receive or can get the source code. And you must show them these terms so they know their rights.

We protect your rights with two steps: (1) copyright the software, and (2) offer you this license which gives you legal permission to copy, distribute and/or modify the software.

Also, for each author's protection and ours, we want to make certain that everyone understands that there is no warranty for this free software. If the software is modified by someone else and passed on, we want its recipients to know that what they have is not the original, so that any problems introduced by others will not reflect on the original authors' reputations.

Finally, any free program is threatened constantly by software patents. We wish to avoid the danger that redistributors of a free program will individually obtain patent licenses, in effect making the program proprietary. To prevent this, we have made it clear that any patent must be licensed for everyone's free use or not licensed at all.

The precise terms and conditions for copying, distribution and modification follow.

GNU GENERAL PUBLIC LICENSE
TERMS AND CONDITIONS FOR COPYING,
DISTRIBUTION AND MODIFICATION

0. This License applies to any program or other work which contains a notice placed by the copyright holder saying it may be distributed under the terms of this General Public License. The "Program," below, refers to any such program or work, and a "work based on the Program" means either the Program or any derivative work under copyright law: that is to say, a work containing the Program or a portion of

it, either verbatim or with modifications and/or translated into another language. (Hereinafter, translation is included without limitation in the term "modification.") Each licensee is addressed as "you."

Activities other than copying, distribution and modification are not covered by this License; they are outside its scope. The act of running the Program is not restricted, and the output from the Program is covered only if its contents constitute a work based on the Program (independent of having been made by running the Program). Whether that is true depends on what the Program does.

1. You may copy and distribute verbatim copies of the Program's source code as you receive it, in any medium, provided that you conspicuously and appropriately publish on each copy an appropriate copyright notice and disclaimer of warranty; keep intact all the notices that refer to this License and to the absence of any warranty; and give any other recipients of the Program a copy of this License along with the Program.

You may charge a fee for the physical act of transferring a copy, and you may at your option offer warranty protection in exchange for a fee.

2. You may modify your copy or copies of the Program or any portion of it, thus forming a work based on the Program, and copy and distribute such modifications or work under the terms of Section 1 above, provided that you also meet all of these conditions:

> a) You must cause the modified files to carry prominent notices stating that you changed the files and the date of any change.

> b) You must cause any work that you distribute or publish, that in whole or in part contains or is derived from the Program or any part thereof, to be licensed as a whole at no charge to all third parties under the terms of this License.

> c) If the modified program normally reads commands interactively when run, you must cause it, when started running for such interactive use in the most ordinary way, to print or display an announcement including an appropriate copyright notice and a notice that there is no warranty (or else, saying that you provide a warranty) and that users may redistribute the program under these conditions, and telling the user how to view a copy of this License. (Exception: if the Program itself is interactive but does not normally print such an announcement, your work based on the Program is not required to print an announcement.)

These requirements apply to the modified work as a whole. If identifiable sections of that work are not derived from the Program, and can be reasonably considered independent and separate works in themselves, then this License, and its terms, do not apply to those sections when you distribute them as separate works. But when you distribute the same sections as part of a whole which is a work based on the Program, the distribution of the whole must be on the terms of this License, whose permissions for other licensees extend to the entire whole, and thus to each and every part regardless of who wrote it.

Thus, it is not the intent of this section to claim rights or contest your rights to work written entirely by you; rather, the intent is to exercise the right to control the distribution of derivative or collective works based on the Program.

In addition, mere aggregation of another work not based on the Program with the Program (or with a work based on the Program) on a volume of a storage or distribution medium does not bring the other work under the scope of this License.

3. You may copy and distribute the Program (or a work based on it, under Section 2) in object code or executable form under the terms of Sections 1 and 2 above provided that you also do one of the following:

> a) Accompany it with the complete corresponding machine-readable source code, which must be distributed under the terms of Sections 1 and 2 above on a medium customarily used for software interchange; or,

> b) Accompany it with a written offer, valid for at least three years, to give any third party, for a charge no more than your cost of physically performing source distribution, a complete machine-readable copy of the corresponding source code, to be distributed under the terms of Sections 1 and 2 above on a medium customarily used for software interchange; or,

> c) Accompany it with the information you received as to the offer to distribute corresponding source code. (This alternative is allowed only for noncommercial distribution and only if you received the program in object code or executable form with such an offer, in accord with Subsection b above.)

The source code for a work means the preferred form of the work for making modifications to it. For an executable work, complete source code means all the source code for all modules it contains, plus any associated interface definition files, plus the scripts used to control compilation and installation of the executable. However, as a special exception, the source code distributed need not include anything that is normally distributed (in either source or binary form) with the major components (compiler, kernel, and so on) of the operating system on which the executable runs, unless that component itself accompanies the executable.

If distribution of executable or object code is made by offering access to copy from a designated place, then offering equivalent access to copy the source code from the same place counts as distribution of the source code, even though third parties are not compelled to copy the source along with the object code.

4. You may not copy, modify, sublicense, or distribute the Program except as expressly provided under this License. Any attempt otherwise to copy, modify, sublicense or distribute the Program is void, and will automatically terminate your rights under this License. However, parties who have received copies, or rights, from you under this License will not have their licenses terminated so long as such parties remain in full compliance.

5. You are not required to accept this License, since you have not signed it. However, nothing else grants you permission to modify or distribute the Program or its derivative works. These actions are prohibited by law if you do not accept this License. Therefore, by modifying or distributing the Program (or any work based on the Program), you indicate your acceptance of this License to do so, and all its terms and conditions for copying, distributing or modifying the Program or works based on it.

6. Each time you redistribute the Program (or any work based on the Program), the recipient automatically receives a license from the original licensor to copy, distribute or modify the Program subject to these terms and conditions. You may not impose any further restrictions on the recipients' exercise of the rights granted herein. You are not responsible for enforcing compliance by third parties to this License.

7. If, as a consequence of a court judgment or allegation of patent infringement or for any other reason (not limited to patent issues), conditions are imposed on you (whether by court order, agreement or otherwise) that contradict the conditions of this License, they do not excuse you from the conditions of this License. If you cannot distribute so as to satisfy simultaneously your obligations under this License and any other pertinent obligations, then as a consequence you may not distribute the Program at all. For example, if a patent license would not permit royalty-free redistribution of the Program by all those who receive copies directly or indirectly through you, then the only way you could satisfy both it and this License would be to refrain entirely from distribution of the Program.

If any portion of this section is held invalid or unenforceable under any particular circumstance, the balance of the section is intended to apply and the section as a whole is intended to apply in other circumstances.

It is not the purpose of this section to induce you to infringe any patents or other property right claims or to contest validity of any such claims; this section has the sole purpose of protecting the integrity of the free software distribution system, which is implemented by public license practices. Many people have made generous contributions to the wide range of software distributed through that system in reliance on consistent application of that system; it is up to the author/donor to decide if he or she is willing to distribute software through any other system and a licensee cannot impose that choice.

This section is intended to make thoroughly clear what is believed to be a consequence of the rest of this License.

8. If the distribution and/or use of the Program is restricted in certain countries either by patents or by copyrighted interfaces, the original copyright holder who places the Program under this License may add an explicit geographical distribution limitation excluding those countries, so that distribution is permitted only in or among countries not thus excluded. In such case, this License incorporates the limitation as if written in the body of this License.

9. The Free Software Foundation may publish revised and/or new versions of the General Public License from time to time. Such new versions will be similar in spirit to the present version, but may differ in detail to address new problems or concerns.

Each version is given a distinguishing version number. If the Program specifies a version number of this License which applies to it and "any later version," you have the option of following the terms and conditions either of that version or of any later version published by the Free Software Foundation. If the Program does not specify a version number of this License, you may choose any version ever published by the Free Software Foundation.

10. If you wish to incorporate parts of the Program into other free programs whose distribution conditions are different, write to the author to ask for permission. For

software which is copyrighted by the Free Software Foundation, write to the Free Software Foundation; we sometimes make exceptions for this. Our decision will be guided by the two goals of preserving the free status of all derivatives of our free software and of promoting the sharing and reuse of software generally.

NO WARRANTY

11. BECAUSE THE PROGRAM IS LICENSED FREE OF CHARGE, THERE IS NO WARRANTY FOR THE PROGRAM, TO THE EXTENT PERMITTED BY APPLICABLE LAW. EXCEPT WHEN OTHERWISE STATED IN WRITING THE COPYRIGHT HOLDERS AND/OR OTHER PARTIES PROVIDE THE PROGRAM "AS IS" WITHOUT WARRANTY OF ANY KIND, EITHER EXPRESSED OR IMPLIED, INCLUDING, BUT NOT LIMITED TO, THE IMPLIED WARRANTIES OF MERCHANTABILITY AND FITNESS FOR A PARTICULAR PURPOSE. THE ENTIRE RISK AS TO THE QUALITY AND PERFORMANCE OF THE PROGRAM IS WITH YOU. SHOULD THE PROGRAM PROVE DEFECTIVE, YOU ASSUME THE COST OF ALL NECESSARY SERVICING, REPAIR OR CORRECTION.

12. IN NO EVENT UNLESS REQUIRED BY APPLICABLE LAW OR AGREED TO IN WRITING WILL ANY COPYRIGHT HOLDER, OR ANY OTHER PARTY WHO MAY MODIFY AND/OR REDISTRIBUTE THE PROGRAM AS PERMITTED ABOVE, BE LIABLE TO YOU FOR DAMAGES, INCLUDING ANY GENERAL, SPECIAL, INCIDENTAL OR CONSEQUENTIAL DAMAGES ARISING OUT OF THE USE OR INABILITY TO USE THE PROGRAM (INCLUDING BUT NOT LIMITED TO LOSS OF DATA OR DATA BEING RENDERED INACCURATE OR LOSSES SUSTAINED BY YOU OR THIRD PARTIES OR A FAILURE OF THE PROGRAM TO OPERATE WITH ANY OTHER PROGRAMS), EVEN IF SUCH HOLDER OR OTHER PARTY HAS BEEN ADVISED OF THE POSSIBILITY OF SUCH DAMAGES.

END OF TERMS AND CONDITIONS

How to Apply These Terms to Your New Programs

If you develop a new program, and you want it to be of the greatest possible use to the public, the best way to achieve this is to make it free software which everyone can redistribute and change under these terms.

To do so, attach the following notices to the program. It is safest to attach them to the start of each source file to most effectively convey the exclusion of warranty; and each file should have at least the "copyright" line and a pointer to where the full notice is found.

<one line to give the program's name and a brief idea of what it does.> Copyright (C) <year> <name of author>

This program is free software; you can redistribute it and/or modify it under the terms of the GNU General Public License as published by the Free Software Foundation; either version 2 of the License, or (at your option) any later version.

This program is distributed in the hope that it will be useful, but WITH-OUT ANY WARRANTY; without even the implied warranty of MERCHANT-ABILITY or FITNESS FOR A PARTICULAR PURPOSE. See the GNU General Public License for more details.

You should have received a copy of the GNU General Public License along with this program; if not, write to the Free Software Foundation, Inc., 59 Temple Place, Suite 330, Boston, MA 02111–1307 USA

Also add information on how to contact you by electronic and paper mail.

If the program is interactive, make it output a short notice like this when it starts in an interactive mode:

Gnomovision version 69, Copyright (C) year name of author Gnomovision comes with ABSOLUTELY NO WARRANTY; for details type 'show w.' This is free software, and you are welcome to redistribute it under certain conditions; type 'show c' for details.

The hypothetical commands 'show w' and 'show c' should show the appropriate parts of the General Public License. Of course, the commands you use may be called something other than 'show w' and 'show c'; they could even be mouse-clicks or menu items–whatever suits your program.

You should also get your employer (if you work as a programmer) or your school, if any, to sign a "copyright disclaimer" for the program, if necessary. Here is a sample; alter the names:

Yoyodyne, Inc., hereby disclaims all copyright interest in the program 'Gnomovision' (which makes passes at compilers) written by James Hacker.

<signature of Ty Coon>, 1 April 1989
Ty Coon, President of Vice

This General Public License does not permit incorporating your program into proprietary programs. If your program is a subroutine library, you may consider it more useful to permit linking proprietary applications with the library. If this is what you want to do, use the GNU Library General Public License instead of this License.

Glossary

ACL Access Control Lists.

AFAIK As Far As I Know—the standard disclaimer.

AMI Alternate Mark Inversion (sometimes known as **bipolar**)—a protocol used on T1 circuits which alternates the polarity of ones being sent. This is done to save power on the transmission line by eliminating the residual DC component of the signal.

APM Advanced Power Management—a set of BIOS features which can be configured to implement power-saving features of the hardware, such as drive spin-down, after a defined period of inactivity.

ARP Address Resolution Protocol (for Ethernet, it's documented in RFC 826).

ATM Asynchronous Transfer Mode—a networking protocol characterized by very small packets.

B8ZS Binary 8 Zero Substitution—protocol used on T1 circuits to maintain the minimum density of ones (used so that clocking remains synchronized during long sequences of zeros). It is an example of an intentional bipolar violation.

BGP Border Gateway Protocol, a dynamic routing protocol (RFC 1164).

BIOS Basic Input Output System, the code used to initially bootstrap the computer so that it can find the operating system. It can also perform functions such as assigning IRQs and base addresses to PCI devices. Some operating systems (e.g., MS-DOS) use functions provided by it for writing to system devices such as the screen or floppy drive.

bit-rot Allowing a piece of software to become antiquated and lose its usefulness by neglecting to maintain it properly.

bridge A network device that connects two segments of the same media type.

BTW By The Way.

CHAP Challenge Handshake Authentication Protocol—also commonly used for PPP authentication mechanisms (See also **PAP**).

CIDR Classless Inter-Domain Routing (RFC 1519).

CIR Committed Information Rate.

CPE Customer Premise Equipment—everything on your side of a digital telco circuit's demarc.

CSU Channel Service Unit—provides physical termination, performs signal amplification, and initiates loopbacks for a digital telco circuits. For T1 circuits, it also performs frame formatting and computes performance measurement statistics. Typically found in a **CSU/DSU**. (See **DSU**.)

D4 A framing technique used on T1 digital circuits. (See **ESF**.)

DLCI Data Link Connection Identifier—the link-layer address of a Frame Relay node within your network. Normally an integer between 16 and 1023.

DHCP Dynamic Host Configuration Protocol.

DMA Direct Memory Access.

DSU Data Service Unit—is located between the CSU and terminal equipment (your router). It converts unipolar digital signals from terminal devices into a bipolar digital format for transmission over the digital network. The DSU also provides timing recovery, control signaling, and synchronous sampling. (See also **CSU**.)

EGP External Gateway Protocol, a dynamic routing protocol (RFC 904).

ESF Extended Super Frame—a framing technique used on T1 digital circuits which provides for collection of performance statistics of the circuit (compare to **D4**).

FDDI Fiber Digital Device Interface—a physical network protocol which runs over optical fiber for LANs up distances greater than 100km.

FQDN Fully Qualified Domain Name—the combination of the hostname (sometimes called the "short name") with that host's domain name. For example, *pongo.mancill.com* is pongo's FQDN.

FSF The Free Software Foundation. (See **GNU**.)

FSE Full Status Enquiry—a message format used between Frame Relay routers to let each other know that all is well.

gen Jargon for "*gen*erate a kernel"—i.e., build a new kernel from the sources.

GNU "GNU's Not Unix." (The infamous lefthand recursive acronym.) A project started by the Free Software Foundation (**FSF**) "to develop a completely free Unix-like operating system." See *http://www.gnu.org/* for more information.

GPL The GNU Public License. See *http://www.gnu.org/copyleft/gpl.html*.

GSS-API The Generic Security Service Application Programming Interface. A network programming API used with SOCKS V5. See RFC 1961 for details.

hand-lib Building and installing software by hand, as in "I had to hand-lib the latest copy of *foo* onto the box because there isn't a package available yet."

HDLC High-level Data Link Control—a layer 2 (link-layer) protocol which provides an error-free connection between two network nodes. All frames terminate with Cyclic Redundancy Check (CRC) bytes which are used to detect any data errors. Frames received correctly are acknowledged by the receiver while erroneous frames are ignored.

hub a network concentrator that acts like a bus.

ICP Internet Cache Protocol, used by caching HTTP proxies such as *Squid*.

IDE Integrated Drive Electronics.

idiot image A pre-canned boot disk that is ready to go, hiding the more complex details of configuring the system.

IETF Internet Engineering Task Force.

IMHO In My Humble Opinion—certainly an oxymoron, since the speaker is not very likely to be humble after this lead-in.

IMO In My Opinion—grip yourself to receive someone else's idea(s).

IP Internet Protocol.

IRQ Interrupt ReQuest.

ISA Industry Standard Architecture.

ISDN Integrated Services Digital Network.

ISO International for Organization Standardardization—*http://www.iso.ch*.

ISP Internet Service Provider—someone with more bandwidth to the Internet than you have, and who would like to sell you part of it.

ITAR International Traffic in Arms Regulations—the U.S. State Department's set of export regulations, wherein certain types of cryptography are deemed illegal for export under the pretext that they are *weapons*. For more information about this sort of thing, visit the *Electronic Frontier Foundation* at *http://www.eff.org/*.

kernel-space Refers to code that is executed by the kernel in its own environment, such as device drivers, routing, and packet-filtering. Compare to **user-space**. Example of usage from *fortune*:

> Our OS who art in CPU,
> UNIX be thy name.
> Thy programs run, thy syscalls done,
> In kernel as it is in user!

LAPB Link Access Procedure Balanced—a bit-oriented synchronous protocol that provides complete data transparency in a full-duplex point-to-point operation. It supports a peer-to-peer link in that neither end of the link plays the role of the permanent master station.

LBO Line Build Out—a CSU setting used to compensate for loss of signal strength over distance for T1 digital circuits interfacing CPE. For each 133 feet (40 meters) your CSU is distant from the terminating point of T1, you should increase this setting.

LDP Linux Documentation Project—a collection of freely distributable documentation including HOWTOs, mini-HOWTOs, and even some books. It is the brainchild of Greg Hankins and the result of hard work by many. Visit it at *http://www.linuxdoc.org/*.

LINUX Linux Is Not User Xenophobic—the obligatory left-hand recursive acronym, just like **GNU** is.

LMI Local Management Interface—the method by which Frame Relay routers keep each other notified regarding the status of the network.

lpr The command used to Line Print Remote—i.e. send jobs to a print spooler.

LRP Linux Router Project—a networking-centric Linux mini distribution. See *http://www.linuxrouter.org/*.

luser A not necessarily derogatory name for a non-admin, non-programmer, non-guru. Reserve this term for a newbie for whom you felt a twinge of pity and compassion because of his or her computer ignorance. When you're having a bad day, everyone is a luser.

MAC Media Access Control—as in *MAC address*, which refers to the 6-byte address assigned to each Ethernet adapter by its manufacturer.

MIB Management Information Base (RFC 1213)—a mapping of numbers to parameters used by **SNMP**. MIBs are databases of parameter descriptions with their associated MIB values.

MINIX A free Unix-like operating system created by and under the direction of Andy Tannenbaum. Much of the early history of Linux is intertwined with discussions on the *comp.os.minix* newsgroup. See *http://www.cs.vu.nl/~ast/minix.html* for more information.

Moore's Law The observation that the logic density of silicon integrated circuits has closely followed the curve *(bits per square inch)* $= 2^{t-1962}$ where t is time in years; that is, the amount of information storable on a given amount of silicon has roughly doubled every year since the technology was invented.

MTA Mail Transfer Agent.

MTBF Mean Time Between Failure—the average operational-life of a component before some part of it breaks.

MTU Maximum Transfer Unit—a network parameter defining the maximum packet size.

NAT Network Address Translator—a router performing IP masquerading.

netiquette   Standards of politeness when interacting with other **netizens**. This used to be quite a strong yet undocumented code, that has somehow fell by the wayside. You can often tell newbies by their (lack of) netiquite. A trivial example is having a *.signature* longer than four 80-character lines. A more serious example is flaming someone in a public forum (e.g., a Usenet newsgroup) without first discussing the matter with him or her via private email. Equally offensive is posting a private message to a newsgroup without the sender's permission.

netizens   Others on the Internet.

NIC   Network Interface Card.

OSPF   Open Shortest Path First—a dynamic routing protocol (RFC 1131).

OTOH   On The Other Hand—whoops, I'm about to contradict myself.

OSI   Open Systems Interconnection (sometimes known as the "OSI Reference Model" or the "OSI Stack")—an ISO standard for implementing networking protocols which logically separates the functions of the network and programs using network into seven layers.

PAP   Password Authentication Protocol—commonly used for PPP authentication mechanisms.

PCI   Peripheral Component Interconnect.

PCM   Pulse Code Modulation—a method used to convert an analog waveform to a series of digital pulses.

PIM   Protocol Independent Multicast—this multicast routing protocol is used widely because Cisco supports it. You need special software to use it (pimd-v1); it comes in two flavors: PIMv1 and PIMv2.

POP   Point Of Presence—this term describes locations where network service providers have installed equipment and are willing to let you connect to this equipment and their network either via a digital circuit or some form of dial-up. **POP** is also used for Post Office Protocol, as in POP3 for the third version of this protocol.

PPP   Point-to-Point Protocol (RFC 1661).

PPTP   Point to Point Tunnelling Protocol—a method of encapsulating IP packets within IP packets for either security purpose (by encrypting the inner packet) or remote network access (by allowing the inner packets to have a source address on the destination network). Typically used for both simultaneously.

PTT   Post, Telegraph, and Telephone—a generic term referring to providers of telephony services.

PVC   Permanent Virtual Circuit.

RFC   Request For Comments.

RFC 1983   This RFC contains the *Internet Users' Glossary*, which is a voluminous glossary of terms from an authoritative source.

RIP   Routing Information Protocol—a dynamic routing protocol (RFC 1058).

RSN   Real Soon Now—as, the time period a vendor promises to have a fix available. Typically meant sarcastically.

RTFM   Read The Darn Manual. As a newbie, you may feel like a lightning rod for this statement. Give it time. . .

SCSI   Small Computer System Interface.

SLARP   Serial Line Reverse Address Resolution Protocol.

SMTP   Simple Mail Transport Protocol.

SNMP   Simple Network Management Protocol (RFC 1908) (plus RFC 1155, RFC 1156, RFC 1157, and others).

SNPP   Simple Network Paging Protocol (RFC 1861).

TCO   Total Cost of Ownership. For any sort of computing solution, this includes not only the initial hardware and software costs, but also the ongoing hardware maintenance and software license costs plus the time that must be spent keeping the system running (e.g., a system that runs on freeware, but requires 10–20 person-hours per month of system administration will eventually cost a company more than a solution which costs $10,000 out of the box but needs 1/10th of the administration).

TCP   Transfer Control Protocol (RFC 675).

TCP/IP   A suite of protocols used over IP networks.

TDM   Time Division Multiplexing—the practice of dividing bandwidth of a channel based on timeslots. Each timeslot is in a frame, which, can then be allocated to different senders. The receiving side demultiplexes the signal back into (ACK!).

TOS   Type Of Service (RFC 1349)—a field in an IP packet header which indicates how network components should treat the packet if they are capable of providing different levels of service.

TTL   Time To Live—in the case of an IP packet, this is the additional number of hops the packet can take before it is discarded as undeliverable. This is done to prevent misconfigured routers from bringing the network to its knees by routing a packet in circles infinitely.

UPS   Uninterruptable Power Supply.

user-space   Refers to processes running on a Unix system, whether they are daemons or normal user processes, and regardless of the UID of the process. If you can see it with `ps fax`, then it's a user-space process. See **kernel-space**.

WRD   Weighted Route Damping (an extension to **BGP**).

YMMV   Your Mileage May Vary—a disclaimer that states "this worked for me, but its applicability to your environment is not known, and therefore it may or may not work for you."

Bibliography

CHAPMAN, D. BRENTAND ZWICKY, ELIZABETH D., *Building Internet Firewalls*. O'Reilly & Associates, Sebastopol, CA, 1995. ISBN: 1–56592–124–0

GARFINKEL, SIMON and SPAFFORD, GENE, *Practical UNIX and Internet Security, Second Edition*, O'Reilly & Associates, Sebastopol, CA, 1996. ISBN: 1–56592–148–8

HELD, GILBERT, *Understanding Data Communications, Fourth Edition*, SAMS Publishing, 1994. ISBN: 0–672–30501–1

PERLMAN, RADIA, *Interconnections: Bridges, Routers, Switches and Internetworking Protocols, Second Edition*, Addison Wesley Longman, Inc., 1999. ISBN: 0–201–63488–1

RAYMOND, ERIC S., with STEELE, GUY L. JR., *The New Hacker's Dictionary*, The MIT Press, Cambridge, MA, 1991. ISBN: 0–262–68069–6

STEVENS, RICHARD W., *Unix Network Programming : Networking APIs: Sockets and XTI (Volume 1), Second Edition*, Prentice Hall, 1999. ISBN: 0–134–90012-X

WALL, LARRY, CHRISTIANSEN, TOM, and SCHWARTZ, RANDAL L., with STEPHEN POTTER, *Programming Perl, Second Edition*, O'Reilly & Associates, Sebastopol, CA, 1996. ISBN: 1–56592–149–6

Index